THE ARCHAEOLOGY
OF IBERIA

Theoretical archaeology group (tag)

In this series:

The Archaeology of Human Ancestry
Power, Sex and Tradition
edited by James Steele and Stephen Shennan

Cultural Identity and Archaeology
The Construction of European Communities
edited by Paul Graves-Brown, Sîan Jones, Clive Gamble

The Cultural Life of Images
Visual Representation in Archaeology
edited by Brian Leigh Molyneaux

Managing Archaeology
edited by Malcolm A. Cooper, Antony Firth, John Carman and David Wheatley

Theory in Archaeology
A World Perspective
edited by Peter J. Ucko

Time, Tradition and Society in Greek Archaeology
Bridging the 'Great Divide'
edited by Nigel Spencer

THE ARCHAEOLOGY OF IBERIA

The dynamics of change

Edited by
Margarita Díaz-Andreu and Simon Keay

ROUTLEDGE

London and New York

First published 1997
by Routledge
11 New Fetter Lane, London EC4P 4EE

Simultaneously published in the USA and Canada
by Routledge
29 West 35th Street, New York, NY 10001

Typeset in Bembo by Florencetype Ltd, Stoodleigh, Devon

Printed and bound in Great Britain by
Biddles Ltd, Guildford and King's Lynn

British Library Cataloguing in Publication Data
A catalogue record for this book is available from the British Library

Library of Congress Cataloguing in Publication Data
The archaeology of Iberia: the dynamics of change / edited by
Margarita Díaz-Andreu and Simon Keay.
p. cm.
Selected papers from the Theoretical Archaeology Group Conference
held in Southampton in 1992.
Includes bibliographical references.
1. Spain – Antiquities – Congresses. 2. Portugal – Antiquities –
Congresses. 3. Man, Prehistoric – Spain – Congresses. 4. Man,
Prehistoric – Portugal – Congresses. 5. Social change – Spain –
Congresses. 6. Social change – Portugal – Congresses.
I. Díaz-Andreu García, Margarita. II. Keay, S. J.
III. Theoretical Archaeology Group (England). Conference
(1992 Southampton, England)
DP44.A694 1997
936.6–dc20
96–7550
CIP

ISBN 0–415–12012–8 (hbk)

CONTENTS

FIGURES AND TABLES

FIGURES

TABLES

CONTRIBUTORS

Margarita Díaz-Andreu, Department of Archaeology, University of Durham

Josefa Enamorado, Departamento de Prehistoria, Centro de Estudios Históricos, CSIC, Madrid

Genís Ribé, Departament de Prehistòria, Universitat Autònoma de Barcelona

Walter Cruells, Departament de Prehistòria, Universitat Autònoma de Barcelona

Miquel Molist, Departament de Prehistòria, Universitat Autònoma de Barcelona

Almudena Hernando Gonzalo, Departamento de Prehistoria, Universidad Complutense de Madrid

Victor Hurtado, Departamento de Prehistoria y Arqueología, Universidad de Sevilla

Susana Oliveira Jorge, Faculdade de Letras, Universidade do Porto

Vítor Oliveira Jorge, Faculdade de Letras, Universidade do Porto

Maria Manuela dos Reis Martins, Unidade de Arqueología, Universidade do Minho

Gonzalo Ruiz Zapatero, Departamento de Prehistoria, Universidad Complutense de Madrid

Arturo Ruiz Rodríguez, Departamento de Territorio y Patrimonio Histórico, Facultad de Humanidades, Universidad de Jaén

Simon Keay, Department of Archaeology, University of Southampton

Isabel Rodà, Department d'Art, Universitat Autònoma de Barcelona

Luis Caballero Zoreda, Departamento de Historia Antigua y Arqueología, Centro de Estudios Históricos, CSIC, Madrid

Vicente Salvatierra Cuenca, Departamento de Territorio y Patrimonio Histórico, Facultad de Humanidades, Universidad de Jaén

Robert Chapman, Department of Archaeology, University of Reading

GENERAL EDITOR'S
PREFACE

Why does the world need archaeological theory? The purpose of *Theoretical Archaeology* is to answer the question by showing that archaeology contributes little to our understanding if it does not explore the theories that give meaning to the past. The last decade has seen some major developments in world archaeology and the *One World Archaeology* series provides a thematic showcase for the current scale of enquiry and variety of archaeological interests. The development of a *Theoretical Archaeology* series complements these thematic concerns and, by focusing attention on theory in all its many guises, points the way to future long-term developments in the subject.

In 1992 the annual Theoretical Archaeology Group (TAG) conference was held in Southampton. Europe was our theoretical theme at this the *Euro*TAG conference from which the first volumes in this series originated. We stressed two elements in the structure of the three-day conference. In the first place 1992 had for long been heralded as the time when the single market would come into existence combined with moves towards greater European unity. While these orderly developments could be planned for and sessions organized around the role of archaeology and the past in the construction of European identity, no one could have predicted the horror of what would occur in former Yugoslavia. Throughout 1992 and beyond, the ideologies of integration and fragmentation, federalism and nationalism vied with each other to use the resources of the past in vastly different ways.

The second element recognized that 1992 was a notable anniversary for theoretical archaeology. Thirty years before, Lewis Binford had published his first seminal paper, 'Archaeology as Anthropology', in *American Antiquity*. This short paper was a theoretical beacon in an otherwise heavily factual archaeological world. From such beginnings came the influential processual movement which, in its early years, was referred to as the New Archaeology. Thirty years has clearly knocked the shine off such bright new futures. In the meantime archaeological theory had healthily fragmented while expanding into many areas of investigation, previously regarded as off-limits to archaeologists and their mute data. Processualism had been countered by post-processualism to either the enrichment or irritation of by now partisan theoretical practitioners. *Euro*-TAG marked the anniversary with a debate involving the views of Lewis Binford, Chris Tilley, John Barrett and Colin Renfrew, supplemented by opinions from the floor. Their brief was to outline the theoretical challenges now set before the subject. The audience heard various programmes of where we might go as well as fears about an uncertain theoretical future. Both optimism and pessimism for another thirty years of theoretical excitement were to be found in almost equal measure. However, the clear impression, exemplified by the number of people, almost 800, who attended *Euro*TAG was that the strength of any future theoretical archaeology now lies in its diversity.

How different in numbers attending and diversity of viewpoints from the early days of TAG, an organization whose aims have always been simple: to raise the profile of discussion about the theories of the past. The need for such a group was recognized at the first open meeting held in Sheffield in 1979 where the programme notes declared that 'British archaeologists have never possessed a forum for the discussion of theoretical issues. Conferences which address wider themes come and go but all too frequently the discussion of ideas is blanketed by the presentation of fact.' TAG set out to correct this balance and achieved it through an accent on discussion, a willingness to hear new ideas, often from people just beginning their theoretical careers.

*Euro*TAG presented some of the influences which must now contribute to the growth of theory in archaeology as the discipline assumes a central position in the dialogues of the humanities. As expected there was strong participation from European colleagues in sessions which focused on Iberia and Scandinavia as well as discussions of the regional traditions of theoretical and archaeological research in the continent, an archaeological perspective on theory in world archaeology, the identity of Europe and multicultural societies in European prehistory. Set beside these were sessions devoted to visual information, human ancestry, food, architecture and structured deposition. Two archaeological periods expressed their new-found theoretical feet. Historical archaeology argued for an escape from its subordination to history while classical archaeology embraced theory and applied it to its rich data. Finally, the current issues of value and management in archaeology were subjected to a critical examination from a theoretical perspective.

Demonstrating and understanding change has always been central to our subject. It is therefore unsurprising that the dynamics of change have probably accounted for more theoretical discussion than any other archaeological issue. We have not been slow in recent years either to borrow theory from other historical disciplines or to situate our own contribution within wider debates. Archaeology, as this volume demonstrates, brings a particular perspective to bear on the issue of change. When conducted at a regional scale, as here with Iberia, it is possible to take the long-term view and seek resonances between political and economic changes that occurred at very different times. What follows is an opportunity to examine the theoretical approaches of prehistorians, classical and historical archaeologists as they examine two of the most diverse countries of Europe. Iberia, with its particular position as a bridge between Africa and Europe and its history of Christianity and Islam, was the obvious region at *Euro*TAG for the investigation of change. The implications these historical studies bring to our understanding of Europe, that polyphonic continent of identities and nations, is here presented in sharp focus and with diverse materials.

Clive Gamble
April 1996

ACKNOWLEDGEMENTS

The *Euro*TAG organizing committee consisted of Clive Gamble, Sara Champion, Simon Keay and Tim Champion. They were helped by many staff and students from the Department of Archaeology at the University of Southampton and particularly by Cressida Fforde and Olivia Forge who did the lion's share of the organization in the final days. Thanks were also due to Peter Philips who videotaped the debate and to Mike Corbishley, Peter Stone and Eric Maddern who organized videos and storytelling, while the art of Carolyn Trant and Sylvia Hays provided the art exhibition. Financial support came from The Prehistoric Society, the TAG travel fund, Oxbow books, Routledge and the University of Southampton.

ACKNOWLEDGEMENTS

The publication of this book has relied upon the cooperation and support of a large number of people. In the first instance we would like to recognize the contribution of Ms Isabel Lisboa during the original TAG session and in its initial transition to publication. The translation of the texts into English was achieved with the valuable assistance of translators Mr Daniel Ribot and Mr Justin Byrne, and Mrs Ruth Daniel. The artwork for the chapters and the cover is the work of Ms Katharyn Knowles and Ms Yvonne Beadnell respectively. We would like to thank especially Ms Debbie Malson, who typed out the many drafts of all the chapters without demur and without whose patience this book would probably never have appeared at all. The editors would also like to acknowledge the support and encouragement they have received from their respective institutions: the Consejo Superior de Investigaciones Científicas, the Departamento de Prehistoria of the Universidad Complutense de Madrid and the Department of Archaeology of the University of Durham (Díaz-Andreu), and the Department of Archaeology of the University of Southampton (Keay).

Margarita Díaz-Andreu and Simon Keay

CHAPTER ONE

INTRODUCTION

SIMON KEAY AND
MARGARITA DÍAZ-ANDREU

This book is an integral part of the project to publish the proceedings of the TAG Conference which was held at Southampton in 1992, and which had European archaeology as its underlying theme. The other volumes in this series focus on the world perspective of European archaeology (Ucko 1995), the archaeology of human ancestry (Steele and Shennan 1995), the role of cultural construction in the identity of Europe (Graves-Brown *et al.* 1995) and theory in Greek archaeology (Spencer 1995). This volume seeks to explore the application of such new theoretical traditions to a particular European region through a number of case studies ranging from the Palaeolithic through to the medieval period.

Iberia is Europe in microcosm. It represents a juxtaposition of north, south, east and west and mirrors a heterogeneous multicultural, multilingual Europe. Throughout the first million years of Iberian prehistory, the Mediterranean and the Atlantic exercised a dual influence over the development of communities in the peninsula. It is within this context that one should understand the appearance in Iberia of such peoples as the Phoenicians, Greeks, 'Celts', Romans, Germanic peoples and Muslims from the protohistoric period onwards. Iberia is, thus, one of the few European regions which provides the archaeologist with a cross-section of the full range of culture contact and culture change in antiquity. This very rich archaeological heritage easily lends itself to the testing of new theoretical models of social, religious, economic and political change.

There are many perspectives from which the archaeological record can be analysed, and that of Iberia has been no exception. In the current context, however, two trends merit special attention. The first is that of a growing acceptance of functionalist (*sensu lato*) perspectives in Iberian archaeology (Gilman 1995: 4). The second concerns the fact that despite this, an underlying culture-historical perspective persists within interpretative frameworks. The practice of using a culture-historical theoretical framework, which dominated Iberian archaeology from the 1920s until the 1970s, emphasized the collection of data and the construction of archaeological 'cultures'. That is not to say that other perspectives were not unknown. Despite the academic restrictions imposed by the dictatorships of Franco and Salazar, the works of authors such as Gordon Childe were familiar to archaeologists. However, they were only consulted selectively and attention was focused upon culture-historical sequences (Díaz-Andreu 1995). Growing opposition to the dictators in Spain and Portugal changed this scenario. It gave rise to a very different understanding of Childe in the late 1960s. His Marxist ideas and conception of history were particularly attractive and laid the foundations of the historical–materialist schools that have played an important role in the interpretations of the archaeology of Iberia. This historical materialism was put into practice in what Antonio Gilman calls functionalism in the broadest sense.

The political embeddedness of the discipline does not explain every change in the theoretical realm in science (Gilman 1995: 1). There is at least one further factor that has to be considered: the structure of the academic profession. It plays a role in the increasing popularity of post-processual archaeology in British and North American universities, the persistence of culture-history in most countries, and the current state of Spanish and Portuguese archaeology. Thus, in most countries, entry to and progress within the academic world is based on a system of patronage (for Germany see Härke 1991). The advancement of an individual's career relies upon the support of superiors already in post. The position of a newcomer in a department with an established 'school' of thought is initially weak, and any new challenging ideas can be controlled by senior academics.

This kind of academic patronage has long prevailed in Spain and Portugal, although it has been interrupted from time to time. This happened in the 1920s with the introduction of prehistoric studies into university curricula by two relative outsiders, Pere Bosch Gimpera and Hugo Obermaier, who nevertheless in turn formed their own circle of disciples. The system of academic patronage was again interrupted for a decade during the later years of the 1970s and the early 1980s. As a result of an earlier demographic increase, a 'baby-boom' generation entered the universities, at that time provoking an urgent need for new staff. Among the new generation of academics were to be found stout defenders of historical materialism. Arturo Ruiz Rodríguez at Jaén and Vicente Lull at the Autònoma University of Barcelona are just two examples. Other 'baby-boomers' linked innovation to the adoption of such new techniques as radiocarbon dating, survey methods, pollen analysis, spatial analysis, etc. However, this was not necessarily accompanied by a complementary emphasis on archaeological method, theory and ecology.

Post-processual approaches to archaeology are not popular amongst academics in Spain and Portugal, with explicit rejections of them appearing in print (Ruiz Zapatero *et al.* 1988, Vicent 1990; see also Vázquez Varela and Risch 1991). The reasons for this are not clear. It may be that it is perhaps unrealistic and inappropriate to expect that a range of theoretical approaches which are best understood in the context of one academic tradition, such as post-processualism, should *necessarily* be adopted by archaeologists working elsewhere and within distinct academic traditions. This is not the appropriate place to attempt to explain the popularity of post-processual approaches in Britain and the United States (where there are at least fifteen practitioners: Thomas 1995: 349). Nevertheless it is possible that it may perhaps be understood in the context of access to and advancement within certain sectors of the profession in both countries.

It is probable that post-processual archaeology and its emphasis upon the role of ideology and the individual may find greater acceptance amongst Spanish and Portuguese archaeologists in the future. Currently, however, there is an implicit belief that archaeological evidence allows us to define the *systems* which generate cultural behaviour and rejects the study of the individual in the creation of cultural symbols. Behind this may lie pessimism about the ability of the individual to bring about change in societies, or the scope of the individual's role in society. This, of course, has to be understood in the context of the recent political histories of both Spain and Portugal.

Currently, functionalist perspectives (in the broadest sense) are gaining increasing acceptance amongst archaeologists in Iberia. This is a trend which Antonio Gilman (1995: 4) explains in terms of 'a guarantee of professional respectability'. This means that analyses of the archaeological record increasingly focus upon socio-political and economic factors, which had hitherto received little attention. This is evident in most of the chapters in this volume.

The origins of this book lie in the TAG session 'The Dynamics of Change' held at Southampton in 1992. The line-up of speakers comprised Margarita Díaz-Andreu, Paloma Gómez Marcen, Almudena Hernando Gonzalo, Susana Jorge Oliveira, Vitor Jorge Oliveira, Simon Keay, Isabel Lisboa, Arturo Ruiz Rodríguez, Gonzalo Ruiz Zapatero and Roberto Risch. All were recognized as having a particular contribution to make to the theme of cultural change in Iberia. In the planning of the book that arose from this meeting, however, it was decided to broaden the range of contributors. The aim was to contrast the theoretical approaches to cultural change adopted by specialists within the key traditional period divisions, such as the Palaeolithic, Neolithic, Chalcolithic, Bronze and Iron Ages, as well as the Roman and early medieval periods. Given the great inherent regionalism of the Iberian Peninsula, care was also care taken to ensure that archaeologists from as many different parts of Iberia as possible were represented: Catalunya (Molist *et al.*, Rodà), Madrid

(Enamorado, Ruiz Zapatero, Díaz-Andreu, Hernando, Caballero), Andalucía (Hurtado, Ruiz Rodríguez, Salvatierra), northern Portugal (Martins dos Reis), southern Portugal (Jorge and Jorge), as well as British scholars working in Iberia (Chapman and Keay). Needless to say, such heterogeneity is also reflected in the theoretical perspectives that they adopt. The aim of this approach was to try and break away from single-period or single-regional period studies which dominate the analysis of Iberian antiquity. While these have many merits they are achieved at the expense of the *longue durée* or the broader picture. Thus, apart from the 'national' histories of Spain and Portugal, this volume represents one of the very few attempts to treat Iberia as a whole and to span its full chronological range of archaeology, especially including the Palaeolithic and medieval periods. This stands in contrast to many syntheses, especially those translated into the English language, which have tended to focus upon the period between the Chalcolithic and Roman periods (Chapman 1990, Fernández Castro 1995, Cunliffe and Keay 1995, Gilman and Thornes 1985, Harrison 1988, Lillios 1995, Mathers and Stoddart 1994).

Apart from an introduction to the history of archaeology in Iberia (Díaz-Andreu), all of the chapters address the theme of change. Some adopt a 'global' perspective within the Iberian peninsula (Enamorado, Ribé *et al.*, Oliveira Jorge and Oliveira Jorge, Rodà, Caballero), while others reflect upon the nature of cultural change from the perspective of regional studies (Hernando, Hurtado, dos Reis Martins, Ruiz Zapatero, Ruiz Rodríguez, Keay and Salvatierra). Moreover some contributors focus upon the transition between one period and another, while others analyse the internal dynamics within apparently 'static' societies. In most contributions the theoretical perspective is implicit and the authors concentrate upon its application to archaeological case studies.

A range of contrasting academic traditions have traditionally governed the development of interpretational frameworks within the prehistoric, protohistoric, classical and medieval periods. Consequently the models invoked by authors in this book invoke a range of models to shed light upon cultural change. In light of the comments above, it will come as no surprise to discover that historical materialism predominates. All of this and its implications in the broader context of recent developments in Iberian archaeology are discussed in the concluding chapter. Theoretical heterogeneity of this kind within individual chronological periods and across the cultural divide is not restricted to Iberia and poses a challenge to those who seek over-arching theories of cultural change in prehistoric and early historical societies.

REFERENCES

Chapman, R. (1990) *Emerging Complexity. The Later Prehistory of south-east Spain, Iberia and the West Mediterranean*, Cambridge: Cambridge University Press.

Cunliffe, B. and Keay, S. (eds) (1995) *Social Complexity and the Development of Towns in Iberia*, Proceedings of the British Academy 86, Oxford: Oxford University Press.

Díaz-Andreu, M. (1995) 'Childe and the Iberian Atlantic Bronze Age', in 'Is There an Atlantic Bronze Age?', Colloquium held at Lisbon, October 1995.

Fernández Castro, M. C. (1995) *Iberia in Prehistory*, Oxford: Blackwell.

Gilman, A. (1995) 'Recent trends in the archaeology of Spain', in K. Lillios (ed.) *The Origins of Complex Societies in Late Prehistoric Iberia*: 1–6. International Monographs in Prehistory, Ann Arbor: University of Michigan Press.

Gilman, A. and Thornes, H. B. (1985) *Land-use and Prehistory in south-east Spain*, University of London Monograph Series, London: Allen and Unwin.

Graves-Brown, P., Jones, S. and Gamble, G. (eds) (1995) *Cultural Identity and Archaeology: The Construction of European Communities*. The Theoretical Archaeology Group, London: Routledge

Härke, H. (1991) 'All quiet on the western front? Paradigms, methods and approaches in West German archaeology', in I. Hodder (ed.) *Archaeological Theory in Europe. The Last Three Decades*, London: Routledge.

Harrison, R.J. (1988) *Spain at the Dawn of History. Iberians, Phoenicians and Greeks*, London: Thames and Hudson.

Lillios, K.T. (ed.) (1995) *The Origins of Complex Societies in Late Prehistoric Iberia*, International Monographs in Prehistory, Archaeological Series 8, Michigan: Ann Arbor.

Mathers, C. and Stoddart, S. (eds) (1994) *Development and Decline in the Mediterranean Bronze Age*, Sheffield Archaeological Monographs 8, Sheffield: J. R. Collis Publications.

Ruiz Rodríguez, A., Chapa, T. and Ruiz Zapatero, G. (1988) 'La arqueología contextual: una revisión crítica', *Trabajos de Prehistoria* 45: 11–17.

Ruiz Zapatero, G. (1991) 'Arqueología y Universidad', *Revista de Arqueología* 118: 6–7.

Spencer, N. (ed.) (1995) *Time, Tradition and Society in Greek Archaeology: Bridging the Great Divide*. The Theoretical Archaeology Group, London and New York: Routledge.

Steele, J. and Shennan, S. (eds) (1995) *The Archaeology of Human Ancestry: Power, Sex and Tradition*. The Theoretical Archaeology Group, London and New York: Routledge.

Thomas, J. (1995) 'Where are we now? Archaeological theory in the 1990s', in P. Ucko (ed.) *Theory in Archaeology. A World Perspective*: 343–62, London and New York: Routledge.

Ucko, P. (ed.) (1995) *Theory and Archaeology: A World Perspective*. The Theoretical Archaeology Group, London and New York: Routledge.

Vázquez Varela, J.M. and Risch, R. (1991) 'Theory in Spanish archaeology since 1960', in I. Hodder (ed.) *Archaeological Theory in Europe. The Last Three Decades*: 25–51, London and New York: Routledge.

Vicent, J. (1990) 'El debat postprocessual: algunes observacions «radicals» sobre una arqueologia «conservadora»', *Cota Zero* 6: 102–7.

CHAPTER TWO

CONFLICT AND INNOVATION

The development of archaeological traditions in Iberia

MARGARITA DÍAZ-ANDREU

INTRODUCTION

Spain and Portugal are located on the southwest edge of Europe. Their extra-centrality has not, however, prevented them from following the main European trends. Therefore, the formation and development of archaeology in both countries has, in general terms, gone through similar periods to the rest of the continent, although without having the might of more developed countries. In Europe at the end of the eighteenth century a powerful interest in history grew up because it could be used as a means of justifying the nation, a concept which was the nucleus of the new emergent political system of nationalism. This attempt to define the nation historically ultimately led to archaeology's formation as a scientific discipline. The fact that history in its widest sense now became a key element in the political legitimation of the different nations represented a new motive for the study of the remote past, already on the increase during the preceding three centuries; so much so, that it attained a new status and history, became a discipline which ranked among the most important and was therefore worthy of specialization. However, this process did not advance at the same rhythm in different countries as it was related to the weight of the middle classes, who had the greatest interest in establishing the liberal system which brought them the right to govern. Spain and Portugal were not the first in the field but amongst a second group of countries, but precisely for this reason the study of the formation of archaeology as a discipline in these countries can serve as an example of a less developed archaeological tradition, so poorly treated in the most famous histories of archaeology.

The evolution of Iberian archaeology draws attention to factors which have scarcely been considered in existing histories of the discipline: the distinct dynamics which have driven archaeology's development in the different European countries; the existence of a colonial archaeology within Europe itself and not just beyond its frontiers; the influence that the dominant political ideologies in each region have had on the hypotheses put forward by archaeologists; the relation between geographical position and the consolidation of distinct theories, and between the degree of economic development and archaeology.

To date, insufficient attention has been paid to the relationship between politics, economy and science in explaining the birth of professional archaeology in the nineteenth century. The situation of Spain and Portugal at that time is, however, a clear example of these relationships. These two countries on the periphery of Europe were marked throughout the last century by the agonizing loss of their empires and chronic political instability. In consequence, archaeology developed relatively late and weakly and it was intellectually subordinate to the archaeology of more advanced countries. But, in addition, a comparison between the evolution of archaeology in Spain and Portugal confirms the distinct dynamics which have driven archaeology's development. Whilst, as stated, both countries were economically and socially backward in contrast with the most advanced countries in Europe, the same was also true of Portugal in relation to Spain, not in intellectual terms but as regards institutionalization. It was the internal development of each country which provided the foundations of the institutional base for emergence of archaeology as a discipline and permitted the creation of a corps of specialists dedicating their efforts to archaeology.

Colonialism could not only be seen in respect to intellectual influences of the type which existed in Spanish and Portuguese archaeology, which were to a large extent dependent on foreign inspiration. The relative backwardness and late professionalization of the discipline also betray the hegemonic countries' failure to accept the real progress achieved. The refusal to recognize the existence of the Palaeolithic art of Altamira, or to include the Iberian Peninsula in the major surveys, testify to the strength of this attitude during the nineteenth century. The Iberian Peninsula was perceived by other European (and North American) archaeologists as a virgin country in which everything had still to be done. Although this was partly true, it is undeniable that their work was largely based on generally unrecognized previous work done by native archaeologists. After an interval in the first half of the twentieth century this situation continued, and only over the last two decades has there been important change. Nowadays foreign archaeologists are integrated into Spanish or Portuguese teams, and some Spanish and Portuguese archaeologists even work in other countries such as France and the United Kingdom.

The influence that political ideologies have had on archaeological interpretations is clearly revealed by the study of Iberian archaeology. Nationalism not only provoked the birth of archaeology as a professional discipline, but, as it was founded on the political will of a particular group to consider itself a nation and hence to demand the right to self-determination, it also gave rise to conflicts between groups with opposing interests. The cultural complexity of the Iberian Peninsula provided fertile ground for the emergence of different types of nationalist sentiments, either unifying (Spanish, Portuguese or Iberian), or fragmented (Catalan, Basque, Galician, etc.), which archaeologists would support through their interpretations.

The archaeology of the Iberian Peninsula also exemplifies the way in which the geographical location of any given country conditions the elaboration of hypotheses. The Iberian Peninsula's position linking two continents has influenced archaeologists' vision of Africa. Europe's systematic contempt for all things African was largely absent in Spain and Portugal, whose intellectuals defended, although not without contradictions and internal struggles, the bonds which tied them to their southern neighbours. This tendency can be appreciated most clearly in two periods of study, the Palaeolithic and the Islamic periods (Díaz-Andreu 1996b).

After a long period of dictatorship in both countries, in which (particularly during the first decades) archaeology followed a fascist model, the transition to democratic political regimes and entry into the European Economic Community (later European Union) have brought both Spain and Portugal closer to their European partners. This has been shown by their previously unimaginable capacity in general, and specifically in archaeology, to respond to new challenges. We are now in a period of change that is leading to the definitive integration of Iberian archaeology into European and world archaeology.

THE FORMATION OF PROFESSIONAL ARCHAEOLOGY IN THE IBERIAN PENINSULA[1]

Following the triumph of nationalism as a political ideology after the French Revolution in 1789, the boom in the study of the past led to its institutionalization as a science. However, in nineteenth-century Europe this process did not advance at the same pace in all countries. The most economically developed of these, and hence those with the most advanced liberal systems, led the way and served as models for the more backward ones. Within the Iberian Peninsula there existed a similar tendency. Spain, albeit with some delay, followed more closely behind the countries of northern Europe. Although both countries were far less industrialized than their northwestern and central European neighbours, Spain's economic development outstripped that of Portugal, so facilitating the growth of the middle classes, the social group most interested in fostering the study of history.

The development of Iberian archaeology was not isolated from that of Europe. This is perhaps obvious in the case of Spain as a consequence

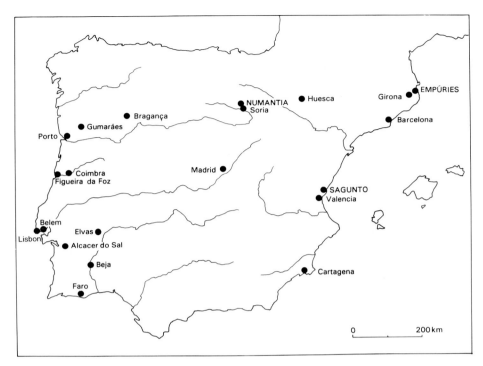

Figure 2.1 Map showing the places and sites mentioned in the text.

of its cultural dependence on France. In archaeology, the foundation in France of Monument Commissions in 1830 (Larousse 1865–90 (II): 532) was followed by a similar development in Spain in 1844. Similarly, the School of Advanced Diplomatic Studies, created in Madrid in 1856 and in which subjects such as archaeology and numismatics were taught (Peiró and Pasamar Alzuría 1991: 144), was merely a reproduction of the French École des Chartes. Whilst between 1861 and 1865 Napoleon III ordered the excavation of Celtic remains in search of the French national past (Trigger 1989: 148), in Spain the Royal Academy of History financed the excavation of Numantia at almost exactly the same time, 1861–66 (Mélida 1922: 106). *The Musée des Antiquités Nationales* (Museum of National Antiquities), established in Paris in 1867, was followed in the same year by the foundation of the *Museo Arqueológico Nacional* (MAN, National Archaeological Museum) in Madrid. Although it is probable that Portuguese archaeology was subject to similar foreign influences, these are not mentioned in the studies carried out by Fabião (1989, 1993) or Jorge (1993), and we can rule out the possibility that they came from Britain (Raposo pers. comm.), despite the close diplomatic relations which existed between the two countries during the last century.

One essential prerequisite for the institutionalization, and hence development, of archaeology in both Spain and Portugal was the transformation of its social base. During the nineteenth century the study of antiquities ceased to be the almost exclusively aristocratic or ecclesiastical pursuit which it had been until then. In its struggle to overthrow the Ancien Regime and define its place in society, the middle class identified its own interests with those of the community, personifying the collective in a single being, the nation. It was only the exclusive personality of the nation that entitled it, or rather its middle classes, to hold political power. For this reason they were very interested in the past, in the genesis of the nation, and members of the middle classes began to organize in order to study it themselves. The associations and societies which would channel this interest in the past began to appear in Spain after 1833. The most notable early examples were the *Sociedad Numismática Matritense* (Madrid Society of Numismatics) (1837), the *Sociedad Arqueológica* (Archaeological Society) (1840) and the *Academia Española de Arqueología* (Spanish Academy of Archaeology) (1844) (Pasamar and Peiró 1991: 73). In Portugal, these societies came somewhat later, the *Sociedade Archeologica Lusitana* (Lusitanian Archaeological Society, a society of dilettanti [Fabião pers. comm.]) in 1849 (Ribeiro 1879) and the *Real Associação dos Architectos Civis e Arqueólogos Portugueses* (Royal Association of Portuguese Civil Architects and Archaeologists) in 1863 (Custódio 1992: 48–9). These were middle-class initiatives, the work of men such as Basilio Sebastián Castellanos de Losada and Francisco Bermúdez de Sotomayor in Spain, and Carlos Ribeiro, Nery Delgado and Pereira da Costa in Portugal.

Before this new-found interest in antiquities could bear fruit a legal framework for the excavation, analysis and exhibition of remains had to be constructed. Portugal had been a pioneer in this respect, since by the eighteenth century a Royal Decree of 1721 had already established principles governing the protection of monuments and ancient remains (Fabião 1989: 17, Soromenho and Silva 1992: 38, but for its lack of success see Fabião 1996). In Spain, the only known step in this direction was an order issued by the Marquis of La Ensenada in 1752 (*La Gaceta*, 8 April) in response to a find made in Cartagena whereby he ordered the recovery, conservation and removal of the remains to the Royal Academy of History (Mora 1994). In the nineteenth century, however, Spain would take the initiative. In 1803, the Royal Academy of History was responsible for the first legislation regulating the conservation of ancient heritage, the Royal Patent of the Court of Charles IV of 6 July 1803. This ordered adherence to the 'instructions issued by the Royal Academy of History concerning the form in which ancient remains discovered, or still to be discovered, in the kingdom shall be collected and conserved' (quoted in Barandiarán 1988: 103). Whilst further measures to protect antiquities were introduced during the ephemeral reign of Joseph Bonaparte (Rodríguez Hidalgo 1991: 93), Ferdinand VII's attempt to re-establish the Ancien Regime brought progress in this respect to a standstill under his rule (1813–33). The situation changed dramatically in both Spain and Portugal after 1833, as the dissolution of the religious orders led to a sudden increase in the number of works of art and antiquities in circulation. In both countries these collections were the beginnings of many archives, libraries and, most importantly for archaeology, new museums.[2] Although, given their origin, these primarily contained works of art, they also possessed some archaeological objects. In Spain, this led to the creation of new museums not just in the larger cities, where what were known as *gabinetes* (small, usually private, museums) already existed, and where these were now joined by entities such as the National Museum which opened in Madrid in 1840, but also in smaller provincial towns such as Castelló, Girona or Huesca, to cite just three examples (Sanz-Pastor 1990). In contrast, in Portugal, archaeological objects brought into circulation by the dissolution of the religious orders were still only sent to museums in the largest cities, Lisbon and Oporto, for example those founded around 1833 by their respective Fine Art Academies (França 1986: 417) or, as in the case of the coin collection which had belonged to the Alcobaça monastery, the *Museu da Casa da Moeda* (Mint Museum) (*Grande* 1935–60 (18): 263). The creation of Monument Commissions in both countries was also linked to this development. The *Comisiones de Monumentos Históricos y Artísticos* established in Spain in 1844 were intended to protect buildings, monuments and artistic objects which either for reasons of the beauty of their construction, or for their age, their origin, the use made of them or their historical importance, were worth preserving (R.O. (*Real Orden*) 2 April 1844). Of the Commissions' three departments, one was devoted to architecture and archaeology. In Portugal, work on an ambitious inventory of antiquities would begin towards the end of the century, in 1894 (Raposo 1993: note 4).

In Spain, the widespread foundation of museums stimulated the professionalization of archaeology. However, an important obstacle had to be overcome before this could take place, namely the scepticism surrounding conclusions drawn from the study of physical remains, compared to those derived from the analysis of written documents. Reflecting the fact that some authorities identify this with the debate between natural and philological models (Schnapp 1991), the professionalization of archivists and librarians preceded that of archaeologists. Hence, although the *Escuela Superior de Diplomática* (ESD, School of Advanced Diplomatic Studies) founded in 1853 had been established to train archivists, librarians and museum conservators, the latter were not included in the name of the corps (which was called the corps of Archivists and Librarians). It was only in 1868, a year after the creation of the *Museo Arqueológico Nacional* (MAN, National Archaeological Museum), that they were included in the renamed Corps of Professional Archivists, Librarians and Antiquarians (Marcos Pous 1993: 25). The bourgeois character of Spanish archaeology was reinforced from then on, as most professional archaeologists came from the middle classes (of more than fifty curators or assistants of the MAN in the nineteenth century it seems that not one was a cleric). Amateur scholars and enthusiasts, among whom members of the clergy predominated, were excluded from the profession, although their activities were endorsed by institutions such as the Royal Academies, which retained much of their prestige. Examples of this group in Spain include Father Fita, member of the Royal Academy of History from 1879 and its director between 1912 and 1916, and Father José Brenha in Portugal.

In Portugal, on the other hand, the small museum established around 1864 by the recently created *Associação dos Architectos Civis e Arqueólogos Portugueses* (Association of Portuguese Civil Architects and Archaeologists) (*Grande* 1935–60 (18): 243) did not advance the professionalization of archaeology there. Only in the 1880s did museums containing archaeological collections begin to appear. In the first half of the decade museums were opened in Elvas, Coimbra and Guimarães, and between 1892 and 1896 these were joined by others in Alcácer do Sal, Beja, Bragança, Faro, Figueira da Foz and Lisbon (*Grande* 1935–60 (18): 223–78). In 1893 Leite de Vasconcellos established the *Museu Etnológico Português* (Portuguese Ethnological Museum) in Lisbon (S. Machado 1964). During the same period, attempts were made to institutionalize the discipline. These included Estácio da Veiga's proposal in 1891 for the creation of a State Archaeology and Fine Arts Office and for archaeology to be included in the syllabus of the Lisbon Lyceum or within the Curso Superior de Letras (Higher Degree in Arts) (Gonçalves 1980a).

The archaeologists' higher education was directed, therefore, at training museum curators. In 1856, their training became the responsibility of the ESD in Spain, which offered a course in Archaeology and Numismatics. However, whilst in France the teaching of these subjects was transferred to the universities, the greater conservatism of Spain meant that this continued within the ESD. This remained the case despite an attempt to establish archaeology within the university curriculum in 1873 (Peiró and Pasamar Alzuría 1991: 145), although there were some exceptions, such as the course on prehistoric sciences given by Vilanova and Tubino in the University of Seville in 1872 (Ayarzagüena 1992: 20). In Portugal, a course on anthropology, palaeontology and prehistoric archaeology was taught in the Faculty of Philosophy at the University of Coimbra after 1885 on the initiative of Bernardino Machado (Fabião pers. comm.). However, this was not recognized as an official course (Raposo pers. comm.).

The prehistorians constitute a special case in both countries (as in most of Europe). Given that archaeology was considered to be the science of studying works of art and industry defined exclusively in terms of their antiquity (Peiró and Pasamar Alzuría 1991: 147), the absence of prehistoric works of art meant that, as in the rest of Europe, prehistorians were excluded from official archaeology courses (for the French case see Schnapp 1984: 49). In nineteenth-century Portugal, the formation of the Geological Commission in 1848 and its subsequent reorganization in 1857 (Castelo-Branco 1985: 195) led geologists to dominate prehistorical studies. A good example of this was the installation of a prehistoric collection in the *Museu dos Serviços Geológicos* (Geological Services Museum) founded in 1857. Geologists and physical anthropologists such as Carlos Ribeiro, Joaquim Filipe, Nery Delgado and Pereira da Costa were the first to carry out fieldwork in the subject (Jorge 1993: 103). Subsequently in Portugal, prehistory joined forces with ethnography through the activities of researchers in a number of provinces, including Martins Sarmento in Guimarães, Estàcio de Veiga in the Algarve, Leite de Vasconcelos in Lisbon and the group based around the journal *Portugalia* (1899–1908) in Oporto (Jorge 1993). This group was characterized by its anti-clerical positivism (Jorge pers. comm.). In Spain, the most important prehistorians were the geologists Casiano de Prado y Vallo and Juan Vilanova y Piera, together with ethnologists working in fields as diverse as journalism, biology or botany.

A new scientific discipline requires its own professional organs. In other European countries, specialized journals had already begun to appear in the eighteenth century, as with the journal *Archaeologia*, founded in Britain in 1770, or in the nineteenth century, as in the case of the French *Annales Archéologiques*, first published in 1844. In Spain, the first attempt came with the *Revista de Bellas Artes e Histórico-Arqueológica* published between 1866 and 1888 (Rueda Muñoz de San Pedro 1991). Only with the professionalization of archaeology would the first regular journals appear, the *Revista de Archivos, Bibliotecas y Museos* in 1871 or the more specialized *Museo Español de Antigüedades* in 1872. The aim of the former was corporatist, to maintain and, if possible, multiply the bonds of fellowship in the profession (quoted in Peiró and Pasamar Alzuría 1991: 143). In Portugal this development came a little later. The generation of the 1870s was responsible for a number of initiatives such as the *Revista de Guimarães* which Martins Sarmento published in 1884. Specialized journals first appeared in the 1890s, the *Boletim da Real Associação dos Architectos Civis e Archaeologos Portugueses* and *O Arqueólogo Português* (1895), along with others which included archaeology, such as *Revista Lusitana* in 1887 or *Portugalia* in 1899.

As a result of their relative underdevelopment, Spain and Portugal acquired a romantic image in northern Europe which was propagated by a stream of foreign travellers. In this way the Iberian Peninsula was also included in the sphere of colonial archaeology. Although it could hardly compete with the success of Greece, the importance of Italy or the exoticism of the East, it had something of all these. Professional foreign and non-professional archaeologists began to visit the Peninsula during the second half of the nineteenth century, the most romantic of these, such as the Anglo-French painter George Bonsor, settling in their adopted homeland. Others, such as the brothers Henri and Louis Siret, Belgian mining engineers, were brought to the Peninsula by their work. A third group only undertook study visits. This was the case with the Frenchmen Louis Lartet, René Verneuil and, a little later, Emile Cartailhac, Léon Heuzey, Arthur Engel and Pierre Paris, the British Hugo Falconer and George Busk, and the German epigrapher Emil Hübner. They all (except perhaps Hübner) shared a number of characteristics, writing most of their works in their native language, publishing them in their respective countries and only exceptionally contributing to Iberian journals. They even created their own professional organs, for example the *Bulletin de la Société Académique Franco-Hispano-Portugaise* in the 1870s. They socialized with each other, creating a network of correspondence to which Spaniards and Portuguese had little access (see for example Maier 1991), and they rarely cited native archaeologists in their works. The acknowledgements given by Pierre Paris in his 1903 book provide a striking example of this tendency. Whilst he thanked a number of anonymous Spaniards for the help they had given him, his French colleagues were individually named and their place of work given. Similarly, in *Promenades* (published in 1910) Paris mentions some Spanish archaeologists in passing whilst he devotes several paragraphs to the Anglo-French Bonsor. In general, foreign archaeologists fostered the image of Iberian archaeology as virgin and unexplored territory which they alone were beginning to chart.

Nevertheless, many of the studies written by these foreign archaeologists became essential works of reference in Iberian archaeology. This was perhaps inevitable given the sheer scale of works such as the second volume of Hübner's *Corpus Inscriptionum Latinarum* of 1869, *Les Âges préhistoriques de l'Espagne et du Portugal* published by Emile Cartailhac in 1886, the Siret brothers' *Les Premiers Âges du métal dans le sud-est de l'Espagne* of 1887, or Pierre Paris's *Essai sur l'art et l'industrie de l'Espagne primitive*, published in 1903. However, Spanish and Portuguese specialists also wrote surveys of Iberian archaeology in the nineteenth century. Examples from Portugal include Pereira da Costa's *Noções sobre o estado prehistorico da Terra e do Homem seguido da descripião de alguns dolmens ou antas en Portugal* (Notions on the prehistoric state of the Earth and of Humankind, followed by a description of some dolmens or antas of Portugal) (1868), or Felipe Simões with his *Introdução à archeologia da Península Ibérica* (Introduction to the Archaeology of the Iberian Peninsula), published in 1878 (Fabião 1989: 12). Less influential were the works by the Spaniards Sales and Ferré, *Prehistoria y el origen de la civilización* (Prehistory and the origin of civilization) of 1890, or Vilanova and Rada's *Protohistoria Ibérica* (Iberian Protohistory), published in 1892.

Iberian archaeologists were not passive in relation to Europe, although their lack of resources and geographical isolation made it harder for them to participate to the same extent as their richer northern neighbours. International prehistory conferences or universal exhibitions without a Spanish representative were exceptions (Ayarzagüena 1992), and in 1880 the Ninth International Conference of Anthropology and Prehistoric Archaeology was held in Lisbon (Gonçalves 1980b, 1993). Despite this, however, the limited resources available to the relatively few Iberian archaeologists meant that they made only a modest theoretical contribution to world and European archaeology. It is nonetheless worth mentioning the most significant of these, namely their contribution to the debate over tertiary man (Daniel 1975), the discovery of Palaeolithic art (Daniel 1975: IV.2) and the identification (Ayarzagüena 1992: 599), or at least defence (Bosch Gimpera 1919: 5),[3] of the existence of a Mesolithic period and the Copper Age.

Finally, the influence which nationalism had in the nineteenth century on Spanish and Portuguese archaeology should also be emphasized. As this has already been considered in detail for each country elsewhere (Díaz-Andreu 1994, 1995b, 1996b; Fabião 1996; Lillios 1995), I only wish to emphasize here the nationalist movement which spanned both countries, that is, Pan-Iberian nationalism. This emerged at the time of the unification of Italy and Germany, in 1870 and 1871 respectively, and aspired to create a single Iberian state. The archaeologists Vilanova y Piera, and de la Rada y Delgado, for example, argued in 1892 that Spain and Portugal were

> territories which, whilst they unfortunately constitute two politically separate nationalities, in terms of their primitive history should form a single unit, as no natural boundary separates them, and as has been said, both their geological structure and the peoples who since ancient time have inhabited them are the same.
>
> (Vilanova y Piera and Rada y Delgado 1892: 22)

Among the Portuguese Pan-Iberian nationalists were Augusto Filippe Simões and Oliveira Martins (Jiménez Díez 1993: 252). However, whether Pan-Iberian nationalist or not (and this was also true of the works written by foreigners mentioned above), most general works published in this period dealt with the archaeology of the Iberian Peninsula as a whole. This would be much less common during the twentieth century, above all in the middle decades of the century.

By the end of the nineteenth century, therefore, the foundations of Iberian archaeology had already been laid, a professional body formed and the first specialist journals published. However, although the contributions of distinguished figures such as Sautuola, Vilanova or Ribeiro were eventually incorporated into the corpus of scientific knowledge of the nineteenth century, the progress made by these two countries, geographically isolated on the edge of Europe and facing serious economic and political problems, was still not comparable to that of central and northern Europe.

NATIONALIST ARCHAEOLOGIES:
THE FIRST THIRD OF THE TWENTIETH CENTURY

In both Iberian countries, the crisis at the end of the century brought with it a critical reappraisal of the national social, political and intellectual situation. In Spain, the loss of the last remaining American and Pacific colonies was perceived as the culmination of a disaster which had been maturing for over a hundred years. In Portugal, the ultimatum issued by Britain in 1890 and the ensuing economic recession, which came after a period of prosperity, prompted a debate among politicians as to the best strategies for escaping underdevelopment and economic dependence on other countries. It was widely felt that Portugal was dominated by Great Britain, an idea echoed by the writer Eça de Queirós. Everything, he said, was imported, 'laws, ideas, philosophies, topics for discussion, aesthetic values, science, style, industry, fashion, manners, jokes, everything reaches us in small crates off the mail steamer' (quoted in Birmingham 1993: 135). It was in reaction to this sense of decadence which existed in both countries that a new spirit of intellectual enquiry emerged which also encompassed archaeology.

Archaeology changed significantly during the first three decades of the century in Spain, although the major advances were made from the 1920s onwards. Teaching was modernized, new legislation introduced, and a whole series of institutions and regular journals created to support the development of the discipline. In terms of methodology, this signified the introduction of the historical-cultural method, whilst the beginnings of organized fieldwork constituted a significant innovation in technique. It should be noted, however, that all this was more important in prehistory than in classical archaeology, as the latter still laboured under the weight of the nineteenth-century antiquarian tradition. The tendency towards ever greater professionalization begun in the preceding century continued, expanding to include prehistorians in the 1920s. The next decade saw women enter the profession in Spain for the first time (Díaz-Andreu and Sanz Gallego 1994), a development which would only come much later in Portugal (Jorge and Jorge 1993).

The anomalous position of the teaching of archaeology, which was still in the hands of the ESD, when in countries such as Denmark it had been taught in the university from the 1850s (Sørensen 1996), was rectified. In 1900 the subject was transferred to the universities, although at first this made little difference as the teachers remained the same, simply moving from one institution to another. In Portugal, some important changes were introduced in the context of the university reform of 1911. An Institute of Anthropology was created in the University of

Oporto that year, and it included prehistoric anthropology (Castelo-Branco 1985: 196; Jorge 1993: 104). In addition, Leite de Vasconcelos began to teach in around 1914 (Raposo pers. comm.), if only at secondary level, a course on archaeology, epigraphy and numismatics in the Ethnological Museum, which by then formed part of the Arts Faculty of the University of Lisbon (S. Machado 1964: 56). After 1923 Vergilio Correia gave a course on archaeology in the University of Coimbra (Fabião pers. comm.).

It was largely thanks to the influence of the prehistorians that in the 1920s Iberian archaeology underwent a revival which enabled it to escape its earlier inertia. In 1922 prehistory officially became part of the Spanish university system (in France this had happened in the 1890s (Fonton 1993: 74)) with the appointment of Hugo Obermaier as Professor of the Primitive History of Man at the University of Madrid. In 1933 this was followed by the addition of prehistory to the title of Pere Bosch Gimpera's chair, which from 1916 until then had been called simply ancient and medieval history, although Bosch Gimpera's work had been focused on prehistory. These innovations in prehistory can only be understood in the context of the broader spirit of renewal which then existed in the Spanish academic world, and the government's policy of establishing closer contacts between Spanish and European science which led to an evident improvement in the quality of teaching. In part this was achieved through foreign study scholarships awarded by the *Junta para la Ampliación de Estudios* (JAE, Council for the Enhancement of Studies), created in 1907 and won by at least twenty-three archaeologists (Díaz-Andreu 1995a, 1996a). Over 43 per cent of those who spent more than six months abroad chose to go to Italy where the JAE maintained a School of Art and Archaeology in Rome between 1910 and 1914. However, those who gained most from this experience and from the contacts maintained with colleagues in the host country were the ten archaeologists, including Pere Bosch Gimpera, who went to Germany. They were responsible for introducing influential theories from the rest of Europe into the Spanish academic system, thus bringing it up to the standard of its counterparts elsewhere. This influence was also felt in Portugal, in part through the works of Bosch Gimpera (Jorge 1993: 105).

All these changes were accompanied by the creation of a new legal framework for the discipline. In response to the sale of the Iberian sculpture the *Lady of Elche* to the Museum of the Louvre in 1897,[4] the Spanish government passed an Archaeological Excavations Act (Bosch Gimpera 1980: 52) in 1911 regulating archaeological activity and prohibiting the sale of antiquities abroad. The following year the *Junta Superior de Excavaciones y Antigüedades* (JSEA, Higher Council for Excavations and Antiquities) was created to enforce the new law. The spirit of the 1911 Act was later incorporated into the Heritage Act passed in 1933. In response to the rise of peripheral nationalisms, this transferred powers to some regions, for example Catalunya, which for a few years enjoyed administrative independence in so far as the regulation of archaeological activities was concerned (Marc-7 1986 (90)). This period also saw the appearance of archaeological services in regions such as Valencia (Pla Ballester 1980) and Catalunya (Marc-7 1986 (90)). In Portugal, however, despite the efforts made at the turn of the century by Estácio da Veiga, and with the exception of a 1901 decree defining the National Monuments (Raposo 1993: note 5), a measure which had been introduced in Spain more than fifty years earlier, in 1844, little progress was made in this respect before the declaration of the First Republic in 1910. New legislation was then enacted establishing the regional administrations' responsibility for the conservation and defence of national heritage, and creating, in 1915, the *Conselho Superior de Arte e Arqueologia* (Higher Council of Art and Archaeology), which had its headquarters in Lisbon, Porto and Coimbra (Ferreira 1993: xviii; Raposo 1993: 38).

The social composition of the discipline had remained largely unchanged since the nineteenth century. Despite a slow increase in the number of professionals in the field, there were still only about forty in the whole of Spain in 1930, including some thirty museum curators and the professors of archaeology and prehistory in the universities. In 1928 a woman was employed in an archaeological museum for the first time, and four more would be appointed before 1936. There were, of course, many more people who, without being professional archaeologists, were active in the field. For example, whilst the great majority of those receiving the substantial excavation grants were professional archaeologists, a number of grants were also awarded to architects and nobles. In fact, the Marquis of Cerralbo, an aristocrat who was not officially considered a professional archaeologist, received more excavation licences from the JSEA, although without grants, than any other person. In Portugal, non-professionals carrying out excavations included architects and clerics such as Father Francisco Manuel Alves and Father José Brenha.

During the first third of the century, and above all after the First World War when the principle of nationalities was incorporated into the peace treaties for the first time, European archaeology came to be profoundly influenced by nationalist ideologies. Germany played a particularly significant role in reinforcing the connection between nationalism and archaeology. In part this was simply a consequence of German academic strength. However, it also reflected the fact that the historical–cultural method had first appeared in Germany in 1898 and that it had become widely disseminated there after 1904 (Zwernemann 1983: 31–7). However, Bosch Gimpera considered that it was only in 1914 that Gustav Kossinna, the method's principal advocate, had come to understand the significance of cultural provinces and their relationship to peoples, and had begun to become interested in the problem of the Indo-Europeans (Bosch Gimpera 1980: 65). As a result of the highly politicized climate of the 1920s and

1930s, the different European archaeologies became impregnated with nationalist ideas. This was reflected in the fact that prestigious archaeologists were no longer to be found only in national capitals, but also in those regions demanding independence or autonomy. In Spain this was the case in Catalunya and the Basque Country, where Pere Bosch Gimpera and José Miguel de Barandiarán respectively guided the archaeologies of these regions, developing distinctly nationalist-type interpretations. In Catalunya, Spain's most prosperous country, Bosch Gimpera was able to organize what became known as the Catalan School of Archaeology.

The influence of German archaeology was also felt in Madrid as a consequence of the direct contacts which the archaeologists working in the city had with German academia. Not only was the first Professor of Prehistory, Hugo Obermaier, a German but a number of his disciples, such as Antonio García y Bellido, also obtained important posts in classical archaeology. Thanks to the scholarships obtained from the JAE, they had established close relations with their German counterparts, for example, García y Bellido with the German archaeologist Gerhart Rodenwaldt (Díaz-Andreu 1996a). As mentioned above, in Portgual nationalism in part entered archaeological discourse through the works of Bosch Gimpera. This development was reflected in studies by A. Mendes Correia – which included titles as significant as *Raça e Nacionalidade* (1919, Race and Nationality) or *As bases geográficas e étnicas da nova carta política de Europa* (1921, The Geographical and Ethnic Foundations of the New Political Map of Europe) – whose work was devoted to the search for Portugal's ethnic and archaeological roots (Castelo-Branco 1985: 196). The creation of Anthropology, Prehistory and Ethnology associations, bodies which had first appeared in Germany in the nineteenth century and which around 1920 were imitated in Catalunya (1923–6), Madrid (1921) and Portugal (1918), were products of this influence.

A continuation of the tendency of the preceding period was the increasing number of specialist journals. They now generally included reports of findings obtained from excavations, whilst the JAE's excavation reports were dedicated exclusively to these. However, not everything had changed in this respect. The journal *Archivo Español de Arte y Arqueología* reflected the continued influence of nineteenth-century conceptions of classical archaeology during the first third of the century. The same was also true in Portugal, as can be seen from the collection devoted to the country's monuments which the *Associação dos Archeologos Portugueses* (Association of Portuguese Archaeologists) began to publish in 1929. These studies were intended to foster popular interest in Portugal's artistic and architectural heritage, and were largely dedicated to monumental buildings rather than archaeological finds. Journals such as *O Arqueólogo Português*, first published back in 1895, or *Arqueologia e Historia* (in its first phase still linked to monument conservation rather than to archaeology) which appeared in 1922, demonstrated a more modern conception of the discipline, although more general journals, such as *Revista de Guimarães*, continued to occupy an important place in Portuguese archaeology.

As far as the role of foreign archaeologists is concerned, two different tendencies can be observed during the first third of the twentieth century. On the one hand, the presence of Frenchmen such as Pierre Paris, Henri Breuil (who exercised a great influence on Spain and especially on Portugal) and Arthur Engel, and the Germans August Frickenhaus and Adolf Schulten, represented a degree of continuity from the nineteenth century. On the other hand, this period was characterized by the first real institutionalization of the archaeological colonization of the Peninsula, a process which developed much later than in Greece or Italy, as Iberia did not form part of traditional constructions of Europe's past. First, *Revue Hispanique* and *Bulletin Hispanique*, which included articles on both Spain and Portugal, began publication in 1894 and 1899 respectively (Niño Rodríguez 1988: 147–64). Then, in 1909, the *École des Hautes Études Hispaniques* (School of Advanced Hispanic Studies) was set up in Bordeaux under the direction of Pierre Paris (Niño Rodríguez 1988: 186). Two decades later, in 1928, when the French School, the *Casa de Velázquez*, was established in Madrid as the first base for foreign archaeologists in Spain, Paris was appointed its director. Through this school, and through those which existed in Athens and Rome, France aspired to lead a kind of Latin union which would counteract the advancing Germanization of northern Europe (Gran-Aymerich and Gran-Aymerich 1991: 184). The creation of the Hispanic Society of America in 1904, which also played a role in the development of archaeology in the Peninsula, should also be mentioned in this context. Although still important, foreign influences became more evenly balanced during this period. Spain, at least, was involved in a number of international projects such as the *Corpus Vasorum Antiquorum* (Olmos 1989) or the *Tabula Imperii Romani* (in which Spaniards were present from the very beginning) (Olmos *et al.* 1993: 58). General works such as Mendes Correa's 1928 volume *A Lusitânia Pré-Romana* (Pre-Roman Lusitania) (Jorge 1993: 104) or Bosch Gimpera's much more important *Etnologia de la península Ibèrica* (Ethnology of the Iberian Peninsula) of 1932, reflected the flourishing health of Iberian archaeology in the 1930s.

ARCHAEOLOGY AND MILITARY DICTATORSHIP: THE MUZZLED DECADES

For forty years, the history of Spain and Portugal was marked by military dictatorships imposed in the 1920s and 1930s. In Spain, the dictatorship established in 1923 fell in 1930, but after the brief democratic interval of the Second Republic, General Francisco Franco's victory in the Civil War led to another dictatorship which only came to an end in 1975. In Portugal, this form of government was established in 1926 and did not disappear until 1974. Both dictatorships shared common characteristics which affected archaeology. In organizational terms, state centralization directed from the Spanish capital led to the elimination of all the steps taken towards autonomous government in those regions with nationalist aspirations. Meanwhile, the discipline increasingly became the preserve of professionals. As for archaeological interpretations, certain subjects were emphasized in an attempt to legitimate the regimes, as was the case with Vila Nova de São Pedro in Portugal (Lillios 1995). However, neither in Spain (Díaz-Andreu 1993, 1994) nor in Portugal (Jorge 1993: 102) did the military regimes consistently foster the development of archaeology, with the result that Jorge (1993) considers this era in Portugal to have been one of stagnation. Finally, it should be noted that fluid relations existed between archaeologists in both countries until at least the 1960s, through the exchange of contributions to the journals that were beginning to appear at this time. This was possible even though Pan-Iberian nationalism had disappeared from their interpretations, to be replaced by a new emphasis on the distinctiveness of each country. This was reflected in the celebration of separate National Archaeological Congresses, held from 1949 onwards in Spain and from 1958 in Portugal (Jorge 1993: 105).

Great changes took place in the administration of archaeology in Spain (Díaz-Andreu 1993) and in Portugal. In Portugal, the *Direcção Geral dos Edifícios e Monumentos Nacionais* (Department of National Buildings and Monuments) was established to promote, organize and execute all the work necessary for the preservation and restoration of the country's heritage. A series of decrees issued in 1932 and 1933 regulated archaeological excavations, which were now made the responsibility of new organizations, the *Junta Nacional de Educação* (National Council of Education), the *Junta Nacional de Excavaçoes e Antiguidades* (National Council for Excavations and Antiquities) (which disappeared in 1936, competence in this field being transferred to the *Junta Nacional del Educação* until 1977) and the *Comissões Municipais de Arte e Arqueologia* (Municipal Art and Archaeology Committees) (Raposo 1993: 38–9). Meanwhile, the Geological Department continued to supervise the collection of data about finds and to serve as host for the foreign archaeologists (Breuil, Roche and to some extent both Leisners) working in the country.

Exclusively archaeological journals also now appeared for the first time. *Ampurias* came out in 1939. It was an initiative promoted by the new professor in Barcelona – who replaced the exiled Bosch Gimpera – Martín Almagro Basch. A year later it was followed by *Archivo Español de Arqueología* (now definitively an archaeological rather than art journal), and *Zephyrus*. A number of Portuguese journals were also launched in the same period: *Revista de Arqueología* (1932), *Ethnos* (1935), *Nummus* (1953), *Viriatis* (1957) and *Conimbriga* (1959). In both countries, however, the quality of publications still left much to be desired (Jorge 1993: 105), as until the 1970s they largely consisted of inaccurate descriptions of sites and only rarely were subjects treated systematically.

It was in this period that archaeology was definitively transformed into a profession, while untrained and amateur archaeologists gradually lost the recognition that they had previously enjoyed. In the 1940s and 1950s, it was still common to find priests, engineers, doctors, etc. engaged in archaeological activity (Lucas Pellicer 1991), one notable example being Eugenio Jalhay, who was responsible for the excavation of Vila Nova de São Pedro in Portugal, and another being the important 'school' formed by geologists such as Georges Zbyszewski, who, together with Henri Breuil, carried out important work on Palaeolithic Portugal (Fabião pers. comm.). After 1970, however, hardly any new figures joined the ranks of the amateur archaeologists, because of the strength of institutional archaeology, which excluded amateurs from doing official archaeology. In the 1970s, following the example set by Barcelona, Spanish universities expanded the teaching of prehistory, now offered as an undergraduate, and not merely postgraduate, course. In Portugal, prehistory had already been reintroduced into the universities in 1957, although as courses were left in the hands of non-specialist lecturers it remained a peripheral subject (Jorge 1993: 102). On the eve of the Civil War women had begun to join the profession in Spain, but this process came to an abrupt halt during the first two decades of the dictatorship. It was not until the 1960s, and particularly the 1970s, that women began to find posts in Spanish universities again (Díaz-Andreu and Sanz Gallego 1994). In Portugal Virgínia Rau in the 1940s became the first woman to publish works on archaeology. She was followed by at least six more women in the 1950s, who later obtained positions in museums (Fabião pers. comm.).

Foreign archaeologists were still active in the Peninsula during this period. Spaniards and Italians collaborated as equals on different projects (and this has a political reading), as was the case with Martín Almagro Basch and Nino Lamboglia at the Roman town of Empúries. These contacts led to the organization of successive international courses at this site from 1947, which played an important role in the development of Spanish archaeology. It was here that Lamboglia's method of excavation was first introduced as an alternative to that of Wheeler (Carandini 1981: 32–3, Without Author 1974). The French box method of excavation was introduced into Portugal by Eduardo Serrão and Prescott Vicente in 1956 (Jorge and Jorge 1993).

Whilst the influence of the French declined, German archaeology remained an important force with the presence first of Vera and Georg Leisner, and later of the *Deutsches Archäologisches Institut* (DAI, German Archaeological Institute), established in Madrid in 1943 (Grünlagen 1979) and in Lisbon in 1972 (Jorge 1993: 106). In this way, the pervasive influence of German archaeology during the first three decades of the century was maintained. The dissemination of excavation techniques in the 1960s was largely the work of these German archaeologists, who built upon the achievements of the courses in Empúries and taught it to Portuguese (Jorge 1993: 104) and Spanish students. On the other hand, in the 1940s British archaeologists, or archaeologists working in Great Britain, began to return to the Peninsula. The most prominent of these were John Evans and Vere Gordon Childe (see, for example, Carvalho 1989), who even sent one of his disciples, Eoin MacWhite, to study in Madrid with Julio Martínez Santa-Olalla. Childe, who made numerous visits to the Peninsula, gained a certain amount of influence in Iberian archaeology thanks to the translation of his works into both Portuguese (Jorge 1993: 105) and Spanish (printed in Mexico and Argentina), and to the publication of a large number of reviews of these. Finally, in 1968, Hubert Newman Savory wrote a prehistory of Spain and Portugal. The French continued to operate from their Madrid head-quarters in the *Casa de Velázquez*, which had reopened in 1959 after being completely rebuilt (Delaunay 1994). In the 1960s they would be responsible for restarting the excavation of the Roman town of Baelo (Bolonia) begun by Pierre Paris and Bonsor before the Civil War. However, since French archaeologists maintained only loose contacts with their Spanish colleagues, their influence in this period was weak (except in Palaeolithic studies). Later, in the 1970s, a new generation of foreign archaeologists began to work in Spain and Portugal, a generation char-acterized by their close relationships with Spanish or Portuguese archaeologists, which would later, in the 1980s, bear fruit in collabora-tive projects.

As a logical consequence of the internal political situation in both countries, the presence of archaeologists from the Iberian Peninsula declined on the international scene. Their participation in the *Corpus Vasorum Antiquorum* and the *Tabula Imperii Romani* projects was frozen, whilst in Spain these were substituted by nationalist-inspired ventures, the *Corpus Vasorum Hispanorum* and the *Cartas Arqueológicas Provinciales*, neither of which met with much success (Olmos *et al.* 1993). Spain and Portugal were not only colonized countries but also colonizers. The colo-nial presence of Spanish archaeologists in Morocco, and the Portuguese in Angola and Mozambique, was characterized by explicitly nationalist perspectives (see for example Pérez de Barradas *et al.* 1940).

Mention should also be made of the new auxiliary archaeological tech-niques introduced from the early 1960s. These included radiocarbon dating, dendrochronology, and silicate, x-ray, neutron and oxygen isotope analyses, all of which were discussed in articles by Martín Almagro Gorbea and others mostly published in *Trabajos de Prehistoria* between 1970 and 1976. In contrast to this technical progress, archaeological theory remained virtually unchanged (Vázquez Varela and Risch 1991:

27–31). The cultural-historical method was still in use, although it gradually lost its ideological character. Ruiz Rodríguez (1993: 307) has described this as archaeology which lay somewhere between highly idealistic historicism and the innocent eclecticism of traditional positivism. Applied mechanically, this gave rise to an 'archaeography' characterized by historicist tendencies, the virtual absence of generalizations, a lack of interest in problems such as those presented by the environment, and bereft of interdisciplinary approaches. In practice, it seems probable that in this respect Iberian archaeology differed little from that of the rest of continental Europe. These basically traditional, if technically updated, archaeologies of Portugal and Spain would be transformed by the major political changes which took place in 1974 and 1975.

IBERIAN ARCHAEOLOGY TODAY

The transition to democracy in both countries in the mid-1970s had far-reaching implications in a number of areas. Political freedom led to the adoption of new theories whilst changes in the law radically altered the way in which the historic heritage was administered. These developments, combined with the prosperity of the 1980s, provoked significant social change within the archaeological profession.

Spain's administrative system has been profoundly modified in recent years. As a result of the division of the country into seventeen autonomous communities with the power to determine their own cultural policies, archaeology has evolved differently in the distinct regions (Dupré i Raventós 1991, García Fernández 1989). In general, since plans of action must now be presented before work can begin, the haphazard excavation of archaeological remains is avoided. New projects, such as Archaeological Parks (Parques Arqueológicos 1993) are also now under way in Spain. New regulations governing archaeological excavations were introduced in 1978, whilst in 1985 these were followed by the Cultural Heritage Act. Similar developments have taken place in Portugal. In 1973 the *Direcção-Geral de Asuntos Culturais* (Department of Cultural Affairs) was established and, within this, the *Divisão de Patrimonio Cultural* (Cultural Heritage Office). The year 1980 saw the creation of the *Instituto Português do Património Cultural* (Portuguese Institute of Cultural Heritage) (replaced in 1992 by the *Instituto Português do Património Arquitectónico e Arqueológico* (Portuguese Institute of Architectural and Archaeological Heritage)), now called IPAR, and *Serviços Regionais de Arqueologia* (Regional Archaeological Departments). Originally set up in order to decentralize archaeological administration, these regional offices were subsequently abolished in 1990 (Jorge 1993: 107; Raposo 1993: 39–42; Real 1991). The number of archaeological journals has also multiplied in this period.

The appearance of rescue archaeology in both countries is a major innovation in recent years (Jorge 1993: 103, Ruiz Zapatero 1993: 61–6).

It has contributed to the expansion of urban archaeology, and hence classical and medieval archaeology, to the detriment of research in more traditional areas of the discipline. This is due to the fact that resources which the state normally obtains from developers are channelled into rescue archaeology (Ruiz Zapatero 1993: Figure 6.7).

The social composition of archaeology has also changed significantly. Although the profession remains small in comparison with countries such as France or Great Britain (see, for example, Schnapp 1984: 51), it has expanded with the number of professional archaeologists rising significantly, above all during the prosperous 1980s. There are now some 200 archaeologists working in Spanish universities and another forty in state museums, a figure which would more than double if those employed in museums of the autonomous communities were taken into account. The consolidation of rescue archaeology at the end of the 1980s has enlarged and profoundly transformed the profession. Whilst this previously consisted almost exclusively of university teachers and those employed in research institutions, at least 50 per cent of archaeologists in Spain now make a living from rescue archaeology. Evidently these constitute a powerful force. In Portugal, the expansion of the profession appears to have followed a similar pattern, where most of the university departments teaching archaeology are very recent creations (Lemos 1992: 54). In terms of the social composition of the profession, the incorporation of women should be noted. In Spain, some 40 per cent of all archaeologists are women, whilst in Portugal the figure is still somewhat lower (Jorge and Jorge 1993). The expansion of professional archaeology has been accompanied by a reduction in the number of amateurs qualified to express their ideas on the subject. The scale of this change is such that even in the bulletin of the Spanish *Asociación de Amigos de la Arqueología* (Association of Friends of Archaeology), an organization originally composed of amateurs, the majority of articles published are now written by professionals.

Great progress has also been made in terms of the techniques employed, which have achieved a high standard. This has meant the definitive consolidation of the Wheeler method in archaeological excavations, the systematic study of material evidence, the spread of palaeo-economic and environmental studies, and, more recently, the use of sophisticated electronic equipment. The *Primeras Jornadas de Metodología de Investigación Prehistórica* (First Workshop on Prehistoric Research Methodology) held in Soria in 1981 marked an important milestone in this respect in Spain, as the majority of papers presented dealt with distinct technical innovations. It should be emphasized that the standardization of techniques spread to all areas of the discipline during this period, even the most resistant of all, medieval archaeology.

The most obvious, if not yet universal, transformation to take place in recent years has been the development and application of archaeological theory, particularly in prehistory. The 1981 Soria Workshop was also important in this respect, as some papers presented there discussed epistemological questions. Subsequent developments have been outlined elsewhere (Vázquez Varela and Risch 1991). The influence attained by the new post-processual archaeology is still unclear, although elements of this can be detected in the most recent work by the Portuguese archaeologist Victor O. Jorge and by others. Nevertheless, reactions to this approach have already begun to appear (Lull *et al*. 1990; Ruiz Rodríguez *et al*. 1988; Vicent 1990). As far as prehistoric archaeology is concerned, the major impact of this development has been a decline in German influence and a rise in that exercised by the archaeology of the English-speaking world.

The incorporation of these new theoretical trends has been reflected in the growing internationalization of Iberian archaeology. One result of this is that foreign archaeologists have now begun to collaborate directly with Spanish and Portuguese teams for the first time. The greater international presence of the archaeological innovations of both countries is demonstrated by their active participation in recent annual meetings of the American Anthropological Association and the Theoretical Archaeology Group in Britain among others. Here, Spanish and Portuguese archaeologists have appeared in the same sessions, whilst the First Congress of Peninsular Archaeology held in Oporto in 1993, in which numerous Spanish scholars took part, was fostered, for example, by the Portuguese archaeologist Victor O. Jorge. This Congress is a further index of the closer relations which now exist between Portuguese and Spanish archaeologists. These represent another important step towards the integration of Iberia into the mainstream of European academic tradition.

ACKNOWLEDGEMENTS

I would like to express my gratitude for the comments which Gloria Mora (CSIC), Vitor Oliveira Jorge (University of Oporto) and Carlos Fabião (University of Lisbon) made on this chapter, and for the help received from my Portuguese colleages Antonio Carvalho (Cascais), José d'Encarnação (University of Coimbra), Teresa Marqués (IPPAR), João Carlos de Senna Martinez (University of Lisbon) and Luís Raposo (Museu Nacional de Arqueología, Lisbon).

NOTES

1   The analysis presented in this chapter is largely possible thanks to the existence of a body of existing work. It should be noted that the majority of these studies have been published during the last two decades and that they represent a dramatic increase in our knowledge of the development of archaeology in both countries. They also reflect the growing maturity of the

discipline in the Peninsula. In Spain, the conference on the Historiography of Spanish Ancient History (eighteenth to twentieth centuries) held in Madrid in December 1988 (Arce and Olmos (eds.) 1991) was an important milestone in this respect. This has been complemented by the appearance of a number of doctoral theses (Ayarzagüena 1992; Cortadella i Morral 1992; Jiménez Díez 1993; Mora 1994), statewide (Cerrillo 1987; Díaz-Andreu 1993, 1994; Dupré i Raventós 1991, 1992; González Morales 1992; Martínez Navarrete 1990; Ripoll 1993; Ruiz Zapatero 1993) or regional studies (on Catalunya (Marc-7 1986; VVAA 1992), Valencia (Goberna Valencia 1981, 1983, 1985, 1990), the Basque Country (Barandiarán 1988) and Galicia (Casal García 1984)) and works on questions such as the history of theory (Lull 1991; Vázquez Varela and Risch 1991) or of institutions (Gran-Aymerich and Gran-Aymerich 1991; Grünlagen 1979; López 1993; Vicent 1993). In Portugal, interest in the subject is also on the increase (Alves 1989; Castelo-Branco 1985; Custódio 1992; Fabião 1989, 1993; Jorge 1993; Lemos 1987, 1992; Raposo 1992, 1993; Ramos *et al.* 1993; Real 1991; Santos 1980, 1981; Soromenho and Silva 1992). This is reflected by the appearance of a number of works considering the political use made of different aspects of the past (Guerra and Fabião 1992), as well as other isolated studies in the field (Carvalho 1989; Gonçalves 1980a, 1980b, 1993; Silva 1980). Figure 2.1 shows the places and sites mentioned in the text.

2 For the above see Sanz Pastor (1990) and Raposo (1992: 18). However, as Fabião (1996) states, this led to a special protection of medieval monuments, leaving aside those from other periods.

3 According to Bosch Gimpera (1980) the idea originated with the Austrian Mateu Muth whilst Daniel (1987: 146) maintains that it was first proposed by other archaeologists, such as François von Pulsky and others including Italian archaeologists.

4 Bosch Gimpera affirms that the Act was a product of the creation of the Higher Council for Excavations, that itself was a product of the 1911 law.

REFERENCES

Alcina Franch, J. (1989) *Arqueología antropológica*, Madrid: Akal.

Alves, F.J.S. (1989) *Museu Nacional de Arqueologia e Etnologia. Portugal das origens à época romana*, Lisbon: Museo Nacional de Arqueologia e Etnologia and Instituto Português do Património Cultural.

Arce, J. and Olmos, R. (eds) (1991) *Historiografía de la arqueología y de la historia antigua en España (siglos XVIII–XX)*, Madrid: Ministerio de Cultura.

Ayarzagüena Sanz, M. (1992) *La arqueología prehistórica y protohistórica Española en el siglo XIX*, Madrid: Universidad Nacional de Educación a Distancia.

Barandiarán, I. (1988) *Enciclopedia General Ilustrada del País Vasco. I. Prehistoria: Paleolítico*, San Sebastián: Auñamendi.

Birmingham, D. (1993) *A Concise History of Portugal*, Cambridge: Cambridge University Press.

Bosch Gimpera, P. (1919) *Prehistòria Catalana*. Enciclopédia Catalana XVI, Barcelona: Catalana.

—— (1980) *Pere Bosch Gimpera. Memòries*, Barcelona: Edicions 62.

Bray, W. and Glover, I.C. (1987) 'Scientific Investigation or Cultural Imperialism: British Archaeology in the Third World', *Bulletin of the Institute of Archaeology* 24: 109–25.

Carandini, A. (1981) *Storïe dalla terra. Manuale dello scavo archeologico*, Bari: De Donato.

Carvalho, A. (1989) 'Para a História da arqueologia em Portugal. O livro de visitantes de Junta de Turismo de Cascais', *Arquivo de Cascais* 8: 75–150.

Casal García, R. (1984) 'Resumen breve de la investigación arqueológica en Galicia hoy', in F. Acuña Castroviejo, R. Casal García, J. J. Eiroa García, J. M. Hidalgo Cuñarro, and J. M. Vázquez Varela, *La prehistoria y arqueología en la actualidad*: 7–15, Vigo: Publicaciones del Museo Municipal Quiñones de León (Castrelos).

Castelo-Branco, F. (1985) 'Arqueologia portuguesa', in J. Serrão (ed.), *Dicionãrio de História de Portugal* 1: 195–8, Oporto: Livraria Figueirinhas [1971, Lisbon: Iniciativas Editoriais].

Cerrillo, E. (1987) 'La arqueología en España', in C. A. Moberg, *Introducción a la arqueología*: 217–32, Madrid: Cátedra.

Corrêa, A. (1947) 'Histoire des recherches préhistoriques en Portugal', *Trabalhos de Antropologia e Etnografia* 11 (1–2): 115–70.

Cortadella i Morral, J. (1992) La *història antiga en la historigrafia catalana*, Edició microfotogràfica, Barcelona: Publicacions de la Universitat Autònoma de Barcelona.

Custódio, J. (1992) 'Salvaguarda do património. Antecedentes históricos. De Alexandre Herculano à Carta de Veneza (1837–1964)', in *Dar Futuro ao Passado*: 34–71, Lisbon: IPPAR.

Daniel, G. (1975) *A Hundred and Fifty Years of Archaeology*, London: Duckworth. 2nd edition [1987, *Un siglo y medio de Arqueología*, México: Fondo de Cultura Económica].

Delaunay, J.M. (1994) *Des Palais en Espagne. L'École des hautes études hispaniques et la Casa de Velázquez au coeur des relations franco-espagnoles du XXe siècle (1898–1979)*, Bibliothèque de la Casa de Velázquez 10, Madrid: Casa de Velázquez.

Díaz-Andreu, M. (1993) 'Theory and Ideology in Archaeology: Spanish Archaeology under the Franco Regime', *Antiquity* 67: 74–82.

—— (1994) 'The Past in the Present: The Search for Roots in Cultural Nationalisms. The Spanish Case', in J. G. Beramendi, R. Máiz and X. M. Núñez (eds) *Nationalisms in Europe: Past and Present* I: 199–218, Santiago de Compostela: Universidade de Santiago de Compostela.

—— (1995a) 'Arqueólogos españoles en Alemania en el primer tercio del siglo XX. Los becarios de la Junta de Ampliación Estudios (I) Pedro Bosch Gimpera', *Madrider Mitteilungen* 36: 13–40.

—— (1995b) 'Nationalism and Archaeology. Spanish Archaeology in the Europe of Nationalities', in P. Kohl and C. Fawcett (eds) *Nationalism, Politics, and the Practice of Archaeology*: 39–56, Cambridge: Cambridge University Press.

—— (1996a) 'Arqueólogos españoles en Alemania en el primer tercio del siglo XX. Los becarios de la Junta de Ampliación Estudios (II)', *Madrider Mitteilungen* 37.

—— (1996b) 'Islamic Archaeology and the Origin of the Spanish Nation', in M. Díaz-Andreu and T. Champion (eds) *Archaeology and Nationalism in Europe*:

68–9, London: UCL Press.

Díaz-Andreu, M. and Sanz Gallego, N. (1994) 'Women in Spanish Archaeology', in M. C. Nelson, S. M. Nelson and A. Wylie (eds) *Equity Issues for Women in Archaeology*: 121–30, Archaeological Papers of the American Anthropological Association 5, Washington: American Anthropological Association.

Dupré i Raventos, X. (1991) 'L'Organisation de l'archéologie territoriale en Espagne', in V. Negri (ed.) *L'Organisation territoriale de l'archéologie en Europe*: 47–57, Douai: Anact.

—— (1992) 'La Protection du patrimoine archéologique en Espagne: aspects légaux', in V. Negri (ed.) *Protection pénale du patrimoine archéologique*. Paris: L'Hermès.

Fabião, C. (1989) 'Estudos para a História da Arqueologia em Portugal', *Penélope. Fazer e desfazer história* 2: 10–26.

—— (1993) 'A arqueologia pré-histórica', in J. Medina and V. S. Gonçalves (eds) *Historia de Portugal* I: 108–15, Lisbon: Ediclube.

—— (1996) 'Nationalism and Archaeology. The Portuguese Case', in M. Díaz-Andreu and T. Champion (eds) *Archaeology and Nationalism in Europe*: 90–107, London: UCL Press.

[Antero] Ferreira, C. (1993) 'Prefácio', *Património Arquitectónico e Arqueológico Classificado*: I–XXV. Lisbon: IPPAR.

Fonton, M. (1993) 'Les Muséums d'histoire naturelle et la préhistoire. Deux cas d'Espèce: le Muséum National d'Histoire Naturelle. Le Muséum d'Histoire Naturelle de Toulouse', in *La Préhistoire en France. Musées, écoles de fouilles, associations du XIXᵉ siècle à nos jours*, Paris: Editions du CTHS.

França, J.A. (1986) 'El siglo XIX', *Summa Artis. Historia General del Arte XXX. Arte Portugués*: 399–482, Madrid: Espasa-Calpe.

García Fernández, J. (1989) 'The New Spanish Archaeological Heritage Legislation', in H. Cleere (ed.) *Archaeological Heritage Management in the Modern World*: 182–94, One World Archaeology, London: Unwin Hyman.

Goberna Valencia, M.V. (1981) 'La Sociedad Arqueológica Valenciana', *Archivo de Prehistoria Levantina* XVI: 575–608.

—— (1983) 'Los estudios de arqueología y prehistoria en el País Valenciano durante la segunda mitad del siglo XIX', *Llansol de Romaní* III (3): 19–22.

—— (1985) 'Arqueología y prehistoria en el País Valenciano: Aportaciones a la historia de la investigación', *Arqueología del País Valenciano: Panorama y Perspectivas*: 9–30, Anejo de la Revista Lucentum, Alicante: Universidad de Alicante.

—— (1990) 'La donación "Vilanova" a la biblioteca del S.I.P', *Archivo de Prehistoria Levantina* XX: 475–9.

Gonçalves, V.S. (1980a) 'Estacio du Veiga; um programa para a instituçã dos estudos arqueológicos em Portugal (1880–1891)', *CEHC/CHUL/IV CNA*.

—— (1980b) *O IX Congresso Internacional de Antropologia e Arqueologia Pré-Históricas (Lisboa, 1880); uma leitura seguida da 'crónica' de Bordalo Pinheiro*, Lisbon: CHUL.

—— (1993) 'O Congresso Internacional de 1880', in J. Medina and V. S. Gonçalves (eds) *Historia de Portugal* I: 99–108, Lisbon: Ediclube.

González Morales, M.R. (1992) 'Racines. La justification archéologique des origines régionales dans l'Espagne des communautés autonomes', in T. Shay and J. Clottes (eds) *The Limitations of Archaeological Knowledge*: 15–27, Liège: Université de Liège.

Gran-Aymerich, E. and Gran-Aymerich, J. (1991) 'La Création des Écoles françaises d'Athènes, Rome et Madrid', *Extraits de Communications* 54: 175–86.

Grande Enciclopédia portuguesa e brasileira (1935–60), Lisbon and Rio de Janeiro.

Grünlagen, W. (1979) 'Zur Geschichte der Abteilung Madrid des Deutschen Archäologischen Instituts von 1929 bis 1979', *Das Deutsche Archäologische Institut. Geschichte und Dokumente* 3: 117–65, Mainz am Rhein: Verlag Philipp von Zabern.

Guerra, A. and Fabião, C. (1992) 'Viriato: Genealogia de um Mito', *Penélope. Fazer e desfazer a história* 8: 9–23.

Jalhay, E. (1947–8) 'Una fase interesante del Bronce inicial portugués', *Ampurias* 9–10: 13–20.

Jiménez Díez, J.A. (1993) 'Historiografía de la pre y protohistoria de la Península Ibérica en el siglo XIX', unpublished Ph.D. thesis, University Complutense of Madrid.

[Oliveira] Jorge, S. and [O.] Jorge, V. (1993) 'Women in Portuguese archaeology', unpublished paper, presented at TAG, session on 'Women in European Archaeology', Durham, December 1993.

[Oliveira] Jorge, S. and [O.] Jorge, V. (1995) 'Theoretical underpinnings of Portuguese archaeology in the twentieth century', in P. Ucko (ed.) *Theory in Archaeology. A World Perspective*: 251–62, London and New York: Routledge.

[Oliveira] Jorge, S. and [O.] Jorge, V. (forthcoming) 'Women in Portuguese Archaeology', in Trabalhos de Antropologia e Etnologia.

[Oliveira] Jorge, V. (1993) 'Presupòsists teòrics de l'arqueologia portuguesa al segle XX: algunes aportacions', *Cota Zero* 9: 102–9.

Larousse, P. (1865–90) *Grand Dictionnaire universel du XIXᵉ siècle*, Paris: Larousse.

[Sande] Lemos, F. (1987) 'As três idades da arqueologia portuguesa', *Forum* 2: 5–11.

—— (1992) 'Arqueologia portuguesa: próximo futor. Previsões para a última década do II milenio', *Forum* 11: 53–64.

Lillios, K. (1995) 'Nationalism and the Historiography of Copper and Bronze Age Portugal', in P. Kohl and C. Fawcett (eds) *Nationalism, Politics, and the Practice of Archaeology*: 57–74, Cambridge: Cambridge University Press.

López, P. (1993) 'El Centro de Estudios Históricos', in M. I. Martínez Navarrete (ed.) *Theory and Practice of Prehistory: Views from the Edges of Europe*: 15–18, Santander: Servicio de Publicaciones de la Universidad de Cantabria.

Lucas Pellicer, Mᵃ R. (1991) 'La arqueología no profesional: antecedentes y panorama actual', in J. Arce and R. Olmos (eds): 237–42.

Lull, V. (1991) 'La prehistoria de la teoría arqueológica en el Estado español', in A. Vila (ed.) *Arqueología. Nuevas Tendencias*: 231–50, Madrid: Consejo Superior de Investigaciones Científicas.

Lull, V., Micó, R., Montón, S. and Picazo, M.(1990) 'La arqueología entre la insoportable levedad y la voluntad de poder', *Archivo de Prehistoria Levantina* 20: 461–74.

[Saavedra] Machado, J.L. (1964) 'Subsídios para a História do Museu Etnológico de D.ᵒʳ Leite de Vasconcelos', *O Arqueólogo Português* 5: 51–448.

Maier, J. (1991) 'El epistolario de Jorge Bonsor; correspondencia con Luis Siret', in J. Arce and R. Olmos (eds): 149–56.

Marc-7 (X. Dupré, O. Granados, E. Junyent, X. Nieto, N. Rafel and F. Tarrats) (1986) 'L'arqueologia catalana', *L'Avenç* 90: 139–45, 91: 224–31 and 92: 291–7.

Marcos Pous, A. (ed.) (1993) *De gabinete a museo. Tres siglos de historia. Museo Arqueológico Nacional*, Madrid: Ministerio de Cultura.

Martínez Navarrete, M.I. (1989) *Una revisión crítica de la prehistoria española. La Edad del Bronce como paradigma*, Madrid: Siglo XXI.

—— (1990) 'La prehistoria española en los últimos cincuenta años', *Hispania* L/2 (175): 439–57.

—— (ed.) (1993) *Theory and Practice of Prehistory: Views from the Edges of Europe*, Santander: Servicio de Publicaciones de la Universidad de Cantabria.

Mélida, J.R. (1922) *Excursión a Numancia pasando por Soria*, Madrid: Ruiz Hnos.

Mora, G. (1991) 'Arqueología y poder en la España del siglo XVIII', in J. Arce and R. Olmos (eds): 31–2.

—— (1994) 'La arqueología clásica en España en el siglo XVIII', Unpublished Ph.D. thesis, Universidad Complutense de Madrid.

Niño Rodríguez, A. (1988) *Cultura y diplomacia. Los hispanistas franceses y España de 1875–1931*, Madrid: CSIC, Casa de Velázquez and Société des Hispanistes Français.

Olmos, R. (1989) 'El Corpus Vasorum Antiquorum, setenta años después: pasado, presente y futuro del gran proyecto internacional de la cerámica antigua', *Archivo Español de Arqueología* 62: 292–303.

Olmos, R., Plácido, D., Sánchez Palencia, J. and Cepas, A. (1993) 'El origen de las cartas arqueológicas y el Mapa del Mundo Romano', *Inventarios y Cartas arqueológicas*: 45–56, Valladolid: Junta de Castilla y León.

Paris, P. (1910) *Promenades archéologiques en Espagne* I, Paris: Ernest Leroux.

Parques Arqueológicos (1993), Madrid: Instituto de Conservación y Restauración de Bienes Culturales.

Pasamar Alzuría, G. and Peiró Martín, I. (1991) 'Los orígenes de la profesionalización historiográfica española sobre la Prehistoria y la Antigüedad (tradiciones decimonónicas e influencias europeas)', in J. Arce and R. Olmos (eds): 73–8.

Peiró, I. and Pasamar Alzuría, G. (1991) 'La "vía española" hacia la profesionalización historiográfica', *Studium. Geografía. Historia. Arte. Filosofía* 3: 135–62.

Pérez de Barradas, J., Alonso del Real, C. and Martínez Santa-Olalla, J. (1940) *Investigación científica de Marruecos. I. Cuestionarios de Etnología, Lingüística y Arqueología*, Madrid.

Pla Ballester, E. (1980) 'Introducción', in *Nuestra Historia*, Valencia: Mas-Ivars.

[Oliveira] Ramos, P., [Maia] Nabais, A.J.C., [Bragança] Gil, F., Rocha-Trindade, M. B., [Cruz] de Carvalho, J. M., [Sommer] Ribeiro, J. A. F., [Elias] Casanovas, L. E., [Baptista] Pereira, F. A., Raposo, L. and [Galopim] de Carvalho, A. (1993) *Iniciação à museologia*, Lisbon: Universidade Aberta.

Raposo, L. (1992) 'Introdução Geral', in A.C. Ferreira da Silva, L. Raposo and C. Tavares da Silva (eds) *Pré-história de Portugal*, Lisbon: Universidade Aberta.

—— (1993) 'A estrutura administrativa do Estado e o património cultural', *Vértice* 54: 38–45.

Real, F. (1991) 'La Recherche archéologique au Portugal', in V. Negri (ed.) *L'Organisation territoriale de l'archéologie en Europe*: 157–61, Douai: Anact.

Ribeiro, J.S. (1879) 'Sociedade Archaeologica Lusitana', in *Historia dos Estabelecimentos Scientificos, Literarios e Artisticos de Portugal nos sucessivos reinados da Monarchia* VIII: 303–24.

32 Margarita Díaz-Andreu

Ripoll Perelló, E. (1993) 'Notas para una historia de la arqueología', in G. Ripoll López (ed.) *Arqueología, hoy*: 15–28, Cuadernos de la UNED 108, Madrid: Universidad Nacional de Educación a Distancia.

Rodríguez Hidalgo, J. M. (1991) 'Sinopsis historiográfica del anfiteatro de Italica', in J. Arce and R. Olmos (eds): 91–4.

Rueda Muñoz de San Pedro, G. (1991) 'Francisco María Tubino (1833–1888) y la Revista de Bellas Artes (1866–1868)', in J. Arce and R. Olmos (eds): 59–63.

Ruiz Rodríguez, A. (1993) 'Present Panorama of Spanish Archaeology', in M. I. Martínez Navarrete (ed.): 307–26.

Ruiz Rodríguez, A., Chapa, T. and Ruiz Zapatero, G. (1988) 'La arqueología contextual: una revisión crítica', *Trabajos de Prehistoria* 45: 11–17.

Ruiz Zapatero, G. (1993) 'The Organisation of the Archaeology in Spain', in M. I. Martínez Navarrete (ed.): 45–73.

Sales y Ferré, M. (1880) *Prehistoria y origen de la civilización*, Sevilla.

Santos, M.F. (1980) 'Estudos de pré-história em Portugal de 1850 a 1880', *Anais da APH* 26(2): 253–97.

—— (1981) 'Antropologia pré-histórica em Portugal', *Anais da APH* 27: 131–58.

Sanz Pastor, C. (1990) *Museos y colecciones de España*, Madrid: Ministerio de Cultura.

Schnapp, A. (1984) 'France', in H. Cleere (ed.) *Approaches to the Archaeological Heritage*: 48–53, New Directions in Archaeology, Cambridge: Cambridge University Press.

—— (1991) 'Modèle naturaliste et modèle philologique dans l'archéologie européenne du XVIème au XIXème siècles', in J. Arce and R. Olmos (eds): 19–24.

Silva, A.C. (1980) 'A questão do Homem Terciário português', *História* 21 Julio: 50–60.

Sørensen, M.L. (1996) 'The Fall of a Nation, the Birth of a Subject: The National Use of Archaeology in Nineteenth Century Denmark', in M. Díaz-Andreu and T. Champion (eds) *Archaeology and Nationalism in Europe*: 24–47, London: UCL Press.

Soromenho, M. and [Vassallo] Silva, N. (1992) 'Salvaguarda do património. Antecedentes históricos. Da Idade Média ao século XVIII', *Dar Futuro ao Passado*: 34–71, Lisbon: IPPAR.

Trigger, B.G. (1989) *A History of Archaeological Thought*, Cambridge: Cambridge University Press.

Vázquez Varela, J.M. and Risch, R. (1991) 'Theory in Spanish Archaeology since 1960', in I. Hodder (ed.) *Archaeological Theory in Europe. The Last Three Decades*: 25–51, London and New York: Routledge.

Vicent, J. (1990) 'El debat postprocessual: algunes observacions "radicals" sobre una arqueologia "conservadora"', *Cota Zero* 6: 102–7.

—— (1993) 'The Department of Prehistory', in M. I. Martínez Navarrete (ed.): 19–36.

Vila, A. (ed.) (1991) *Arqueología. Nuevas tendencías*, Madrid: CSIC.

Vilanova y Piera, J. and Rada y Delgado, J. de D. (1892) 'Geología y proto-historia ibéricas', *Historia general de España* I, Madrid: El Progreso Editorial.

VVAA (1992) 'Dossier. 10 anys d'arqueologia a Catalunya. 1981–1990', *Cota Zero* 9.

Without Author (1974) 'Crónica de los Cursos Internacionales de Prehistoria y Arqueología en Ampurias', *Miscelánea Arqueológica. XXV Aniversario de los Cursos Internacionales de Prehistoria y Arqueología en Ampurias (1947–1971)*: IX–XXIV, Barcelona: Diputación Provincial de Barcelona.

Zwernemann, J. (1883) *Culture History and African Anthropology. A Century of Research in Germany and Austria*, Uppsala Studies in Cultural Anthropology 6, Uppsala: Acta Univ. Ups.

CHAPTER THREE

BEHAVIOURAL TRANSFORMATIONS DURING THE PLEISTOCENE

An Iberian perspective

JOSEFA ENAMORADO

INTRODUCTION

In this chapter the behavioural evolution and adaptive changes of hunters, gatherers and fishers in the Iberian Pleistocene will be discussed in terms of variations in the distribution and organization of energy and social life.[1] Both a synchronic and diachronic perspective will be adopted. This chapter follows the ecological approach of Jochim (1981) and the regional perspective of Gamble (1986), where the Iberian Peninsula is understood to comprise part of the southwest and west Mediterranean regions. I will also use the settlement history of these populations as a framework to deal with differences in their distribution across the landscape. At the same time I will argue that differences in social organization (Gamble 1986; 1993) help to explain changes of behaviour in the hunter-gatherers of Iberia.

This is the first synthesis of Pleistocene sites in Iberia in English since Obermaier published *The Fossil Man in Spain* (1924). A brief summary article exists in Spanish (Santonja 1989), but this only deals with the data from Spain. Although from the general perspective of this article it would be unnecessary to mention every site, I do think that it is useful for archaeologists – especially for those who do not know the Spanish language – to introduce the richness of Pleistocene human-settlement evidence in the Iberian Peninsula and how it changed through time. This allows us to explain changes in human behaviour during the course of the Pleistocene, which is the aim of this chapter.

THE ARCHAEOLOGICAL RECORD IN THE
IBERIAN PENINSULA

The archaeological record of the Pleistocene in the Iberian Peninsula (Figure 3.1) varies in distribution, density and preservation, and with it our understanding of different periods and regions. Nevertheless, there is a continuous sequence throughout the entire period. From the chronostratigraphic point of view the Iberian Palaeolithic archaeological record corresponds to the Middle and Upper Pleistocene, including the Tardiglacial, and the time range stretches between 500,000 BP and 10,000/8000 BP. However, there are general difficulties of interpretation, some of which are derived from the context of archaeological data, as for instance those recorded on excavations undertaken at the beginning of this century, as well as methodological and theoretical problems.

There are additional problems with the geological characteristics of the Iberian Quaternary, which was formed from dynamic processes of dissection rather than sedimentation. Deposits are not very thick, except in the Guadix–Baza basin, and coarse detritic sediments are dominant.

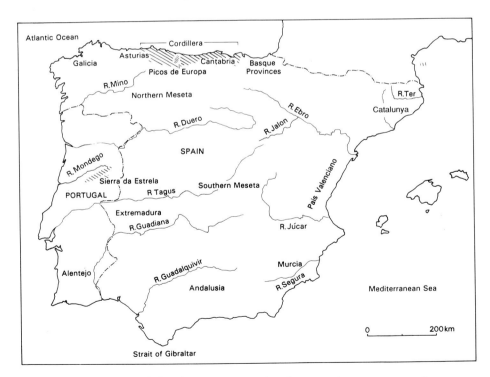

Figure 3.1 Map of the Iberian Peninsula showing the regions and rivers mentioned in the text.

This prevents accumulation and the preservation of the floral and faunal record, as well as the utilization of other techniques of correlation or dating.

Lower and Middle Pleistocene: a brief review

Until the recent publication of the Atapuerca TD6 fossil, no human remains and artefacts had been found pre-dating 780,000 BP (Carbonell *et al.* 1995; Parés and Pérez González 1995), in the Pleistocene of the Iberian Peninsula. Lithic artefact occurrences are sporadic and samples are numerically poor and without clear stratigraphic context. Their chronology is thus unclear (Santonja 1981, 1989; Raposo 1985; Santonja and Villa 1990). Hence it can be said that the current evidence supports the short-chronology hypothesis for the colonization of Europe (Roebroeks 1994; Roebroeks and Van Kolfochoten 1994). These authors argue that all finds before the Early Pleistocene come from a disturbed and coarse matrix, and that the first primary context sites with good archaeological evidence in Europe and Iberia (Figure 3.2) that occur in abundance date to the Middle Pleistocene. Some scholars think that the reason for that abundance is the better preservation of remains, others believe that there was a real change in human settlement density and continuity in Europe at some time during the Middle Pleistocene. Dennell (1987) among others suggests that fundamental changes in human behaviour were the cause of the effective colonization of Europe. However, most Middle Pleistocene sites are accumulations of lithics in fluvial deposits; well-preserved archaeological sites which provide information on human behaviour and subsistence strategies are still few, which makes it difficult to establish a broad understanding of the behaviour of mobile populations. In addition, the density of Middle Pleistocene sites in the interior of the Iberian Peninsula, the Meseta, differs from that in the littoral. To some extent this is a reflection of varying intensity of survey as well as the differential preservation of sediments of this period.

Some syntheses of the Middle Pleistocene archaeological record have been published already, such as those by Santonja (1989, 1992); Santonja and Villa (1990); Raposo (1989); Zilhão (1992). More recently, regional data have been made available by Arnáiz (1990, 1991); Enamorado (1992, forthcoming a); Fernández Peris (1993); Fullola (1992); Montes Barquín (1994); Villaverde (1992); Santonja and Raposo (1993); Carbonell and Rodríguez (1993); Vega *et al.* (1994) and references in them.

Upper Pleistocene

The Iberian Early Upper Pleistocene (Figure 3.3) is documented in the long sequences of fluvial terraces, such as those of the rivers Tagus, Manzanares, Tormes and Guadalquivir, although there are some cave sites,

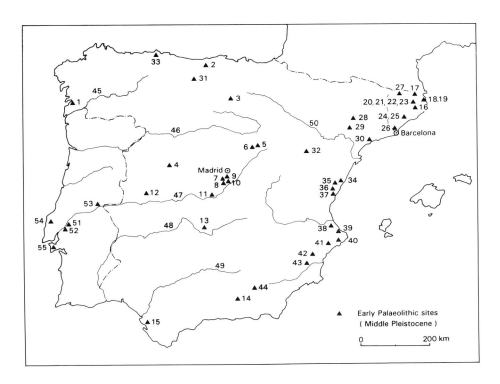

Figure 3.2 Location of Early Palaeolithic sites (Middle Pleistocene) in Iberia.

Spain: 1) Gándaras de Budiño (Pontevedra). 2) Cueva del Castillo (Cantabria). 3) Atapuerca (Burgos). 4) La Maya (Salamanca). 5) Torralba (Soria). 6) Ambrona (Soria). 7) San Isidro (Madrid). 8) Las Delicias (Madrid). 9) Arenero de Arriaga (Madrid). 10) Arenero de Aridos (Madrid). 11) Pinedo (Toledo). 12) El Sartalejo (Cáceres). 13) Porzuna (Ciudad Real). 14) Solana del Zamborino (Granada). 15) El Aculadero (Cádiz). 16) Puig d'en Roca (Girona). 17) Mollet I (Serinyá, Girona). 18) Cau del Duc de Torroella (Baix Empordá, Girona). 19) Cau del Duc d'Ullá (Baix Empordá, Girona). 20) Mas d'en Galí (Gironés, Girona). 21) Can Rubau, (Gironés, Girona). 22) Can Garriga (Gironés, Girona). 23) Pedra Dreta (Gironés, Girona). 24) Puig d'Esclats (La Selva, Girona). 25) Complejo de La Selva (Girona). 26) Can Albareda (Baix Llobregat, Barcelona). 27) La Vinya (Alt Urgell, Lleida). 28) Farfanya (La Noguera, Lleida). 29) Complejo de la Femosa (Segriá, Lleida). 30) Mas Blanc (Tarragona). 31) San Quirce de río Pisuerga (Palencia). 32) Cuesta de la Bajada (Teruel). 33) Bañugues (Asturias). 34) Cau d'en Borrás (Oropesa, Castelló). 35) Cova del Tossal de la Font (Vilafamés, Castelló). 36) El Pinar (Artana, Castelló). 37) Casablanca I (Almenara, Castelló). 38) Cova de Bolomor (Tavernes de la Valdigna (Valencia). 39) Cova del Corb (Ondara, Alicante). 40) Cova de les Calaveres (Benidoleig, Alicante). 41) Valles de Alcoi (Alicante). 42) Vinalopó (Aspe, Alicante). 43) Hurchillo (Alicante). 44) Cullar Baza (Granada). Occurrences in fluvial terraces: 45) Miño river. 46) Duero river and tributaries. 47) Tagus river and subsidiaries. 48) Guadiana river and subsidiaries. 49) Guadalquivir river and tributaries. 50) Ebro river and tributaries. **Portugal**: 51) Alpiarça. 52) Milharós. 53) Monte Famaco. 54) Siexosa. 55) Belverde.

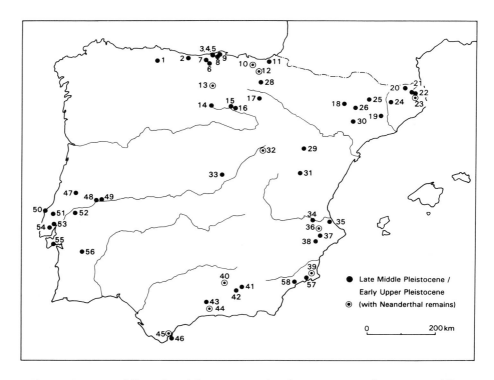

Figure 3.3 Middle Palaeolithic sites in the Iberian Peninsula. Late Middle Pleistocene/Early Upper Pleistocene.

1) El Conde (Asturias). 2) Unquera (Cantabria). 3) El Pendo (Cantabria). 4) Cobalejos (Cantabria). 5) El Ruso (Cantabria). 6) Hornos de La Peña (Cantabria). 7) El Castillo and La Flecha (Cantabria). 8) Cueva Morín (Cantabria). 9) Fuente del Francés (Cantabria). 10) Axlor (Vizcaya). 11) Amalda (Guipúzcoa). 12) Lezetxiki (Guipúzcoa). 13) Valdegoba (Burgos). 14) Atapuerca (Burgos). 15) Cueva de la Ermita (Burgos). 16) Cueva Millán (Burgos). 17) Peña Miel (La Rioja). 18) Gabasa (Huesca). 19) Abric Romaní (Capellades, Barcelona). 20) Els Ermitons (La Garrotxa, Girona). 21) L'Arbreda (Serinyá, Girona). 22) Mollet I (Serinyá, Girona). 23) Banyoles (Girona). 24) Cova del Toll (Bages, Girona). 25) La Roca dels Bous (La Noguera, Lleida). 26) Cova de L'Estret de Tragó (Os de Balaguer, Lleida). 27) Cova del Gegant (Sitges, Barcelona). 28) Arrillor (Alava). 29) Eudoviges (Alacón, Teruel). 30) Complejo de la Femosa (Segriá, Lleida). 31) Cuesta de la Bajada (Teruel). 32) Cueva de los Casares (Guadalajara). 33) Arenero de Arriaga (Madrid). 34) Las Fuentes (Navarrés, Valencia). 35) Cueva de Bolomor (Tavernes de Valdigna, Valencia). 36) Cova Negra (Játiva, Valencia). 37) Cova Beneito (Muro, Alicante). 38) El Salt (Alcoi, Alicante). 39) Cabezo Gordo (Murcia). 40) Cueva de la Carihuela (Piñar, Granada). 41) Solana del Zamborino (Fonelas, Granada). 42) Cueva Horá (Darro, Granada). 43) Cueva de las Grajas (Archidona, Málaga). 44) Cueva del Boquete de Zafarraya (Alcaucín, Málaga). 45) Devil's Tower (Gibraltar). 46) Gorham's Cave (Gibraltar). 47) Caldeirão (Tomar, Portugal). 48) Vilas Ruivas (Rodão, Portugal). 49) Foz de Enxarrique (Rodão, Portugal). 50) Gruta Furninha (Portugal). 51) Grota Nova da Columbeira (Bombarral, Portugal). 52) Alpiarca (Vale do Forno, Portugal). 53) Cuevas de Salemas (north of Lisboa, Portugal). 54) Santo Antão do Tojal (Lisboa, Portugal). 55) Figueira Brava (Sesimbra, Portugal). 56) Gruta do Escoural (Montemor-o-Novo, Alentejo, Portugal). 57) Cueva Vermeja (Almería). 58) Cueva Perneras (Murcia).

such as Atapuerca (Aguirre *et al.* 1990) and Cabezo Gordo (Gibert *et al.* 1994), which do contain sediments of this age. At the present, there are some archaeological sites from the Late Middle Pleistocene which have yielded lithic assemblages with Middle Palaeolithic technological and typological features (levallois and blade technique, no bifaces). These include, for instance, Solana del Zamborino, the lower levels of Cueva Horá, Bolomor, Cuesta de la Bajada, Arriaga II, Atapuerca, Mollet I, Toll and Vale do Forno. Therefore, it can be said that the Middle Palaeolithic technology appears to start in the latest stages of the Middle Pleistocene (around 250,000 BP) and showed a great deal of variability (Vega Toscano *et al.* 1994). In turn, human settlement of the Early Upper Pleistocene with Middle Palaeolithic assemblages ('Mousterian') is present all over the Peninsula, both along the coast and towards the interior (Meseta). It is mainly found in rock-shelters and caves. Its chronological range is from oxygen isotopic stage 5 to 3/2 in some places (128,000–ca. 35,000 BP) (Figure 3.3).

In Cantabria and the Basque Country (Figure 3.1), the most remarkable human occupation with large lithic assemblages and long stratigraphic sequences has been found in the caves Morín, El Pendo, La Flecha, El Castillo and El Conde (the only site in the Asturias region). However, there are other sites whose archaeological record is attributed to this technocomplex, for instance Hornos de la Peña and Otero (Cantabria), and the rock-shelter of Axlor (Vizcaya), which yielded Neanderthal remains, as well as Lezetxiki (Guipúzcoa), the only site situated in truly mountainous terrain, and Amalda (San Sebastián) in the Basque Country. In addition, some open-air sites have been found, notably at Kurtzia (Vizcaya) near the shore and Unquera (Santander) (Vega Toscano 1983; Santonja 1989; Straus 1992a).

Along the north of the Mediterranean coast, in Catalunya, the assemblages exhibit some similarities to regions in the south of France. The most important sites are those at Mollet I, Abric Romaní, L'Arbreda, Roca del Baus, Abric de L'Estret de Tragó (Mora 1988; 1992). There are also some open-air sites in fluvial terraces, as for instance at La Femosa (Fullola 1992). Further south along the Mediterranean coast in Castelló there are finds of this age in El Pinar de Artana, La Fuente de San Luis (Villaverde 1992) and La Cova del Tossal de La Font. The last site was previously considered to be Lower Palaeolithic but is now attributed to the Middle Palaeolithic (Gusi *et al.* 1984). The greater concentration of Middle Palaeolithic sites in the Iberian Peninsula lies in the provinces of Valencia and Alicante, with the most important stratigraphic sequences being found at Cova Negra (with Neanderthal remains), El Salt (Villaverde 1992) and Cova Beneito (Iturbe *et al.* 1993), where research is currently being carried out. There are other sites at Cova Foradada and Penya Roja, and Cova de les Cendres, which have not yet been published in detail (Villaverde 1992; Villaverde and Martínez-Valle 1992).

In Murcia, further south, the site of Cabezo Gordo has yielded both Middle Palaeolithic and Neanderthal remains (Gibert *et al.* 1994), as well as the sites of Cueva Perneras and Cueva Vermeja (Vega Toscano 1990). Along the Mediterranean coastal region of Andalucía there is a range of archaeological sites, such as Zájara I (Almería), Cueva de las Grajas and Boquete de Zafarraya (Málaga), Gorham's Cave and Devil's Tower (Gibraltar), all of which yielded Neanderthal remains. The most interesting group is located in Granada, comprised by the sites of Cueva de la Carihuela, with late Neanderthal remains, and Cueva Horá. Both have yielded remarkable Mousterian assemblages (Vega Toscano 1990, 1993). They are near the Guadix–Baza basin, a region with a long Quaternary history, which allows research into the changes in human behaviour from a regional perspective to be developed.

In the Atlantic region the major concentration of sites is restricted to Portugal. Here the Middle Palaeolithic sites are mainly located in the littoral region between the Tagus and Mondego rivers. Among them are: Vilas Ruivas (Rodão) and Estrada do Prado (Tomar), both open-air sites. Recently, an Early Upper Pleistocene deposit has been recorded in the karstic system of Almonda, the Cone Mousteriense site (Zilhão *et al.* 1991). There are also some sites with younger chronologies (30,000/ 40,000 BP) at Figueira Brava (Sesimbra), Columbeira (Bombarral), Caldeirão (Tomar), Foz do Enxarrique (Rodão), Beira Interior, Gruta do Escoural (Montemor-o-Novo) in the Alentejo region (Zilhão 1992). In Galicia (Figure 3.1) the absence of Early Upper Pleistocene evidence is largely explained by the destruction of sites by geomorphological and edaphological factors. Most of them are in the open air with small assemblages, although it is expected that settlement in caves and rock-shelters also took place (Criado Boado *et al.* 1991).

In the interior of the Peninsula (Meseta) some occurrences have been documented in the Upper Pleistocene lower terraces of the Tormes river (northern Meseta), at La Maya and Calvarrasa I and in the lower terraces of the Manzanares and Guadiana rivers (southern Meseta) at Cerro Arzóllar. Some lithic assemblages which are considered to have been lithic workshops have been found on the surface of the lower fluvial terraces in both Mesetas. All of this shows that some human settlement during the Early Upper Pleistocene took place in the open air. In addition to these fluvial sites there are some cave-sites and rock-shelters in the interior at La Ermita, Cueva Millán and Valdegova (Burgos). Neanderthal remains have been found at the latter (Díez *et al.* 1989–90) and at the Cueva de los Casares (Guadalajara) (Vega Toscano 1983, 1988) (Figure 3.3). In the Ebro Valley there are thirty sites with Mousterian assemblages. These are grouped according to natural regions, among which nine are caves and rock-shelters, thirteen are surface occurrences and eight sporadic finds. The caves and rock-shelters are: Arrillor, Peña Miel, Eudoviges, Cantavieja, El Pudial, Fuente del Trucho and Gabasa.

All of them have interesting stratigraphic sequences but only Peña Miel (La Rioja) and Gabasa (Pre-Pyrenees) have been published in detail. Other surface occurrences are discussed by Utrilla and Montes (1993).

Late Upper Pleistocene

Recent chronostratigraphic dating of the archaeological record and human remains in some sites has shown that the transition from the Middle to Upper Palaeolithic was neither synchronic nor uniform across the Peninsula. Moreover, in some locations it was extremely abrupt. There is clear evidence for late surviving Neanderthals – 30,000/28,000 BP – and their associated Mousterian tool-kits at some sites in southeast and southern Spain. These include Cova Negra, El Salt, Beneito (Villaverde 1992) and Carihuela, Cueva, Horá, Zafarraya, Gorham's Cave, Devil's Tower (Vega Toscano 1990, 1993), as well as in Portugal along the Tagus river the sites of Columbeira, Caldeirão, Figueira Brava (Zilhão 1993).

These Late Neanderthal remains and Mousterian assemblages are also interesting because of recent work in north and northeastern Spain at Cueva del Castillo (Cabrera *et al.* 1993) and at L'Arbreda (Bischoff *et al.* 1989). Here Early Upper Palaeolithic (EUP) assemblages (Aurignacian) are associated with anatomically modern humans dated to between 38,000 BP and 40,000 BP. In the southeast of the Peninsula the EUP is much more recent, suggesting that Spain was divided culturally and anatomically. These facts imply that Neanderthals and modern humans inhabited the Iberian Peninsula side by side for several thousand years, during which the former were the latest and the last in southwest Europe, whereas the modern humans are the earliest in the same region. This is important for our understanding of the transitional process between early and modern behaviour, and the implications related to the replacement of the former by the latter (Stringer and Gamble 1993; Aitken *et al.* 1993). However, recently Zilhão (1993) has argued that this period of coexistence was short.

After this transition period, the EUP populations with a widespread and distinctive set of cultural features (blade technology, use of bone and antler as raw material, symbolism and art, body ornaments) spread the length of the littoral of the Peninsula. It is noticeable, however, that there are only a few findspots in the interior. The EUP assemblages (Aurignacian and Gravettian) (see Figure 3.4) in the northwest of Spain are scarce, mainly due to the geomorphological and edaphological factors mentioned above, which affected the open-air sites. Thus, sites quite often comprise only a single, thin, stratigraphic layer, sometimes altered, and lacking any organic material (i.e. no bones) on account of the acid soils. These 'thin' deposits stand in marked contrast to those of the Cantabrian region (Asturias, Santander and the Basque Country) where EUP assemblages occur in caves and rock-shelters that had been occupied earlier during the Middle Palaeolithic (the sites of Morín, Pendo, Castillo, Conde). It is most interesting to note that there is no change in the low number of camp-sites or in settlement patterns at the time of the transition. Some of them were occupied regularly throughout the course of the EUP and into the Late Upper Palaeolithic. However, many other sites were occupied only at a later date. Most sites are located in the coastal zone, although some of them are in the mountainous interior (Straus 1992a: 75; Figure 4.2).

Moving to the Mediterranean coast, in the northeast (Catalunya) there are EUP assemblages in caves, rock-shelters and at a few open-air sites, as for example Can Garriga and a few in the La Selva region. The degree of preservation has ensured that the former have the most complete stratigraphic sequences. L'Arbreda is one of the most important sites, and together with Reclau Viver, which contains human remains, has yielded the first evidence for the new technology. Mollet and Abric Romaní are other important sites. All of them can demonstrate continuous occupation from the Middle Palaeolithic onwards. However, there are other sites where occupation first occurs in the EUP. The provinces of Girona and Tarragona have the largest concentrations, although recently some settlements have been found in western Catalunya (Fullola 1992). In the Valencian Country the EUP assemblages are younger than in Catalunya according to evidence from Mallaetes, although the number of sites is small, e.g. Penya Roja, Cova Beneito (Iturbe *et al.* 1993), Parpalló and Barranc Blanc (Villaverde 1992). The identification of EUP material in the southeast and south of Spain is much more controversial, and concerns such sites as Cueva Perneras (Murcia), Zájara II and Cueva Ambrosio (Almería), Cueva Horá (Granada), Cueva de Nerja and Cueva del Higuerón (Málaga). Certainly, the Late Upper Palaeolithic assemblages are the first sure Upper Palaeolithic evidence in this Mediterranean region. Gorham's Cave (Gibraltar) yielded an age of around 40,000 BP and is therefore the oldest EUP in this region (Vega Toscano 1993).

On the Portuguese coast the EUP is documented in a few sites. These are open-air settlements rather than caves: Gato Preto (Aurignacian), which yielded a controversial thermoluminescence age of around 38,000 BP; Vale de Porcos, Caldeirão, Cabeço de Porto Marinho and Vale Comprido, mainly spread along the littoral region between the Tagus and Mondego rivers, although Gruta do Escoural and Monte da Fainha are located in the Alentejo; some of these sites were first occupied in the Middle Palaeolithic (Zilhão 1992, 1993).

The Late Upper Palaeolithic (LUP) (Figure 3.5) consists of Solutrean and Magdalenian assemblages. The former (Solutrean, ca. 20,000/16,000 BP) is one of the most characteristic and controversial periods of the Upper Palaeolithic in Iberia, due mainly to a set of technological innovations (leaf-points, barbed and tanged arrowheads, notched points, bone and antler artefacts) whereby the use of the bow is inferred. Straus (1992a)

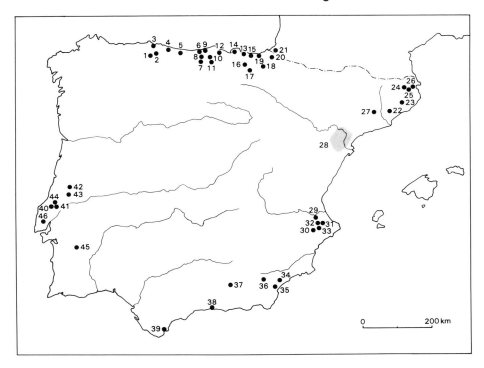

Figure 3.4 Early Upper Palaeolithic sites (Aurignacian) in the Iberian Peninsula.

1) El Conde (Asturias). 2) La Viña (Asturias). 3) Cueva Oscura de Perán (Asturias). 4) El Cierro (Asturias). 5) Cueto de La Mina, La Riera and Arnero (Asturias). 6) El Cudón (Cantabria). 7) Hornos de la Peña (Cantabria). 8) El Castillo (Cantabria). 9) El Pendo, Camargo (Cantabria). 10) Cueva Morín (Cantabria). 11) El Salitre and El Rascaño (Cantabria). 12) El Otero (Cantabria). 13) Santimamiñe (Vizcaya). 14) Kurtzia (Vizcaya). 15) Lumentxa and Atxurra (Guipúzcoa). 16) Bolinkoba (Vizcaya). 17) Lezetxiki and Labeko (Guipúzcoa). 18) Usategi (Guipúzcoa). 19) Ekain and Amalda (Guipúzcoa). 20) Aitzbitarte (Guipúzcoa). 21) Lezia (Guipúzcoa). 22) Can Garriga (Barcelona). 23) La Selva region (Girona). 24) L'Arbreda (Girona). 25) Reclau Viver (Girona). 26) Mollet (Girona). 27) Abric Romaní (Barcelona). 28) Tarragona region. 29) Cova de les Mallaetes (Valencia). 30) Cova Beneito (Alicante). 31) Penya Roja (Valencia). 32) Parpalló (Valencia). 33) Cova del Barranc Blanc (Valencia). 34) Cueva Perneras (Murcia). 35) Cueva de Zájara II (Almería). 36) Cueva de Ambrosio (Almería). 37) Cueva Horá (Granada). 38) Cueva de Nerja (Málaga). 39) Gorham's Cave (Gibraltar). 40) Gato Preto (Portugal) open air. 41) Vale do Porcos (Portugal) open air. 42) Gruta de Caldeirão (Portugal). 43) Fonte Santa (Portugal) open air. 44) Cabeco de Porto Marinho; Casal do Felipe; Terra do Manuel; Vale Comprido (Portugal) open air. 45) Gruta do Escoural (Alentejo, Portugal). 46) Gruta do Pego do Diabo (Lisboa, Portugal).

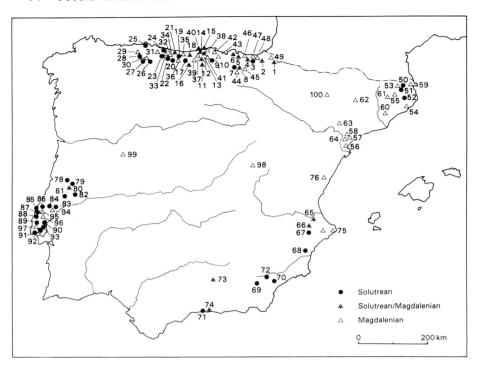

Figure 3.5 Late Upper Palaeolithic sites in the Iberian Peninsula (Pleniglacials, Last Maximum Glacial and Tardiglacial).

1) Abauntz (Navarra). 2) Aitzbitarte, Torre (Guipúzcoa). 3) Amalda (Guipúzcoa). 4) Ermittia, Urtiaga (Guipúzcoa). 5) Santimamiñe (Vizcaya). 6) Atxeta (Vizcaya). 7) Atxuri (Vizcaya). 8) Bolinkoba (Vizcaya). 9) El Mirón (Cantabria). 10) La Haza (Cantabria). 11) El Salitre (Cantabria). 12) La Bona, El Rascaño (Cantabria). 13) Fuente del Francés (Cantabria). 14) Cueva Morín, El Pendo (Cantabria). 15) Cobalejos, Camargo, El Ruso (Cantabria). 16) El Castillo, La Pasiega, Hornos de la Peña (Cantabria). 17) Peña de Carranceja (Cantabria). 18) Altamira (Cantabria). 19) Cueva Chufín (Cantabria). 20) Cueva del Sel (Asturias). 21) Balmori, Tres Calaberes, La Riera, Cueto de la Mina and Coberizas (Asturias). 22) El Buxú, Corao (Asturias). 23) Salumula, Aviao (Asturias). 24) Cova Rosa, El Cierro (Asturias). 25) Cueva Oscura de Perán (Asturias). 26) La Viña (Asturias). 27) La Lluera, Las Caldas (Asturias). 28) Peña de Canadamo (Asturias). 29) Ancenia, La Paloma, Sofoxó, Cueva Oscura de Ania (Asturias). 30) Entrefoces (Asturias). 31) Peña Ferrán (Asturias). 32) La Cuevona, La Lloseta, San Antonio, Tito Bustillo, Viesca (Asturias). 33) Los Azules (Asturias). 34) Fonfría, Brizia (Asturias). 35) Juan de Covera, La Loja, Cueva de la Peña (Asturias). 36) Coimbre, Trauno, La Hermida (Asturias). 37) Linar, Cualventi, Cuco (Cantabria). 38) La Pila (Cantabria). 39) Sovilla (Cantabria). 40) El Juyo, Loreto (Cantabria). 41) Truchino, El Piélago (Cantabria). 42) La Chora, el Otero (Cantabria). 43) El Valle (Cantabria). 44) Sailluenta (Vizcaya). 45) Salibranka, Lezetxiki (Guipúzcoa). 46) Atxurra, Laminak, Abittaga, Goikolau (Guipúzcoa). 47) Ekain (Guipúzcoa). 48) Erralla (Guipúzcoa). 49) Sporquinem, Berroberia (Guipúzcoa). 50) Reclau Viver, Cova d'en Pau (Girona). 51) L'Arbreda (Girona). 52) Cau de les Goges (Girona). 53) La Bora Gran d'en Carreras (Girona). 54) Sant Benet (Girona). 55) Coma d'Infern (Girona). 56) La Mallada (Tarragona). 57) Abric dels Colls, L'Hort de la Boquera,

has examined recently the variability among lithic artefact assemblages from this period as well as the similarities between the EUP and the LUP industries in Cantabria. The Solutrean of the Mediterranean coast of the Iberian Peninsula seems to be as early as, if not earlier than, comparable industries in the southwest region (France and Cantabria), but exhibits some very particular characteristics (Iberian Solutrean, see p. 48). Wall and portable artistic representations and ornaments developed during this period and continued during the Magdalenian. The distribution of both LUP human occupations in the Mediterranean provinces confirms that they are essentially western cultural complexes. In the Iberian Peninsula they are mainly a coastal phenomenon although some Magdalenian has been found in the Meseta, i.e. at Verdelpino (Cuenca) and La Dehesa (Salamanca).

The archaeological record for the early LUP in the Cantabrian region is located almost exclusively in rock-shelters or caves, and generally near their entrances. Some of these caves were first occupied in this period. There is only one open-air site, La Vega de Corao, that is said to have yielded Solutrean remains. There was an increase in the number of sites occupied, and they are distributed throughout the region, from central Asturias in the west to the Basque Country in the east, and from the north coast to the south of the Cordillera Cantábrica, with no large break in the distribution along the major river valleys (Straus 1992a: 96, Table 5.1, Figure 5.2). The early LUP assemblages in Catalunya, northeast Spain, have been found so far in the northern region (e.g. Cau de les Goges, Gironés). Long stratigraphic sequences have been found at the classic sites of Reclau Viver and L'Arbreda (Serinyá). After that period (middle Solutrean) a stratigraphic discontinuity is documented at all the

---

Figure 3.5   (cont.)

L'Hort d'en Marquet (Tarragona). 58) Picamoixons (Tarragona). 59) Cau de les Guilles (Girona). 60) Can Garriga (Barcelona). 61) Roc de Migdia (Barcelona). 62) Cova del Parco (Lleida). 63) Bauma de la Peixera d'Alfés (Lleida). 64) Cova del Boix (Tarragona). 65) Mallaetes (Valencia). 66) Parpalló (Valencia). 67) Cova Beneito (Alicante). 68) Abric de la Ratlla del Bubo (Alicante). 69) Cueva de Ambrosio (Almería). 70) Palomarico (Murcia). 71) Tajo del Jorox (Málaga). 72) Cueva Bermeja (Almería). 73) Cueva de la Carihuela (Granada). 74) Cueva de Nerja (Málaga). 75) Cova de les Cendres (Alicante). 76) Cova Matutano (Castellón). 77) Abric del Tossal de la Roca (Alicante). 78) Ourão (Portugal). 79) Furos (Portugal). 80) Caldeirão (Portugal). 81) Almonda (Portugal). 82) Casal do Cepo (Portugal). 83) Arneiro, Passal, Quintal da Forte (open air, Portugal). 84) Areeiro III, Olival da Carneira, Vale Comprido (open air, Portugal). 85) Furninha (Portugal). 86) Casa da Moura (Portugal). 87) Porto Dinheiro (open air, Portugal). 88) Lapa da Rainha (Portugal). 89) Santa Cruz, Baio, Vale Almoinha (open air, Portugal). 90) Salemas, Correio–Mor (Portugal). 91) Cascais (Portugal). 92) Ponte da Laje (Portugal). 93) Vila Pouca (Portugal). 94) Vascas, Carneira, Cabeco de Porto Marinho, Areeiro I (Portugal). 95) Casa da Moura (Portugal). 96) Suão (Portugal). 97) Rossio do Cabo, Vale da Mata Port (open air, Portugal). 98) Verdelpino (Cuenca). 99) La Dehesa (Salamanca). 100) Fuente del Trucho, Chaves (Huesca).

Table 3.1 Last Interglacial/Glacial chronostratigraphy

Age in 10^3 yr BP	Oxygen isotope stages	Alpine glacial divisions	General glacial division	European pollen zones	Age in 10^3 yr BP
	1	Holocene	Postglacial	Subboreal	5–3
				Atlantic	8–5
				Boreal	9–8
10				Preboreal	10–9
	2	Würm IV	Tardiglacial ($\sim$13–10 $\times$ 10^3 BP)	Dryas III Alleröd	11.8–10.8
				Dryas II Bölling	13–12.4
			Upper Pleniglacial	Dryas Ic Prebölling	14.5–14
				Dryas Ib Angles	15.5–15
			(Last Glacial Maximum at $\sim$19–18 $\times$ 10^3 BP)	Dryas Ia Lascaux Laugerie	18–16.5 / 20–19
		Würm III		Tursac Kesselt	24–23 / 29–27

Table 3.1 (cont.)

Age in 10^3 yr BP	Oxygen isotope stages	Alpine glacial divisions	General glacial division	European pollen zones	Age in 10^3 yr BP
30–35	3	Würm interstadial (38–34 × 10^3 BP)	Inter-pleniglacial	Arcy Cottés Hengelo Moershoofd	31.5–30 36–34.5 40–38 ~50
61	4	Würm II	Lower Pleniglacial (maximum at ~65 × 10^3 BP)		
73	5a			St Germain I	
	5b	Würm I	Early Glacial		
	5c			St Germain II	
	5d				
118	5e	Riss/Würm	Last Interglacial	Eem	
128	6	Riss III	Penultimate Glacial		

Source: after Straus 1992a

sites, some exhibiting post–Palaeolithic assemblages after a sterile layer, whilst at others the latest Solutrean and the earliest Magdalenian phases are not recorded (Fullola 1992: 46–7).

The early LUP in the Valencian Country is called the 'Iberian Solutrean', a facies with distinctive technological features ('flat-faced' points), as well as body ornaments and artistic representations. Moreover, it is considered to have a regional evolutionary process. The most important sites are Parpalló and Mallaetes (Valencia) which yielded early dates for the LUP of 20,490 and 21,710 BP, and contained middle and evolved Solutrean habitation. The latter is one of the most interesting and studied periods of the Mediterranean Upper Palaeolithic on account of its chronological (19,000/16,000 BP) and geographical range. It is subdivided into Upper Solutrean and Solutro-Gravettian (Villaverde and Peña 1981). Both industries are largely documented in the centre and south of the Mediterranean coastal strip, not only in the Valencian sites mentioned above but also at Beneito (Iturbe *et al.* 1993), Ratlla del Bubo (Alicante), Palomarico (Murcia), Ambrosio (Almería), Pantano de Cubillas (Granada), Tajo del Jorox (Málaga), and its presence at some Portuguese sites (Zilhão 1987) shows that its influence extended as far as the Atlantic coast. There are also some similarities to the Solutrean assemblages of the Chaves cave and the artistic representations at La Fuente del Trucho in Huesca, which points to some human occupation during the Upper Pleniglacial in the Ebro Basin (Utrilla 1989; Villaverde 1992) (Figure 3.5).

In the south of the Peninsula the LUP is less well known. However, a few sites have yielded Solutrean occupation. One of the most important is Cueva Ambrosio (Ripoll López 1988), which has recently yielded rock-art representations (Ripoll López 1994), Cueva Vermeja and Tollos (Almería), Cueva de la Carihuela and Los Ojos (Granada), and the Cueva de Nerja to the southwest (Málaga) (Santonja 1989). On the Atlantic coast of Portugal, the early LUP cave and open-air sites are concentrated between the Tagus and the Mondego rivers as in earlier periods. In the interior some are located close to the calcareous mountains, as is the case with Ourão, Furos, Caldeirão, Almonda, Cascais, Ponte da Laje and Vila Pouca (Zilhão 1992).

The later LUP (Magdalenian) is characterized by an increase in microlithic-backed bladelets and a variety of geometric shapes, together with bone and antler artefacts, the most important of which are harpoons. In the Cantabrian region sites with attested later LUP occupation (Last Glacial: ca. 16,000/10,000 BP; see Table 3.1) are more common than in the earlier period, which points to continued population growth. These Magdalenian sites are located both on the coastal plain and in the mountains, both in the intermontane and the upper valleys as well as on the Cordillera slopes (Straus 1992a: 129; Figures 6.1 and 6.2). It is worth noting that Abauntz in Navarra is an LUP human settlement using the high interior, which together with the archaeological and artistic signatures of Chaves and Fuente del Trucho (Huesca) in the Ebro Basin, supports the hypothesis of Upper Pleniglacial and Tardiglacial communications between Vasco-Cantabrian and Mediterranean populations through the Ebro basin along the south of the Pyrenees (Utrilla 1989, 1992; Fullola 1992).

The stratigraphic hiatus which follows the Solutrean in the Serinyá region (Catalunya) has already been mentioned. There is some later LUP occupation, as at Bora Gran d'en Carreras. Magdalenian occupation throughout the whole of Catalunya is later as, for instance, at La Mallada (Baix Ebre), Sant Benet (Baix Empordá) and Coma d'Infern (La Garrotxa). In the Montsant river the later LUP occupation has been documented in the Abric dels Colls (Priorat) and also at two open-air sites, L'Hort de la Boquera and L'Hort d'en Marquet. In the Francolí area the occupation of the rock-shelter of Picamoixons has been assigned to that period on the basis of the technology and faunal remains. At 12,000 BP intensive occupation existed throughout the northeastern Peninsula, at the sites of Bora Gran d'en Carreras, Cau de les Guilles (Roses), La Teulera and Cova de L'Arpó (Roselló), and Can Garriga in middle Catalunya, the Cova del Boix in the south and the Bauma de la Peixera d'Alfés and Cova del Parco to the west (Fullola 1992).

As far as the archaeological signatures of the later LUP in the Valencian Country are concerned, the most notable sites are Parpalló and Mallaetes, although there is also occupation at Les Cendres, Matutano and Mejillones. All these assemblages are very similar in typological terms, as can be corroborated at other sites along the Mediterranean coastal strip as far south as Málaga, i.e: Tossal de la Roca, Caballo, Algarrobo, Hoyo de la Mina and Nerja (Villaverde 1992). In the interior of Andalucía, the Cueva de la Carihuela has also yielded some evidence for later LUP occupation. On the Portuguese coast later LUP occupation tends to be more concentrated near the coast, but between the Tagus and Mondego rivers as in earlier periods at such sites as Caldeirão, Vascas, Carneira, Cabeço de Parto Marinho, etc. (Zilhão 1992), due to survey intensity, preservation and concentration of population in coastal lowlands.

ENVIRONMENTAL CHARACTERISTICS

The climate of the Iberian Peninsula can be sub-divided into two different zones, the Atlantic and the Mediterranean. This is evident in the modern vegetation, with deciduous mixed forest and warm Mediterranean forest respectively, and coniferous forest, bushes and pastures above 1000/1500 m. Most information about the ancient environment comes from geomorphology, marine and continental faunas, pollen and OIS (Oxygen Isotope Stages) data, and largely derives from the last Interglacial/Glacial cycle.

Middle Pleistocene

The evidence for Middle Pleistocene environments comes exclusively from the interior and south of the Peninsula, and is provided by faunal and pollen associations (Soto and Sesé 1987; Aguirre 1989; Alberdi and Bonadona eds 1989; Enamorado 1992). Almost all the localities are related to aquatic biotopes, although the moisture conditions sometimes could only be local. In other cases humidity is clearly regional or even climatic over a long time span. This is inferred from the development of mature forest, as for example at Aridos (Enamorado forthcoming a). The avian associations also indicate areas of humidity in the interior of the Peninsula, in places where it is not the case today (Sánchez Marco 1993). It is also clear that during the Iberian Middle Pleistocene a very rich fauna was associated with open landcapes.

During this period, therefore, the human populations in Iberia lived under the influence of a temperate, humid climate. In contrast to the northern and continental European regions, the Middle Pleistocene in the Peninsula was distinguished by climatic constancy where the gradient between Interglacial and Glacial was less pronounced due to its southern location and the oceanic effect, with only occasional variations towards more instances of more rigorous continental conditions. These were more or less synchronic with the advance of the ice-sheets (Enamorado 1992).

Last Interglacial/Glacial cycle in the Atlantic zones

The last Interglacial/Glacial cycle is marginally better known in the Peninsula. There were ice-caps in the Cantabrian region during the Upper Pleistocene in some zones of the Cordillera Cantábrica and Picos de Europa (OIS 4 and 2), with high amounts of snow and rain together with low annual temperatures. Both the pollen and mammal records exhibit evidence for open grasslands that disappeared with the onset of the Postglacial. The climatic characteristics of OIS 5 are not well recorded in this region. In turn the Lower Pleniglacial (OIS 4; see table 3.1) analyses reveal harsh cold and dry conditions, which were later (OIS 3 or Interpleniglacial) more temperate and humid, interspersed with colder oscillations. Parkland dominated the landscape, with some wood patches (pine, hazel, oak, etc.). The mammalian faunas were not very significant in climatic terms (roe deer, wild pig, rhino and elephant, but not reindeer), indicating a warming and drying trend.

During the glacial maximum, polar waters moved southward to latitude 42° and hence an abrupt thermal front developed off the coast of central Portugal. Consequently the climate was more temperate towards the south. The climatic features were colder than at present, and throughout the Last Glacial Maximum (OIS 2 *c.* 18,000 BP, hereafter the LGM) the Cantabrian sea and the north Portuguese Atlantic surface-water temperature was around 10 degrees centigrade cooler than today. In the Bay of Biscay the difference was around 11 degrees centigrade higher than in other parts of the north Atlantic. In addition, the Gulf Stream was pushed southeastward by the Labrador Current and did not flow into the Cantabrian sea but onto the western coast of the Peninsula. During the Pleniglacial in the south of Portugal the surface sea–water temperature was only 2 to 3 degrees centigrade cooler than at present. At the LGM there were glaciers on the Sierra de la Estrella in the north central region of Portugal. The climatic aspects during that period were more severe in terms of temperature and humidity than in the Mediterranean and similar to the Cantabrian region (Uchupi 1988; Straus 1992a, 1992b). On the south slopes of the Cantabrian mountains the high rainfall enabled pine forests and deciduous trees to develop. Although harsh, these landscapes were rich in game as well as in fish and shell-fish, from which the hunter-gatherer–fisher groups could easily make a living.

Throughout the Tardiglacial (Table 3.1) the Polar Front changed its position and on occasions reached Galicia and the north half of Portugal. As a result steppe environments dominated the periods (e.g. Dryas III) when the Polar waters were closer. The fluctuations were always more abrupt than in the Mediterranean region (Straus 1992b). Nonetheless, the data for the Cantabrian region show an increasing improvement, with the advent of humid conditions on account of the oceanic effect. The woodlands had not yet completely developed. The temperatures, in general, were still cold, as is demonstrated by the presence of a northern vole (*Microtus oeconomus*) and reindeer. However, after the Tardiglacial, warm conditions returned and there was a swift rise in arboreal vegeta-tion which ended with the mature forests of the Postglacial. At the same time the ice-caps would have started to melt, although the sea did not yet reach high levels (Straus 1992a).

Last Interglacial/Glacial Cycle in the Mediterranean zone

During the last Interglacial/Glacial period the palaeotemperature in the Mediterranean sea (Monastir, Tunisia, and Mallorca) was 3 degrees centigrade warmer than now (Cornu *et al.* 1993). The climatic aspects of this cycle in Catalunya and the Valencian Country were very similar. There was an increase in temperature and humidity (Lower Pleniglacial) with woods of pine and Mediterranean deciduous trees (birch, hazel, ilex, etc.) appearing in the Interpleniglacial; although it should be pointed out that open conditions were dominant. Horses and red deer are the most commonly recorded animal species. The Upper Pleniglacial and LGM climatic features were cold and dry, even steppe conditions, some-times with an expansion of pine and birch. In Catalunya there were some cold-climate mammal species, such as the musk ox and reindeer, while horses and red deer were present in both regions and roe deer and ibex are attested in the mountains. The sedimentological and palaeobiological evidence suggests that the Tardiglacial oscillations were not very marked in this Mediterranean region and a temperate rather than cold and humid climate was characteristic of that period (Fullola 1992; Villaverde 1992; Fumanal 1986; Aura *et al.* 1993).

The south Mediterranean region of the Peninsula (eastern Andalucía) had a predominantly temperate Mediterranean climate, due to its latitude and the oceanic effect. However, some minor cooler episodes are detectable (OI Stage 4 and 2; see Table 3.1) mainly through changes in the vegetation and micromammals. These are caused by changes in humidity/aridity, but are never the result of a reaction to extreme cold. It has to be noted that during these phases some of the highest mountains in the Sierra Nevada were covered by ice-caps, although a broad range of temperatures was not evident. Nevertheless, conditions near the coast were more temperate, with Atlantic influences and higher amounts of rain. The landscape was formed by open grasslands and some pine woods. Even though the main temperature fell, some Mediterranean taxa survived in sheltered zones. The climatic ameliorations were more humid, hence the Mediterranean deciduous woods (birch, ilex, hazel, *Oleacea*) developed. The faunal evidence also supports these conclusions (Dupré 1988; Ripoll López 1988; Vega Toscano 1993; Vega Toscano and Carrión 1993). In Andalucía the Tardiglacial climatic pattern is similar to that of other regions.

There are only a few data on the Last Interglacial/Glacial cycle which are representative of the Meseta. However, both Atlantic and Mediterranean influences reached this region, so that climatic conditions would be constantly temperate with some cold and steppe episodes. It must be understood that during Glacial periods, ice-caps covered the central mountains, although the climatic factors exhibited a less continental pattern than in other European regions. It has to be borne in mind that the Interglacial/Glacial thermal gradient was rather constant before the Last Interglacial/Glacial cycle, and that subsequently it was higher, although more temperate than in northern European regions, and of course more marked in the north than in the rest of the Peninsula.

In summary, cold temperatures were the outstanding feature, with some temperate and humid fluctuations, of the Late Upper Pleistocene (ca. 35,000/10,000 BP; Interpleniglacial, Upper Pleniglacial and Tardiglacial; Table 3.1), of the Cantabrian region and the northern half of Portugal. Along the Mediterranean coast temperatures were milder, despite some cool/arid episodes. Pine trees dominated the vegetation in the Peninsula and in general they were more abundant in the temperate Mediterranean region. In the north, deciduous trees marked the climatic improvements (hazel, birch, oak, elm), whereas in the Mediterranean, termophile species had that role (*Oleacea*, ilex, etc). The Peninsular landscape therefore comprised open grassland with large steppe regions and some patches of trees which never developed into mature forests. The Tardiglacial was distinguished by cold–warm oscillations with grasslands and some woods of pine, ilex, box and birches. The climate then underwent an amelioration process which reached its peak in the course of the Postglacial.

It is worth mentioning the transitional role that Iberia occupies between Europe and western Africa, thereby becoming a refuge for Quaternary flora and fauna, containing a large number of endemisms (Dupré, 1988). The Mediterranean region of Iberia can be regarded as a refuge during cold phases in continental Europe, not only for plants and animals but also for humans, e.g. the Neanderthals (Vega Toscano 1993; Zilhão 1993) who inhabited this area until the begining of OIS 2 (ca. 28,000 BP). At this time anatomically modern humans were in the north and northeast of the Peninsula and throughout Europe. Both the Mediterranean and Cantabrian regions acted as refuges. This is reflected in the high population densities attested during the LGM, on account of the climatic conditions (Straus 1992a).

BEHAVIOURAL TRANSFORMATIONS OF PLEISTOCENE HUNTER-GATHERER POPULATIONS IN IBERIA

Following this review of the history of environment and settlement in the Iberian Peninsula throughout the Pleistocene some inferences can be made about hunter-gatherer behaviour. This framework and the approaches of specialists in human ecology and social organization (Jochim 1981; Gamble 1986 and 1993, Enamorado 1995), provide the basis for examining the dynamics of adaptation among these populations.

The first extensive human settlement took place in the Peninsula during the Middle Pleistocene. Since then occupation was continuous, although in the north there is little evidence until the Last Interglacial. Different reasons have been claimed for this, e.g. erosion and natural alteration. However, in my opinion another explanation may be the lack of social and organizational responses to the particular environmental problems of the northern region of the Peninsula. For example, the harsh climatic conditions in the glacial phases of the Pleistocene ensured that resources would be to some extent unpredictable and only available in dispersed patches. This would prevent an intense and continuous human settlement before the Last Interglacial. In fact, until that period some human occupation was always present south of the Cantabrian mountains, e.g. San Quirce, Atapuerca and sites in the Duero Basin. The environment could bring selective pressure to bear (duration of seasons, distribution of resources, competitors) upon human behaviour, resulting in the development of social and cultural mechanisms in the form of networks of alliances, mating, interchange and new technologies, which enabled occupation to continue in that north Peninsular region after the Last Interglacial.

I suggest that the permanent settlement that took place in much of the Peninsula throughout the Pleistocene may be a result of the existence of environmental mosaics (Guthrie 1984) with different regional habitats (plains and uplands) in addition to the aforementioned climatic constancy. The landcape of Iberia was irregular, comprising the northern Meseta, southern Meseta, interior and coastal plains, high mountains, river basins and lakes, and giving rise to some differences in the environment and resources. When climatic conditions became harsher during the Pleistocene and there were food shortages, as for instance in the Atlantic zone (north of Portugal, Galicia and Cantabria), populations could reduce risk and survive either by moving to southern habitats or by using social solutions (social ties and alliances) to cover their needs.

At a local level, the signatures from the Iberian Middle Pleistocene archaeological record show that the foragers (early forms of *Homo sapiens*) lived in ephemeral camps at which the accumulation of debris essentially represents butchering and tool-making activities. Most of these sites were established near streams and lakes and it is not possible to talk about a pattern of home bases and satellite locations, given the lack of 'structure' in the spatial distribution of the bones and stones, or evidence for any structures. Indeed these people had an 'off-site' settlement pattern. As Gamble claims (1994: 2), 'we are dealing with locales within the landscapes'; hence the term 'site' is not applicable to the study of the behaviour of these people.

Given the predictable environment in Iberia, these hominids developed a foraging adaptation system (Binford 1980) with high mobility (to prevent risk) throughout the landscape in those areas where staple resources were readily available, to obtain food and raw materials, and also formed dispersed groups (Foley 1985). In this sense, their life appears to have been organized in self-sufficient local units and was opportunistic (using whatever habitat was available). Small territories were occupied, although the size of settlements was dictated by the influence of ecological factors on behavioural organization (Gamble 1993), and in large measure these were related to the density of resources. Their spatial and social systems seem to have been compact and exclusive (Gamble 1986, 1993) due to the low densities of population, group size and distribution in a predictable environment with enough resources accessible and an even climate. From this we can infer that few social relationships outside the local group would be needed to ensure survival (biological and cultural) during lean seasons. Information about the landscape or the social group itself was limited.

The tool-kit produced by these human groups was dominated by expedient tools. These were knapped on the spot and discarded after use.

Assemblages were formed by stone artefacts with sharp edges for use in different tasks (multipurpose) and most of them direct, that is, used for procurement of food (Enamorado 1992, forthcoming b). However, this does not mean that they lacked forward planning, because we can assume that all hominids had a form of anticipation based on memory. They had a conception of time distinct from ours and, as a result, this forward planning would have had a short time depth, e.g. one or two days.

In the Early Upper Pleistocene, Neanderthals were widespread in Iberia. There were some changes in behaviour but, as mentioned above, also some technological overlap between this period and the late Middle Pleistocene. Some archaeological sites from this last period yielded assemblages with older Middle Palaeolithic technological and typological features: generalization of the Levallois technique, blade technique, absence of bifaces.

In spite of such behavioural changes as the use of rock-shelters and caves as habitats (Castillo, Atapuerca, Carihuela), the lack of spatial structure in such Middle Palaeolithic sites is still a major feature. In most places no built hearths are recorded, and there are instead only levels with accumulations of ashes which confirm the use of fire. However, built hearths are not recorded until the latest phases, as at Vilas Ruivas, an open-air site in Portugal. The settlement pattern tends to be more concentrated in fixed places, either in the open or in shelters (caves and rock-shelters).

During this period the environment in Iberia was more predictable in the Mediterranean region than in the north. However, human occupation in the north was also continuous from this period. The adaptive system of these hominids was essentially foraging (plants and animals), combined with some interception (hunting and scavenging) of herd animals watched from fixed places in the landscape. Obviously, there were some variations in species, dependent upon the regional constraints of the Peninsula. Indeed, this behaviour involved a higher level of forward planning in order to organize moves in the landscape to obtain food, and even involved the use of artificial storage to keep meat for lean seasons or just for a few days after a successful catch. The latitude and climate of Iberia during the Pleistocene made it impossible to acquire meat from animals covered in and preserved by natural storage in the frost, as in northern European latitudes. Furthermore, mobility would still have been a behavioural strategy to prevent shortages of food and other problems in the human group.

The available records suggest that population density was low. Group size was small although social and economic necessities demanded that larger areas were inhabited, even though these were always variable in size because of ecological circumstances. The life of these hunter-gatherers was still predominantly self-sufficient and local. In all probability the social system was closed and exclusive with few contacts outside the group, because the predictable temperate environment in the Peninsula obviated the necessity to insure against any kind of failure through social ties. In this regard they did not need symbolic communication outside their local group, hence the lack of art and external visual symbols for strangers. Possibly they used body paintings merely to show status within the group. Indeed there is no clear evidence of symbolic behaviour in the form of personal ornaments in Neanderthal contexts in Europe, although the lithic styles could be used in such a way (White 1993).

The artefactual assemblage of these Early Upper Pleistocene human groups is more varied and diverse than in the earlier period. But again it served mainly immediate needs. Some stone tools were multipurpose and others specialized, but almost all of them had direct functions as before, hand-axes, flakes, blades, points, etc. Consequently these populations of hunter-gatherers were still 'tool-assisted'.

Neanderthals and modern humans coexisted in different regions in the Iberian Peninsula, as has already been discussed. Indeed the latest Neanderthals in the southwest of Europe are those from eastern Andalucía in the southeast of Spain. Here the Early Upper Palaeolithic (EUP) assemblages (Aurignacian) are poorly represented, with the Solutrean being the first widespread Upper Palaeolithic assemblage (Vega Toscano 1993: 165). In addition, according to Zilhão (1993: 141), the EUP in Portugal and in southern (Gorham's Cave) and southeast Spain (Mallaetes) is also younger − 28,000 BP − than in the north and northeast of Spain. Thus, it seems clear that the Neanderthals in Iberia during the Lower Pleniglacial (OIS 4; Table 3.1) were living in a southerly refuge. Modern humans reached these areas later than the north of Iberia and other parts of southwest Europe. When environmental conditions became harsher in the northern regions, e.g. Cantabria and Portugal, these Neanderthal populations decided to move to those temperate areas where resources were sufficient to maintain population densities with the same lifestyle. They were therefore constrained, like the early *Homo sapiens*, by the environment (Stringer and Gamble 1993). This affected their occupation and settlement in different regions within Iberia.

The earliest evidence for modern human occupation in the Iberian Peninsula is recorded at Castillo (Cantabria) and the L'Arbreda cave (northeast Catalunya) (Cabrera *et al.* 1993 and Bischoff *et al.* 1989). There is some evidence of Chatelperronian assemblages and, at the Morín cave, Mousterian in association with Aurignacian, although it should be noted that the Chatelperronian and Aurignacian are inter-stratified (González Echegaray 1993). Some scholars (see Hayden 1993: 120) have argued for technological continuity between the Middle Palaeolithic and the Early Upper Palaeolithic in the north of Spain, while others point out that not all the Chatelperronian necessarily had to be manufactured by Neanderthals, as for example was the case at St Césaire (Freeman 1993).

Furthermore, it has also been noted that anatomically modern human remains are usually associated with Aurignacian assemblages (Straus 1992a). Therefore the replacement theory, which claims that Neanderthals imitated some aspects of modern human behaviour once contact had occurred, is more likely than the model of independent development of modern behaviour in different regions.

The archaeological evidence for modern humans in Iberia tends to be found in caves and rock-shelters, some of which have evidence for a structured use of space (Cabrera *et al.* 1993: 94; Freeman 1993: 184; Ripoll López 1988: 503). The wider settlement pattern was highly concentrated with home bases and secondary locales. However, they continuously occupied large and varied geographical areas. Occupation was constant in both the Atlantic and Mediterranean regions and continued throughout the Upper Pleniglacial and Last Glacial Maximum (Table 3.1). This was probably due to changes in social behaviour — more complex and dynamic — as well as new technology.

Their tool-kit still consisted of such stone tools as flakes, blades and bladelets, although they now used other sorts of raw materials, bone and ivory, to manufacture points, and animal teeth for pendants and personal ornaments. Hence the assemblages can to some extent be described as *curated*: tools are manufactured in anticipation of future use, repaired and maintained. They also comprised *direct* (manufactured for food procurement) and *indirect* objects (created to make objects not related to the subsistence procurement, such as ornaments and needles) (Enamorado 1995). The artefacts are more standardized in shape and at the same time specialized for different tasks. Some artefactual assemblages (e.g. Solutrean) now exhibit distinct styles in shaping the tools in different regions, as for example Solutrean laurel-leaves and points. We are therefore dealing here with stylistic diversity within technological uniformity. In addition, modern *Homo sapiens* utilized art and symbolism as a social element. Here, as elsewhere in Europe, it can be said that they developed symbolically organized behaviour patterns in contrast to the preceding Neanderthals (Stringer and Gamble 1993).

The environment of Iberia during the Upper Pleniglacial, although temperate in the Mediterranean, was cooler than in earlier periods: in the Cantabrian and Atlantic regions it was harsher. Nevertheless, the resources were sufficient for survival and populations could develop an adaptive system based on foraging and hunting. These tasks now involved long-term planning to intercept the animal herds in logistical places, process animals and store part of the supply to ensure subsistence at other times of the year. As a result of these developments settlement in any one region would be more permanent than had been the case before. Consequently these populations started to use poorer and more expensive (in terms of energy outcomes and labour) resources (fish and shellfish) in an intensive manner, as is evidenced by the presence of harpoons in the assemblages. At the same time they diversified their use of the resources and habitats they exploited (Straus and Clark 1986; Straus 1992a).

There were other ways that hunter-gatherer–fishers could secure resources and avoid risks at lean periods. The case of the LGM in Cantabria is a good example. This region probably had a high population density. This could be achieved by developing social networks and alliances (friendships, tasks groups, mating relationships, etc.) outside the local group, strategies which Jochim (1981: 177) called 'storage of credit and value'. It is in this context that symbolic culture and social organization played their main role. As a result social life became more open and inclusive (Gamble 1993) because contacts with strangers were needed to create an 'insurance' against subsistence failure. For instance, Straus (1992a: 99) argues that the Cantabrian region underwent an increase in population density as a consequence of a movement of people southwards during the glacial advances over northern and northwestern Europe. This population employed diversification and intensification in the use of resources and habitats as a survival strategy. I would suggest that in order for these hunter-gatherer–fishers from Cantabria to avoid competition, they established contact with the Mediterranean region. This was another way to achieve a secure subsistence by means of a social solution. These interregional contacts might follow the easiest route of the Ebro Basin according to the archaeological record so far (Abauntz and Chaves caves: see Utrilla 1992). Moving to distant regions might be one means by which modern human populations obtained not only food supplies, but also raw materials and prestige goods such as shells, ivory, and ornaments (Flébot-Agustins and Perles 1991), which contain social information by virtue of their rarity. Therefore, these social relationships served not only as a form of insurance to supply resources, but also to transmit knowledge about the group or region to which individuals belonged and to construct mating connections.

In addition, Gamble (1993: 42) has argued that by linking local networks modern humans generated 'social landscapes'. In this regard, artistic representations and symbolic communication and behaviour (by means of body ornaments and artefact style) are important elements for charting the dynamic of change. In Iberia, as well as throughout Europe (Mellars 1990; Bosinski 1990), art and symbolism arose during the EUP (Aurignacian). The widespread paintings and engravings in caves and rock-shelters, personal ornaments and portable art (stone, antler, bone, etc.) occurred around the LGM (18,000 BP) in Cantabrian, Atlantic and Mediterranean regions (see Straus 1992a: Figure 7.1). In contrast to these claims, Clark and Lindly (1989) argue that the artistic explosion only occurs after 20,000 BP.

If Jochim's (1983: 217) interpretation of rock art as 'land claims' is assumed, it is the high population density in the Cantabrian region which made people use paintings and visual representations to mark their territory in order to survive successfully. According to this model artistic representation 'serves as a measure of the intensity of competition between these populations and their physical and social environment' (Gamble 1986: 340). Moreover, from the social perspective it can be regarded as a measure of the integration of groups from a regional population – the construction of identity – as Conkey (1980) posited in her study of Altamira. In referring to the high number of personal ornaments in the Early Upper Palaeolithic contexts in contrast to the Neanderthal contexts, White (1993: 351) states that this is evidence of a transformation from 'internally un- or weakly-differentiated social systems to ones in which a variety of social identities was being constructed and communicated by means of carefully selected and worked materials'.

One aspect that should be pointed out is that there are differences in the art representation between regions in Iberia: in the north wall paintings and engravings dominated whereas in the Mediterranean region stone plaquettes with engravings (portable art) were similarly important. At this point in the discussion a few questions can be posed. Why did the Mediterranean hunter-gatherers employ other types of blanks to represent their social range? Is the answer a matter of population density and less competition, or is it just that they had a distinctive way of claiming the land as a result of variations in environmental constraints? Even more important is the question as to whether symbolic and artistic representations had any other meaning, or whether only the blank slabs or plaquettes varied. Why is there no evidence of these kinds of depiction in Neanderthal and Late Neanderthal contexts in Iberia? In my opinion, one profitable issue for future enquiry may be the integration of rock art with archaeological investigations. If scholars in Iberia approach rock art from the perspective of human ecology and social organization, the answers to those questions might eventually be forthcoming. These approaches appear to have been useful in furnishing some explanations of the dynamics of change in human behaviour throughout the Iberian Pleistocene and have not required any misapplication of ethnography.

ACKNOWLEDGEMENTS

I am very grateful to Professor Clive Gamble for his encouragement, advice and comments on this chapter. I would also like to express my thanks to Antonio Sánchez Marco for assisting me with the environmental inferences, and to the editors of this book for their invitation to participate in the volume.

NOTE

1 The chapter was written during the author's stay in the Department of Archaeology, University of Southampton, funded with a Postdoctoral Scholarship by the Consejo Superior de Investigaciones Científicas (C.S.I.C.), Madrid, Spain.

REFERENCES

Aguirre, E. (1989) 'Vertebrados del Pleistoceno continental', in *Mapa del Cuaternario de España*: 47–69, Madrid: Instituto Tecnológico y Geominero de España.

Aguirre, E. Arsuaga, J.L. Bermúdez de Castro, J.M. Carbonell, E. Ceballos, M. Díez, C. Enamorado, J. Fernández-Jalvo, Y. Gil, E. Gracia, A., Martín-Nájera, A., Martínez, I., Morales, J., Ortega, A.I., Rosas, A., Sánchez Marco, A., Sánchez Chillón, B., Sesé, C., Soto, E. and Torres, T. (1990) 'The Atapuerca Sites and the Ibeas Hominids', *Human Evolution* 5: 55–73.

Aitken, M.J., Stringer, C. and Mellars, P. (eds) (1993) *The Origin of Modern Humans and the Impact of Chronometric Dating*, Princeton: Princeton University Press.

Alberdi, M.T. and Bonadona, F.P. (eds) (1989) *Geología y paleontología de la cuenca de Guadix-Baza*, Trabajos sobre Neógeneo/Cuaternario, Madrid: Museo Nacional de Ciencias Naturales.

Arnáiz, M.A. (1990) 'Las ocupaciones de San Quirce de río Pisuerga: reflexiones sobre la utilización del espacio y sus implicaciones', *Boletín del Seminario de Arte y Arqueología* LVI: 25–37.

—— (1991) 'La ocupación humana en la cuenca alta del río Pisuerga durante el Pleistoceno inferior y medio', unpublished Ph.D. thesis, University of Valladolid.

Aura, J.E., Fernández Peris, J. and Fumanal, M.P. (1993) 'Medio físico y corredores naturales: notas sobre el poblamiento paleolítico del País Valenciano', *Recerques del Museu D'Alcoi* II: 89–101.

Binford, L.R. (1980) 'Willow smoke and dog tails: hunter-gatherer settlement systems and archaeological site formation', *American Antiquity* 43: 330–61.

Bischoff, J., Soler, N., Maroto, J. and Juliá, R. (1989) 'Abrupt Mousterian/ Aurignacian boundary at ca. 40 kyr. BP: accelerator radiocarbon dates from L'Arbreda Cave', *Journal of Archaeological Science* 16: 553–76.

Bosinski, G. (1990) *Homo sapiens: l'histoire des chasseurs du Paléolithique supérieur en Europe (40,000–10,000 av. J.C.)*, Paris: Errance.

Cabrera, V., Hoyos, M. and Bernaldo de Quirós, F. (1993) 'La transición del Paleolítico Medio/Paleolítico Superior en la Cueva de El Castillo: características paleoclimáticas y situación cronológica', in V. Cabrera (ed.) *El Origen del Hombre Moderno en el Suroeste de Europa*: 81–101, Madrid: Universidad Nacional de Educación a Distancia.

Carbonell, E., Bermúdez de Castro, J. H., Arsuaga, J. L., Díez, J. C., Rosas, A., Cuenca-Bescós, G., Sala, R., Mosquera, M. and Rodriguez, X. P. (1995) 'Lower Pleistocene Hominids and Artifacts from Atapuerca – TD6 (Spain)', *Science* 269: 826–30.

Carbonell, E. and Rodríguez, X. P. (1993) 'Early Middle Pleistocene deposits and artefacts in the Gran Dolina site (TD4) of the 'Sierra de Atapuerca' (Burgos, Spain)', *Journal of Human Evolution* 26: 291–311.

Clark, G.A. and Lindly, J. (1989) 'The case for continuity: observations on the biocultural transition in Europe and western Asia', in P. Mellars and C. Stringer (eds) *The Human Revolution: Behavioural and Biological Perspectives in the Origins of Modern Humans*: 626-76, Edinburgh: Edinburgh University Press.

Conkey, M. (1980) 'The identification of prehistoric hunter-gatherer aggregation sites: the case of Altamira', *Current Anthropology* 21: 609–30.

Cornu, S., Pätzold, J., Bard, F., Meco, J. and Cuerda Barceló, J. (1993) 'Paleo-temperature of the last interglacial period based on O18 of *Strombus bubonius* from the western Mediterranean sea', *Palaeogeography, Palaeoclimatology, Palaeoecology* 103: 1–20.

Criado Boado, F., Bonilla, A., Cerqueiro, D., Díaz, M., González, M., Infante, F., Méndez, F., Penedo, R., Rodríguez, E. and Vaquero, J. (1991) *Arqueología del Paisaje. El área de Bocelo-Furelo entre los tiempos paleolíticos y medievales. Campañas 1987–88 y 89*, Colección Arqueoloxía/Investigación 6, Santiago de Compostela: Xunta de Galicia.

Dennell, R. (1987) *La prehistoria económica de Europa*, Barcelona: Crítica.

Díez, J.C., García, M.A., Gil, E., Jordá, J.F., Ortega, A.I., Sánchez, A. and Sánchez, B. (1989–90) 'La cueva de Valdegoba (Burgos). Primera campaña de excavaciones', *Zephyrus* XLI–XLII: 55–74.

Dupré, M. (1988) *Palinología y paleoambiente. Nuevos datos españoles. Referencias*, Trabajos del S.I.P. 84, Valencia: Servicio de Investigación Prehistórica.

Enamorado, J. (1992) 'Aprovechamiento del entorno por los grupos humanos del Pleistoceno en la Península Ibérica', unpublished Ph.D. thesis, Complutense University of Madrid.

—— (1995) 'Lithics in a human ecological context: a critical review of recent Spanish approaches', in J. Schofield (ed.) *Lithics in Context*: 55–70, London: British Museum and HMSO.

—— (forthcoming) 'El Paleolítico de Madrid', *Revista de Arqueología*.

Fernández Peris, J. (1993) 'El Paleolítico Inferior en el País Valenciano. Una aproximación a su estudio', *Recerques del Museu D'Alcoi* II: 7–21.

Flébot-Agustins and Pérles, J. (1991) 'Perspectives ethno-archéologiques sur les échanges à longue distance', Unpublished MS, Colloques 'Ethnoarchéologie', Antibes.

Foley, R. (1985) 'Optimality theory in archaeology', *Man* 20: 222–42.

Freeman, L.G. (1993) 'La "transición" en Cantabria. La importancia de Cueva Morín y sus vecinos en el debate actual', in V. Cabrera (ed.), *El Origen del Hombre Moderno en el Suroeste de Europa*: 171–93, Madrid: Universidad Nacional de Educación a Distancia.

Fullola Pericot, J.M. (1992) 'El Paleolítico en Cataluña', in P. Utrilla (ed.) *Aragón/Litoral Mediterráneo: Intercambios culturales durante la Prehistoria. Homenaje a J. Maluquer de Motes*: 37–53, Zaragoza: Instituto Fernando el Católico.

Fumanal, M.P. (1986) *Sedimentología y clima en el País Valenciano. Las cuevas habitadas en el Cuaternario reciente*, Trabajos Varios del S.I.P. 83, Valencia: Servicio de Investigación Prehistórica.

Gamble, C.S. (1986) *The Palaeolithic Settlement of Europe*, Cambridge, Cambridge University Press.

—— (1993) 'Exchange, foraging and local hominid network', in Ch. Scarre and F. Healy (eds) *Trade and Exchange in Prehistoric Europe*: 35–44, Oxford: Oxbow Books.

—— (1994) 'Middle Palaeolithic Biotopes OIS 8-3 (300 Kyr – ca. 35 kyr)', paper presented to the European Science Foundation Workshop, 'Middle Palaeolithic settlement patterns', Arras, Holland.

Gibert, J., Walker, J.M., Malagosa, A., Sánchez, F., Pomery, P.J., Hunter, D., Arribas, A. and Maillo, A. (1994) 'Hominids in Spain: Ice Age Neanderthals from Cabezo Gordo', *Research and Exploration* 10 (1): 120–3.

González Echegaray, J. (1993) 'La evolución histórica del concepto de transición a los cazadores recolectores del Paleolítico superior', in V. Cabrera (ed.), *El Origen del Hombre Moderno en el Suroeste de Europa*: 105–16, Madrid: Universidad Nacional de Educación a Distancia.

Gusi, F., Gibert, J., Agustí, J. and Pérez Cueva, A. (1984) 'Nuevos datos del yacimiento Cova del Tossal de la Font (Vilafamés, Castellón)', *Cuadernos de Prehistoria y Arqueología Castellonenses* X: 7–18.

Guthrie, R.D. (1984) 'Mosaics, allelochemis and nutrientes: an ecological theory of late Pleistocene megafauna extictions', in P. Martin and R. Klein (eds) *Quaternary Extinctions: A Prehistoric Revolution*: 259–98, Tucson, Arizona: Arizona University Press.

Hayden, B. (1993) 'The cultural capacities of Neanderthals: a review and re-evaluation', *Journal of Human Evolution* 24: 113–46.

Iturbe, G., Fumanal, M.P., Carrión, J.S., Cortell, E., Martínez, R., Guillem, P.M., Garralda, M.D. and Vandersmeersch, B. (1993) 'Cova Beneito (Muro, Alicante): Una perspectiva interdisciplinar', *Recerques del Museu D'Alcoi* II: 23–88.

Jochim, M.A. (1981) *Strategies for Survival. Cultural Behaviour in an Ecological Context*, New York: Academic Press.

—— (1983) 'Palaeolithic cave art in ecological perspective', in G. N. Bailey (ed.) *Hunter-gatherer Economy in Prehistory*: 212–19, Cambridge: Cambridge University Press.

Mellars, P.A. (ed.) (1990) *The Emergence of Modern Humans*, Edinburgh: Edinburgh University Press.

Montes Barquín, R. (1994) 'Los complejos industriales del Paleolítico Inferior en el centro de la región Cantábrica', *Raña* 16: I–IV.

Mora, R. (1988) 'El Paleolítico Medio en Cataluña', unpublished Ph.D thesis, Central University of Barcelona.

—— (1992) 'Aproximación a los procesos de trabajo en el Paleolítico Medio catalán', in A. Moure Romanillo (ed.) *Elefantes, Ciervos y Ovicaprinos: Economía y aprovechamiento del medio en la Prehistoria de España y Portugal*: 97–116, Santander: Universidad de Cantabria.

Obermaier, H. (1924) *The Fossil Man in Spain*, New Haven: Yale University Press.

Parés, J.M. and Pérez-González, A. (1995) 'Paleomagnetic age for hominid fossils at Atapuerca Archaeological Site, Spain', *Science* 269: 830–2.

Raposo, L. (1985) 'Paléolithique inférieur archaique au Portugal. Bilan des connaissances', *Bulletin de la Société Préhistorique Française* 82 (6): 173–80.

—— (1989) 'Problemas actuais no estudo do Paleolitico Inferior e Médio Portugues', *Lusiada* 2: 5–28.

Ripoll López, S. (1988) *La Cueva de Ambrosio (Almería, España) y su posición cronoestratigráfica en el Mediterráneo occidental*, British Archaeological Reports International Series 462, Oxford: BAR.

—— (1994) 'The Palaeolithic rock art of the Cueva Ambrosio (Almería, Spain)' *International Newsletter on Rock Art (INORA)* 7: 1–2.

Roebroeks, W. (1994) 'Updating the earliest occupation of Europe', *Current Anthropology* 35, 3: 301–5.

Roebroeks, W. and Van Kolfochoten, T. (1994) 'The earliest occupation of Europe. A short chronology', *Antiquity* 68: 489–503.

Sánchez Marco, A. (1993) 'Paleoecology of the Iberian Pleistocene as related by its Taphornitothenoses', *Síntesis del medio ambiente en España durante los dos ultimos millones de años*, Report to the European Community, Contract CECFI2W-CT91-0075: 305–19. Madrid.

Santonja, M. (1981) 'Características generales del Paleolítico inferior de la Meseta española', *Numantia*: 9–65.

—— (1989) 'Visión general de la Arqueología del Pleistoceno', in *Mapa del Cuaternario de España*: 71–85, Madrid: Instituto Tecnológico y Geominero de España.

—— (1992) 'La adaptación al medio en el Paleolítico Inferior de la Península Ibérica. Elementos para una reflexión', in A. Moure Romanillo (ed.) *Elefantes, Ciervos y Ovicaprinos: Economía y aprovechamiento del medio en la Prehistoria de España y Portugal*: 37–76, Santander: Universidad de Cantabria.

Santonja, M. and Raposo, L. (1993) 'The Earliest human occupation in Spain and Portugal', paper presented to the European Science Foundation Network, 'The Earliest occupation of Europe', Tautavel, France.

Santonja, M. and Villa, P. (1990) 'The Lower Paleolithic of Spain and Portugal', *Journal of World Prehistory* 4, 1: 45–94.

Soto, E. and Sesé, C. (1987) 'Mamíferos del Pleistoceno del Municipio de Madrid', *Estudios de Prehistoria y Arqueología Madrileñas* 1987: 11–38.

Straus, L.G. (1992a) *Iberia before the Iberians. The Stone Age of Cantabrian Spain*, Albuquerque: University of New Mexico Press.

—— (1992b) 'To change or not to change: the late and postglacial in the southwest of Europe', *Quaternaria Nova* II: 161–85.

Straus, L.G. and Clark, G.A. (1986) *La Riera Cave: Stone Age Hunter-Gatherer Adaptations in Northern Spain*, Anthropological Research Papers, 36, Tempe: Arizona State University.

Stringer, Ch. and Gamble, C.S. (1993) *In Search of the Neanderthals. Solving the Puzzle of Human Origins*, London: Thames and Hudson.

Uchupi, E. (1988) 'The Mesozoic–Cenozoic geologic evolution of Iberia. A tectonic link between Africa and Europe', *Revista de la Sociedad Geológica de España* 1, 3–4: 257–294.

Utrilla, P. (1989) 'Los niveles paleolíticos de la Cueva de Chaves (Bastarás, Huesca)', in *Cien años después de Sautuola*: 361–77, Santander.

—— (1992) 'Aragón/Litoral Mediterráneo. Relaciones durante el Paleolítico', in P. Utrilla (ed.) *Aragón/Litoral Mediterráneo: Intercambios culturales durante la Prehistoria. Homenaje a J. Maluquer de Motes*: 9–35, Zaragoza: Instituto Fernando el Católico.

Utrilla, P. and Montes, L. (1993) 'El final del Musteriense en el Valle del Ebro. Datos y reflexiones', in V. Cabrera (ed.) *El origen del hombre moderno en el suroeste de Europa*: 219–46, Madrid: Universidad Nacional de Educación a Distancia.

Vega Toscano, L.G. (1983) 'El Hombre de Neandertal y el Paleolítico Medio en España', *Revista de Arqueología* 29: 42–55.

—— (1988) *El Paleolítico Medio del sureste español y Andalucía Oriental*, Serie Tesis Doctorales, Madrid: Universidad Complutense.

—— (1990) 'La Fin du Paléolithique Moyen au Sud de L'Espagne: ses implications dans le contexte de la Péninsule Ibérique, *Mémoires du Musée de Préhistorie d'Ile de France* 3: 169–176.

—— (1993) 'El tránsito del Paleolítico Medio al Superior en el sur de la Península Ibérica', in V. Cabrera (ed.), *El origen del hombre moderno en el suroeste de Europa*: 147–70, Madrid: Universidad Nacional de Educación a Distancia.

Vega Toscano, L.G. and Carrión, J.S. (1993) 'Secuencia paleoclimática y respuesta vegetal durante el Pleistoceno superior de la cueva de la Carihuela (Piñar, Granada, SE. de España)', *Estudios sobre Cuaternario* 1993: 131–8.

Vega Toscano, L.G., Raposo, L. and Santonja, M. (1994) 'Medio ambiente y asentamientos en el Paleolítico Medio ibérico', Paper presented to the European Science Foundation Workshop, 'Middle Palaeolithic settlement patterns', Arras, Holland.

Villaverde, V. (1992) 'El Paleolítico en el País Valenciano', in P. Utrilla (ed.), *Aragón/Litoral Mediterráneo: Intercambios culturales durante la Prehistoria. Homenaje a J. Maluquer de Motes*: 55–87, Zaragoza: Instituto Fernando el Católico.

Villaverde, V. and Martínez-Valle, R. (1992) 'Economía y aprovechamiento del medio en el Paleolítico de la región central del Mediterráneo español', in A. Moure Romanillo (ed.) *Elefantes, ciervos y ovicaprinos: economía y aprovechamiento del medio en la Prehistoria de España y Portugal*: 77-97, Santander: Universidad de Cantabria.

Villaverde, V. and Peña, J.L. (1981) *Piezas con escotadura del Paleolítico valenciano (Materiales del Museo de Prehistoria de Valencia)*, Trabajos Varios del S.I.P. 69, Valencia: Servicio de Investigación Prehistórica.

White, R. (1993) 'A technological view of Castelperronian and Aurignacian body ornaments in France', in V. Cabrera (ed.) *El Origen del hombre moderno en el Suroeste de Europa*: 327–57, Madrid: Universidad Nacional de Educación a Distancia.

Zilhão, J. (1987) *O Solutrense da Estremadura portuguesa. Una proposta de interpretacão palaeoantropológica*, Lisbon: Dpto. de Arqueología do Instituto Portugues de Patrimonio Cultural.

—— (1992) 'Estrategias de povoamento e subsistencia no Paleolítico e Mesolítico de Portugal', in A. Moure Romanillo (ed.) *Elefantes, ciervos y ovicaprinos: economía y aprovechamiento del medio en la prehistoria de España y Portugal*: 149–62, Santander: Universidad de Cantabria.

—— (1993) 'Le Passage du Paléolithique moyen au Paléolithique supérieur dans le Portugal', in V. Cabrera (ed.) *El Origen del hombre moderno en el suroeste de Europa*: 127–46, Madrid: Universidad Nacional de Educación a Distancia.

Zilhão, J., Mauricio, J. and Souto, P. (1991) 'A Arqueología da Gruta da Almonda (Torres Novas): Resultados das escavacoes de 1988–89', *Actas das IV Jornadas Arqueológicas*: 161–71.

CHAPTER FOUR

THE NEOLITHIC OF THE IBERIAN PENINSULA

GENÍS RIBÉ, WALTER CRUELLS AND
MIQUEL MOLIST

INTRODUCTION

The history of archaeological research into the Neolithic has given rise to problems which complicate our understanding of its origins and development. Research has traditionally focused upon pottery identification and establishing regional chronological and cultural sequences. This has severely limited interpretations of economic and social themes. Pottery has served as the main frame of reference and research. Its presence, absence and decoration have been used as the indicators of cultural and economic change. Some archaeozoological and palaeobotanical studies (including pollen analysis and anthracology) have been carried out during the last twenty years, and through them it is now possible to say something about how the environmental context of Neolithic communities developed. These kinds of data refer mainly to the Iberian eastern Mediterranean area, however, and environmental evidence from other areas is still needed. This makes comparisons difficult and complicates any attempt at synthesis.

THE PALAEO-ECOLOGICAL FRAMEWORK

It is difficult to attempt a palaeo-ecological synthesis and reconstruction for the Iberian Peninsula. Not only is there great regional climatic, geographical and vegetational diversity, but palaeo-ecological studies are rare, except in eastern Spain. However, the data do allow us to outline the general evolution of the Early Neolithic period and its immediate aftermath.

The beginning of the Atlantic climatic period throughout the Mediterranean region is documented between the eighth and sixth millennia BP, and is characterized by higher temperatures (Boreal period) and humidity than in preceding periods. Optimal conditions (*optimum* Atlantic) appeared and allowed deciduous forests to grow and expand in coastal areas. Due to latitudinal differences and distance from the sea there was a mixed-type Mediterranean wood with holm-oak, pine, thicket and kermes oak in other coastal areas (Parra 1993). The climate with stabilized alluvial deposits and wind-blown deposits generated rich soils and established an appropriate basis for the first agricultural practices. Studies of pollen, charcoal, fauna and sediments demonstrate that by the seventh and the sixth millennia BP the first signs of productive human activities, such as farming, herding and deforestation, appeared (Ros and Vernet 1987; Dupré 1988; Fumanal 1986). The first human impact on plant environments, such as changes to the arboreal mass or fired forest, has been detected near settlement and cave-sites (Riera 1994; Badal *et al.* 1994).

Three stages can be established in the development of the palaeo-ecological framework. The first comprised a climatic improvement which started in the pre-boreal period and continued into the boreal itself, with a slow deforestation. The second stage was characterized by the Atlantic *optimum* climate, and the expansion of deciduous wooded areas. In the third and final stage, the first human attempts to modify the environment began, and there was a process of woodland degradation. This basic scheme will, of course, be further refined and developed by future research.

THE ORIGIN OF SUBSISTENCE PRODUCTION IN THE IBERIAN PENINSULA: THE EARLY NEOLITHIC

Socio-economic changes were not synchronic throughout the whole of the Iberian Peninsula. In the Mediterranean area generally, changes appeared rapidly. In the interior areas such as the Meseta and the northwest these changes occurred at later periods (Martí 1978; Muñoz 1984; Rincón 1987; López 1988). Everywhere the dynamics and the economic structure of hunter-gatherer societies were the main cause of transformation. In some places these groups adapted and developed new economic strategies (food production); in other places, hunter-gatherer groups progressively acquired the knowledge and techniques to transform the basis of their subsistence.

In the Mediterranean region of Iberia, the move towards the Neolithic was similar to that observed throughout the western Mediterranean, although the date of the advent of domestication is still disputed. The first period is characterized by the impressed-cardial pottery dated to the eighth and especially the seventh millennia BP. Material culture generally reveals regional diversity, with impressed pottery being rare in Andalucía and abundant in the Levant and Catalunya (Figure 4.1). In the latter areas, assemblages of cardial pottery conformed to regional patterns.

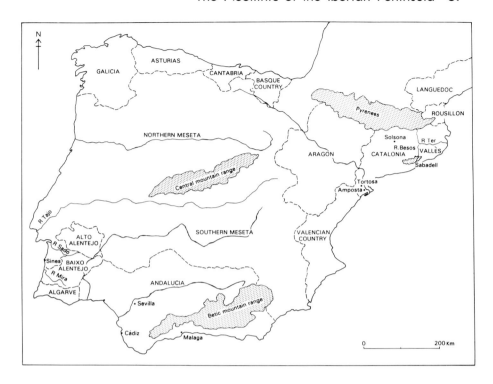

Figure 4.1 Map showing principal regions and places mentioned in the text.

It is difficult to equate individualized pottery styles with cultural groups, or chronological and geographical phases. However, it does allow us to observe a phenomenon documented in the rest of Europe: the progressive regionalization of pottery styles. This could be understood as a result of the consolidation and gradual expansion of new economic and social practices, as well as a sign of the rapid intensification of the occupation of space by the first agricultural and herding communities (Molist *et al.* forthcoming).

In the regions of Valencia and Aragón (Figure 4.1) archaeological research has demonstrated the simultaneous existence of Epipalaeolithic tradition (late phase or geometric 'Cocina' type) and full Neolithic hunter-gatherer groups. Hence such sites as Cueva de la Cocina, Botiquería dels Moros and Abrigo de Costalena (Figure 4.2) have provided Neolithic pottery and polished stone in levels considered to be Epipalaeolithic on the basis of their technology, as well as evidence of a wide-ranging predatory economy. At the same time sites such as Cova de l'Or, Cova de la Sarsa, Cova de les Cendres and Cueva de

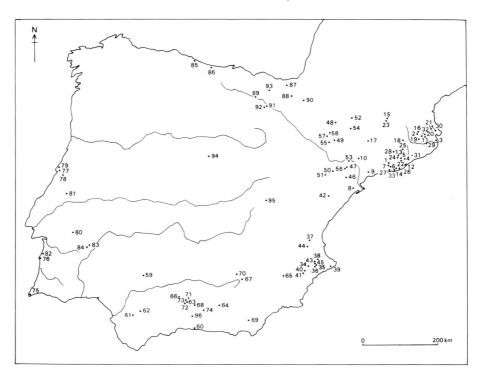

Figure 4.2 Map showing the archaeological sites cited in the text.

Catalunya: 1. Les Guixeres de Vilobí, 2. Plansallosa, 3. Puig Mascaró, 4. Can Banús, 5. Pla de la Bruguera, 6. Pujolet de Moja, 7. Hort d'en Grimau, 8. Barranc d'en Fabra, 9. Timba del Bareny, 10. Vall de la Femosa, 11. La Draga de Banyoles, 12. Sant Pau del Camp, 13. Cova del Frare, 14. Cova de Can Sadurni, 15. Balma Margineda, 16. Cova 120, 17. Cova del Parco, 18. Font de la Vena-Tavertet, 19. Cova de l'Avellaner, 20. Cova de Mariver de Martís, 21. Ca n'Isach, 22. Bòbila Madurell, 23. Feixa del Moro, 24. Cova dels Lladres, 25. Toll, 26. Gavà-Can Tintorer, 27. Bòbila d'en Roca, 28. Pla de les Marcetes, 29. Puig d'en Roca, 30. Serra de Roda-Les Alberes, 31. El Coll, 32. Serinyà, 33. Cova Verda. **Valencian country**: 34. Cova de la Sarsa, 35. Mas del Pla, 36. Bancal Satorre, 37. Cueva de la Cocina, 38. Cova de l'Or, 39. Cova de les Cendres, 40. Lara, 41. Arenal, 42. Cova Fosca, 43. Les Jovades, 44. La Ereta del Pedregal, 45. Alcoià. **Aragón**: 46. Botiquería dels Moros, 47. Abrigo de Costalena, 48. Cueva de Chaves, 49. El Torrollón, 50. Alonso Norte, 51. Las Torrazas, 52. Espluga de la Puyascada, 53. Barranc de la Mina Vallfera, 54. Cueva del Moro, 55. El Villar, 56. Pontet, 57. Peña del Agua, 58. El Portillo. **Andalucía**: 59. Cueva Chica de Santiago, 60. Cueva de Nerja, 61. Cueva de Parralejo, 62. Cueva de la Dehesilla, 63. Cueva de Mármoles, 64. Cueva de la Carihuela, 65. Abrigo del Barranco de los Grajos, 66. Cueva de los Murciélagos, 67. Cueva del Nacimiento, 68. Peña de los Gitanos, 69. Terrera Ventura, 70. Hornos de Segura, 71. Murcielaguina, 72. Inocentes, 73. Huerta Anguita, 74. La Molaina, 96. Cueva del Agua. **Portugal**: 75. Ponta de Sagres, 76. Vale Pincel, 77. Junqueira, 78. Forno do Cal, 79. Várzea do Lirio, 80. Gruta do Escoural, 81. Grota do Caldeirão, 82. Salema, 83. Poço da Galeira 1, 84. Gorginos 2. **Asturias**: 85. Les Pedroses, 86. Mazaculos. **Basque country**: 87. Marizulo, 88. Abauntz, 89. Fuente Hoz, 90. Cueva de Zatoya, 91. Peña Larga, 92. Los Husos, 93. Cueva de Urtao II. **Meseta**: 94. Cueva de la Vaquera, 95. Abrigo de Verdelpino.

Chaves have a clear early Neolithic sequence (seventh and sixth millennia BP). They exhibit a mature productive economy involving cereal crops and the domestication of ovicaprines as well as technological innovations comprising pottery, lithic and bone industries. This duality and the existence of these two different cultural traditions have been the subject of different interpretations. Some authors explain this period as one in which the last hunter-gatherers coincided with the first producers, the latter of whom had adopted an economy of external origin. The two cultural traditions would remain independent and be the result of a process of a Neolithic acculturation over Epipalaeolithic groups, which would have adopted several traits of Neolithic economy and technology (Martí 1988; Juan 1992). An alternative interpretation has been suggested by Barandiarán and Cava (1992). These authors explain the differences as the outcome of different adaptations to specific ecological territories by the same human group.

Interpretational problems remain in Andalucía (Figure 4.1) on account of the scarcity of research into this period and published stratigraphic sequences. Great dynamic geographical and historical differences exist between its eastern and western sectors. Traditionally it was maintained that the Neolithic appeared first in the east and afterwards in the west. Recent evidence, however, reveals a more complex pattern. The existence of very early radiocarbon dates of the early eighth millennium BP[1] in several caves of western Andalucía suggests that there was a nucleus of Neolithic development here which was independent from that observed in the rest of Iberia (Acosta 1987). These sites (Cueva Chica de Santiago, Cueva de La Dehesilla, Cueva de Nerja and Cueva del Parralejo, Figure 4.2) have pottery decorated with their own techniques (coating and slip pottery), but *cardium*-impressed pottery is rare. However, new open-air settlements with cardial pottery have recently been discovered in coastal and mountainous areas of Andalucía. The appearance of these has been related to the introduction of a productive economy and they are considered to be contemporary with the cave-occupation sites in the peripheral interior highlands discussed earlier.

In Portugal the Neolithic has traditionally been related to the appearance of cardial pottery. During the seventh millennium BP early cardial Neolithic settlements were essentially distributed along the coast (Figure 4.2). These were either open-air sites (Ponta de Sagres, Vale Pincel, Junqueira, Forno do Cal and Várzea do Lirio) or caves (Grota do Escoural and Grota do Caldeirão). However, sites with cardial pottery seem to have been slightly overvalued: they are always ephemeral and seem to be of little significance when compared to other pottery assemblages. Sites of the productive economy seem to be contemporary with local hunter-gatherer groups exploiting the inland ecological niches of the Tajo (Tejo in Portuguese), Sado and Mira estuaries and whose subsistence strategies survived up to the end of the eighth millennium BP (Straus 1991; Zilhão

1993). Several authors argue in favour of a Neolithic formation process 'by development' from small settlements with cardial pottery, domesticated animals and plants. Others suggest the existence of a somewhat endogenous process to explain the acquisition of an agricultural way of life distinct from that of Mesolithic communities. The latter interpretation suggests that these groups developed the new socio-economic patterns themselves. Items related to food production have also been found at Mesolithic sites, but are not necessarily explained by diffusionist-acculturation models, and may in fact be the result of other factors, such as exogamic exchange and territorial mobility (Tavares 1989).

Information about the rest of Iberia is scarce, but in general terms it seems that development towards a farming economy took place at a later date. A regional assessment reveals a lack of information for the central areas, where the site of Cueva de la Vaquera, dated to the sixth millennium BP, seems to be the only site that can be certainly considered as Neolithic. In northern Spain (the regions of Galicia, Asturias, Cantabria and the Basque Country) the presence of the first farming activities is attested by the appearance of pottery and new flintwork techniques. Neolithic sites in this area appeared just before the emergence of megaliths (about 5500 BP), the development of which can be interpreted as representing the consolidation of this new farming pattern.

Territory and settlement

In the landscape Neolithic human groups operated through new strategies of economic exploitation. These comprised the development and expansion of new farming technologies, the continuity of the traditional subsistence activities of hunting, fishing and gathering, and the exploitation of new raw materials for the manufacture of new tools. The territory was increasingly organized in a more complex way, and in several cases very differently from the prevailing Epipalaeolithic period. However, no clear rupture was initially attested in the settlement pattern. The consolidation of the Neolithic gave rise to a higher settlement density and an increase in interdependent relationships. In light of this, the relationship of farming communities to their 'living space' and the degree to which the new way of life affected the archaeological record is a matter of some interest. Unfortunately, however, this analysis would have benefited greatly from more palaeo-ecological studies.

Early Neolithic settlements with cardial and postcardial pottery in Catalunya date to between the second half of the seventh and the sixth millennia BP, and are concentrated in the Precoastal Depression and neighbouring chains. At a later date they are to be found more extensively in the interior and in the valleys of the Pyrenees. In the former area, the Precoastal Depression and neighbouring chains, some open-air settlements were located on the top of lower-lying hills, on fertile alluvial land suitable for crop cereals, near water sources and close to natural routes of communication. Close to those settlements there were low- and medium-lying mountain areas suitable for breeding practices. This was especially relevant on open-air sites such as Les Guixeres de Vilobí and Plansallosa. Sites have also been documented in different ecological contexts outside the Precoastal Depression, such as in the interior lowlands and Segre valley (area of Vall de la Femosa), the high plateau areas (Plansallosa), lacustrine zones (La Draga in Banyoles) and coastal areas (Sant Pau del Camp).

Despite the scarcity of evidence for habitation sites, there is evidence to suggest that architectural elaboration consisted of perishable material (clay, straw and wood branches) and the occasional use of stone. The construction of simple dwelling huts has been deduced from post holes, oval and circular pits, and combustion pits. Settlements also contained groups of storage-pits, of short duration, as well as other pits of unknown function. Complete sedentarization has been stated at such sites as Barranc d'en Fabra, where great oval huts built from dry-stone walls, floors, support and combustion structures have been documented (Bosch *et al.* 1991).

It is difficult to document the processes whereby farming activities were established. Deforestation has been documented through palaeo-ecological reconstruction, the existence of polished axes, and the use of sickle blades, adzes, hand grinders and pounders for farming. It is similarly difficult to establish the types of crops and crop-rotation schemes, and to ascertain the existence of short-fallow land and roving crops in woodlands. However, the evidence of legumes at Iberian Mediterranean sites suggests the existence of crop rotation/alternation as in traditional Mediterranean agriculture (Buxó 1991).

In mountainous areas breeding activities were important, as is evident at the sites of Cova del Frare, Cova de Can Sadurní and Balma Margineda. The occupation of caves and shelters was generally seasonal or for specific and specialized economic activities. It is possible to establish different site categories in relation to the pattern of exploitation of the territories of main settlements. The use of caves has to be understood as an economic complement to farming activities. Some of these caves could be used as cowsheds or for the shelter of animals, mainly ovicaprines. In other cases, such as Cova 120, the discovery of pits and large vessels in caves suggests that they may have been used for cereal storage. Ovicaprines seem to have been the prevailing animal type and we can assume that there were migrations over short distances, exploiting the highlands in summer and the lowlands in winter. Highland sites such as Balma Margineda or Cova del Parco are far from the main settlements. Hunting activities also took place, serving to minimize risk in such an undeveloped subsistence/productive economy, and at the same time were a means of controlling directly cultivated lands. As will be shown, the Catalan pattern reflected a similar situation found in the remaining areas during this period.

Recent micro-regional studies in the Valencian region have deeply modified the traditional understanding of the local early Neolithic. Sites are found in caves and shelters, and, on the basis of new discoveries in Alcoià, also coexisted with open-air settlements such as Mas del Pla and Bancal Satorre. As mentioned previously, there was an economic duality in the earlier period. Thus, on the one hand, there were sites such as Cueva de la Cocina, Lara and Arenal, with geometric Epipalaeolithic lithic industries and where hunting and gathering activities were the economic mainstays. On the other, there were sites with a productive economy, seemingly based on ovicaprine herding (Fortea 1973; Fortea *et al.* 1987; Martí *et al.* 1987; Bernabeu 1989; Bernabeu *et al.* 1993). These sites were located either in places never previously occupied, or in places occupied at the end of an important occupational hiatus (Cova de l'Or, Cueva de la Sarsa and Cova de les Cendres). We can reject the traditional hypothesis based on the mechanistic association between cave occupation and herding activities. Throughout the Valencian country open-air settlements and caves were in use, and their joint presence involves a change in our assumptions about Neolithic economy and the social uses of landscape.

A similar pattern of territorial exploitation has been suggested for Aragón during the early Neolithic. Notwithstanding the scarcity of data, Balldellou points to the existence of a socio-economic duality based on two types of settlement pattern. On the one hand there is occupation in mountainous areas with herding activities, and on the other there are open-air settlements with agriculture as the economic basis, such as El Torrallón (Baldellou *et al.* 1989). Recently, open-air settlements such as Alonso Norte and Las Torrazas have been documented in southern Aragón. These were involved in agricultural activities and are characterized by the presence of non-cardial-impressed pottery. They are dated to the late seventh millennium BP.

A predominance of wild-fauna exploitation has been attested at sites in western Andalucía up to the later Neolithic at such sites as Cueva de la Dehesilla and Cueva del Parralejo in the province of Cádiz. In eastern Andalucía, however, the storage of cereals in pits in natural caves has been documented at such sites as the Cueva de Mármoles. It has been suggested that cereal cultivation in the Subbetic mountain-range could have taken place in lowland areas close to natural caves, and that it was complemented by the hunting of deer and livestock-breeding. However, recent excavations in open-air settlements located in southern coastal areas of Andalucía will probably change our hypothesis about this economic pattern.

There is a very different pattern in southern Portugal. No clear break is attested between Mesolithic and Early Neolithic settlements. In both periods dwellings were occupied for short periods, and have yielded scanty archaeological remains. The sites occupied large open and sandy areas close to coastal cliffs or river courses. The inhabited nuclei comprised a set of small domestic units: hut floors and combustion structures were the most common. The former were built with perishable elements. Combustion structures filled with burned stone, flat stone-paved pits and ovens have been interpreted as hearths (Morais 1982; Tavares and Soares 1987). Recent archaeological excavations of caves located in the mountains of eastern Extremadura and new data on open-air settlements provide information about complementary territorial exploitation.

In the Basque Country and western Cantabria, Neolithic processes appeared at a very late date; in the sixth millennium BP agricultural practices can be inferred from the presence of polished axes. However, animal domestication is well attested with the presence of ovicaprines, bovines and pigs, and complemented by hunting. In mountainous settlements, animal grazing initially had a greater importance than agriculture. Settlements were mostly situated in caves, such as Les Pedroses, Mazaculos, Marizulo, Abauntz and Fuente Hoz (Cava 1990; Arias 1991).

Palaeo-economy

From the Early Neolithic period there was a modification in the patterns of resource exploitation. Domestication of either animals or plants appeared to be closely related to the rest of the Neolithic technocultural system. However, strategies of territorial exploitation would depend on a large number of elements which diverged from general dynamics (regional-local palaeo-ecological frame, settlement pattern, functional character of occupation). 'Exceptions' usually appeared: complementary and equilibrated exploitation of multiple resources, predominance of hunting and gathering activities over productive ones, and animal exploitation to the detriment of agricultural practices.

In that sense it has been observed that wild sheep, goat (*Capra aegragus*) and horse did not originally exist in the Iberian Peninsula, and that the domestication of the latter seems to have taken place at a late date. However, data from some sites such as Cova Fosca could be taken to suggest an earlier appearance. There were wild dogs (*Canis lupus*), cattle (*Bos primigenius*, aurochs) and pigs (*Sus scrofa*, wild boar), although too little is presently known about the last to allow us to confirm whether they were domesticated in Iberia. It is broadly accepted that animal domestication did not take place in the Peninsula. In certain areas, however, conditions were advantageous for domestication during the Epipalaeolithic or geometric Mesolithic periods. Experimentation and changes in resource exploitation occurred, probably on account of ecological and subsistence strategies. These new economic patterns provoked a change in settlement distribution, material culture and fauna (small-size deer and goat (*Capra pyrenaica*)). It also marks the appearance of evidence for hunting at sites such as Zatoya, deer during the Asturiense period,[2] and goat-hunting in the Mondúver massif.

Domestication largely involved ovicaprines, followed by pig, cattle and dog, as is documented at the sites of Les Guixeres de Vilobí and La Cova del Frare (Catalunya), Cueva de Chaves and Espluga de la Puyascada (Aragón), Cova de la Sarsa (Valencia), and at Cueva de la Cariguela (also called Carihuela), Cueva de Nerja and Cueva de Mármoles (Andalucía). However, recent faunal studies at some sites in Catalunya suggest a greater importance of cattle (La Draga) and pigs (Sant Pau del Camp). The importance of hunting activities varied according to region, but red deer, goat, wild boar, roe deer, aurochs, rabbit and horse prevailed. Skins, leather, horns and meat were obtained from these animals. Fishing has also been documented as a supplementary food source at such sites as Cova de les Cendres and in the coastal area of Sines in southern Portugal.

A range of shell foods has also been documented, although their contribution to the diet was very limited, as is shown by data from sites such as Cova de les Cendres: however, the contrary is true of some exceptional sites such as Vale Pincel I and Salema. In most cases, therefore, the presence of shells at Iberian Neolithic sites has to be interpreted as raw material for ornaments (*Columbella rustica*, *Sphincteochilla candidissima*, *Rumina decollata* and *Cepaea*). Their use extended beyond coastal areas and was introduced to inland sites such as Cueva de Chaves, Abrigo de Costalena, Cueva del Agua, Abrigo de Verdelpino, Abrigo del Barranco de los Grajos and Cueva de Zatoya: at the last site, shells were found in pre-Neolithic levels.

Domestication of plants was not carried out in the Iberian Peninsula. In the Early Neolithic cultivation was based on wheat (*Triticum*) and barley (*Hordeum*), of which a rich range of types have been found: einkorn (*T. monococcum*), emmer (*T. dicoccum*), and bread wheats (*T. aestivum*), barley (*H. vulgare var. nudum*) and hulled barley (*H. vulgare var. polystichum*). All of these are documented in the fifth millennium BP and attested at such sites as Cova de l'Or, Cueva de los Murciélagos de Zuheros, Cueva de Mármoles and Cova 120. The vegetal diet was complemented by legumes (such as *Vicia sp.*, found at Cova 120) and wild fruits including acorns, which have been discovered at Cova de l'Or and Cueva de los Murciélagos. The increasingly common identification of new legumes (broad beans, lentils and peas) in archaeological contexts promises us a better understanding of farming and its relationship to cereal crops. A range of archaeological data allow us to reconstruct Early Neolithic agricultural activities. These include spade-handle weights, adzes (made from hard stones), woodworking chisels, sickle blades, hand querns, axes (pricked and polished combined manufacture that would be used primarily in forest clearance) and large pottery vessels, as well as storage-pits excavated in caves or open areas, and which confirm that cereals were harvested.

Burial

In the Valencian region and Catalunya there seems to have been a trend in the use of caves for inhumation burials. In spite of the scarce documentation for the cardial period, there is evidence that burial rites consisted of single and double burials with rare grave goods. An example of this was found in the Cova de la Sarsa. From the last quarter of the seventh millennium BP caves continued to harbour burials, although the cavities selected were smaller and had narrow passages (Cova de l'Avellanor and Cova de Mariver de Morti). The burial rite seems to have been collective inhumation. Grave goods were rich and consisted of pottery, beads (the site of Cova dels Lladres was exceptional in having more than 2000 beads made of various materials), and food tributes of wild boar, rabbit, tortoise and birds. From the first third of the sixth millennium BP, there was an anticipation of future developments with open-air burials that were either isolated or grouped together in ceme-teries for the first time as at Hort d'En Grimau, Sant Pau del Camp, Pujolet de Moja, Tortosa, Amposta and Barranc de la Mina Vallfera. Megalithic tombs also appeared in this period. They comprised a central cist with a substantial earth mound and an external stone ring. Initially they housed single inhumations (the megalithic tombs of Font de la Vena). Skeletons were in a crouched position and the grave goods consist of pottery (plain and corded, combed and with relief), large numbers of shell bracelets and food tributes of bovids, ovicaprines, pig, wild boar and deer. In this latter phase of the Early Neolithic period, the burial pattern is better known: inhumation, simple oval pits, circular pits covered by small stone mounds and pits with benches and cists.

The Valencian region burial rites are not so well known. In Aragón, cave burial is well attested and is sometimes associated with settlements. Two examples can be mentioned: Cueva de Chaves, where there was an inhumation in a crouched position, but without significant grave goods, and Cueva del Moro, where human remains have been associated with cardial pottery and beads, although in no clear stratigraphic context.

In the Basque Country several sites with collective burials, such as Cueva de Zatoya I and Cueva de Fuente Hoz, have been dated to the seventh millennium BP (Armendáriz 1990). However, the stratigraphic sequence of these caves does not seem to be clear. In the rest of the Iberian Peninsula, in Andalucía (except in La Molaina), Portugal, Galicia, Cantabria and both Mesetas, no Early Neolithic burial sites have yet been discovered.

MIDDLE NEOLITHIC: THE CONSOLIDATION OF A PRODUCTIVE ECONOMY

In general terms the period dating to the second half of the sixth millennium BP and first half of the fifth represents the consolidation of a socio-economic way of life whose development began during the Early Neolithic. This period saw the evolution of social and economic features, a technical and economic change, an increase in the complexity of the organization of inhabited space, greater ritual and structural diversity in burials, and a greater development and dispersion of territorial exploitation. However, there was also important continuity between what we have defined as the Early and Middle Neolithic, and external influences cannot be made responsible for the changes we observe from the second half of the sixth millennium BP.

Aspects of chronology and terminology

There is great diversity and indeed confusion in the terminology used by Spanish and Portuguese archaeologists. In Catalunya the *sepulcros de fosa* culture ('pit-grave' culture) developed between the second half of the sixth and the first half of the fifth millennia BP. In Andalucía this period is labelled 'Middle–Late Neolithic' by scholars and is dated to the last quarter of the sixth and the second half of the fifth millennia BP. Its most evident feature was a change in pottery traditions, with the replacement of cardial and impressed pottery by plain ware at such sites as Carihuela, Nerja and Nacimiento. The Middle Neolithic of Aragón is dated to between 6000 BP and 5000 BP. However, for the period we are considering as Middle Neolithic (from the second half of the sixth millennium BP onwards) data are scarce. Only three radiocarbon dates are available, at the site of Pontet, where the b level has been dated to 5450 ± 290 BP, and to 4810 BP and 4370 BP at the cemetery of Mina Vallfera. More terminological confusion exists in the Valencian region. Archaeologists here label our Early Neolithic as Middle Neolithic, a period with incising, no cardial-impressed and channelled-ware predominance. Valencian archaeologists also divide our Middle Neolithic into phases A and B of Neolithic II, characterized by plain and graffitoed wares, which show a new range of forms (plates, bowls and carinated vessels), and by bigger lithic blades and the appearance of arrowheads.

Settlement, economy and social context

This period was characterized by a spread of open-air settlements, an increase in settlement size and a progressive abandonment of caves and shelters. In Catalunya recent investigations carried out at sites such as

Ca n'Isach, Bòbila Madurell and Feixa del Moro have provided new information. The location of settlements and cemeteries allows us to characterize the distribution of population. There was a continuity of settlement patterns in the main fertile areas (valleys, precoastal lowlaïs or coastal areas) which had already begun in the late phases of the Early Neolithic, but with some differences. These are a colonization of new and isolated areas, such as the central area of Catalunya and the Catalan Pyrenees, an increase in the number of settlements and the general abandonment of caves (although there are some exceptions such as the caves of Toll and Molinot). The sites at Bòbila Madurell and Ca n'Isach provide information about the architectural organization of settlements. At Bòbila Madurell circular pits (probably storage pits reused for rubbish), excavated rectangular structures with post holes and combustion pits have been found (Alaminos *et al.* 1991; Bordas *et al.* 1994). Ca n'Isach had several habitation areas associated and delimited by wall footings with post holes, combustion sites (plain hearths and pits), storage areas (pits) and fireplaces. This has several occupation floors dating to between the late sixth and beginning of the fifth millennia BP (Tarrús *et al.* 1992).

In the Valencian region the same pattern of rupture is to be found from the second half of the sixth millennium BP. There was a population expansion and open-air settlements emerge, such as those of Les Jovades and Ereta del Pedregal, which occupied new territories. However, caves continued to be used (Cova de l'Or and Cova de les Cendres) (Bernabeu *et al.* 1989), as was also the case in Aragón (Abrigo del Pontet). A similar phenomenon has been observed in Andalucía where there was a survival of cave occupation (Nerja and Nacimiento), but where we can also observe the appearance of the first open-air settlements, as at Peña de los Gitanos, Terrera Ventura and probably Hornos de Segura.

Palaeo-ecological analysis of this period indicates that there was an improvement in herding throughout the Iberian Peninsula, and an increase in *suidae* and *bovinae* at the expense of goats and sheep. Ground and freshwater molluscs were also gathered. Hunting activities were carried out but played a secondary role. Agriculture was dominated by cereal crops and there was an increase in barley, surely on account of its better ecological adaptability. There was also an increase in the number of hand querns, and this may indicate a development of farming. As in the previous period, sickle blades, storage-pits and great storage vessels attest to the importance of productive activities.

The exchange of raw materials and manufactured products is also documented in this period, and has to be seen as playing an important part in the economy. In Catalunya this was based on shells and callaïs (variscite), materials used in the manufacture of ornamental beads and pendants that would form part of grave goods. Good-quality lithic materials, especially flint and obsidian, were also exchanged. The recent discovery and excavation of the Can Tintorer (Gavà) callaïs mines has yielded a great deal of information concerning exchange networks during the Middle Neolithic period. This mine operated from approximately 5400 to 4600 BP. It was very complex in architectural terms and formed from pools and galleries. Beads and bracelets made of callaïs, carved instruments of lyddite and polished items in stone such as schist were manufactured there. Production and distribution took place on a large scale, and covered the whole of Catalunya and, probably, Aragón, and Rousillon and Languedoc in France (Villalba *et al.* 1986; Blasco *et al.* 1991; Bosch and Estrada 1994). The increase of these exchanges and the presence of specialized production centres such as that at Can Tintorer points to the emergence of an incipient social organization of work. This is not only visible in the manufacture of luxury items, but also may be expected in other specialized sectors such as basket-making, building and tool manufacture.

Death: spaces and ritual

Throughout the Middle Neolithic new types of graves appeared. They consolidated the separation between burial space and settlements. However, previous ritual forms continued in caves, characterized by the collective burial ritual at Los Husos, Peña Larga and Cueva de Urtao II in the Basque Country and other sites in the Valencian region. Spatial organization, however, was partially modified and there was greater diversity.

Burials are very well known in Catalunya and have given their name to the *sepulcros de fosa* or 'pit-grave' culture. Recent research has systematized burial forms, and two basic types have been suggested: the pits used in the region around Sabadell, and the cists near Solsona. At the same time the first megaliths appear in pre-Pyrenean and Pyrenean areas. Pits are distributed throughout the precoastal and coastal areas of central Catalunya, the lowlands and the valleys of the Besòs and Ter rivers. Known cemeteries such as Pla de les Marcetes, Bobila d'en Roca and Puig d'en Roca are numerous, but undoubtedly the most emblematic site is Bòbila Madurell in the Vallès area. This site has about 130 pit-graves. Generally speaking, the burial structures are not homogeneous. They were simple pits covered with earth, or took the form of flagstone-lined pits with a stone roof, and were circular or rectangular in form. In each grave was placed a single or double inhumation (exceptionally formed by three or four individuals). There are a large number of burials, most of which belong to infants. Unfortunately relationships between grave goods, sex, age and morphology are still not clear, but seem to be a promising area of future research. Grave goods were characterized by their variety. Plain wares with completely new forms, including carinated forms, are present. Flintwork consisted of knives, prismatic cores, and triangular and trapezoidal microlithic tools, axes, adzes and chisels made of hard stones such as sillimanite, serpentine, schist and porphyry. There were also a great number of hand mills and evidence of bone industries; punches, spatulae and doubled-edged axes. Finally, grave goods included luxury items such as callaïs necklace beads (Bordas *et al.* 1994; Pou *et al.* 1994). Cist-burials are to be found in the Catalan interior high plateau. Single-burial inhumations are the most frequent, but double inhumations also occurred. With the appearance of megaliths these cists were sometimes covered with a cairn or earth mound. Goods found within them consisted of a range of transverse, subtriangular and trapezoidal arrowheads and products of a bone industry (punches, spatulae and daggers) (Castany 1992). A new hypothesis concerning the origin of megaliths in Catalunya has been formulated recently. It points to an indigenous development of Early Neolithic funeral traditions. The earliest megaliths were distributed across the north Pyrenean region. There are two different structural types. The first consists of a central stone-chamber burial beneath a large and complex earth tumulus in the high plateau of Tavertet, and has a radiocarbon date of about 5,700 BP. The second is comprised by the well-documented passage-graves of the Serra de Roda-Les Alberes, one of which has a radiocarbon date of 5,400 ± 100 BP (Molist *et al.* forthcoming).

In the southeast, and especially in Portugal, Megaliths have early dates: indeed the Portuguese examples are amongst the earliest in Europe. They were either dry-stone or chambered grave tombs with collective burials. Their appearance has traditionally been linked to the development of complex societies in the fifth millennium BP. Georg and Vera Leisner's work has shown that there was an important link between the origins of this burial tradition and indigenous rites, thereby eschewing any possible orientalizing influences. Research carried out over the last twenty years has confirmed the existence of an archaic megalithic development in Portugal, especially in the Algarve, Baixo and Alto Alentejo (Tavares 1987). Burial forms were initially simple with either a rectangular or a square plan, and later evolved towards more complex polygonal chambers (Poço da Galeira 1, Gorginos 2). The chronology of this early phase is still in dispute because of the existence of two thermoluminescence dates of 6,510 ± 360 BP and 6,440 ± 360 BP, with which not all scholars are in agreement. Megalithic development seems to be indisputable from at least the first half of the sixth millennium BP. The second half of the sixth and the first half of the fifth millennia BP represent the climax of megalithic development in Portugal. The tombs become monumental and more complex (larger chamber and horseshoe chamber), and reveal a diversification of grave goods and new types of lithic items. In Galicia, Cantabria and the Basque Country there was a similar spread of megalithic phenomena thoughout the sixth millennium BP and the emergence of the first agricultural practices (Criado and Fábregas 1989).

THE LATE NEOLITHIC AND TRANSITION TO THE CHALCOLITHIC

By the end of the Neolithic period, agriculture not only involved wheat and barley but also included a great range of resources such as legumes (broad beans and lentils). Livestock exploitation embraces bovines and pigs, predominating over ovicaprines. Hunting was on the wane, except in various areas of Andalucía. A general intensification of agriculture and herding is also observed. There were regional differences in settlement patterns and territorial exploitation. In areas such as the Valencian region, there was a break in settlement patterns. Some authors have suggested that incipient social stratification was emerging, and this was to consolidate during the Valencian Bronze Age. Urbanism developed with the appearance of the Beakers (Bernabeu *et al.* 1989). In Aragón there was technocultural continuity between the Neolithic and Chalcolithic, a period which was characterized by settlements such as El Villar, Peña del Agua and El Portillo, which were located in lowlands and have yielded Beaker pottery.

In Catalunya two different assemblages have been differentiated for the second half of the fifth millennium BP: the Veraza horizon and the Treilles group. The latter is characterized by pottery decorated with engraved triangles. The former is characterized by 'tulip-form' vessels, hemispherical bowls, carinated forms, large jars, cordon decoration, superimposed buttons, pastille applications and ornamental items (pendants, and beads of bone and callaïs) (Tarrús *et al.* 1985). The best-known sites of the Late Catalan Neolithic are El Coll, an open-air settlement with a radiocarbon date of between 4,775 ± 80 BP and 4,640 ± 130 BP, Bóbila Madurell, radiocarbon dated to between 4,020 ± 130 BP and 3,870 ± 110 BP, and the caves of Cova del Frare (4,450 ± 100 BP) and the cave ensemble of Serinyà and Cova Verda.

In Andalucía a decreasing use of geometric tools has been attested alongside a continuity in blade industries, axes, adzes and smoothing tools. Pottery assemblages show an increase of non-decorated vessels and the emergence of painted, slip and combed pottery found at sites such as Mármoles, Murcielaguina, Inocentes and Huerta Anguita. In the period of transition to the Chalcolithic there is continuity in the production of decorated pottery, but new shapes in the form of large hemispherical bowls have been documented. Flintwork is characterized by long blades with an abrupt and bilateral retouch, sickle flint (Mármoles), a continuity of arrowhead types, the appearance of pressure-flaking (*retouche couvrante*), flat retouch, scrapers, the use of tabular flint and the presence of large blades.

Burial rites at the end of the fifth millennium BP and in the early fourth millennium did not change substantially. There was an important increase in secondary collective inhumation burials either in caves or in megalithic tombs (passage-graves, simple chambered tombs, para-dolmens). The understanding of stratigraphic levels, especially those in caves used as collective burials, is one of the main current problems.

CONCLUSIONS

Currently, the direction of research into the Neolithic of Spain seems to have altered and can be summarized in terms of three main areas. In the first place, investigation into the appearance of agriculture and livestock management in Iberia is not so much concerned with when and how it took place, as how and why. As regards the consolidation of new socio-economic forms in agricultural contexts, priority in analysis is now given to the following themes in the transition from the Early to Middle Neolithic: the occupation and exploitation of the territory, the transformation of the landscape, the configuration of living and funerary spaces, and, finally, social and cultural change. Finally, as far as the end of the 'Neolithization process is concerned, we are aware that there are many questions about the transition from the Late Neolithic to Chalcolithic. Hitherto, different authors have focused their attention upon the funerary world, in terms of the material culture. Current research into settlements has opened new perspectives in which the sites themselves begin to provide an important source of information which allows us to have a broader understanding of social and economic change at the threshold of the metal age.

NOTES

1 Non-calibrated dates, as are all the dates in this chapter.
2 The Asturiense is a Mesolithic culture located on the Cantabrian coast, in which all sites are dated between Boreal and Atlantic climatic periods.

REFERENCES

Acosta, P. (1987) 'El Neolítico en Andalucía: Estado actual de su conocimiento', *Trabajos de Prehistoria* 44: 63–85.

Alaminos, A., Blanch, R.M. and Lázaro, P. (1991) 'Bòbila Madurell. Su contribución al Neolítico Medio en Cataluña', *Revista de Arqueología* 128: 14–23.

Arias, P. (1991) *De cazadores a campesinos. La transición al Neolítico en la región cantábrica*, Santander: Publicaciones de la Universidad de Cantabria.

Armendáriz, A. (1990) 'Las cuevas sepulcrales en el País Vasco', *Munibe* 42: 153–160.

Badal, E., Bernabeu, J. and Vernet, J.L. (1994) 'Vegetation changes and human action from the Neolithic to the Bronze Age (7000–4000 BP) in Alicante, Spain, based on charcoal analysis', *Vegetation History and Archaeobotany* 3, 3: 155–66.

Baldellou, V., Mestres, J., Martí, B. and Juan, J. (1989) *El Neolítico Antiguo. Los primeros agricultores y ganaderos en Aragón, Cataluña y Valencia*, Huesca: Diputación de Huesca.

Barandiarán, I. and Cava, A. (1992) 'Caracteres industriales del Epipaleolítico y Neolítico en Aragón: su referencia a los yacimientos levantinos', in P. Utrilla (ed.) *Aragón/Litoral Mediterráneo. Intercambios culturales en la prehistoria*: 181–96, Zaragoza: Institución Fernando El Católico.

Bernabeu, J. (1989) *La tradición cultural de las cerámicas impresas en la zona oriental de la Península Ibérica*, Trabajos varios 86, Valencia: Servicio de Investigación Prehistórica and Diputación de Valencia.

Bernabeu, J., Aura, J.E. and Badal, E. (1993) *Al Oeste del Edén. Las primeras sociedades agrícolas en la europa mediterranea*, Madrid: Síntesis.

Bernabeu, J., Guitart, I. and Pascual, J.L. (1989) 'Reflexiones en torno al patrón de asentamiento en el País Valenciano entre el Neolítico y la Edad del Bronce', *Saguntum* 22: 99–123.

Blasco, A., Edo, M. and Villalba, M.J. (1991) 'Les Perles en callaïs du Sud de la France proviennent-elles des mines de Can Tintorer?', in *Le Calcholithique en Languedoc. Ses relations extra-régionals*, 279–89, Montpellier: Fédération Archéologique de l'Hérault.

Bordas, A., Díaz, J., Pou, R., Parpal, A. and Martin, A. (1994) 'Excavacions arqueològiques 1991–1992 a la Bòbila Madurell–Mas Duran (Sant Quirze del Vallès, Vallès Occidental)', in *Tribuna d'Arqueologia 1992-1993*: 31–47, Barcelona: Generalitat de Catalunya.

Bosch, J. and Estrada, A. (eds) (1994) *El Neolític Postcardial a les mines prehistòriques de Gavà (Baix Llobregat)*, Gavà: Museu de Gavà.

Bosch, J., Miró, J.M. and Molist, M. (1991) 'El marc històric i arqueològic dels orígens de l'agricultura a Catalunya', *Cota Zero* 7: 77–87.

Buxó, R. (1991) 'Nous elements de reflexió sobre l'adopció de l'agricultura a la Mediterrània occidental peninsular', *Cota Zero* 7: 68–76.

Castany, J. (1992) 'Estructures funeràries dels megàlits neolítics del Solsonès', in *IXè Colloqui Internacional d'Arqueologia de Puigcerdà. Estat de la Investigació sobre el Neolític a Catalunya*: 249-54, Puigcerdà-Andorra: Institut d'Estudis Ceretans.

Cava, A. (1990) 'El neolítico en el País Vasco', *Munibe* 42: 97–106.

Criado, F. and Fábregas, R. (1989) 'The megalithic phenomenon of northwest Spain: main trends', *Antiquity* 63, 241: 682–96.

Dupré, M. (1988) *Palinologia y Paleoambiente. Nuevos datos españoles. Referencias*, Trabajos varios 84, Valencia: Servicio de Investigación Prehistórica and Diputación de Valencia.

Fortea, J. (1973) *Los complejos microlaminares y geométricos del Epipaleolítico Mediterráneo Español*, Memorias del Seminario de Prehistoria 4, Salamanca: Universidad de Salamanca.

Fortea, J., Martí, B., Fumanal, M.P., Dupré, M. and Pérez, M. (1987) 'Epipaleolítico y neolitización en la zona oriental de la Península Ibérica', in J. Guilaine, J. Courtain, J.-L. Roudil and J.-L. Vernet (eds) *Premières communautés paysannes en Méditerranée Occidentale*: 581–91, Paris: CNRS.

Fumanal, M. P. (1986) *Sedimentología y clima en el País Valenciano. Las cuevas habitadas en el cuaternario reciente*, Trabajos varios 83, Valencia: Servicio de Investigación Prehistórica and Diputación de Valencia.

Juan, J. (1992) 'La neolitización de la vertiente mediterránea peninsular. Modelos y problemas', in P. Utrilla (ed.) *Aragón/Litoral Mediterráneo. Intercambios culturales en la prehistoria*: 255–68, Zaragoza: Institución Fernando El Católico.

López, P. (ed.) (1988) *El Neolítico en España*, Madrid: Cátedra.

Martí, B. (1978) 'El Neolítico de la Península Ibérica. Estado actual de los problemas relativos al proceso de neolitización y evolución de las culturas neolíticas', *Saguntum* 13: 59–98.

—— (1988) 'Early Farming Communities in Spain', *Berytus. Archaeological Studies*, XXXVI: 69–86.

Martí, B., Fortea, J., Bernabeu, J., Pérez, M., Acuna, D., Robles, F. and Gallart, M.D. (1987) 'El Neolítico antiguo en la zona oriental de la península Ibérica', in J. Guilaine, J. Courtain, J.-L. Roudil and J.-L. Vernet (eds) *Premières communautés paysannes en Méditerranée Occidentale*: 607–19, Paris: CNRS.

Molist, M., Ribé, G. and Saña, M. (forthcoming) 'Les changements du Néolithique en Catalogne durant le Vème millénaire', in *La Culture de Cerny. Colloque de Nemours*, Nemours: APRAIF and Musée de Préhistoire d'Ile de France.

Morais, J. (1982) 'Le Néolithique Ancien et les processus de Néolithisation au Portugal', in *Le Néolithique ancien méditerranéen*: 29–48, Montpellier: Fédération Archéologique de l'Hérault.

Muñoz, A.M. (1984) 'La neolitización en España: problemas y líneas de investigación', in *Scripta Praehistorica. Francisco Jordà. Oblata*: 349–69, Salamanca: Universidad de Salamanca.

Parra, I. (1993) 'Desplaçaments latitudinals de la vegetació al litoral mediterrani durant els darrers 8500 anys. Un enfocament pol.línic i climàtic', *Revista Catalana de Geografia* 21: 36–44.

Pou, R., Martí, M., Díaz, J., and Bordas, A. (1994) 'Estudio de la necrópolis del grupo de sepulcros de fosa del yacimiento de "Bòbila Madurell" (Sant Quirze del Vallès, Barcelona) en el contexto del Neolítico Medio reciente en Catalunya', in *1⁰ Congresso de Arqueologia Peninsular, Trabalhos de Antropologia e Etnologia* 34, 3–4, 61–76, Porto: Sociedade Portuguesa de Antropologia e Etnologia.

Riera, S. (1994) 'Paleobiogeografia, pertorbacions i acció antròpica durant l'holocè mitjà al delta del riu Llobregat', *Rubricatum* 0: 195–214.

Rincón, M. A. (1987) 'El Neolítico y el Calcolitico en la Península Ibérica', in J. Lichardus, M. Lichardus-Itten, G. Baillud and J. Cauvin (eds) *La protohistoria de Europa. El Neolítico y el Calcolítico*: 354–414, Barcelona: Labor.

Ros, M.T. and Vernet, J.L. (1987) 'L'Environnement végétal de l'Homme, du Néolithique a l'Age du Bronze, dans le Nord-Est de la Catalogne: analyse anthracologique de la Cova del Frare, St. Llorenç del Munt (Matadepera, Barcelona)', in J. Guilaine, J. Courtain, J.-L. Roudil and J.-L. Vernet (eds) *Premières communautés paysannes en Méditerranée Occidentale*: 125–9, Paris: CNRS.

Straus, L.G. (1991) 'The "Mesolithic–Neolithic transition" in Portugal: a view from Vidigal', *Antiquity* 65: 899–903.

Tarrús, J. (1985) 'Consideracions sobre el Neolític final–Calcolític a Catalunya (2500–1800 a.C.)', *Cypsela* V: 47–57.

Tarrús, J., Chinchilla, J., Aliaga, S. and Mercadal, O. (1992) 'Ca n'Isach (Palau-Saverdera): un assentament a l'aire lliure del Neolític Mitjà', *Tribuna d'Arqueologia 1990–1991*: 27–39, Barcelona: Generalitat de Catalunya.

Tavares, C. (1987). 'Megalitismo do Alentejo Occidental e do sul do Baixo Alentejo (Portugal)', in *El Megalitismo en la Península Ibérica*: 85–93, Madrid: Ministerio de Cultura.

—— (1989) 'Nuovos dados sobre o Neolítico Antigo do sul de Portugal', *Arqueologia* 20: 24–32.

Tavares, C. and Soares, J. (1987) 'Les Communautés du Néolithique ancien dans le Sud du Portugal', in J. Guilaine, J. Courtain, J.-L. Roudil and J.-L. Vernet (eds) *Premières communautés paysannes en Méditerranée Occidentale*: 663–71, Paris: CNRS.

Villalba, M.J., Bañolas, L., Arenas, J., and Alonso, M. (1986) *Les mines neolítiques de Can Tintorer (Gavà). Excavacions 1978–1980*, Barcelona: Departament de Cultura de la Generalitat de Catalunya.

Zilhão, J. (1993) 'The spread of agro-pastoral economies across Mediterranean Europe: A view from the far west', *Journal of Mediterranean Archaeology* 6, 1: 5–63.

CHAPTER FIVE

The funerary world and the dynamics of change in southeast Spain (fourth–second millennia bc)

ALMUDENA HERNANDO GONZALO

An analysis of the funerary world of the western Mediterranean between the fourth and second millennia bc[1] reveals a logic consistent with the establishment of a 'peasant way of life'[2] and the need to create new models for a community's relationship with its environment.[2] But what is more important is that it reveals a complete process of cultural transformation of the greatest significance and that this is repeated with minimal variations. It also clearly demonstrates that the traditional structuring of prehistory needs to be modified and that traditional periodization is obsolete. That first conclusion has already been reached and defended by various authors in Spain, particularly by Vicent (1990) and Criado (1991, 1993). I do not intend, therefore, to repeat what we already know, but to try to suggest how the different processes of cultural change that mark the beginning of a 'peasant way of life' in three specific areas are clearly reflected in the particular characteristics that the funerary world developed in each case, and how this process invalidates the traditional periodization of prehistory. The three areas that will be considered here are: the islands of the central Mediterranean, as exemplified by Sardinia, southeast Spain (mainly Almería, Murcia and Granada, but including also Málaga and Jaén for comparison), and the La Mancha region of Spain (Ciudad Real, Albacete and part of Cuenca) (see Figures 5.1 and 5.2).

To begin with, we could list the three areas suitable for a 'peasant way of life' in decreasing order of risk. First, the islands, simply because of what they are, with a clearly defined and non-extendable land mass.

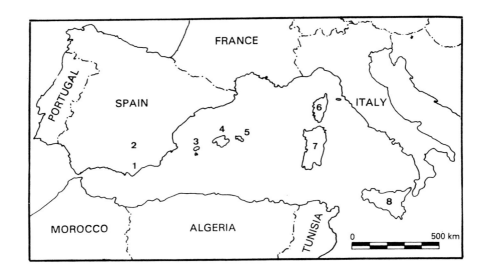

Figure 5.1 Map showing the main areas of the western Mediterranean.
1: Southeast Spain. 2. La Mancha region. 3. Ibiza. 4. Mallorca. 5. Menorca. 6. Corsica.
7. Sardinia. 8. Sicily.

Therefore when the population increases, as was the case at the end of the Neolithic (end of the fourth millennium BC), the land becomes a critical resource. As is known (Waldren 1984: 915), islands often become paradigms that attest the processes of transformation in surrounding areas: since they are subjected to strict territorial limits, these processes are much more evident.

The second most exposed area was southeast Spain. Its geographical characteristics isolate it from the Mediterranean and Atlantic cyclone-generating activity, thus making it a more arid region than its neighbours (Geiger 1973: 183). The question of whether geoclimatic conditions in southeast Spain during the period between the fourth and second millennia can be extrapolated from its present characteristics has been the subject of extensive debate (see Lull 1983: 23–49; Gilman and Thornes 1985: 11–15; Hernando 1988: 400–513). Differences in forestation in the region between then and now would certainly have affected the climatic characteristics of the area. In fact, the archaeological record of the southeast between the fourth and second millennia BC displays an extremely varied woodland fauna, some aquatic animals and abundant arboreal species (Driesch 1972: 175, 1973: 330; Driesch and Morales 1977: 23, 30; Boessneck 1969: 172–87). Today, however, southeast Spain displays the most arid conditions of the entire European continent (Vilá Valentí 1961: 25), together with a semi-desert landscape that, in the driest areas, is characterized by xerophytic and sparse vegetation (Terán

Figure 5.2 Map showing the regions of La Mancha and southeastern Spain.

La Mancha region: 1. Ciudad Real. 2. Region of Cuenca. 3. Albacete; southeast Spain: 4. Murcia. 5. Almería. 6. Granada. 7. Jaén. 8. Málaga.

and Solé Sabarís 1978: 436). Thus it would seem clear that, although it would be inappropriate to compare the characteristics of the past and the present in absolute terms, it can be accepted that the differences between the sub-areas comprising this region and its surrounding areas must have remained stable (Gilman and Thornes 1985: 12–13), since the general orographic and cyclone-generating characteristics have not changed (Lamb 1971; Geiger 1973: 183–5). In view of its low rainfall, southeast Spain would have been an area of evident risk for the establishment of a farming economy. Moreover, studies undertaken (Hernando and Vicent 1987) show that the basic difference between this and neighbouring damper regions is that it has a smaller proportion of arable land. Overall, therefore, there were inherent difficulties for agricultural strategies in this region which were absent in other parts of the Peninsula and Europe.

The least risk was encountered in La Mancha. Although it presents far less risk for a peasant way of life than the other two, it is characterized by a notable temperature oscillation during the year. The summer heat contrasts with the length and severity of the winter (Terán and Solé

Sabarís 1978: 176), and the low rainfall. At the same time the annual average of about 400 mm (Sabaté *et al.* 1981: 18) makes it more arid than other parts of the Peninsula: in fact, water is such a critical resource that the name 'La Mancha' comes from the Arabic word 'ma'ancha' meaning 'without water' (Chapman 1991: 322).

If we look at the period between the fourth and second millennia BC, it is evident that the whole of western Europe saw the transition from hunter-gatherers to a peasant way of life. The traditional sequence for this period is Neolithic–Chalcolithic–Bronze Age. Thus, a period division organized on the basis of technical criteria (such as the beginning of polished stone, the use of copper and the alloy of bronze) has been equated with more socio-economic criteria (the beginning of food production, metallurgy and social hierarchy). However, these conceal more far-reaching processes which deny the validity of this periodization.

As has been argued in various works (see, for example, Ingold (1986, 1990), Criado (1991, 1993), Vicent (1990) and Hernando (1994)) the beginning of agriculture, which has traditionally and erroneously been associated with a set of features (such as polished stone, pottery, weaving, permanent or semi-permanent settlements, etc.) does not in fact mark the beginning of any distinguishable stage in the history of humanity, but rather represents the development of a process of using the resources necessary for survival. However, as that process intensifies as a consequence of an increase in demographic density, mobility necessarily becomes limited, and human groups become more closely linked to land, which is increasingly crucial for their survival. This link between people and land brings with it a profound ideological change, in that it implies a concept of compartmentalized, controlled and organized time and space, and a relationship of domination with the means of production (Criado 1991, Ingold 1990). It is this new stage, therefore, which would seem significant in the history of humanity, and not that marked by the beginning of agriculture which, as Barbara Bender (1978) stated so well at the time, would only have been the unforeseen and unforeseeable result of the development of strategies of economic intensification. Thus, this new stage could be described as a 'peasant way of life', whose main characteristic has been defined (Vicent 1990) as the permanent connection of primary producers to their means of production, namely the land.

Thus in those areas where land is scarcer or production less efficient, one would expect that the establishment of a link with the land would become a factor in survival to be defended above all else. The principal means of establishing such a connection with the land claimed was to demonstrate the rights bestowed by long occupation, which would be visible in the archaeological record in the development of burial traditions (Vicent 1990: 285–6). Evidently, outside a system in which the 'ancestor' is important in the regulation of access to the means of production, funerary practices can only have been sporadic. Thus the turning point is not the existence of burials, but the development of funerary traditions (Vicent 1990: 285). These would become a visible indicator of a new economic and ideological relationship with the environment, and thus the outward sign of the beginning of a new cultural stage (Criado 1991). In the period during which such a transformation took place, the dead become a crucial weapon in the power struggle of the living to link themselves to their main means of production.

This implies a complex process of symbolic transformation. When people did not need to defend a link with a defined territory, because they were hunter-gatherers, the dead belonged to a separate world and were unconnected with the world of the living (Clastres 1987: 74–7; Criado 1991: 93–5). Clastres (1987: 76) offers various examples of strategies practised by these groups, through which he shows how 'death is completely denied' by the living: although the dead are normally buried, cemeteries rarely exist and there are abundant cases of endocannibalism, ritual exposure of the corpse, etc. The dead belong to the mythic world of the ancestors-founders, while the community of the living dissociates, denies and excludes itself from that mythic world (Clastres 1987: 77).

Thus, when the land became a basic means of production, and the presence of the dead began to be used to legitimize the land claims of the living, it was necessary to connect the two worlds, which meant developing an awareness of time and establishing the link between the living and the dead. We would, thus, expect this process to be expressed in the development of a sophisticated ritual at funerary sites, representing all the processes by which the living individual became the ancestor, and the establishment of that connection between the generations, and between the two worlds of the living and dead. The human body has been used in most cultures throughout history to symbolize every kind of moral and social 'truth' (Huntington and Metcalf 1979: 15), so that its even more forceful symbolic use after death should come as no surprise.

Consequently, my claim here is that the greater the risk there was in ensuring access to a 'peasant way of life', the more sophisticated was the ritual at funerary sites during the Late Neolithic/Chalcolithic phases, during which that transcendental cultural change also took place. If my assumptions are correct, we would expect the developmental sequence of the funerary ritual between the end of the fourth and the beginning of the second millennia BC (i.e. between the Late Neolithic and the beginning of the Bronze Age) in the three areas mentioned to mirror these varying degrees of difficulty, insecurity or possible risk in the development of a 'peasant way of life' in the context of a demographic increase which is evident in the archaeological record (Atzeni 1985: xxix; Molina 1988; Nájera 1984). The greater the difficulty, the greater was the investment of energy in the symbolic use of the world of the dead. Moreover, if we analyse the characteristics of the funerary sites in these three areas and list them in decreasing order of sophisticated ritual, we will see that the results would once again be: the islands, southeast Spain and the La Mancha region.

There was no permanent and stable occupation in either the islands or southeast Spain until the Late Neolithic, i.e. the second half of the fourth millennium BC (Molina 1988: 258–9). Systematic occupation began in this period, coinciding with the generalization of domesticated species (Cherry 1981: 58; Atzeni 1985: xxvii; Trump 1984: 513; Chapman 1985: 145; Molina 1988: 258–9; several authors in López García (ed.) 1988). Until then, the way of life was mainly based on hunting and gathering, although some domesticated species did exist, primarily animal in the case of the islands (Chapman 1985: 145). However, settlement continued to be unstable throughout the whole period until the Late Neolithic, as is demonstrated by the continued occupation of caves and the absence of stable villages in the Iberian Peninsula (López García (ed.) 1988). Thus, just at this time, there was increasing dependence upon productive land. This process can be seen in the archaeological record, since both in southeast Spain and in Sardinia the burial traditions began at the very end of the Neolithic, defining what has been called the Ozieri culture in Sardinia and the Almería culture in the southeast, the first truly agrarian cultures.

Sardinia was the area where land could have been the most crucial resource, as it was an island. The emergence of an arable and pastoral economy can only really be seen in the Ozieri culture (Late Neolithic for some authors and Chalcolithic for others). This occurred at the same time as the first indications of mining appeared, all of which coincided with clear signs of a notable population increase (Atzeni 1985: xxix). It is just at this time that the first of thousands of tombs appeared on the island, mainly in natural caves, and certain structures were built which have been interpreted as places of worship. The development of a sophisticated ritual was extremely rapid, much more so than in the other two regions. Tombs resembling the houses of the living were built and comprised separate chambers and doors with lintels etc., and some structures have even been interpreted as 'sanctuaries' because of the complexity of their ground plans and the space available for ritual activity (Atzeni 1985: xxi–xl). At the end of the Ozieri culture, around the end of the third millennium, the development of the funerary world culminated with the appearance of the first defended settlements, precursors of the later Bronze Age *nuraghi*.

The first funerary traditions of the Late Neolithic in southeast Spain, dated to the second half of the fourth millennium, are represented by structures that were not very visible, but very accessible, such as the so-called *Rundgräber* of Almería, or the first megalithic cists (Molina 1988:

262), situated outside the settlements. They included individual and collective burials. Examples of the former are the Late Neolithic pit-graves at Los Castillejos de Montefrío in Granada (Arribas and Molina 1979) and the *Rundgräber* or cist-type tombs of the Cerro de las Canteras (Almería) (Motos 1918). Examples of the latter are the megalithic cists associated with the village of Los Millares, used as collective ossuaries (Savory 1977: 171; Mathers 1984a: 22).

If we now focus our attention on the Chalcolithic period, i.e. the second half of the third millennium BC, we can observe that as the agrarian economy becomes consolidated and the number and stability of villages increase (Vicent 1990: 289), the ritual elaboration of burials rises in the same proportion. To begin with, the monumentality of some tombs increases (dolmens and *tholoi*, for example) and in other cases, the tomb is located in inconspicuous natural and artificial caves in the land-scape. Thus, we can find megalithic tombs in Málaga, Jaén and Murcia (Ferrer Palma 1986: 98–9). However, they are particularly notable in two provinces (Figure 5.2). First, in Granada, where systematic surveys have revealed numerous groups of the most varied types in the eastern and western mountain regions (Arribas and Molina 1984: 92) in addition to the traditional cemeteries (Gor-Gorafe, Fonelas or the group of Las Peñas de los Gitanos in Montefrío). Second, in Almería, where surveys carried out by the University of Granada have revealed more dolmens than *tholoi*, a discovery which contradicts traditional assumptions (Molina 1987). Furthermore, the greater the aridity of the land, the more monumental was the appearance of the tomb, as is demonstrated by the *tholos* ceme-teries of Almería (Los Millares, El Barranquete, Almizaraque and El Chuche) (Arribas and Molina 1984: 96).

The burial ritual is collective at all these, and gradually spread over the whole area: it then became progressively more complex until it finally developed into full individualization. In Murcia, for example, it seems clear that very fragmented collections of bones were deposited in caves (Bollaín 1986: 94), including natural and semi-artificial (Murviedro) caves, and dolmens. Partial cremation is recorded both in *tholoi* (Almizaraque, Los Millares, El Barranquete), dolmens (Bagil), natural caves (La Represa), artificial caves (Blanquizares de Lébor) or in mixed structures (Murviedro) (Idáñez Sánchez 1986: 166). García Sánchez and Spahni (1959) also report the presence of charred bones in many Granadan dolmens, although they are most common in the driest part of the region, namely eastern Granada, Almería and western Murcia (Idáñez Sánchez 1986), where a greater degree of cranium cremation also appears to be widespread, as can clearly be seen in the semi-artificial cave of Murviedro and in the *tholos* cemeteries of El Barranquete (Idáñez Sánchez 1986: 167), Los Millares and El Chuche (Olaria de Gusi 1979: 531). The analysis of these features led Idáñez Sánchez (1986) to conclude that partial cremation of corpses is not an isolated and fortuitous phenomenon, but was standard practice in the Chalcolithic cemeteries of southeast Spain. Sometimes grave goods also appear to have been partially or completely cremated after deposition (Idáñez Sánchez 1986; Olaria de Gusi 1979: 524), with layers of ashes scattered over the whole burial area in the caves, or concentrated at the passage entrance of passage graves.

Thus there are no major differences in burial ritual, which, in all the cases, implies a very significant symbolism. Although the deficiencies in the available information prevent us from making definitive conclusions, the absence of intact inhumations suggests that the corpses were left to decompose, possibly at the entrance of the tomb, and were then later moved into the burial chamber (Vázquez Varela 1992–3). This may explain the function of the *tholos* entrances with their betyls (*betilos*), and may also have been the kind of ritual undertaken in caves. Corridors and passages could have been the metaphor of the path from the world of the living to the world of the dead, and the perforated stones inside them (Moñita *et al.* 1986) would emphasize progressive stages along that symbolic journey (Thomas 1988: 550; Vázquez Varela 1992–3). In fact, the symbolic and ritual complexity of tombs seems to reach its highest level when the segmentation of the corridors, niches and lateral chambers appears in them. These features characterize the Late Chalcolithic phases of collective tombs, particularly in the Almerían lowlands (Mathers 1984a: 22, 1984b: 1,170).

In southeast Spain, therefore, the few tombs associated with Late Neolithic occupation (*Rundgräber*, cists) did not stand out in the landscape. They did not have structures that might act as a framework for funerary rituals in themselves, but were used only for the final deposition of the dead. However, with the beginning of metallurgy the inner spaces of the tombs were enlarged and the tomb itself became more conspicuous for the living community. This was achieved by means of greater monumentality (as in the cases of dolmens and *tholoi*) or through the location of tombs in caves suitable for collective celebrations or having difficult access and requiring the participation of part of the community in transporting the remains. In general, by the time of the Late Chalcolithic, segmented tombs began to be associated with individual burials in niches or lateral chambers, including those of children, which has been considered an indication of the progressive social differentiation (Mathers 1984a, 1984b) that would become apparent with the individualization of burial, characteristic of the Bronze Age El Argar culture.

Third, La Mancha (Figure 5.2) was mentioned as the region presenting the fewest problems for the establishment of a peasant community (as well as being the least known to archaeologists (Martín *et al.* 1993: 24)). The limited data available indicate that communal cave tombs also represented the first burial traditions, although the rituals in this region were far less sophisticated than those in southeast Spain or Sardinia (Fernández Vega and Galán Saulnier 1986). It does seem clear that the ritual features present in the cave tombs in the southeast (total or partial cremations, and layers of ashes) were not found in the same type of burials of La Mancha Chalcolithic (Fernández Vega and Galán Saulnier 1986), suggesting that these features were independent of the type of monument, and instead represent the degree of conflict and social stress experienced in each area. Only in the Bronze Age does the occupation of La Mancha seem to have exceeded its conflictive limit. The previous Neolithic and Chalcolithic occupation is only attested by some 'pits' and scanty settlement remains (Nájera 1984: 22), highlighting the absence of notable structures. It was in the Bronze Age that settlements appeared. They were located either in lowland areas or in the highlands, but they always exhibited defensive structures and contained individual burials with separate grave goods, as in the Bronze Age of the southeast (Nájera 1984; Martín *et al.* 1993: 25–8). Thus, it appears that at some point during the Bronze Age, but not before, the La Mancha region reached its conflictive limit, at which point the archaeological manifestations achieved matched those that had characterized the other two regions.

CONCLUSIONS

The analysis presented in this chapter suggests the following conclusions. There seems to be a direct relationship between the difficulties encountered in ensuring a link with the productive land in a 'peasant way of life' and the degree of sophisticated ritual in the funerary world from the end of the fourth to the beginning of the second millennia BC. By this time, the world of the dead seems to have greater symbolic potential for transforming society, and therefore its limits are defined very clearly. The burial is sited away from the settlement and located in an inaccessible place (such as a cave), thereby increasing the sense of privacy and concealment (see Whittle 1988: 181) (this is also reflected by burial in small and hidden caves), or by architecturally defined structures (dolmens and *tholoi*). Furthermore, the increase in ritual spaces that characterizes the evolution of the megaliths (Criado and Fábregas 1989; Thomas 1988) and caves seems to act as a setting for the transition from 'forebears' to 'ancestors', the connection between the world of the living and the world of the dead (Vázquez Varela 1992–3). This is symbolized by corridors and passages, and slabs of stone cut to resemble doorways in the case of constructed tombs, or by distant locations in the case of caves. An advanced stage of this process is where the tomb comes to represent the ancestors' 'house', their place of residence, as happens in the Ozieri culture, thus definitively linking land to the lineage that works it. The ancestors 'live' there: the descendants as a group are thus linked with that land.

But once an awareness of time had developed from approximately 1800 BC, reinforced by the link with ancestors amongst other things, and the possibility of passing on rights and powers from one generation to the next had been established, the funerary world seems to lose that symbolic potential. The increasing exploitation of mineral, timber, animal and vegetable resources would also demonstrate that control had been consolidated over the land claimed previously. Moreover, the construction of fortifications, which began to appear in all the regions under consideration, gradually became more complicated until they were as effective as the Argaric settlements, the Sardinian *nuraghi*, the Corsican *torre* and the villages of La Mancha. In this way they make up a 'political map' of centres of power and regional control. By this time, settlements usually contained the tombs of individuals whose position in the group demonstrated the emergence of economically differentiated ranks. At the end of this process, i.e. at the beginning of the Bronze Age, around 1800 BC, the world of the dead was no longer needed to symbolize and strengthen the ideological transformation of society: the fundamental conflict then took place on economic, social and ideological bases that had been accepted and institutionalized.

The main turning point in the whole process of cultural transformation that occurred in the western Mediterranean between the fourth and the beginning of the second millennia BC thus appears to be the transition from a hunter–gatherer way of life to that of the peasant, and this process does not begin with the introduction of agriculture or stock-raising in these areas. As Vicent (1990: 263–4) has stated, the introduction of these strategies should be read more as a technique for stabilizing the production of hunter-gatherer groups in times of social stress or in areas with a high degree of unpredictability and risk, rather than as a technique for optimizing production. The archaeological record appears effectively to support this interpretation, since there is no evidence for substantial changes in the way of life and relationship with nature until an advanced stage of the Late Neolithic. In this respect, it is worth emphasizing once again that the traditional periodization of European prehistory is obsolete, and supporting those scholars who have been trying to offer alternatives more in keeping with what appears to be the reality of the process (Criado 1993; Ingold 1980, 1986, 1990; Vicent 1990, for example).

NOTES

1 Non-calibrated dates, as are all the dates in this chapter
2 Literally translated from the Spanish expression 'modo de vida campesino'.

REFERENCES

Arribas, A. and Molina, F. (1979) *El poblado de Los Castillejos en Las Peñas de Los Gitanos (Montefrío, Granada). El corte 1 (Campaña de 1971)*, Cuadernos de Prehistoria de la Universidad de Granada, Serie monográfica 3, Granada:

Secretariado de Publicaciones para el Departamento de Prehistoria de la Universidad.

—— (1984) 'Estado actual de la investigación del megalitismo en la Península Ibérica', in J. Fortea (ed) *Francisco Jordá Oblata: Scripta Praehistorica*: 63–112, Salamanca: Universidad de Salamanca.

Atzeni, E. (1985) *Ichnussa. La Sardegna dalle origini all'età classica*, Milano: Grazanti.

Bender, B. (1978) 'Gatherer-hunter to farmer: a social perspective', *World Archaeology* 10, 2: 204–22.

Boessneck, J. (1969) 'Restos óseos de animales del Cerro de la Virgen, en Orce, y del Cerro del Real, en Galera (Granada)', *Noticiario Arqueológico Hispánico* 10–12: 172–89.

Bollaín, A. (1986) 'Los yacimientos funerarios del Calcolítico de Murcia: una revisión bibliográfica', *Trabajos de Prehistoria* 43: 85–98.

Chapman, R. (1985) 'The later prehistory of Western Mediterranean Europe: recent advances', in F. Wendorf and A. Close (eds) *Advances in World Archaeology* 4: 115–87, London: Academic Press.

—— (1991) *La formación de las sociedades complejas. El sureste de la península ibérica en el marco del mediterráneo occidental*, Barcelona: Crítica. [(1990) *Emerging Complexity. The Later Prehistory of south-east Spain, Iberia and the West Mediterranean*, Cambridge: Cambridge University Press.]

Cherry, J.F. (1981) 'Pattern and process in the earliest colonization of the Mediterranean islands', *Proceedings of the Prehistoric Society* 47: 41–68.

Clastres, P. (1987) *Investigaciones en Antropología Política*, 1st reprint, Barcelona: Gedisa. [(1980: *Recherches d'Anthropologie politique*, Paris: Editions du Seuil.]

Criado, F. (1991) 'Tiempos megalíticos y espacios modernos', *Historia y Crítica* I: 85–108.

—— (1993) 'Límites y posibilidades de la Arqueología del Paisaje', *SPAL* 2: 9–55.

Criado, F. and Fábregas, R. (1989) 'The megalithic phenomenon of northwest Spain: main trends', *Antiquity* 63: 682–96.

Driesch, A. von den (1972) *Osteoarchäologische Untersuchungen auf der Iberischen Halbinsel*, Studien über frühe Tierknochenfunde von der Iberischen Halbinsel 3, München: Institut für Palaeoanatomie, Domestikationforschung und Geschichte des Tiermedizin der Universität München and Deutsches Archäologisches Institut Abteilung Madrid.

—— (1973) 'Tierknochenfunde aus dem frühbronzezeitlichen Gräberfeld von El Barranquete, Provinz Almería, Spanien', *Säugetierkindliche Mitteilungen* 21: 328–35.

Driesch, A. von den and Morales, A. (1977) 'Los restos animales del yacimiento de Terrera Ventura (Tabernas, Almería)', *Cuadernos de Prehistoria y Arqueología de la Universidad Autónoma de Madrid* 4: 15–34.

Fernández Vega, A. and Galán Saulnier, C. (1986) 'Las denominadas cuevas sepulcrales colectivas eneolíticas del País Valenciano y la Meseta', *Boletín del Museo Arqueológico Nacional* 4: 7–26.

Ferrer Palma, J.E. (1986) 'El Megalitismo en Andalucía Oriental: Problemática', *Actas de la Mesa Redonda sobre Megalitismo Peninsular*: 97–110, Madrid: Asociación Española de Amigos de la Arqueología.

García Sánchez, M. and Spahni, J.C. (1959) 'Sepulcros megalíticos de la región de Gorafe (Granada)', *Archivo de Prehistoria Levantina* 8: 43–113.

Geiger, F. (1973) 'El Sureste español y los problemas de la aridez', *Revista de Geografía* 7: 166–209.

Gilman, A. and Thornes, J.B. (1985) *Land Use and Prehistory in south–east Spain*, University of London Monograph series, London: Allen and Unwin.

Hernando, A. (1988) *Evolución interna y factores ambientales en la interpretación del Calcolítico del Sureste de la Península Ibérica. Una revisión crítica*, Colección Tesis Doctorales 188/88, Madrid: Universidad Complutense.

—— (1994) 'El proceso de neolitización. Perspectivas teóricas para el estudio del Neolítico', *Zephyrus* 46: 123–42.

Hernando, A. and Vicent, J.M. (1987) 'Una aproximación cuantitativa al problema de la intensificación económica en el Calcolítico del Sureste de la Península Ibérica', *El origen de la metalurgia en la Península Ibérica* I: 23–39, Papeles de Trabajo, Arqueología 1, Madrid: Instituto Universitario José Ortega y Gasset.

Huntington, R. and Metcalf, P. (1979) *Celebrations of Death: The Anthropology of Mortuary Ritual*, Cambridge: Cambridge University Press.

Idáñez Sánchez, J.F. (1986) 'Incineración parcial en los enterramientos colectivos del Sudeste español', *Actas de la Mesa Redonda sobre Megalitismo Peninsular*: 165–6, Madrid: Asociación Española de Amigos de la Arqueología.

Ingold, T. (1980) *Hunters, Pastoralists and Ranchers: Reindeer Economies and their Transformations*, Cambridge: Cambridge University Press.

—— (1986) *The Appropiation of Nature. Essays on Human Ecology and Social Relations*, Manchester: Manchester University Press.

—— (1990) 'Society, nature and the concept of technology', *Archaeological Review from Cambridge* 9, 1: 5–17.

Lamb, H.H. (1971) 'Climates and circulation regimes developed over the northern hemisphere since the last Ice Age', *Palaeogeography, Palaeoclimatology, Palaeoecology* 10: 125–62.

López García, P. (ed) (1988) *El Neolítico en España*, Madrid: Cátedra.

Lull, V. (1983) *La 'cultura' de El Argar (Un modelo para el estudio de las formaciones económico–sociales prehistóricas)*, Col. Akal Universitaria 49, Madrid: Akal.

Martín, C., Fernández-Miranda, M., Fernández-Posse, M.D. and Gilman, A. (1993) 'The Bronze Age of La Mancha', *Antiquity* 67: 23–45.

Mathers, C. (1984a) 'Beyond the grave: the context and wider implications of mortuary practice in south-eastern Spain', in T.F.C. Blagg, R.F.J. Jones and S.J. Keay (eds) *Papers in Iberian Archaelogy*: 13–44, British Archaeological Reports, International Series 193 (1), Oxford: BAR.

—— (1984b) 'Linear regression, inflation and prestige competition; second millennium transformations in south-east Spain', in W.H. Waldren, R. Chapman, J. Lewthwaite and R.C. Kennard (eds) *The Deya Conference of Prehistory. Early Settlement in the West Mediterranean Islands and the Peripheral Areas* I: 1167–96, BAR International Series 229, Oxford: BAR.

Molina, F. (1987) 'Los Millares and the begining of metallurgy in the South East of Spain'. Unpublished seminar held at the Fundación José Ortega y Gasset on 17 February 1987.

—— (1988) 'El Calcolítico en la Península Ibérica. El Sudeste', *Rassegna di Archaeologia* 7: 255–62.

Moñita, R. Corral, M. Díaz, M.A. Colmenarejo, M.R. and Sánchez, M.M. (1986) 'Espacios de habitación y funerarios en el S.E. durante el Calcolítico',

Arqueología Espacial. Coloquio sobre el Microespacio 2: 139–56, Teruel: Colegio Universitario de Teruel.

Motos, F. de (1918) *La Edad Neolítica en Vélez Blanco*, Memorias de la Comisión de Investigaciones Paleontológicas y Prehistóricas 19, Madrid: Comisión de Investigaciones Paleontológicas y Prehistóricas.

Nájera, T. (1984) *La Edad del Bronce en la Mancha Occidental*, Tesis Doctorales de la Universidad de Granada 458, Granada: Universidad de Granada.

Olaria de Gusi, C. (1979) 'Dos nuevas tumbas megalíticas en Almería: el ritual funerario en la cultura de Los Millares y su problemática de interpretación', *Estudios dedicados a Carlos Callejo Serrano*: 511–32, Cáceres: Diputación Provincial de Cáceres.

Sabaté, A. Méndez, R. and del Canto, C. (1981) *A través de Castilla. Itinerarios geográficos*, Madrid: Penthalon.

Savory, H.N. (1977) 'The role of Iberian communal tombs in Mediterranean and Atlantic prehistory', in V. Markotic (ed.) *Ancient Europe and the Mediterranean*: 161–80, Warminster: Aris and Phillips.

Terán, M. de and Solé Sabarís, L. (1978) *Geografía regional de España*, Barcelona: Ariel.

Thomas, J. (1988) 'The social significance of Cotswold–Severn burial practices', *Man* 23: 540–59.

Trump, D. (1984) 'The Bonu Ighinu project', in W.H. Waldren, R.R. Chapman, J. Lewthwaite and R.C. Kennard (eds) (1984) *The Deya Conference of Prehistory. Early Settlement in the West Mediterranean and the Peripheral Areas* I: 511–32. BAR International Series 229, Oxford: BAR.

Vázquez Varela, J.M. (1992–3) 'El simbolismo del espacio en la arquitectura megalítica del Noroeste de la Península Ibérica', *Tabona. Revista de Prehistoria y Arqueología* 1: 611–17.

Vicent, J.M. (1990) 'El Neolític. Transformacions socials i economiques', in J. Anfruns and E. Llobet (eds) *El canvi cultural a la prehistoria*: 241–93, Barcelona: Columna.

Vilá Valentí, J. (1961) 'La lucha contra la sequía en el Sureste de España', *Estudios Geográficos* 22: 25–44.

Waldren, W.H. (1984) 'Chalcolithic settlement and beaker connections in the Balearic Islands', in W.H. Waldren, R. Chapman, J. Lewthwaite and R.C. Kennard (eds) *The Deya Conference of Prehistory. Early Settlement in the West Mediterranean Islands and the Peripheral Areas* I: 911–67, BAR International Series 229, Oxford: BAR.

Whittle, A. (1988) *Problems in Neolithic Archaeology*, Cambridge: Cambridge University Press.

CHAPTER SIX

The dynamics of the occupation of the middle basin of the river Guadiana between the fourth and second millennia BC

An interpretational hypothesis

VICTOR HURTADO

INTRODUCTION

This chapter is a reflection upon hypotheses for explaining transformations in the socio-economic structures of sedentary populations in the middle Guadiana river basin, in southwestern Iberia, between the fourth and second millennia BC. Inherent difficulties are brought sharply into focus when one considers the dearth of information as a result of, amongst other things, a lack of theoretical perspectives, interdisciplinary planning and active teams in the field. One need only mention the absence of palaeoenvironmental studies, the scarcity of faunal and anthropological analyses and the fact that accurate dating has been obtained from only five sites. This highlights the difficulty of investigating cultural dynamics without empirical data.

I am conscious of the need to be explicit about most of the hypotheses put forward and, of course, to justify and contrast them both empirically and theoretically. The fundamental aim of this work is to propose a synthetic interpretation of available documentary evidence and, thus, to expose gaps in our knowledge and highlight future research opportunities.

The geographical context

The middle Guadiana river basin (MGB) is situated in the province of Badajoz in southwestern Spain (Figure 6.1), crossing it from east to west towards the Portuguese frontier, at which point it heads southwards. The river basin is some 150 kilometres in length and widens towards the west at the frontier with Portugal. The depression falls within a great peninsular plain of low relief, comprising a few isolated hillocks of between 200 and 400 metres, but which rarely rise above 600 metres. To the north, the Guadiana plain is bounded by high ground lying to the south of the river Tagus. To the south it is bordered by the edge of the Sierra Morena, and to the east by relief which separates it from the plain of La Mancha.

The territory in which the populations of the period developed lies principally to the south, or the left bank, of the river Guadiana where land is flatter and the soil more fertile. The two most important regions are the Tierra de Barros to the west and La Serena to the east. The first is uniformly flat and characterized by a clay soil very apt for cereal production. The second is a more undulating, slaty plain with dark southern soils that have good grazing potential (Enríquez 1990 II; Vegas 1971: 351–8).

Historiographical context of the MGB

A symposium on the archaeology of southwestern Iberia took place in 1978 (Setúbal, Portugal). During this a three-phase periodization was proposed as a frame of reference for identifying Copper-Age sites from new surveys. It was based on key characteristic ceramic styles, such as the 'carenated casserole' for the initial phase, the 'plate with thickened rim' for the full Chalcolithic phase and the Bell-Beaker for the final phase. The absolute chronologies obtained from some sites were used as reference points for initial dating, so that the first phase roughly spans the first half of the third millennium BC, the second ranges from 2600 to 2100 BC and the third and final phase ranged from 2100 to 1800/1700 BC.

At the beginning of the 1980s, the first excavations at the sites of El Lobo and La Pijotilla gave rise to a periodization specifically for the Chalcolithic of the MGB. This largely coincided with the aforementioned discussions (Hurtado 1987; Enríquez and Hurtado 1986). At the same time new research trends that were beginning to be accepted in Spain in the second half of the 1980s engendered a reaction to traditional research techniques. But these offered no clear theoretical alternatives and did not affect the proposed periodization. Early advances of these kinds are occasionally reflected in field-surveys, through the mechanistic application of techniques stemming from spatial archaeology (Rodríguez 1986; Enríquez 1990). They are also implicit in some

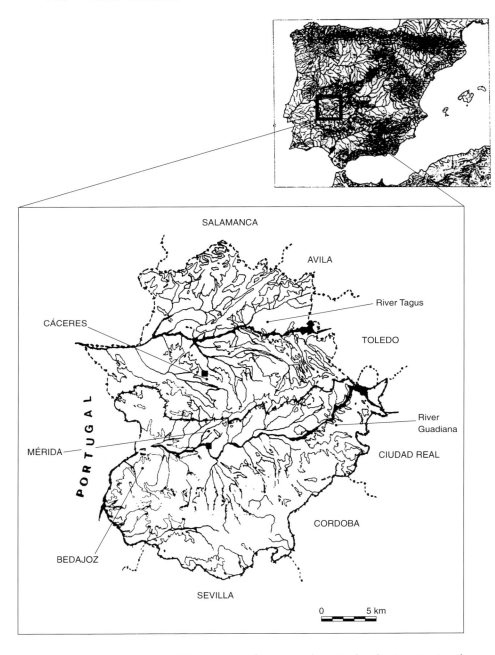

Figure 6.1 Location of the region of Extremadura in the Iberian Peninsula.

open-area excavations, which applied a more modern, and exceptionally interdisciplinary, methodology. However, the focus of investigation centred almost exclusively on the *interior* of sites (Hurtado 1991). A recent study of Chalcolithic settlements in the MGB could serve as a reference point for the present state of research (Enríquez 1990). Similarly a compilation of succinct reports on archaeological activities in Extremadura (*Extremadura Arqueológica* II, 1991) contains the basic information for this study.

THE END OF THE NEOLITHIC: THE ARAYA–LOBO PHASE (2800–2300 BC)

Ever since the diffusionist theories that claimed an oriental origin for the Chalcolithic of the Iberian peninsula (Blance 1971; Savory 1968) and later research which refuted them (Renfrew 1967), most contemporary studies have discarded the east–west argument. Instead they emphasize the importance of the underlying substratum in the analysis of specific territories and in explaining the process of change towards more developed forms of production in Neolithic communities. The new theoretical developments of the 1980s contributed to the rejection of positivist explanations for cultural change based on typological criteria alone.

In Extremadura the earliest evidence of Neolithic settlement is thinly represented at natural cave sites scattered in mountainous areas to the north and south of the MGB. The traditional view of these settlements has altered in view of the discovery of open-air settlements in different parts of the southwest of the peninsula. Although they are sporadic, some settlements in the Alentejo region are known to have been associated with dolmen burials which provide evidence for a first attempt at occupying territories better suited to agriculture and livestock management than mountainous areas had been.

The geology of the MGB is not well suited to the natural formation of caves, which might explain why the first settlements were situated in the open air. Until recently, however, the available archaeological data suggested that the earliest signs of human occupation were to be found in the very few existing caves. Thus, although the stratigraphic record of Cueva de la Charneca (Oliva de Mérida) has been disturbed by modern activity, human remains have been found associated with Neolithic and Chalcolithic material. The excavator does not rule out that this might be a burial cave (Enríquez 1986) but finds it impossible to determine when the burial might have taken place, or to discuss ritual, or whether it represented a single burial. The lack of Neolithic burials in the region would have made this a matter of great interest.

Occupation takes place in the first half of the third millennium BC. This would be the moment when the colonization of better lands brought about an increase in production. This development is signified by the distribution of settlements and the number of quern which would complement traditional livestock raising (documented in the village of Araya) with the rearing of goat, sheep and pig.

The settlement pattern at this time was of limited extent and characterized by a total lack of natural and artificial defences: sites appear on fertile alluvial soils in flat lands next to the river Guadiana. Even though few surveys have been carried out in the region, the distribution of these first settlements around the principal fords of the river (Badajoz and Mérida) suggests that there was a progressive occupation of territories inwards from the Guadiana. However, settlements are relatively close to one another and their stratigraphy is shallow. This endorses the hypothesis proposed for the Portuguese Alentejo in which these semi-nomadic populations practised slash and burn and were displaced when lands became exhausted (Silva 1987; Jorge 1990). Assuming that the settlements belonging to different groups are contemporary, their proximity to one another points to a peaceful coexistence. In this context the fords would have acted as crossings, a development which implies the existence of a degree of strategic control, as was the case in subsequent epochs.

The best-known sites belonging to this phase are found in the region of Mérida (Araya) and Badajoz (Alcazaba, Santa Engracia, El Lobo). They date to around the first half of the third millennium BC. The predominance of undecorated ceramics and open forms (including the casserole or dish with sloping sides) now supplements ceramics with form and decoration appropriate to the Neolithic. These were important for the whole of the third millennium BC and reflect collective participation in the consumption and preparation of foodstuffs. Querns are frequent and arrowheads with bifacial retouching also begin to appear.

The first known anthropomorphic fired-clay figurine was discovered at Araya (Enríquez 1981–2). Only the lower half remains, which represents a thick-set woman whose female sexual characteristics have been emphasized. It is stylistically similar to Neolithic examples from other parts of the Mediterranean. However, it is a single example and we cannot yet be drawn about its significance, or make inferences about the nature of representation in Neolithic societies. Nevertheless, it is pertinent to draw attention to the contrast between this figure and the schematic type of representations already documented at the beginning of the third millennium in the neighbouring Alentejo (the typical 'plaque idols' of the dolmen burials), and the first discoveries of (plain) 'cylindrical idols' at Papa Uvas.

There were no absolute chronologies in this phase of the MGB that allowed temporal relationships to be established between this and other regions, or between both types of representation. On the basis of scarce discoveries alone it would seem that it is the small settlement of El Lobo where the first 'plaque idols' and 'staves' of the region appear. It also continues the stratigraphic sequence established at Araya. Evidently, however, this is impossible to confirm without more solid chronological evidence.

The site of El Lobo (Molina 1980) is occupied to a later date than Araya. New kinds of material begin to be incorporated alongside the typical repertoire of the first horizon. In the sequence formed by Araya–El Lobo–La Pijotilla, there is a tendency towards more stability in the settlements and a transition without interruption into the second half of the third millennium. Notwithstanding this, the stratigraphic deposition at El Lobo seems to have been caused by harnessing the periodic floodings of the river. In this context it would be interesting to learn whether a drier climate[1] and the normal channelling of the river contributed to the abandonment of the site and a population movement from the Badajoz ford to new territories further south in the subsequent phase. El Lobo also has the best examples of houses of the period. These comprise small round or oval huts (1.6–2.0 metres in diameter), with a sunken pebble floor (*c.* 0.60–0.80 metres deep), and cane and mud walls. This construction technique is common in areas where stone is rare and has been documented at many sites near the rivers Guadiana and Guadalquivir.

One of the problems posed by this horizon concerns the type of burial and the settlement/cemetery relationship. The apparent divergence between burial grounds and settlements in the southwest of the peninsula is also manifest in the MGB. The oldest megalithic tombs are distributed in the vicinity of the Portuguese frontier and at villages concentrated around the river Guadiana. The evidence is made more substantial by noting the different agricultural potential of the soils. Thus, whilst the settlements appear on the more fertile alluvial plains of the Guadiana depression, the tombs generally appear in terrain less suitable for cultivation, with slaty soils and better livestocking potential. It is probable that there was a gradual reoccupation of territories eastwards from the Alentejo in search of lands suitable for agriculture and livestock. Bueno (1986), who has centred her research on the megaliths of Extremadura, considers them to have been an extension of the Alentejo culture. She also estimates that the high point in the development of the short corridor dolmens took place in the second half of the fourth millennium, while the long corridor appeared at its end. Both persisted into the first half of the third millennium.

There is a great concentration of dolmens in the Alentejo zone of Reguengos de Monsaraz and on the right bank of the river Guadiana. During their initial-phase expansion into the Extremadura region the river must have constituted an obstacle, although not an insurmountable one, and the number of long-corridor dolmens on the opposite shore diminishes considerably. The greatest spread, however, must have been in the north, where there would have been no need to cross the river towards the Cáceres zone of Valencia de Alcántara, where the oldest short-corridor dolmens in the region of Extremadura are the most common type (Bueno 1988). Further to the east, megalithic burials start to decrease. Close to the Guadiana, there are very few burials related to known settlements. This is a total contrast to the situation along the river Tagus where only megalithic burials are found. A recent spatial analysis of the region has interpreted the location of the 'megaliths in relation to points where the river basin was crossed, as constituting a symbol of transient communities' (Galán and Martín 1991–2: 193).

Although the 'absence' of the settlements corresponding to dolmen concentrations is in large part due to a lack of systematic survey, it seems certain that they were rare and that they were not necessarily located centrally. In the surveys of Valencia de Alcántara, only one settlement datable to the first half of the third millennium BC was found (Bueno 1987). Recent surveys in Reguengo de Monsaraz have revealed some open-air settlements associated with groups of dolmens similar to those in Extremadura. These have been ascribed to the 'initial and middle phases of megalithism in Reguengos' and to the later Neolithic to Early Chalcolithic (Soares and Silva 1992: 48–51). They lie towards the outer edge of the grouping at some distance from the dolmens. Other Chalcolithic settlements opt for riverside locations and are not associated with known groups of dolmens (Soares and Silva 1992: 52). In the Alentejo differences become noticeable with the appearance of the first great megalithic burials (whose grave goods are the same as material found in frontier settlements, as at the second phase of El Lobo) and may reflect internal inequalities that are not as yet palpable in the MGB.

Dolmen burials have been repeatedly interpreted as a medium that symbolised possession of a territory by societies practising itinerant agriculture (Soares and Silva 1992: 46) and where this 'cannot be suggested by a permanent habitat which does not exist' (Galán and Martín 1991–2: 199). Their importance to the societies which constructed them is also implicit in the labour invested, while their monumentality signifies possession of the territory by cohesive family groups interred collectively.

THE FULL CHALCOLITHIC:
THE PIJOTILLA PHASE (2300–2000 BC)

Most of the few absolute chronologies obtained from the MGB correspond to this phase and, with only one exception, do not pre-date 2300 BC. The appearance of metallurgy is first documented in the last occupation level at El Lobo. Throughout the second half of the third millennium there is a rise in the number of settlements throughout the Guadiana basin, implying a demographic increase. The mobility of people between the Guadiana and Tajo rivers, population pressure and, most important, the search for fertile terrain could have influenced the abandonment of old lands and the occupation of new territory to the south alongside small streams and rivers.

Despite the lack of systematic survey there are gounds for believing that there may have been a settlement hierarchy. This assumes that sites were contemporary and takes into account differences in size. The levels of functionality, however, still have to be established. La Pijotilla is the largest settlement, not only in the MGB but also in the southwest of the Peninsula, and can be considered alongside Valencina de la Concepción in the Guadalquivir valley and Ferreira de Alentejo in Portugal. Together with this great settlement and those in the valley, other fortified sites appear around 2200 BC. In the area of Plasenzuela, to the north of the Guadiana, some excavated settlements have provided absolute dates (González *et al.* 1991). Two unfortified examples are dated to 2265 and 2110 BC: two fortified settlements and a strategic hill-top lookout post for a nearby valley settlement have been given a later date on the basis of finds. However, the absence of Bell-Beakers[2] was taken to suggest that they were earlier (González *et al.* 1991: 25). Nevertheless, there is no reason to think that they could be contemporary, as the analysis of Tierra de Barros will show.

Logically, fortifications develop when settlements need to defend themselves, as can be detected in this phase. The distribution map of Chalcolithic settlements published by Enríquez (1990: 319), upon which Figure 6.2 is based, suggests that fortified settlements are distributed in the south of Badajoz province, the northern border area of the Sierra Morena and in the region of Llerena. These are upland areas with mineral resources and defences would have been constructed for their strategic value, controlling access to the Guadalquivir valley and its metal resources. There are, however, other fortifications, in the peninsular plain (Figure 6.2: marked with an asterisk) whose regular spacing is interesting. Their distribution seems to comprise two lines which converge on the Guadiana river in a 'V' formation. These divide Tierra de Barros and La Serena regions into two zones. The more westerly of these comprises settlements situated strategically on hill tops (6.2: triangles). In this way the Tierra de Barros is circumscribed by the river Guadiana to the north and west, fortifications to the east and the mountains of the Sierra Morena to the south. It should be remembered that this analysis is not able to make use of much systematically collected data. This drawback could be justified, however, by arguing that the data are based on existing knowledge which was obtained under similar conditions. Thus, they constitute a sample which could prove invaluable in formulating a settlement-model, although this would have to be later confirmed or rejected following more specific research.

The inferences that can currently be gleaned from the distribution of fortified settlements principally concern their regularity and linear distribution. These suggest that they might have formed a barrier that would

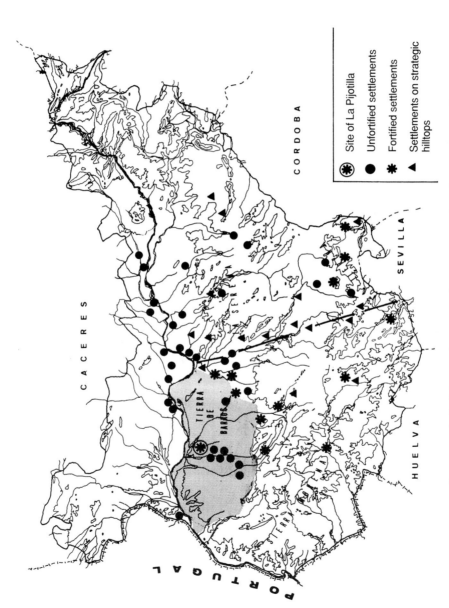

Figure 6.2 Map showing Chalcolithic settlement in the province of Badajoz (Extremadura).

have defended the least protected western edge of a homogeneous territory which largely coincides with the modern-day county of Tierra de Barros (Figure 6.2: shaded zone). This territory comprised some 30 × 60 kilometres, would have been well structured and was dominated by the area which focuses upon La Pijotilla. This particular site would have been the principal centre in the territory and the underlying basis of its control would have been its agricultural wealth. This was a region of optimum agricultural conditions, especially suited to the cultivation of cereals and legumes. Within the territory there are other small settlements which lie on level terrain and are unfortified. At its eastern edge, the line of walled settlements controls movement from the main ford over the Guadiana to the nearest high ground. They also protect the most vulnerable side of the territory. Survey in the county of Mérida (Enríquez 1990) revealed contemporary settlements lying adjacent to the right bank of the river Guadiana. They are absent on the left bank, apart from those lying in the eastern zone and outside the line of fortified settlements. This hypothesis does little more than define a unit of territorial analysis. To understand its socio–economic formation, it is necessary to define the articulation of its internal dynamics and the core–periphery relationships that would have allowed the organization of the political territory to be defined (Castro and González 1989; Nocete 1984).

Comparative analysis of the counties of Tierra de Barros and La Serena is impaired by imbalances in the archaeological record. Few sites are known in the west, despite recent surveys, and it is possible that this may not have constituted a well-defined territory in this phase. Nevertheless, settlement equilibrium shifts to this area in the first millennium BC. This hypothesis raises many questions about the development of social complexity and the mechanisms of the power structure in this phase. Evidence is still insufficient and the dilution of social stratification by kin-based ideology makes characterization difficult. Nevertheless, some points can be made, particularly with reference to the burial record.

Other settlements classed as strategic by Enríquez (Figure 6.2: triangles) on the basis of their altitude and their dominance over large tracts of land are distributed in a regular line, linking the ford at Mérida with the Llerena area. This would have been the route of communication (traced by a line in Figure 6.2) between the Guadiana and the Guadalquivir. Contacts between both regions become very clear towards the end of the third millennium and were maintained in subsequent periods. The Llerena area is probably the area of transition for this route. Its mineral wealth would have provided a source of metal for the interior and the settlement pattern would have replicated that focused upon Huerta de Dios in the Tierra de Barros. A more detailed study is needed to explore this.

The size of the site at La Pijotilla has been established by the distribution of surface finds and by aerial photographs. It is defined by a ditch which runs for nearly 1 kilometre (Figure 6.3) and encloses an area of some 1,000 × 800 metres (Hurtado 1981). Photographs show that within this outer circle there was an inner ring that has not yet been fully excavated and within which dwellings appear to be concentrated. In the eastern sector between the two circular enclosures, there are a number of tombs, which suggests that it was used as a cemetery. The external ditch appeared to define the limits of the entire site. It has not yet been possible to clarify its chronology or function, as it is in the process of being studied. However, the lack of strategic reasoning is surprising, given that its location on the plain would have left it undefended in the event of an attack. The rationale of site location would appear to lie in the proximity of the river course, while its defences may have served to protect the surrounding lands rather than the settlement itself. Nevertheless, it does have a walled access and an isolated stone construction that narrows at the ends and which would have been connected to other structures which have not survived. The interpretation of this is not clear.

This period sees the advent of greater stability in the settlements. This suggests that better use of subsistence resources had been achieved through the use of new cultivation techniques that allowed the intensive exploitation of agricultural lands. Thus, the large number of storage-pits points towards food surpluses and the intensification of agricultural production. These features provide some idea of socio–economic structure in so far as it is reflected in the better control of resources by these populations. Additionally, large storage-pits are grouped in specific areas of the settlement, and small ones sometimes appear within houses, possibly signifying differential access to resources. The huts of this phase are larger and, by and large, continue to be constructed by means of a sunken floor and walls of mud and branches. At sites where stone was abundant more solid structures begin to be built, like the Cabaña de Cabrerizos. This was 6 metres in diameter and had a stone hearth (90 cm) in its interior (González et al. 1991: 21).

A greater diversification can now be observed in the range of artisanal activities. The open-form plates and dishes characteristic of the previous phase continue, and constitute one of the most characteristic forms of the true Neolithic. They also reflect changes in diet and the means of supply. The volume of some storage jars was equal to the capacity of the smallest silos and permitted better preservation. The plate is now the most representative of the ceramic assemblage, but new forms express functional variety as well as interaction with other regions. This is also manifest in the acquisition of new products, the development of new aesthetic tastes evident in certain classes of ceramic decoration (predominantly plain during all the third millennium) and decorative objects, and the use of raw materials from further afield. The lithic industry is notable for its typological range, the greater size of tools (especially axes and

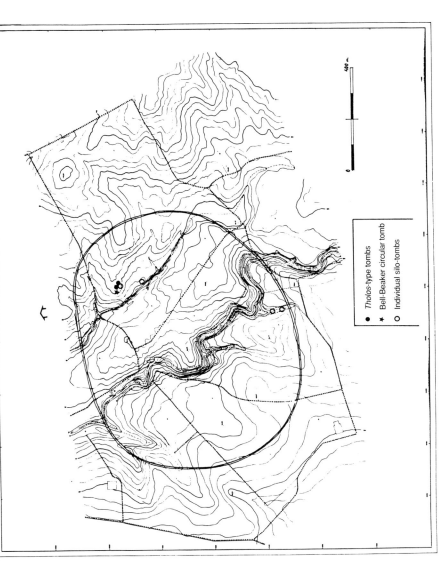

Figure 6.3 Plan of the settlement of La Pijotilla (the circle marks the line of the ditch surrounding the enclosure).

polished adzes or blades) and the diversity of raw materials used. Although an analysis of these industries is lacking, as is a comparison between different settlements, typological differences hint at the variety of purposes for which they were made. The many hoe blades and fittings and the considerable quantities of querns found at La Pijotilla suggest that these were principally agricultural. To these must be added a high proportion of copper hoes in the metalwork assemblage.

La Pijotilla is a consuming centre where we can find an enormous variety of products typical of other regions of the southwest, together with others of local origin. The quantity of objects from this site could be a function not only of internal requirements, but also of distribution to neighbouring settlements. Such a variety and concentration of products at one settlement would have ensured that it had a dominant commercial role and that all other settlements were dependent upon it. It is interesting to contrast the scarcity of raw materials in areas around such sites as Valencina de la Concepción and La Pijotilla, and the variety employed in the manufacture of artefacts in the interior regions. Although analyses of the economic structure are lacking it is clear that there are no copper mines in the MGB and that this metal must have been imported from more distant regions, possibly from the south of Badajoz province. The majority of metal artefacts would have arrived there already manufactured (Figure 6.4). However, the presence of the occasional crucible at La Pijotilla suggests that some metalworking activity did take place, such as re-smelting or possibly creating small pieces from ingots. The number of metal pieces found at La Pijotilla was large when compared to other contemporary sites. In terms of social context, weapons and decorative items have represented prestige goods acquired by an elite. The impact of bronze tools would have been limited, given their scarcity in relation to the overall assemblage of tools. Nevertheless, they do point to a technical improvement in certain activities.

The production of objects with social and ideological overtones is characteristic of La Pijotilla. This is especially true for marble, the technical mastery of which could be taken as an index of the degree of specialization emerging in this society. Plain and decorated marble vessels are abundant (Figure 6.4, top), although their function is difficult to establish. However, their context suggests that they had a connection with the funerary world. The repertoire of idols is very varied. The types known in previous phases, such as the plaque idols typical of the Alentejo, were supplemented with others like the Alentejo 'staves', the '*linulas*' and 'artichokes' of Portuguese Extremadura, 'cruciform' and 'betyls' from the southeast, 'hoppers', 'phalanxes', etc. The most representative pieces, however, are the marble 'cylinder idols of the MGB'. This type can be found throughout the Peninsular southwest, although there are curious regional stylistic differences in form and representation. Generally, the

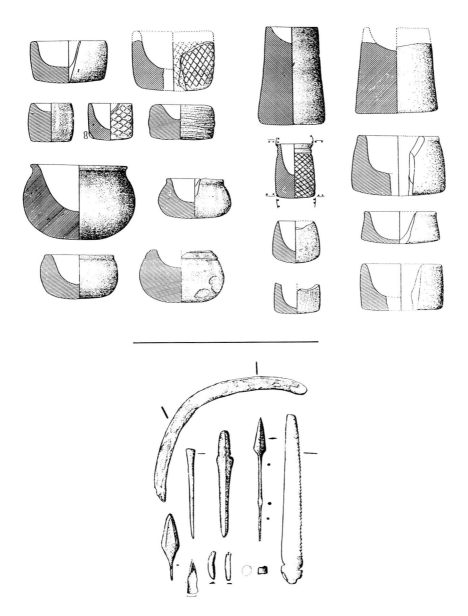

Figure 6.4   Marble vessels (above), metal objects (below).

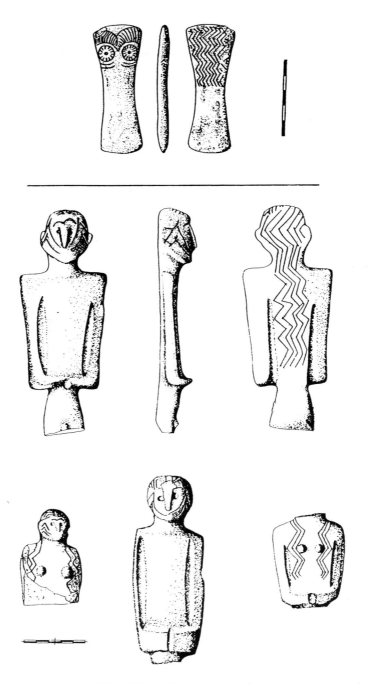

Figure 6.5   MGB marble idols. Above: idol with eyes. Below: male and female human figures.

type has a circular section and cylindrical form. In the MGB, it has a flattened section with a rectangular or 'palette-shaped' form (Figure 6.5, top) and, apart from the characteristic image of eyes, facial tattoo and zigzag hairstyle, it has peculiar wide eyebrows. In truth all representations of idols in the southwest have a single common theme, namely the depiction of a pair of eyes that schematically symbolize the Chalcolithic divinity. This theme is expressed in different ways and on a range of forms such as cylinders, phalanxes and plaques, but the essential idea remains the same. It is the symbol of a deity, probably feminine (judging by the sexual attribute that accompanies it in some representations), which became so ingrained in the mind of Chalcolithic populations that even a smooth pillar (an undecorated cylinder or phalanx) would have had the same significance.

The enormous variety of idol types discovered at La Pijotilla makes this an exceptional site. Most of those known from different regions of Iberia are represented here. It is also the site with the greatest number of examples. This is important for our understanding of the intensification of inter-site relations during this phase. Other observations can also be made. For example, the 'embossed tablets' ceramic decoration, together with 'comb' decoration on pottery, had a distribution which marks a connection between the Peninsular southwest and the French southeast (the *Fontbuisse* culture). It also points to a possible network of relationships outside the Peninsula: thus a cylindrical idol similar to the southwestern type has been found in the Haute-Garonne region of southeastern France. One might also add the introduction of the corded Bell-Beaker into the Peninsula, which was also present at La Pijotilla. Levels containing the 'embossed tablets' have been dated absolutely to between 2265 and 2110 BC at the settlements of Cerro de la Horca II and Cabrerizas II in Cáceres (González *et al.* 1991).

The analysis of tombs and differences in burial ritual are especially relevant in evaluating models of the societies that develop between the third and second millennia. Megaliths, for instance, are diluted by the very nature of collective burial. Nevertheless, the implementation of more refined excavation techniques allows more acute observations to be made and raises the possibility of being able to infer differences in a funerary context. Again it is the site of La Pijotilla which provides the best information on this matter. During this phase its cemetery was situated near to the settlement and was visible from it.[3] Such proximity suggests that it was stable settlements like these that were now the principal centres of territorial control. The investment of labour which had earlier been employed in the construction of tombs was now translated into greater complexity and technical improvement. This can be seen in the raising of a false dome, a covering mound and the implementation of new building techniques, such as dry-stone masonry, that prepare the way for the appearance of the *tholos*-type tomb characteristic of this phase.

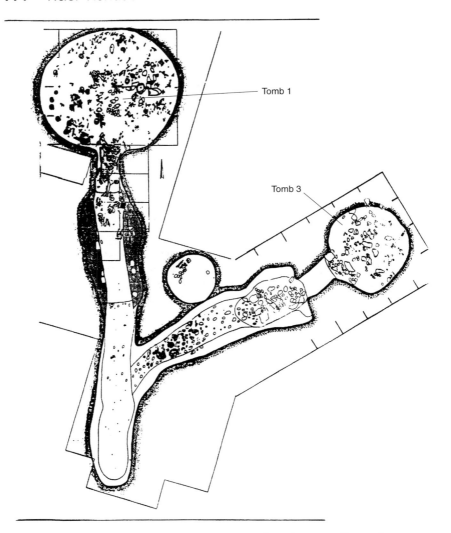

Tomb 1

Tomb 3

Figure 6.6 *Tholos*-type tombs numbers 1 and 3 of La Pijotilla. In the centre: A silo-tomb.

The tradition of collective burial continues, sometimes in some numbers, as is the case in La Pijotilla, where one of the tombs contained over 200 burials. Two intact *tholoi* have been excavated at this site (Hurtado 1991). Both (Figure 6.6) were dug into the chalky soil, so that stone was used solely for the construction of the false dome and the entrance portal. The burial rite consisted in the deposition of the deceased in the foetal position and, as new cadavers were added, the bones of earlier bodies (especially the skulls) were placed along the perimeter of the chambers. In this way the tombs filled up and formed authentic *ossaria* in which the bones of different individuals were superimposed and often mixed.

One of the most significant characteristics of the *tholoi* at La Pijotilla is that although they housed collective burials, the body furnishings are individualized. Despite displacements of remains within the same tomb, and the enormous accumulation of bones, each individual is accompanied by grave goods, even when removed from the initial location. The grave-good assemblages are largely repetitive, although it is interesting to note some differences. First, there is the contrast between the two *tholoi*. In 'tomb 1' each individual is accompanied by a flint plaque and on occasions an arrowhead or a piece of ochre, while in 'tomb 3' a ceramic vessel is more usual. Inside 'tomb 3' further differences can be seen: necklace beads, bone drinking vessels, phalanx idols, anthropomorphic figurines, sea-shells, etc. Some of these items could have formed part of collective grave goods, as in the case of the idols: this could be true of some large drinking vessels found near the entrance. Only one copper dagger has been found next to an individual. In this case, the person was accompanied by two drinking vessels and fragments of ochre and lemonite, although no discernible preferential treatment in his/her interment is noticeable. One cannot discuss all the implications raised by the analysis of these two tombs here, particularly since excavation is still in progress. Although 'tomb 3' was built before 'tomb 1' in stratigraphic terms, it is possible that both tombs could have been contemporary. This raises the question of social differentiation and whether this is based on heredity as Chapman suggests for the cemetery of Los Millares (Chapman 1991: 267). The first anthropological analyses carried out on the remains from 'tomb 3' suggest that this may have been the case, given that there were common morphogenetic characteristics in the one population sample studied.

A new insight into burial rituals is provided by the presence of human remains in rubbish trenches inside the settlement. In Valencina de la Concepción (Sevilla) bodies had been hurled into rubbish ditches without any kind of ritual (Fernández and Oliva 1980) and at La Pijotilla only the crania were present, among animal remains and other debris. The apparent violence of these deposits suggests that they were cases of punishment against transgressors or external enemies. This interpretation has implications for our understanding of the social organization of these peoples, although one should be cautious and seek corroborating evidence.

THE BELL-BEAKER HORIZON (2000–1800/1700 BC)

At the end of the third millennium BC there was an increase in social complexity brought about by an increase in inequality between sectors of the population and the consolidation of elite groups. In territorial terms, these inequalities are reflected in the development of a settlement hierarchy and the emergence of La Pijotilla as a major centre. It absorbs the largest share of products and would have controlled the circulation of goods. This is a situation common to all regions of the southwest, each of which now exhibits a strong cultural identity.

In this period the Bell–Beaker appears in the MGB and there is a greater dynamism in social difference. The archaeological record does not differ substantially from the previous period, suggesting that the same ethnic group was manufacturing artefacts, even though there is no supporting anthropological evidence. The reason for these changes must be sought fundamentally in socio-political aspects. They emerge as a consequence of increasing social inequalities. In the first half of the second millennium BC there emerged a hierarchical order in which power was concentrated in the hands of small groups. The distinctiveness of the MGB rests on the observation of this process through the gradual transformation in burial ritual. On the other hand, the MGB was also a geographical enclave upon which extensive commercial networks converged. This explains the growing similarity and intensification of cultural goods in the region during the Bell–Beaker period, as well as the absorption of different ceramic 'assemblages'.

There are few sites with Bell–Beaker pottery in the MGB and the majority are only known through excavation. This limits the chances of being able to discover whether the changes of the first half of the second millennium BC stem from developments in the region as a whole (and are thus susceptible to division into different phases), or if they are different responses to similar conditions. In the first case, regarding the source of certain items that do not have the necessary dating evidence or corroboration, there is the danger of falling into linear evolutionism. In the second, there is the risk of precipitately assuming polymorphism on account of the dating of certain structures (dwellings or funerary) from a wide chronological spectrum. Here the intention is to emphasize the complexity confronting research in the first half of the second millennium in this region. Even though information is very limited, once the documentary base becomes consistent, it offers us the possibility of understanding the mechanisms of change.

Available information suggests that the organization of the territory of Tierra de Barros continues as in the previous phase. Settlements in the plains and fortified sites are maintained. In the Mérida area, next to the river Guadiana, the Bell–Beaker habitats are all situated on the left bank, although out of line of the fortified towns. This shows that the defensive limit was still maintained with vigour. In this zone there is a fortified settlement on a gentle hill, at La Palacina (Enríquez 1990: 166), whose only occupation level shows that it was constructed at this time, perhaps as some kind of observation post at the principal ford of the river.

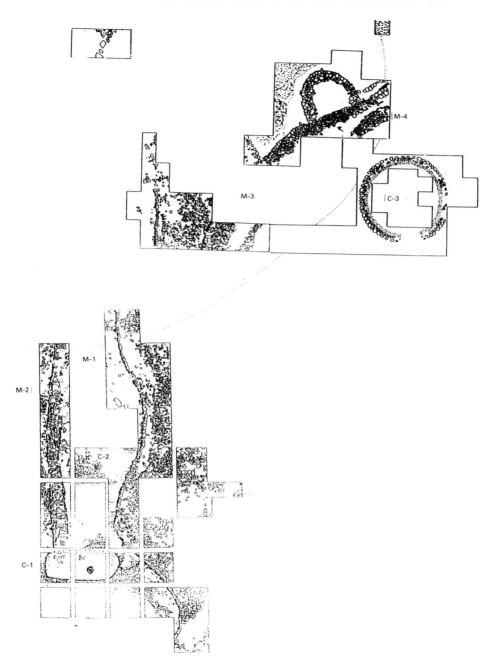

Figure 6.7 Plan of the excavation of the fortified settlement of Palacio Quemado.

Palacio Quemado (Figure 6.7) is one of the few walled sites at which archaeological excavations have taken place (Hurtado and Enríquez 1991). It consists of a small walled settlement (1 ha.) situated on a slight elevation, very vulnerable to attack, and in which two phases of fortification have been documented. The second of these took place after a violent destruction that left the first-phase structures covered with ashes (dated to 2100 BC). Amongst these have been found dry-stone wall bastions and oval dwellings with raised mud-brick floors and internal hearths. The second phase is characterized by late Bell-Beaker pottery and has an absolute date of ca. 1600 BC. The settlement is enclosed by a wall approximately 1 metre wide built from limestone blocks and slate bound with a mud-based mortar. The dwellings are circular (6 m. in diameter) and are built on stone footings 50 cm wide against which rests an interior mud-brick wall. Contemporary huts at La Pijotilla may have been similar.

La Pijotilla continues to be occupied during this phase and is once again the key to understanding the cultural dynamics of the region. The archaeological remains corresponding to this phase of the site are very disturbed due to the alteration of the topsoil. In the ceramic record there was a drop in the number of plates with almond-shaped rims, and an increase in bowls and metal objects. On the surface of the site, vessels with Bell-Beaker decoration are well represented. These are typical of the two traditional typological phases of the Bell-Beaker (Maritime and Continental). At the same time they are characteristic of regional groupings, illustrating the continuity of supra-regional interaction and the concentration of prestige goods at this site. One should also note a local style of Bell-Beaker decoration, typified by a profusion of motifs on the inside and outside of the vessels. They are a characteristic element of the material culture of the region, as was the case of the 'cylinder idols'. There is a continuity of the earlier ceramic repertoire during this phase although it varies in percentage terms. Worthy of note is a carenated vessel, whose development into a more pronounced form can be traced in the stratigraphic sequence at La Pijotilla and Palacio Quemado. This is the type of vessel which characterizes the grave goods of cist burials and which has been used to characterize the Bronze Age in southwest Iberia (Schubart 1975).

Amongst the large assemblage of 'idols' found on the surface of La Pijotilla the 'anthropomorphic', or human figure, type has also been discovered (Figure 6.5, lower). This is difficult to date as we lack contextual data. It has parallels with examples in Andalucía. In the southeast, the idol of Malagón pre-dates the appearance of Bell-Beaker pottery (Arribas 1977). At Valencina de la Concepción two idols were found in a well that contained no Bell-Beaker material and with an absolute chronology of around 1900 BC (Fernández and Oliva 1980). The type belonging to this, or the previous, phase is short-lived and does not continue into subsequent periods. What is clear, however, it that it implies a new conception of representational form that is distinct from the schematic prototype that had prevailed on artefacts and in cave-painting throughout the third millennium. Again it is the settlement of La Pijotilla which is outstanding in this respect, given that more examples of this type have been found here than anywhere else in the whole Peninsula (Hurtado 1981). This does not mean that they were common in the region as a whole, since examples have only been found sporadically at other sites. The large number of idols at this one site suggests instead that La Pijotilla may have been their distribution centre. These human figurines are also the finest exponent of the degree of technical mastery achieved in the crafting of marble, and could be interpreted as evidence for specialist labour (without assuming task exclusivity), which has already been observed in respect to the manufacture of 'cylinder idols' and stone vessels.

It is particularly interesting to contrast this type with those mentioned earlier. By way of hypothesis it may be suggested that they reflect social changes taking place at the end of the Chalcolithic. Amongst the human figurines from La Pijotilla were those with clear indications of sexual identity. For the first time clearly male and female groups were defined and the figures found at other sites belonged to the former group.

Differences in the social structure arise at the end of the third millennium. It is possible to distinguish social groups that would have attempted to control the production of surplus and the use of prestige goods. At the same time there is an increase in conflict, with the figure of a chief acquiring a central role. All these social changes should be translated into the ideological sphere. Schematic representation is substituted by naturalism, and the abstract concept of a female signifier detailing only the eyes is replaced by a complete effigy in which the sexual character is directly identifiable, but in which the masculine form predominates. These changes do not happen drastically, however, nor do traditional forms of representation disappear. The appearance of the 'anthropomorphic idol' would have served to inculcate a new value that is found already introduced as a social concept and that would possibly be the reflection of the chief or warrior figure. This carried strong echoes in the carved stone representations of Bronze Age *stelae* in southwest Iberia.

These changes are also reflected in burials. Some earlier tombs are reused in this phase by the insertion of new burials in the corridors. This implies a loss of interest in building new funerary monuments and, as a consequence, a notable decrease in the investment of labour in this type of enterprise. The same tendency can be observed in the tomb of La Pijotilla (Hurtado 1985). This is located close to the *tholoi*, and is circular in shape with a diameter of 3 to 5 metres. It is of very simple construction and consists of a circle of slates placed upright and partially sunk into a small earth ditch for stability. It seems that these were unsuitable for bearing any weight and that their function was to limit the exterior of the tomb and possibly to contain the covering of the mound. However, this raises the problem as to how the later burials were introduced into the tomb, and consequently the question as to whether it had a covering. It was impossible to determine the siting of the burials and the grave goods, and the number of individuals (thirty-four) could only be established through the quantification of bone remains. Grave goods were dominated by prestige objects comprising, among other things, Bell-Beakers and different types of idol. There are no other known Bell-Beaker tombs in Extremadura, apart from reused earlier tombs (Schubart 1973). This poses the problem as to whether or not the circular burial of La Pijotilla should be considered as the model for this phase of the MGB. After the Bell-Beaker period notable changes take place in burial practice. Account has to be taken of these and of changes in the regional variation in social formation.

THE GUADAJIRA–SOLANA I PHASE: REFLECTIONS ON THE TRANSITION TO THE BRONZE AGE (1800/1700–1500 BC)

The lack of research into the MGB and the positivist rigidity of a cultural classification based upon the identification of characteristic artefacts has excessively compartmentalized periodization. As a result the Bronze Age is explained in terms of some rather reductionist assumptions. The fundamental problem is that models from other areas (Argaric or Portuguese) have been applied to this region. As a result an opportunity to develop a regional model for processes of change in the region has been lost.

Some of the Chalcolithic ceramic types continue and, as mentioned earlier, it is often difficult to ascribe sites to a particular cultural horizon on the basis of surface materials alone. It has been pointed out that the stratigraphy of La Pijotilla allows us to observe how certain artefacts continued in use, and how their frequency varied. Alternatively new artefacts had to be judged against the overall cultural assemblage in order to isolate items that were specific to a particular phase and distinct to that of the Bell-Beakers. This will be evident later from the discovery at Guadajira (Hurtado 1985) and comparison of this with data from the stratigraphic sequence at La Pijotilla. A difference in the funerary assemblage at the former (Hurtado 1985), which was revealed by comparison with La Pijotilla, could have corresponded to Bell-Beakers and the Bronze Age transition. The small 'thin-walled' carenated vessels with reduced firing and semi-polished finish (Figure 6.8), similar to that typifying Schubart's Atalaia horizon (Schubart 1975), became indicative of a new phase. Its development can be followed in the stratigraphic sequence of La Pijotilla, although it cannot date a site to a particular phase when it is found out of its cultural context.

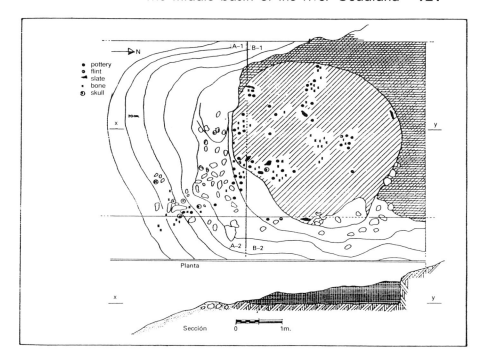

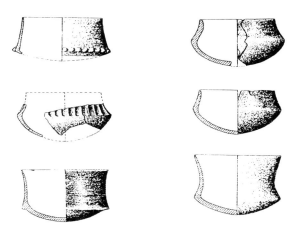

Figure 6.8 Tomb 1 at Guadajira (above) and ceramic grave goods (below).

Perhaps the most salient point concerning this phase in the MGB is the continuity from the previous phase reflected in its materials. According to Barceló (1991: 17) this process of slowing-down is observed principally in the transformation of funerary rites in the region. There are no brusque changes between the ritual of collective and individual burial at the circular tomb of La Pijotilla, the tombs of Guadajira, and in the finds assemblages of different phases. Little can be said, however, about the other settlements in the territory.

From this moment onwards, available information is very scarce. Only two sites can be used to attempt territorial analysis. Some settlements of the previous phase now disappear. This is the case of La Palacina, the walled settlement closest to the Guadiana river, which abandons its position on the high ground. It is replaced by a new settlement at La Solana del Castillo de Alange, located in a strategic position on the side of a nearby hill (Calero and Márquez 1991; Pavón 1991–2), at the confluence of two rivers. Palacio Quemado, however, continued, judging by the dating of 1620 BC obtained for its second phase. The same is possibly also true for La Pijotilla, although the principal source of information is found at another site, Guadajira, situated 5 kilometres to the north. The settlement of Los Cortinales (Gil-Mascarell and Rodríguez 1987) should also be mentioned, although with certain reservations. It is situated outside the limit of the Tierra de Barros and could be ascribed to this phase on the basis of its finds assemblage, from which Bell-Beaker pottery is absent, although there is no absolute dating or sufficient comparative data from that zone.

The stratigraphic sequence of the second millennium can be observed at Solana del Castillo de Alange, and a more detailed analysis could provide important information about the cultural dynamics of the zone in the second half of the millennium (Pavón 1993). Solana's oldest horizon is characterized by a strong degree of 'chalcolithisation' (Pavón 1993: 156). Within the ceramic repertoire the Bell-Beaker and plates with enlarged rims disappear and there is a greater presence of bowls and 'thin-walled' wares.

The changes are more evident in the burial types, as was demonstrated by the tomb of Guadajira (Hurtado 1985) and to which two more must be added, both excavated recently but still unpublished. These are probably contemporary with Solana I, having certain characteristics that accord closely with those already present in 'tomb 2' of La Pijotilla (with Bell-Beakers). The Guadajira tombs (Figure 6.8, above) are partially excavated into a hillside and are circular in shape. Only one of them retained the spring of a false dome and, although they had all been looted, some scattered burials and part of the grave goods were found. They consisted largely of small globular or carenated 'thin-walled' drinking cups, the majority of which had been polished and fired in reducing conditions. In one of the tombs a fragment of a Bell-Beaker was found and in another there were four copper arrowheads of the 'Palmela' type. The carenated vessel was to become one of the most characteristic grave goods of the southwestern cist tombs (Schubart 1975).

There are no absolute dates that would allow connections between different types of tombs to be made with precision, or other data to help explain their diversity. However, it is clear that towards the mid-second millennium, the process towards individual burial is complete. Moreover, the circular tombs suggest that although it did not happen abruptly in some places, the practice of individual burial must have been assimilated with some speed by the population.

The variety of individual tombs is again highlighted at La Pijotilla where an eight-sided pit was found to contain two crania and the remains of a bowl. This was sited at one end of the round Bell-Beaker tomb and caused the destruction of part of the slate perimeter wall. Individual burials also appear in silos, the majority having no grave goods. However, a globular and burnished conical vessel was found in one burial. This type of burial, which is also documented in the Guadalquivir valley, seems to be a form of individual burial which pre-dates the consolidation of the well-known cist burials of the full Bronze Age, because of its limited presence in places with Chalcolithic tradition, as is the case of La Pijotilla and El Gandul (Hurtado and Amores 1984). It is useful to reflect upon the fact that the process of change between the circular Guadajira-type tomb and the silo burial could have taken place in a brief timespan, and in this respect our explanation favours chronological variation based upon a formal diversity of tomb types rather than upon their possible contemporaneity.

On the other hand, one must not forget that the Guadajira and Pijotilla tombs are located in a territory that was of great regional importance during the Chalcolithic. Conversely, all the known cist-burials (Gil-Mascarell et al. 1986) are distributed in the outer area and more precisely in the hinterland between Tierra de Barros and La Serena. With the exception of a few examples we know little about their grave goods, which makes it difficult to establish the chronology and to contrast them with silo burials. The proximity of such settlements as Palacio Quemado and Cortinales has begged the possibility of labelling them as 'epicalcholithic' (Gil–Mascarell et al. 1986: 40; Pavón 1991–2, 1993). But this is a precipitate evaluation, given that little is known about their relationship to the cemeteries or the dynamics of their territory. Moreover, the absolute dating invalidates the (uncalibrated) chronologies proposed for this type of burial at around 1500 BC.

At the settlement of La Pijotilla, all evidence for occupation disappears after the Bell-Beaker period. Nevertheless, certain artefacts found on the surface suggest that these settlements continued up to the middle of the second millennium. These include sophisticated metal objects, such as a dagger with central binding and riveting, or the 'pastora'-type javelin tips. From this time onwards all the settlements in the territory of Tierra de Barros disappear and the equilibrium of occupation is displaced eastwards. This must be related to the changes that were taking place in the socio–economic structure throughout the first half of the second millennium. From what has been discussed above, these changes do not appear to have taken place in a traumatic fashion. The data from the region, however, are scarce indeed. The recent discovery of a stratigraphic sequence continuing into the Late Bronze Age at La Solana de Alange (Pavón 1991–2; 1993) provides an important step in recognizing the process in the cultural record. Nevertheless, in order to understand the cultural dynamics of this region more information integrated into theoretical frameworks and well-defined projects is needed. There is a particularly urgent need for surveys that will allow a more coherent analysis of the territory.

CONCLUSION

Despite the scarcity of material evidence in this region it is possible to outline a processual sequence between the fourth and second millennia BC for the occupation dynamics of the Middle Guadiana Basin. It is also possible to gain some idea of the general process of hierarchization of social structures evident at the emergence of social complexity in other regions during the same period, although confirmation of this would clearly require a rather more detailed analysis. Nevertheless the social change implicit in the peaceful transition from family and communal to the individual is evident in the funerary record. It can be attested in the difference between collective burials and individual cist-burials. Moreover, the emergence of leaders can be identified through differences in burial goods or in sculptural representations. In a region like that of Extremadura, in which prehistoric research is still in its infancy, perspectives for the study of the formation of complex societies are good, as this chapter has tried to demonstrate. They will only improve if there is an increase in projects which focus upon broad analyses of social dynamics, rather than the more traditional interests in cultural development derived through the excavation of stratigraphic sequences alone.

NOTES

1 There is insufficient paleoenvironmental data to allow differences between these two phases to be drawn. Some pollen analyses reveal the existence of oak and cork trees in the lands to the south of the Guadiana, whilst to the north the presence of chestnut trees indicates a somewhat more humid climate than at present.
2 Since the number of sites where Bell-Beaker pottery appears is low, dating based upon the presence or absence of Bell-Beaker pottery in deposits known from surveying our region could be erroneous.

3 Even though research is still limited the tendency for tombs to concentrate around the settlement becomes generalized in this phase. For the moment it can be observed in the large settlements of Valencina de la Concepción and El Gandul in the Guadalquivir valley.

REFERENCES

Arribas, A. (1977) 'El idolo de El Malagón (Cúllar–Baza, Granada)', *Cuadernos de Prehistoria de la Universidad de Granada*, 11: 63–86.

Arteaga, O. (1992) 'Tribalización, jerarquización y estado en el territorio de El Argar', *SPAL* 1: 179–208.

Barceló, J. (1991) 'El Bronce del Sudoeste y la cronología de las estelas alentejanas', *Arqueologia* 21: 15–24.

Blance, B. (1971) *Die Anfänge der Metallurgie auf der Iberischen Halbinsel*, Berlin: Römisch-Germanisches Zentralmuseum.

Bueno, P. (1986) 'Megalitos en Extremadura', in *Actas de la Mesa Redonda sobre Megalitismo Peninsular*: 45–50, Madrid: Asociación de Amigos de la Arqueología.

—— (1987) 'Megalitismo en Extremadura. Estado de la cuestión', in *El Megalitismo en la Península Ibérica*: 73–84, Madrid: Ministerio de Cultura.

—— (1988) *Los dólmenes de Valencia de Alcántara*, Excavaciones Arqueológicas en España 155: 7–210, Madrid: Ministerio de Cultura.

Calero, J.A. and Márquez, A. (1991) 'Prospecciones, sondeos y excavaciones en Alange (1984–1987)', in *Extremadura Arqueologica II. I Jornadas de Prehistoria y Arqueologia en Extremadura (1986–1990)*: 577–98, Mérida–Cáceres: Junta de Extremadura and Universidad de Extremadura.

Castro, P.V. and González, P. (1989) 'El concepto de frontera: Implicaciones teoricas de la noción de territorio político', in F. Burillo (ed.) *Arqueología espacial 13. Fronteras*: 7–18, Teruel: Seminario de Arqueología y Etnología Turolense.

Chapman, R. (1991) *La formación de las sociedades complejas. El sureste de la península ibérica en el marco del mediterráneo occidental*, Barcelona: Crítica. [(1990) *Emerging Complexity: The later Prehistory of south-east Spain, Iberia and the West Mediterannean*, Cambridge: Cambridge University Press.]

Enríquez, J.J. (1981–2) 'Avance al estudio de los materiales procedentes de Araya. Mérida (Badajoz)', *Pyrenae* 17–18: 191–200.

—— (1986) 'Excavación de urgencia en la Cueva de la Charneca (Oliva de Mérida, Badajoz)', *Noticiario Arqueológico Hispánico* 28: 9–24.

—— (1990) *El Calcolítico o Edad del Cobre de la Cuenca Extremeña del Guadiana: Los poblados*, Badajoz: Museo Arqueológico Provincial de Badajoz.

Enríquez, J.J. and Hurtado, V. (1986) 'Prehistoria y Protohistoria', in *Historia de la Baja Extremadura I*, Badajoz: Real Academia de las Artes y Letras de Extremadura.

Fernández, F. and Oliva, D. (1980) 'Los ídolos calcolíticos de El Cerro de la Cábeza (Valencina de la Concepción, Sevilla)', *Madrider Mitteilungen* 21: 20–44.

Galán, E. and Martín, A. (1991–2) 'Megalitismo y zonas de paso en la cuenca extremena del Tajo', *Zephyrus* XLIV–XLV: 193–205.

Gil-Mascarell, M. and Rodríguez, A. (1987) 'El yacimiento calcolítico de Los Cortinales en Villafranca de los Barros (Badajoz)', *Homenaje a D. Fletcher*.

Archivo de Prehistoria Levantina XVII: 123–45.

Gil-Mascarell, M., Rodríguez, A. and Enríquez, J.J. (1986) 'Enterramientos en cista de la Edad del Bronce en la Baja Extremadura', *Saguntum* 20: 9–41.

González, A., Castillo, J. and Hernández, M. (1991) 'La secuencia estratigráfica en los yacimientos calcolíticos del área de Plasenzuela (Cáceres)', *Extremadura Arqueólogica II. I Jornadas de Prehistoria y Arqueología en Extremadura (1986–1990)*: 11–26, Mérida–Cáceres: Junta de Extremadura and Universidad de Extremadura.

Hurtado, V. (1981) 'Las figuras humanas del yacimiento de La Pijotilla (Badajoz)', *Madrider Mitteilungen* 22: 78–88.

—— (1985) 'El Calcolítico en la Cuenca Media del Guadiana y la necrópolis de la Pijotilla', in *Actas de la Mesa Redonda sobre Megalitismo peninsular (Madrid 1984)*: 51–75, Madrid: Asociación de Amigos de la Arqueología.

—— (1987) 'El Megalitismo en el Suroeste peninsular: problemática en la periodización regional', in *El Megalitismo en la Peninsula Iberica*: 31–43, Madrid: Ministerio de Cultura.

—— (1991) 'Informe de las excavaciones de urgencia en la Pijotilla. Campaña de 1990', in *Extremadura Arqueológica II. I Jornadas de Prehistoria y Arqueología en Extremadura (1986–1990)*: 45–68, Mérida–Cáceres: Junta de Extremadura and Universidad de Extremadura.

Hurtado, V. and Amores, F. (1984) 'El tholos de las Canteras y los enterramientos del Bronce en la necrópolis de El Gandul', *Cuadernos de Prehistoria de la Universidad de Granada* 9: 147–74.

Hurtado, V. and Enríquez, J.J. (1991) 'Excavaciones en Palacio Quemado (Alange, Badajoz) Informe preliminar', *Extremadura Arqueológica II. I Jornadas de Prehistoria y Arqueología en Extremadura (1986–1990)*: 69–89, Mérida–Cáceres: Junta de Extremadura and Universidad de Extremadura.

Jorge, S.O. (1990) 'Desenvolvimento da hierarquizacão social e da metalurgia', in J. Serrão and A. Marques (eds) *Nova Historia de Portugal, vol. I*: 102–97, Lisbon: Preseca.

Molina, L. (1980) 'El poblado del Bronce I El Lobo', *Noticiario Arqueológico Hispánico* 9: 93–127.

Nocete, F. (1984) 'Jefaturas y Territorio: Una vision crítica', *Cuadernos de Prehistoria de la Universidad de Granada* 9: 289–304.

Pavón, I. (1991–2) 'La Solana del Castillo de Alange: Una propuesta de secuencia cultural de la Edad del Bronce en la Cuenca Media del Guadiana', *Norba Revista de Historia 11–12*: 75–98.

—— (1993) 'La Solana del Castillo de Alange: Un yacimiento de la Edad del Bronce en la Cuenca Media del Guadiana', *SPAL* 2: 147–68.

Renfrew, C. (1967) 'Colonialism and Megalithism', *Antiquity* 41: 276–88.

Rodríguez, A. (1986) *Arqueología de Tierra de Barros*. Zafra: Editora Regional de Extremadura.

Savory, H.N. (1968) *Spain and Portugal*, London: Thames and Hudson.

Schubart, H. (1973) 'Tholos-Bauten von Colada de Monte Nuevo bei Olivenza', *Madrider Mitteilungen* 14: 11–42.

—— (1975) *Die Kultur der Bronzezeit im Südwesten der Iberischen Halbinsel*, Madrider Forschungen 9, Berlin: de Gruyter.

Silva, C.T. (1987) 'Megalitismo do Alentejo Oxidental e do Sul do Baixo Alentejo (Portugal)', in *El Megalitismo en la Peninsula Iberica*: 85–93, Madrid: Ministerio de Cultura.

Soares, J. and Silva, C.T. (1992) 'Para o conhecimento dos povoados do Megalitismo de Reguengos', *Setubal Arqueológica* IX–X: 37–88.

Vegas, R. (1971) 'Geología de la region extremeña comprendida entre la Sierra Morena occidental y Las Sierras del Norte de la Provincia de Cáceres (Extremadura Española)', *Boletín del Instituto Geológico Minero de España* 82–4: 350–60.

CHAPTER SEVEN

THE NEOLITHIC/ CHALCOLITHIC TRANSITION IN PORTUGAL

The dynamics of change in the third millennium BC

SUSANA OLIVEIRA JORGE AND
VÍTOR OLIVEIRA JORGE

INTRODUCTION

Throughout most of Portuguese territory during the period ranging from *c.* 2700–2500 to *c.* 1800–1700 BC[1] there emerged communities which created new kinds of relationships between the elites and their populations. Such new 'behaviour' has to be linked to a global change in the traditional ideology of power. In some areas, tendentially hierarchical societies took steps towards a quite significant level of social complexity.

Regional variability, however, does not allow us to envisage Portuguese territory in an all-embracing perspective. In addition, some areas have not yet been sufficiently researched as to be characterized in archaeological terms. We will thus assess four major areas independently: the Alentejo/Algarve, Estremadura, Beiras and the north of Portugal. Multiple symbiotic contacts in these regions can be observed, and the formation of cultural areas does not always coincide with the administrative divisions referred to above. Nevertheless, we believe that this geographical partition is appropriate to the scale of our enquiry.[2]

THE ALENTEJO AND THE ALGARVE (FIGURE 7.1)

Three main aspects appear as novelties in the archaeological record during the second half of the third millennium BC. The first concerns the recent identification of several hill-top settlements within which occupation was concentrated in areas protected by defences. Some of these settlements are quite impressive and have walls, towers and bastions. In many cases their architecture seems to be clearly inspired by Mediterranean proto-types, and seems to indicate a climate of social instability common to a large part of southern Portugal.

The second aspect has to do with an important technological inno-vation: the still incipient metallurgy of copper, gold and silver. Thus, from the second half of the third millennium BC, these new materials are used to make prestige artefacts (flat axes, chisels, awls, 'saws' and daggers, etc. in the case of copper), which are as yet rare but still impor-tant since in certain cases they may both reflect and instigate significant social changes. It is quite obvious that such knowledge would not have been shared by all the populations in the south of Portugal at this stage. Some communities are merely recipients of ready-made artefacts which are acquired as elements enriching the social status of the local elite. Essentially, metal can circulate over more traditional areas as an item which is exchanged for subsistence products; but this has no clear influ-ence upon the structure of some of the populations who receive it. It is just another raw material of extraneous origin. The ambivalence which characterizes metal determines that its presence alone does not enable us to evaluate and define the degree of technological knowledge and social complexity of populations which merely manipulate it. Therefore it is understandable that the word 'Chalcolithic' can encompass a vast range of meanings which should be more clearly distinguished. However, we do consider that, for the south of Portugal, metallurgy renewed the cultural scene of the area in a remarkable way, not only as a techno-logical innovation but above all as an exchange network. It acted as an element which implemented certain changes and even triggered cultural processes that could not have easily been anticipated earlier. The third aspect is less obvious and harder to recognize in the archaeological record. It has to do with the renovation of 'ideological structures'. It is connected with the evolution of mortuary architecture and rituals and also with the symbolism of certain ideo-technic items which are present in mortuary and domestic contexts.

At this stage the re-utilization of megalithic monuments coexists with the construction of false-vaulted tombs of the so-called *tholos*-type. Several architectural typologies can be found; but the predominant type in Alentejo and in the Algarve is that which combines orthostatic cham-bers and passages with corbelled roofs. Consequently these monuments have a hybrid character, with a strong local component of megalithic tradition. Their construction could imply new ways of organizing communal work. The size of these monuments could vary, but they would generally be smaller than most earlier Neolithic megalithic tombs. Some authors believe that the building of these *tholoi* would not require

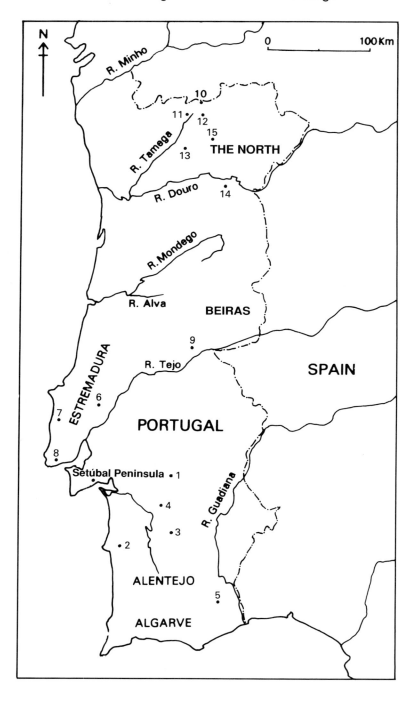

a system of reciprocal work in the community structured in the same way as that which would have existed in the case of megalithic monuments, especially the large examples (Soares and Silva 1992). Therefore, the community as a whole needed a lower energy input for the building of these monuments and certainly a completely different kind of relationship with the elites buried there.

Amongst the artefacts found in these tombs, those stand out which introduce symbolic readjustments: the decorated wares (the so-called 'symbolic' pottery, containing eye or face motifs), traditionally seen as representing a new emerging entity, a putative 'Mother-Goddess', the presence of which is due to interaction with the Mediterranean. These eye motifs can also be found on engraved schist idol plaques which are sometimes understood in terms of solar symbolism (Vilaça 1984). Within this new symbolic system one should mention not only the engraved rocks of the Tagus valley (most of which must have been conceived at this stage), but also the 'anthropomorphic' *stelae* from Crato and N. Sra da Esperança, for instance, which are of Mediterranean inspiration. These structures have parallels in the adjacent region of Cáceres (Spain). Other specimens of the same 'family' are documented in the southwest, the northern Meseta and the northwest of the Peninsula. Several authors (Gomes *et al.* 1983) have recently stated firmly that a hypothetical religious rupture occurred in the south of Portugal, evident in the differences between the symbols of the Late Neolithic and those of the Chalcolithic. The former would be represented by the images of the phallus (menhir) and of the ox (engraved bucrania). The latter, by the image of the 'Mother-Goddess', which would be engraved or sculpted on different materials (ceramic vessels, stone or bone idols, stone *stelae*, etc.). The same authors support this symbolic rupture with two events. The first one would be the ritual 'destruction' of the Escoural rock engravings by populations which then built a Chalcolithic settlement over them. The second event has to do with the recent discovery of menhirs 'destroyed' by Chalcolithic communities which built their settlements in places that had hitherto been sacred (for instance, Monte Novo or Herdade dos Perdigões).

In the meantime, the archaeological record suggests a changing social system encompassing all of southern Portugal, regional details notwithstanding. Two of the most striking features of this cultural process are demographic growth and the proliferation of communities with different

Figure 7.1   Map showing the location of sites mentioned in the text.

Alentejo and **Algarve**: 1. Escoural, 2. Monte Novo, 3. Ferreira do Alentejo, 4. Monte da Tumba, 5. Santa Justa. **Estremadura**: 6. Vila Nova de S. Pedro, 7. Zambujal, 8. Leceia. **Beiras**: 9. Charneca de Fratel. **The North**: 10. Vinha da Soutilha, 11. Pastoria, 12. S. Lourenço, 13. Castelo de Aguiar, 14. Castelo Velho, 15. Buraco da Pala (Mirandela).

cultural identities (Jorge 1990: 167–8). These communities were installed in territories with a smaller area, and their settlement patterns were largely dependent upon the resources they exploited (Jorge 1990: 168). The apparent homogeneity of the material culture should not blind us to this regional diversity. Research in these different regions should enable settlement 'networks' to be defined and allow the characterization of the ecosystems which supported them and made possible the diversified social and economic investment achieved in each sub-area.

We will now make some general comments about the cultural changes noted in southern Portugal throughout the third millennium BC, namely settlement patterns, subsistence technologies and inter-communal exchanges. Some unenclosed settlements which have no natural defences persist, as in the case of those on the coast of the Alentejo (Silva *et al.* 1986). They are rather small in size. The site of Ferreira do Alentejo is an exception, for it might have occupied an area of 50–100 hectares. One can compare it, both in its extent and topography, to other settlements in the southwest of the Peninsula, like Valencina de la Concepción or La Pijotilla (Arnaud 1982). Most of the settlements were built on hilltops and were therefore provided with natural defences, although not all of them were walled. Morais Arnaud argued that such settlements would have enclosed an area of 1 to 5 hectares and could have maintained a population of 150 to 350 people. Finally, one can find fortified hill-top settlements occupying less than 1 hectare with a probable population of between thirty and fifty people. These settlements exhibit some degree of specialization in the defence of fertile land or in mining activities (Jorge 1990: 169–70). We consider, however, that it is appropriate to distinguish several degrees of complexity regarding defensive structures. Therefore, settlements such as Monte da Tumba (Jorge 1990: 169–70) and Santa Justa (Jorge 1990: 175–6), with successive building phases and defensive strategies testifying to a long period of occupation, should probably belong to a different category from that of the majority of the Alentejo's fortified settlements. The simplicity of the latter may be the result of short periods of occupation, which would have meant that this enlargement of structures was never necessary.

A brief analysis of the above-mentioned settlements leads us to another conclusion: the vast majority appear in territories whose intensive agricultural economy would require a somewhat developed technology. This means a probable use of rudimentary ploughs, perhaps an increased harnessing of bovids and equids for carriage and traction, and, eventually, the development of wet-farming which requires the use of small ditches and dams. There are other settlements (e.g. Santa Justa or Corte de João Marques (Jorge 1990: 174–5)) which are located on poor soils, and close to copper mines that were exploited by their communities. Despite the fact that there is no direct archaeological evidence to support this hypothesis, it is possible that both these communities might have resorted to more advanced agricultural techniques to overcome environmental constraints. Thus the location of settlements was no longer totally dependent upon the fertility of farming land. Multiple, and perhaps contradictory, social and economic stimuli, which it would be necessary to determine, caused the communities to expand in every direction. Hence, we can state that farming communities which manipulated copper metallurgy are responsible for the second and decisive 'colonization' of southern Portugal. Such social stimuli are barely recognizable in the archaeological record. However, from the Late Neolithic (i.e. the first half of the third millennium BC) some regions were populated by groups whose dependence on agriculture was quite strong (Jorge 1990: 176–7). The density of the population of sedentary farmers was already quite substantial during the first half of the third millennium in regions such as Reguengos, Portel/Vidigueira and even Ourique (Jorge 1990: 176–7). Several authors (e.g. Gonçalves 1991) suggest that, from the first half of the third millennium, communities in overpopulated areas might have fused. In view of this and the technological development made possible by the so-called 'Secondary Products Revolution', some of the populations would have moved to marginal environments where they could raise or reuse subsistence resources and/or engage in mining activities. This is confirmed when we observe the process of 'colonization' of the eastern Upper Algarve by groups from the southern Lower Alentejo. Several other areas of the Alentejo and the Algarve are quite likely to have followed the same pattern (Gonçalves 1991). These groups, which occupied territories with diversified critical resources, possessed new technologies, enabling them to establish hierarchical settlement networks (Gonçalves 1991; Jorge 1990: 177). These settlements would have had different functions corresponding to the ranking mentioned above. The fortification of some of these settlements could be explained by a need to protect both the copper mining and the adjacent arable fields. In the long run these would be enriched through the effort invested in many social innovations. We cannot, of course, neglect a fundamental question which arises at this point. The fortifications had defensive capabilities beyond their emblematic value. Did the contending groups come from the same cultural system, or were they less-developed farmer groups which shared the new territories? Since the diffusionist hypothesis of extra-Peninsular 'colonies' is no longer acceptable, no current explanatory mechanism enables us to solve this problem.

This cultural process raises a pertinent question, namely the adoption of architectural, artefactual and even ritual patterns of Mediterranean origin by local populations. We believe that this might be connected to a new emergent elite. Chalcolithic communities promote systems of leadership which are progressively more stable and require the leaders to have a growing individual status. The new elites take the protection and the leadership of the communities into their hands, therefore investing in the strengthening of their power display. This is accomplished through the possession of prestige artefacts and the exhibition of supra-regional architectural patterns (Jorge 1990: 178). The presence of votive objects made out of rare raw materials, and of domestic or burial architecture following Mediterranean 'types', indicates that these communities are now part of large-scale interaction interconnecting quite distant areas at several levels, such as the southwest and southeast of the Peninsula and the Portuguese Estremadura (Jorge 1990: 178). The assimilation of 'Mediterranean patterns' as a source for prestige and power might have been the result of the local elites' desire to legitimate their leadership through the display of a ritual, artefactual and architectural symbolism whose parameters extend beyond the Peninsula. This implies that each community is part of a large-scale interdependency system. Thus we can explain, for instance, the system of interactions that took place in the third millennium involving the areas of Alentejo and Estremadura, mainly those concerning commodity exchange, either of subsistence goods or, primarily, of exceptional ones (Jorge 1990: 178). The adoption of Mediterranean 'archetypes' does not call for an explanation which would resort to events occurring outside the internal dynamics of the populations of southern Portugal. The main issue is the attempt to understand the complex tissue of causes which led to the integration of local communities into a wider sphere of cultural standards. This issue is connected to the necessity of critical reflection upon concepts such as 'acculturation' and 'cultural influences'.

Finally, we would like to make some brief comments on the Bell-Beaker contexts. In a first stage (between c. 2200 and 2000 BC), Bell-Beakers appear in traditional Chalcolithic communities, where they are regarded as one kind of prestige good amongst others, for the purpose of enhancing the social status of some elites in southern Portugal. This stage, during which Bell-Beaker wares are imported and copied, corresponds to the end of the Chalcolithic period. In some areas, this process may persist into the beginning of the second millennium BC (Jorge 1990: 179–81).

In a second stage (first half of the second millennium BC), new Bell-Beaker elements, namely metallic artefacts, the so-called 'Beaker package', appear in the context of communities whose settlement strategies, patterns of social interaction and power-relationships testify to the development of the first small chiefdoms. Our view is that these chiefdoms must already be integrated within what is conventionally called the Bronze Age.

ESTREMADURA

In considering the cultural evolution of the Chalcolithic in Estremadura, it is imperative to point out the following aspects. First, we must stress the building of fortified settlements, namely those of the kind exemplified by Vila Nova de São Pedro, Zambujal and Leceia (Jorge 1990: 181–91).

They exhibit impressive walls, towers and bastions which were the product of long construction programmes. One can find many general parallels for such defensive architecture all over the Mediterranean world. Despite these formal resemblances and the originality of such structures at a local and regional level, however, we do not consider that it can be proved that these architectural types relate to foreign or local mediator groups concerned with the exchange of metal or other prestige goods. It is now well known that not only have no overtly 'imported' objects been found at these settlements, but that they also yield a high percentage of artefacts of indisputably local tradition (Jorge 1990: 181–91). Other elements such as vessels called 'copos' and 'idols with horns' can easily be inserted into the category of prestige goods, conceived after Mediterranean prototypes. The presence of such objects does not demand a 'colonial' or diffusionist explanation to any degree. Although they follow a rather generic Mediterranean pattern as in the case of defensive architecture, they also display several construction strategies symptomatic of the internal dynamics of each community. They seem to indicate local settlement formulae, which assimilate foreign archetypes which have been spread in the context of long-distance exchanges – an 'interaction sphere' – something in which Estremadura has always been premature. The Mediterranean 'family resemblance' that these fortifications exhibit should not take anyone by surprise. The south of Portugal is, in several ways, a Mediterranean part of the Peninsula. Consequently, it is not unusual to observe that some groups and elites should have adopted prestigious architectural defensive patterns in order to intensify their power 'display' by virtue of stronger supra-regional contacts. Some aspects are still unexplained. The reason why the populations of Estremadura surrounded themselves with walls and why settlements varied in size, complexity and duration is unclear. Generally speaking, Zambujal and Vila Nova de São Pedro can most probably be regarded as 'central places'. Nevertheless, the importance and function of these places can only be determined by characterizing the settlement system to which they belong. We must also emphasize the mediator role played by groups from Estremadura in connections between Mediterranean stimuli and local tradition.

The settlements in the landscape were camouflaged and located near watercourses halfway between the sea and the hinterland. Most of these were navigable, due to the effects of the Flandrian Transgression (Daveau 1980). Thus, both Zambujal and Vila Nova de São Pedro are remarkable examples of a premeditated settlement strategy which facilitated the exchange of goods between different ecosystems and cultural areas. The former, using the nearby Sizandro river, would in this way have a privileged access to the coast. The latter would have been strongly linked to the sea, having recourse to some tributaries of the Tejo river, which were then navigable up to a distance measurable as one and a half hours' travelling time from the settlement (Daveau 1980; Jorge 1990: 189).

Among the exchange goods referred to above, flint and copper stand out, copper being almost non-existent in Estremadura and rather abundant in Alentejo. This metal would have been used by the elites of Estremadura not only for their own consumption but also for trading at the coast for foreign raw materials, such as ivory from North Africa. Many other types of exchange between Estremadura and Alentejo could have been established, yet have left no archaeological trace.

On the other hand, the new social and economic structures were consolidated through the renewal of ideological patterns. These patterns express themselves through 'religious' symbols which can be found both in funerary and domestic contexts. Different votive objects systematically represent the so-called Mediterranean 'Mother-Goddess'. The 'recycling' capacity of ideological patterns is what gives Estremadura its special cultural personality within the scope of Chalcolithic communities along the Atlantic seaboard.

The third aspect concerning these communities that should be underlined is a strong cultural identity. This is strikingly manifested in the burial and domestic contexts of this area. In the settlements and tombs of Estremadura, artefacts exhibit a distinctive regional character. Once we accept that material culture (mainly that which has to do with day-to-day activities) generally expresses the cultural identity of the groups that produce it, we must come to the conclusion that Estremadura was a cultural reality clearly distinct from those of adjoining areas. In this way one can explain the difference between the inventory of settlements like those of the Setúbal peninsula (which are still part of the region of Estremadura) and Monte da Tumba (Jorge 1990: 190–1) (already located in Baixo Alentejo, but only a few kilometres distant from the ones in Setúbal). As far as artefacts are concerned, such differences between neighbouring areas that always maintained strong links during the Chalcolithic might be due to the fact that such culturally different, yet economically and socially, interdependent, communities needed to preserve their cultural autonomy at any cost. This hypothesis, which is probable within a framework of rather competitive social relations for securing certain raw materials, would justify its own research programme, in order to identify both the 'boundary' or 'boundaries' of the above-mentioned territories and the mechanisms which would have enabled the flow of information in both directions.

THE BEIRAS

In the province of Beira Baixa we can observe the persistence of a cultural pattern which may be connected to that of the Alto Alentejo and the southwest of the Peninsula generally. Some hill-top settlements, a number of which are fortified, such as Charneca de Fratel (Soares 1988), appear in association with reused megalithic tombs of complex architecture. Both the settlements and the tombs yield artefacts. Nevertheless, and despite some essentially southern characteristics of this area (such as the persistence of schematic rock-art at the Tejo 'complex'), we believe that one should look for distinguishing features in this region. The Beiras are an area of passage between the south and the north, by way of an internal route which lies away from the innovating centres of the Chalcolithic on the Estremadura coast.

The cultural reality of Beira Alta seems to us rather more diversified than we might suppose from the massive reuse of megalithic monuments. Thus, the material found in a passage grave like Moinhos de Vento (Senna-Martínez 1989), in the Alva basin, suggests the possible existence of Late Neolithic/Chalcolithic groups which would have been strongly acculturated by artefacts of southern origin. As far as artefacts are concerned, such influence is not, however, specific to Moinhos de Vento. It is also present to a certain degree in every known burial assemblage (namely in reused long passage graves), mainly in the typology of lithic artefacts and certain personal ornaments. Nevertheless, the regional and particular character of this area is yet to be determined.

From this brief analysis of the cultural evolution in the Beiras, one can conclude that no sedentary settlements have been identified which could be linked, in terms of cultural aspects, to the megalithic monuments mentioned above. This stands in contrast to the situation observed in south Portugal. We nevertheless believe that such a void is due to information gaps rather than to insubstantial settlement, following the tradition of the Middle–Late Neolithic.

We firmly consider the second half of the third millennium BC in Beira Alta to be a period of high conservatism with regard to the survival of ancient monumental tombs, though it is simultaneously open to the assimilation of southern artefact patterns in certain areas. However, contrary to the opinion of some archaeologists, this openness is not connected with the rise of elites whose power was based upon metal control, but should be related to the settlement of certain groups in areas propitious for agriculture and animal husbandry. The emergence of communities favoured by an economy based on agriculture and pasture must then be linked to long-distance interaction, which is ultimately responsible for the presence of supra-regional burial assemblages of prestige goods (Jorge 1990: 196–7).

THE NORTH

During the second half of the third millennium BC traditional megalithic monuments, namely passage graves, would have been reused. In the Aboboreira plateau, for instance, the passage grave known as Chã de Parada 1 might have been utilized at least until the end of the third and the beginning of the second millennia BC, when Beaker pottery of Maritime style appears in the tomb (Jorge and Bettencourt 1988). In Trás-os-Montes (Sabrosa), the presence of Beaker pottery in the Madorras 1 passage grave has provided evidence for reuse over time, and for the conclusion that the final stage of burial activities in this monument must have occurred at the beginning of the second millennium BC (Gonçalves and Cruz 1994).

In this same period, the north of Portugal might have witnessed the construction of large undifferentiated passage graves in lower-lying areas. Santa Marta (Pemafiel), Barrosa (Caminha), São Romão do Neiva and Eireira (Viana do Castelo) (Silva 1988; Jorge 1990: 197–8) are examples of this. The last three monuments are located on the coastal plain, a few metres above sea level. The undifferentiated monuments, generally scattered about the landscape, contrast with the clustered character of the cemetery observed in the highlands of the interior. They might be symbolic markers of fertile land. Unfortunately, we still have no evidence for the settlements which correspond to these tombs, for later intense agricultural activities must have destroyed them.

During this second half of the third millennium, we can apparently observe a significant demographic growth of communities in the Late Neolithic tradition, which continued to lead a sedentary life. These settlements are located either on slopes facing valleys of major rivers, or on the coastal plain. Some even mark the first agricultural occupation of certain territories (Jorge 1990: 200–1).

In the region of Chaves/Vila Pouca de Aguiar, settlements like Pastoria, S. Lourenço or Castelo de Aguiar (Jorge 1990: 200–1) exhibit more concentrated and limited types of spatial organization, and use promontories with natural defensive conditions for their setting. Their houses were still quite fragile, being defined by post-holes with clay revetment. On the other hand, these settlements are closer to the valleys of Tâmega and Corgo than earlier ones. These valleys might have played an important role as channels of communication between different regions.

We have little evidence concerning the economy of these settlements, particularly regarding the eventual agricultural intensification or the secondary use of domestic animals. In Pastoria and Castelo de Aguiar – as in the fortified settlement of Castelo Velho, Vila Nova de Foz Côa (Jorge 1993) – we can observe traces of weaving in the late third and early second millennia. A stone structure for the storage of wheat was found in Castelo de Aguiar. In the rock-shelter known as Buraco da Pala (Mirandela) (Sanches 1987) several occupation levels of the late third millennium have been identified, thus uncovering storage-pits and storage pots containing large quantities of wheat, broad beans and acorn seeds.

During this period, inter-communal contacts are quite clear, if we consider the presence of raw materials which are either rare or non-existent in a certain area, such as variscite (callaïs – to make beads), copper (to make awls, chisels, knives, daggers, etc.) or flint (for arrow-heads etc.). Besides, from the middle of the third millennium BC up to the beginning of the second, mainly in the region of Chaves, these communities seem clearly receptive to artefactual prototypes of southern origin. Domestic pottery is predominantly decorated: the basic motifs (alternating metopes) have clear affinities with those of the Chalcolithic vases of Estremadura. Even vessels decorated with the classic eye-motif symbol have been found at the settlements of Vinha da Soutilha, S. Lourenço (Chaves) and Buraco da Pala (Mirandela) (Jorge 1990: 204). Yet vessels decorated with techniques and motifs of a more remote origin (Southern Iberia Middle Neolithic) persist, in even smaller quantities.

In general we can distinguish a tighter network of inter-regional contacts involving the area of Chaves/Vila Pouca de Aguiar, and probably the north of Portugal as a whole. This particular feature is connected with others, such as demographic growth, the spread to areas with good means of natural interaction, the investment in agriculture and husbandry, and the building of settlements with natural (and sometimes artificial) defences. The fortified settlement of Castelo Velho, in the High Douro region (Vila Nova de Foz Côa), whose study has been in progress since 1989, is particularly important in relation to this issue. It comprises two lines of stone walls, built in the Chalcolithic period, and several storage and weaving structures around a central tower, located at the head of the inner enclosure. Meanwhile, the emergence of more stable elites, based on the control of rare raw materials and the use of prestige objects (namely of southern 'style'), may also have occurred.

Finally, Beaker pottery of both the Maritime style and its local variants appear in the basin of the High Tâmega at the end of the third/beginning of the second millennia BC (Jorge 1990: 205–6).

We shall now conclude this analysis of northern Portugal with some general accounts concerning the second half of the third millennium BC. The first aspect we would like to stress has to do with the proliferation of sedentary settlements. Pottery found in the context of these settlements reveals a stylistic setting which goes back at least to the Late Neolithic. Against this background emerge different realities which can be reduced to two distinctive types. While more apparently archaic domestic tools persist in some areas, in other areas, such as Chaves/Vila Pouca de Aguiar) we can find pottery profusely decorated, with metopes, which indicates affinities with the southern Chalcolithic styles. A general statement such as this must not allow us to overlook the fact that there is an increasing regional settlement diversity regarding topographical location, size, defensive strategies, probable production levels, etc.

The second aspect, which constitutes one of the major problems in late prehistoric research concerning the north of Portugal, is the apparent geographical and artefactual dichotomy between settlements and tombs. There is, thus, a general lack of information about the burial procedures of the communities living at these settlements. Nor do we have any information about the way of life of the megalith builders, as was the case in the preceding period.

The third aspect concerns the fact that tombs and, to a certain extent, settlements were not the only symbolic landmarks in the second half of the third millennium BC. Painted rock-shelters and open-air sites with engraved rocks, both of a more or less schematic character, and places with anthropomorphic *stelae* or statue-menhirs, helped create a new 'cultural landscape'. An outstanding example of an open-air sanctuary with numerous anthropomorphic *stelae* is that of Cabeço da Mina located on a hill inside the Vilariça valley (Vila Flor). Once again we are confronted with motifs and styles which show clear affinities to central and southern areas of the Iberian Peninsula.

Finally, the fourth aspect concerns the decorative pattern of Beaker pottery. At first assimilated as an exceptional type of decoration (Maritime complex – linear variant and/or local styles) it was later absorbed as a common decorative element of domestic vessels.

CONCLUSIONS

The transition from the Late Neolithic to the Chalcolithic in Portugal occurred during the second half of the third millennium BC (uncalibrated dates). It is in this period that the following archaeological trends can be observed. First, the reuse of megalithic tombs all over the country and, in some areas, the building of others according to evolved prototypes. This is an aspect which clearly distinguishes the north from the south because of the exclusive presence in the latter area of *tholoi* and rock-cut tombs whose layout is similar to that of the classical passage graves. Second, both the south and the north have hill-top settlements with natural defensive conditions. To these can be added others, particularly in the south, which have artificial defences, such as walls, bastions and towers. These begin to appear in the north as at the settlement of Castelo Velho (Freixo de Numão, Vila Nova de Foz Côa), but in small numbers.

Finally, copper artefacts tend to spread over the country. However, they occur in a wide range of economic and technical contexts, from sporadic discoveries at a particular site, to evidence for production activities for internal and external use at other sites: this explains the spread of copper mentioned. We do not find it misleading to consider all these communities to be Chalcolithic, including those which would obtain copper through exchange, or those which produced it. We justify this statement by observing that the presence of copper artefacts, irrespective of the quantity, may be linked to greater changes.

In broader terms we observe the systematic occupation of new territories during this period, the progressive sedentarism connected with intensification of agriculture and husbandry, the probable development of a social hierarchy and strengthening of the elites, which were possibly interdependent on a regional scale, and an increasing communal exchange of raw materials and prestige artefacts.

In fact, we know very little about this period. As with any transition process, it is a difficult task trying to characterize it. Quality monographs on crucial sites are scarce, and some sites are still being researched. Further, regional research projects are lacking. Entire areas of the country have only recently been approached in archaeological terms. As such, the account we have tried to present in this chapter might stimulate the development of research, not only by Portuguese researchers but also, and perhaps primarily, by fellow West European archaeologists, who systematically seem to ignore the up-to-date Portuguese bibliography on these matters.[2]

NOTES

1 In this chapter all C^{14} dates are uncalibrated. The text was translated from the Portuguese by Alexandra Abranches and revised by Paula Mota Santos.

2 We recommend Jorge (1990) for a development of the matters analysed in this chapter as well for a longer bibliography.

REFERENCES

Arnaud, J. M. (1982) 'O povoado calcolítico de Ferreira do Alentejo no contexto da bacia do Sado e do Sudoeste peninsular', *Arqueologia* 6: 48–64.

Daveau, S. (1980) 'Espaço e tempo. Evolução do ambiente geográfico de Portugal ao longo dos tempos pré-históricos', *Clio* 2: 13–37.

Gomes, R. V., Gomes, M. V. and Santos, M. F. (1983) 'O santuário exterior do Escoural. Sector NE (Montemor-o-Novo, Évora)', *Zephyrus* XXXVI: 287–307.

Gonçalves, A. A. H. B. and Cruz, D. (1994) 'Resultados dos trabalhos de escavação da Mamoa 1 das Madorras (S. Lourenço de Ribapinhão, Sabrosa)', *Actas do Seminário 'O Megalitismo no Centro de Portugal'*: 22–45, Viseu: Centro de Estudos Pré-históricos da Beira Alta.

Gonçalves, V. S. (1991) *Megalitismo e Metalurgia no Alto Algarve Oriental. Uma Aproximação Integrada*, Lisbon: INIC.

Jorge, S. O. (1990) 'Desenvolvimento da hierarquização social e da metalurgia', in J. Alarcão (ed.) *Nova História de Portugal, vol. I, Portugal. Das Origens à Romanização*: 163–212, Lisbon: Presença.

—— (1993) 'O povoado de Castelo Velho (Freixo de Numão, Vila Nova de Foz Côa) no contexto da Pré-história Recente do Norte de Portugal', *Actas do 1º Congresso de Arqueologia Peninsular I, Trabalhos de Antropologia e Etnologia* XXXIII (1–2): 179–216.

Jorge, S. O. and Jorge, V. O. (1990) 'Trois millénaires de vie préhistorique dans le Nord du Portugal', *Revista da Faculdade de Letras–História* III Serie, 7; 325–33.

Jorge, V. O. and Bettencourt, A. (1988) 'Sondagens arqueológicas na Mamoa 1 de Chã de Parada (Baião, 1987)', *Arqueologia* 17: 73–118.

Sanches, M. J. (1987) 'O Buraco da Pala, um abrigo pré-histórico no concelho de Mirandela (notícia preliminar das escavações de 1987)', *Arqueologia* 16: 58–77.

Senna-Martinez, J. C. (1989) 'Pré-história Recente da Bacia do Médio e Alto Mondego. Algumas contribuições para um modelo sociocultural', unpublished Ph.D. thesis, University of Lisbon.

Silva, C. T. da, Soares, J., Cardoso, J. L., Cruz, C. S. and Reis, C. S. (1986) 'Neolítico da Comporta: aspectos cronológicos (datas C14) e paleoambientais', *Arqueologia* 14: 59–82.

Silva, E. J. L. (1988) 'A Mamoa de Afife: breve síntese de 3 campanhas de escavação', *Actas do Colóquio de Arqueologia do Noroeste Peninsular, vol. I, Trabalhos de Antropologia e Etnologia* XXVIII (1–2): 127–36.

Soares, J. (1988) 'O povoado da Charneca de Fratel e o Neolítico Final – Calcolítico da região Ródão – Nisa – notícia preliminar', *Alto Tejo* 2: 3–6.

Soares, J. and Silva, C. T. da (1992) 'Para o conhecimento dos povoados do Megalitismo de Reguengos', *Setúbal Arqueológica* IX–X: 37–88.

Vilaça, R. (1984) 'Sobre uma placa de xisto do Concelho de Ponte-de-Sor', *Arqueologia* 9: 53–9.

CHAPTER EIGHT

THE DYNAMICS OF CHANGE IN NORTHWEST PORTUGAL DURING THE FIRST MILLENNIUM BC

MARIA MANUELA DOS REIS MARTINS

INTRODUCTION

Continuity and change are deeply rooted concepts in the evolutionary perspective of the physical and social world which lies at the heart of the European perception of the world, and which constitutes the conventionalism that is essential to the domestication of time (Fabian 1983; Shanks and Tilley 1987: 211). In spite of the unsuitability of the historical process to segmentation on the basis of technological, economic or social criteria, continuity and change are the operational concepts used in the construction of archaeological discourse, to the point of superseding the narrative and search for explanation.[1]

Assuming that all the social formations which comprise continuity and change (Tilley 1990: 24–5) embody an evolutionary dynamic, it is possible to use these concepts in cultural analysis if we define the criteria through which continuity and discontinuity can be read into the archaeological record. This is how we intend to use the empirical data available for the northwest of Portugal in the first millennium BC in the first part of this chapter. In the second part the criteria which underlie the traditional view of this period are examined, while the third proposes an alternative reading of the cultural dynamics for that region during the period concerned. Throughout this chapter a critical perspective has been adopted. In the first instance this is because of the scarcity of empirical data available for the region.[2] However, it is also because the rationalization of the processes of continuity and change is always limited by the relative and truncated character of the archaeological data, and because the phenomena which form the object of an analysis at a given moment in time[3] have been selected subjectively.

SPACE, TIME AND CULTURAL EVOLUTION: THE TRADITIONAL VIEW

Space

The geographical area analysed in this chapter corresponds broadly to the Portuguese province of Entre-Douro-e-Minho. To the south, it is bounded by the Douro river valley and to the north by the river Minho. To the east, the area is delimited by the natural boundary of the Serras of Padrela, Alvão and Marão, which separate it from Trás-os-Montes. This is an extensive natural area, well defined by geographers (Girão 1933; Birot 1950; Ribeiro 1963), where open valleys alternate with the residual relief of the great inland mountains of the Minho province. An extensive hydrographic network assures the region a plentiful supply of water resources. In addition, its granitic soils provide good potential for forests, grazing and agricultural exploitation. From the lithological point of view the granite–greywacke formations of the region are rich in gold and silver ores and cassiterite, all of which were intensively exploited in antiquity. The extensive hydrographic network, combined with a natural relief oriented northeast/southeast in the form of a huge amphitheatre, opens up the landscape to maritime influence, giving rise to an Atlantic climate.

This vast region was chosen as a subject of study because of the practical impossibility of satisfactorily defining smaller units within the Portuguese northwest.[4] While the synthetic studies of the evolution of this region during the first millennium BC stress its cultural homogeneity, as represented by an archaeological entity known by the name of *cultura castreja* (*castro* culture)[5] (Almeida 1983; Silva 1986; 1992; Fabião 1992), different rhythms of development and sub-regional cultural expressions in the course of this period can be detected. Future work will enable us to shed light on these matters.

Time and cultural evolution

The systematization of the cultural evolution of the first millennium BC has been constructed within a historical-cultural perspective,[6] which has supported the definition of the historical-archaeological entity known as 'the *castro* culture of the Iberian northwest' (*cultura castreja*). This rests upon the characteristic settlement type in this area (*castro* meaning fortified settlement) during the first millennium BC.

The *cultura castreja* was first defined by Bosch Gimpera (1921) in the context of the late European and Iberian Iron Age. This 'culture' has been the subject of chronological refinements and attempts at defining its material culture. Over a hundred years of effort have concentrated upon establishing a uniform culture and identifying a 'Celtic' influence in the cultural and ethnic make-up of the population of the region. There are two main phases in the systematization of the evolution of this 'culture': in the first, the Indo-European migrations have constituted the fundamental support for the establishment of an evolutionary chronology of the *castros* and explained the cultural evolution of the entire first millennium BC (Bosch Gimpera 1932, 1933, 1939, 1945; Correa 1924; López Cuevillas 1953, 1954; Blanco Freijeiro 1960; Cardoso 1962). Within this framework the emergence of fortified settlements was seen as the consequence of the instability caused by Celtic invasions, which were also seen as responsible for the introduction of iron into the region (Martínez Santa-Olalla 1946).

Later analyses provided a more sophisticated chronological model. These stressed some of the internal expressions of this 'culture', such as fortifications (Cardoso 1958; Hawkes 1971, 1984), and rested on premises such as Celtic and Hallstattic influences over the Iberian northwest, and events associated with Roman conquest. This model is implicit in all the chronological proposals put forward even during the 1970s and 1980s,[7] with new empirical data being added as they became available.

By contrast, few have recognized the distinctive characteristics of the Iron Age in northwest Iberia. Within a functionalist perspective Maluquer de Motes (1973) saw the *cultura castreja* as the result of a local cultural process, representing a particularly successful adaptation to the regional environment.[8] In assigning the origins of the *cultura castreja* to the Late Bronze Age, Maluquer de Motes understood the new settlement structure as a result of an internal cultural process (Maluquer de Motes 1975). However, in the end, his chronological proposal was established with reference to external cultural events, such as the fall of Tartessos, the Celtic expansion to the northwest (*c.* 500 BC) and the campaign of Decimus Junius Brutus (138–136 BC). This interpretation has become widely accepted (Acuña Castroviejo 1977: 249; Tranoy 1981: 77; Silva 1986).

The growth of research into the *castros* during the 1980s both in Portugal (Silva 1986, 1992; Martins 1990) and Galicia (Carballo Arceo 1986, 1990; Fernández Ochoa 1987; Maya 1988; Peña Santos 1992) helped to establish the internal chronology of the *castros*, as new radiocarbon dates became available, especially for the first half of the first millennium BC (Carballo Arceo and Fábregas Valcarce 1991). It was then generally accepted that the first fortified settlements emerged within the context of the flourishing Late Bronze Age 'industry' of the northwest (Calo Lourido and Sierra Rodríguez 1983). Nevertheless, the later cultural sequence was established on the basis of technological influences from central and southern Europe and through the presence of parallels and historical facts. Based as it was on the hegemony of the historical-cultural paradigm, this model privileged diffusion and migrations as the key to explaining processes of change. It ignored the economic and social contexts which could give significance to these processes and which would allow the dynamics of change within those communities over a long period of time to be understood.

THE DYNAMICS OF CHANGE:
AN ALTERNATIVE VIEW

In approaching the dynamics of change in northwest Portugal during the first millennium BC we need to abandon the current systematizations established for that period, based as they have been on the creation of a cultural universe characterized by long periods of practically timeless stability, interspersed with events which generate sudden changes. The alternative model entails the construction of a social time, less fragmented by historical events and artefacts, but close to the socio-economic dynamics of the communities of the region and to its distinctiveness in relation to contemporary European cultural contexts. As there are no available funerary data for the period under consideration, one has to rely only upon settlement evidence for generalizations about the dynamics of cultural change.[9] One begins by assuming that cultural systems are not isolated but rather are part of a broader system (Gledhill and Rowlands 1982: 146), where different effects are generated at different levels, local, regional and interregional.[10] In the long term and for such an extensive area as Entre-Douro-e-Minho, we can assume the presence of a reasonable degree of variability within the sub-regional cultural systems.

The beginning of the first millennium BC is characterized by the presence of Late Bronze Age communities (1250–700 BC). The archaeological record for this period is varied. It consists of a reasonable quantity of metal artefacts and some settlements first identified in the 1980s (Silva 1986; Jorge 1987; Martins 1990). The former show that the region was integrated into a broad network of Atlantic and Mediterranean relationships (Ruiz Gálvez Priego 1984, 1987; Coffyn 1985), which intensify from 1250 BC and continue down to the eighth and seventh centuries BC (Jorge 1988; 1990b: 48–52). The typology of these artefacts and their parallels elsewhere in Europe have provided the basis for the construction of an evolutionary chronology, and have enabled the routes of diffusion for both raw materials and artefacts to be identified. The settlement evidence has been used to generate hypotheses about patterns of settlement, economic exploitation of the land and the cultural diversity of these communities (Jorge 1990b: 48–58; Martins 1990). In spite of the scarcity of data, Susana O. Jorge (1990b: 48–57; 1990a) has proposed the division of the Late Bronze Age of northern Portugal into two phases, based on the typology of metal artefacts, settlement strategies and socio-economic structures. The first phase dates from 1250–1000/900 BC and the second from 900–700/600 BC.

In the first phase there would have been an increase in the production (particularly of heeled axes and jewellery in the Villena–Estremoz style) and circulation of bronze artefacts and jewellery. Settlement sites so far identified for this period are scarce, but they seem to favour mountain areas in what seems to be a Middle Bronze Age settlement tradition in this region.[11] They are open sites with perishable structures which comprise a large number of post-holes and ditches, some of which have been interpreted as silos. For the first phase of the Late Bronze Age (1250–1000/900 BC), Susana O. Jorge (1990a: 50) used the Serra da Aboboreira data to suggest that there would have existed a hierarchical settlement system, which could be associated with the economic intensification of a mixed economy. She used the distribution and characteristics of settlements and the discovery of a child burial in a small thirteenth/twelfth-century BC cemetery (Jorge 1980) associated with an open settlement (Jorge 1987) to support her hypothesis, and this suggested the emergence in this period of an inherited social status based upon land ownership. Land could thus be seen as the basis of formation and support of the new social elite. The iconography of the statue-menhirs is further understood as celebrating the leadership of individuals over the social group (Jorge and Jorge 1990). The socio-economic context of the northwest of Portugal during the first millennium BC also seems to fit into a broader intensification in the exploitation of agricultural and mineral resources. This process, together with the establishment of territorial hierarchies, the hereditary transmission of leadership and the mythification of regional leaders, is supposed to continue and spread during the second phase of the Late Bronze Age.

The second phase of the Late Bronze Age (1000–700/600 BC) reveals a scattered pattern of settlement which includes open and fortified sites occupying different geomorphological niches. The former follow the earlier pattern but open sites are now also settled on slopes and valleys. Fortified sites appear for the first time in the northwestern Late Bronze Age context on hill-tops or along the crests of the valleys. They are strategically located at dominant and easily defended points in the landscape with artificial defences being added.[12] Excavations of defended and open settlements dating to the early centuries of the first millennium BC suggest that all these sites were supported by a mixed largely self-sufficient economy. Evidence for agriculture in the archaeological record is provided by querns and macro-organic material, such as a range of seeds and pulses.[13] The paucity of evidence for wood in the pollen register of sites (Aira Rodríguez and Ramil Rego 1992) suggests that there was also a process of deforestation during this period (Aira Rodríguez et al. 1989). Metalwork increases in quantity and reveals a progressive diversification.[14] However, evidence for an intensification of exchange with the

Atlantic and Mediterranean regions is rare in settlement contexts (Jorge 1988), although moulds have been identified at some of them (Silva 1992: 68). Despite this, the settlement evidence is central to understanding economic intensification, the development of the manufacture of bronze artefacts and the resulting processes as a growth in social complexity and the integration of communities between 1000 and 700/600 BC.

In spite of the limited empirical evidence available, it is possible to identify a settlement hierarchy,[15] based upon an efficient control of resources and the circulation of raw materials and finished products. In fact, the development of trans-regional relations from the tenth to ninth centuries BC reflected in artefacts must have fuelled local and regional interaction, thus favouring an increase in economic and social complexity. This is characterized by a growing agricultural and craft specialization at settlements, evident in inter-site diversity and in the concentration of wealth at a minority of settlements, which suggest a vertical differentiation between communities. The development and enrichment of sites could have favoured the centralization of power by the formation of socio-political units at a regional level. However, the limited area of the known settlements, their degree of self-sufficiency, and the homogeneity of residential structures and artefacts does not suggest that emerging socio-economic complexity would have created intra-site status differentiation. Contexts of the early first millennium BC associated with the presumed change from inhumation to cremation ritual also suggest that social status during this period would have been dependent upon the possession and manipulation of prestige goods. These would have allowed regional elites to maintain a system of alliances and retain power, in tandem with the management of the main resources and economic activities.

The conditions which had allowed metallurgical production to thrive in northwest Portugal during the Late Bronze Age disappeared with the dismantling of the complex long-distance exchange network from the eighth to the seventh centuries BC. Bronze metalwork subsequently became rare. However, in contrast with other areas of Europe, it was not immediately superseded by iron artefacts.[16] From the seventh and sixth centuries BC onwards, there is a notable impoverishment in the range of portable artefacts in the archaeological record, which is reduced almost to domestic pottery. The prestige goods previously present in the region now comprise only jewellery and rare ornaments.[17] Imported artefacts are rarer and geographically circumscribed, contradicting the hypothesis that the reorientation of power would have relied upon contact with the Mediterranean. While certain artefacts, techniques, ideas and tastes were introduced into the Iberian northwest from the Mediterranean and may have been used to signify differing social status at regional level, they also signal reduced mobility. Even considering that local workshops producing bronzes survived through contacts with the area of Tartessos in southern Iberia, suggested by the oriental character of some of the jewellery,[18] the shrinkage of the exchange networks from the seventh to sixth centuries BC seems to have caused the disappearance of the socio-economic systems established in the Late Bronze Age. This process of change could be linked to the collapse of power centres and regional elites which had relied upon the control of exchange networks and the manipulation of prestige goods (Jorge 1990b; Martins 1990), a process that could have been responsible for the abandonment of some settlements more directly involved in the production and distribution of metal artefacts.

The disintegration of socio-political systems in the Late Bronze Age would be congruent with reduced interaction. This would have engendered the growth of self-sufficiency at the local level, at least initially, which would account for the impoverishment of the archaeological record of settlements around the middle of the first millennium BC. Changes evident in the material culture are also present at settlement level. Alterations to the settlement pattern comprise the generalized and irreversible abandonment of mountain settlements in favour of the intensification of valley occupation and the replacement of open with fortified settlements. Indeed, the latter become the only known kind of settlement in the second half of the first millennium BC. These developments seem to reflect the consolidation of the system of land exploitation first evident in the Late Bronze Age, when fortified sites were established in dominating positions on the crests of hills bordering the valleys.[19]

The emergence of fortified settlements at the beginning of the first millennium BC and their widespread diffusion from the seventh century BC onwards is an important factor in our understanding of the cultural dynamics of the region. The positioning of the fortified sites on hill-tops signals a radical change in the settlement pattern and a new preference for river valleys. This rupture seems to be linked with the intensification of the use of the resources of the river basins which offer dense forest cover[20] and heavier soils, with greater potential productivity than mountain soils (Bouhier 1979; Criado Boado 1989b). One can consider the emergence of this type of settlement in the Late Bronze Age to have resulted from demographic expansion and the increasing paucity of mountain soils.[21] It is also possible that the new settlements were sited in such a way as to ensure the visibility of the domestic space, so that they symbolized the human transformation of the landscape. Although there is as yet insufficient empirical data, one can establish a relationship between the emergence of defended settlement sites in the Late Bronze Age, the consolidation of socio-economic hierarchies of communities and the need to make domestic space visible. In fact, there is nothing to suggest that the fortifications were constructed for defensive needs. The appearance of fortified settlements from the tenth/ninth centuries BC onwards could represent the emergence of a new ideology linked to the appropriation and intensive exploitation of land. The process of territorialization of communities could then be reflected in the occupation of pre-eminent sites, in which the construction of fortifications gave greater visibility to the domestic space. This suggests that while the land continued to be an economic space, it ceased to be seen as merely the object of labour and became a means of ensuring it.

In the context of the socio-economic change established after the collapse of long-distance exchange networks in the eighth and seventh centuries BC, the spread of fortified settlements and the systematic occupation of valleys are the most important structural features of the new cultural organization. They generated economic, social and ideological dynamics which are significant for our understanding of change in north-west Portugal up to the end of the first millennium BC. The territorialization of these communities failed to guarantee the retention of land through time, requiring the inheritance of economic and social space and the institutionalization of social solidarities within and between communities at the local and regional levels. Only then could they guarantee the restricted access to resources necessary to social reproduction. The disintegration of the Late Bronze Age socio-political system, the greater self-sufficiency of the communities and the greater value that would have been attached to the land could have reinforced this process from the seventh/sixth centuries BC onwards. Nevertheless, self-sufficiency could have become critical as the occupation of the valleys intensified. Moreover, land could have become a vital resource, the main system of value and the basis of support of the new regional elites.

Stronger economic and social interaction must have been established between the communities which systematically settled and occupied the river valleys. As a result of this, economic boundaries, requiring a rigorous definition of resource areas and social links, must have been drawn. These could have been established through kinship systems, marriage alliances and ideology, reflected in the self-image of the communities and in territorial entities linked to socio-economic and symbolic spaces. While visibility remained a fundamental element in the structuring of the landscape throughout the first millennium BC, the early preoccupation with the strategic control of the landscape implicit in the earlier fortified sites seems to diminish and disappear completely in later centuries (Martins 1988b). The new settlements appearing during the second half of the first millennium BC become more closely linked to the maximization of the agricultural resources and increasingly choose locations closer to the lowlands of the valleys (Martins 1990: 211–16). This trend is presumably linked to a process of economic intensification bound up in the exploitation of cereals and increased interaction between the communities settled in northwestern Iberia. It seems to have favoured an increase in social complexity at the local and regional level, with a new phase of inter-site horizontal and vertical differentiation which is clearly visible in the archaeological record from the second century BC onwards.

The transformations undergone in the last two centuries of the first millennium BC have been interpreted as the effect of the expedition of Decimus Junius Brutus in the northwest (138–136 BC) (Silva 1986: 33). This event was traditionally understood to have opened up the region to products and people from southern Iberia, and to have put an end to the endemic warfare between regional chiefs mentioned in literary sources. A more credible explanation would be that the region underwent economic intensification during this period. This would have begun earlier, as reflected in the foundation of new settlements all along the valleys, and would have favoured the production of a surplus able to support a greater degree of regional interaction. Brutus' punitive expedition to the northwest could have reinforced regional solidarity and played an integrating role, reinforcing the power of certain sub-regional chiefdoms and stressing the differences in development between them. Although the material culture of the last two centuries BC seems to be very homogeneous, in reality this masks substantial variability, as is shown in the size and internal organization of settlements, the symbolic decoration of pottery and the degree of availability of metal artefacts.

The archaeological record of this period reveals the existence of a marked settlement hierarchy in which some sites become far more visible than others by virtue of substantial and complex systems of fortifications linked extensively to reorganized internal spaces. This persists up until the middle of the first century AD. Such changes imply the availability of labour for non-productive tasks which could only have taken place through stronger interaction between communities, some of which could have performed specialized economic functions, thus supporting a process of vertical and horizontal differentiation, which is not recognizable at intra-site level. At many settlements the need for construction is accompanied by considerable technological development. This is evident in pottery, bronze and iron metallurgy, and the greater circulation of raw materials and products at the regional and interregional level. There was also greater human mobility and a concentration of population in some *castros*, signalling the appearance of new central places.

This new phase of territorial expression, settlement visibility, interaction with southern Iberia and the affirmation of socio-political units (referred to as *populi* by Roman authors) took place from the second century BC, and was, in fact, underwritten by economic and social developments which had taken place earlier.

WHAT CHANGE AND WHY DURING THE FIRST MILLENNIUM BC? SOME CONSIDERATIONS ABOUT CONCEPTS AND DATA

At the beginning of this chapter it was stated that the concepts of continuity and change are relative and depend upon the available evidence, or variables, that can be used to read the cultural processes. Two questions can thus be asked. What significant changes can be observed when considering long periods of time? What significance can be attributed to them? If we look at the archaeological record of the last millennium BC in northwest Portugal we can identify changes in artefact morphology (pottery, metalwork, jewellery). Overall, some of these changes are difficult to date either in archaeological time or in the social time of the communities which used them. In fact, changes can only be detected once they are present. The amount of time lost in trial and error, in the process of learning, or in the process of innovation and experimentation, which may give rise to new objects and socio-economic structures, will always remain unknown. But what value can be placed upon artefacts when dealing with the analysis of the dynamics of change? Considering that they do not always change in connection with economic, social or ideological transformations, their value can only be gauged by reference to other cultural aspects. The emphasis on other indicators, such as settlement patterns, mobility and the strategies of exploitation of territory, makes it clear that social changes occur at a different rhythm to that of portable artefacts. The former change more slowly, as they respond to the stabilization of the communities in space, the exploitation of the available resources, and ideological constraints.

What significance can then be extracted from the cultural dynamics of the first millennium BC in terms of the value of the concept of change? In the long term, changes in artefacts, exchange networks, settlement patterns, the elites and their systems of alliances can be detected. Nevertheless, underlying these phenomena, which could support the division of our archaeological time, a long continuity can also be stressed. It is related to the slow sedimentation of an agrarian and human landscape, resulting from socio-economic, ideological and symbolic structures, with long-term cultural effects. In fact, the role played by the protohistoric communities discussed in this chapter was crucial in creating a special social and economic network in the river basins of northwest Portugal.[22]

In this way one can conclude that any reading of continuity and change is always arbitrary, when it is based on contingent logics. This results from our inability to deal with the depth of different social times, and its multiple significance, through which communities construct their lives.

NOTES

1 As the evolution of societies is always understood through a succession of present times, questions and discourses are merely a reflection of the evolution of social theory (Shanks and Tilley 1987: 137–85).

2 Although the century-old tradition of the study of *castros* (fortified settlements) initiated by Martins Sarmento is still very influential, we have enough archaeological data to overcome the well-tried classic cultural-historical vision which has been used to construct the cultural evolution of the Iberian northwest in the first millennium BC and which still underlies recent regional syntheses (Silva 1986, 1992; Fabião 1992). However, this is not the case in Jorge's approach to the problems underlying the Late Bronze Age of the region (Jorge 1990b: 48–58, 1990a).

3 The assessment of any cultural reality in terms of its cultural dynamics is always theoretically limited. I agree with the growing criticism of the objectivity of archaeological interpretation being put forward by post-processual archaeologists (Shanks and Tilley 1992).

4 Some of the studies carried out in the 1980s concerned the river basins of some of the large valleys in the region, such as the Cávado (Martins 1990), the Lima (Almeida 1990) and Minho (Marques 1987: 77–120). The evidence is too uneven to allow comparisons to be drawn between the different case studies.

5 The suggested borders for this culture go beyond the Portuguese province of Entre-Douro-e-Minho (López Cuevillas 1953; Esparza Arroyo 1983).

6 As was the case for the whole of Europe (Champion and Megaw 1985), the chronology of the first millennium BC was built upon a historical framework, with reference to literary sources and by adopting an ethnic and regionalist perspective. This view has only recently been questioned (Pereira Menaut 1992).

7 With the exception of the model proposed by Almeida (1983), which seeks to develop a model based on the internal development of the culture.

8 The stress on the adaptive aspects underlying the long duration of the fortified settlements is found in the works of Martins (1990), Carballo Arceo (1990) and, in an original form, in Criado Boado (1989a, 1989b).

9 The absence of funerary data makes this approach questionable in contrast with the rest of central and western Europe where the interpretation of change has relied largely on such data (Haselgrove 1982; Wells 1985, 1988, 1990; Champion *et al.* 1984; Champion and Megaw 1985; Collis 1989; Cunliffe 1988).

10 This model has been used by Brun (1987) and Wells (1985, 1988).

11 Currently, there is only reference to settlements of this period excavated in the Serra da Aboboreira (Baião), where the site at Bouça do Frade has provided the earliest radiocarbon date known (1500 BP) (Jorge 1987).

12 Data provided by excavations show polymorphic defences in Late Bronze Age settlements, which include earth walls and ditches (S. Julião, Vila Verde) (Martins 1988b), stone walls (Coto da Pena, Caminha) (Silva 1986) and wooden walls (Barbudo, Vila Verde) (Martins 1989).

13 Species identified so far include: *Panicum millaceum L., Setaria italica L., Secale cereale L., Hordeum vulgare L., Triticum compactum Host., Triticum aestivum*

L. S. I., *Triticum parvicorum K.*, *Triticum dicoccum S.*, *Vicia faba L. var. minor*, *Vicia faba L. celtica mana*, *Pisum sativum I.* (Silva 1986; Silva 1988; Aira Rodríguez and Ramil Rego 1992).

14 Characteristically, heeled and socketed axes, socketed arrowheads, daggers, everyday items such as sickels, knives, chisels and cauldrons, while jewellery is represented by bracelets and spirals.

15 For Serra da Aboboreira this hierarchy seems to be already present in the previous phase (Jorge 1990a: 47).

16 In fact it is impossible to speak of the existence of a true iron metallurgy in northwest Portugal before the last two centuries BC, the period during which iron artefacts begin to be produced in most settlements (Silva 1986; Martins 1990).

17 In particular, the bell-shaped and ankle pendants found in some of the settlements and dating to between the seventh and sixth centuries BC.

18 Oriental tastes are evident in the technical, morphological and thematic characteristics of the Baião hoard, and in the auriculated necklace of Malhada, Vila Real (Silva 1992: 76).

19 In spite of the small number of excavations it seems that the majority of these settlements were occupied throughout the first millennium BC (Silva 1986; Martins 1990; Bettencourt 1993).

20 The pollen evidence for the middle Cávado registers significant percentages of tree pollen in the lowlands, predominantly *Quercus* and *Castanea* (Aira Rodríguez and Ramil Rego 1992).

21 Soil erosion on the hill-tops has been the object of work in Galicia (Díaz-Fierros *et al.* 1988).

22 The complexity of the agrarian system of northwest Iberia was studied in depth by Bouhier (1979). Criado Boado (1989a, 1989b) has undertaken interesting reflections about the different historical moments in the development of this particular agrarian landscape.

REFERENCES

Acuña Castroviejo, F. (1977) 'Panorama de la Cultura castrexa en el NO de la Península Ibérica', *Bracara Augusta* 31: 235–53, Braga: Câmara Municipal de Braga.

Aira Rodríguez, M. J. and Ramil Rego, P. (1992) 'Datos paleobotánicos del Norte de Portugal (Baixo Minho). Estudio polínico y palaecarpológico', *Lagascalia* 18, 1.

Aira Rodríguez, M. J., Sáa, P. and Taboada, T. (1989) *Estudios palaebotánicos y edafológicos en yacimientos arqueológicos de Galicia*, Arqueoloxia/Investigación 4, Santiago de Compostela: Xunta de Galicia.

Almeida, C. A. B. (1990) *Proto-História e romanização da bacia inferior do Lima*, Viana do Castelo: Centro de Estudos Regionais (Estudes Regionais 7/8).

Almeida, C. A. F. (1983) 'Cultura castreja. Evolução e problemática', *Arqueologia* 8: 70–4, Porto: GEAP.

Bettencourt, A. (1993) 'A transição Bronze Final/Ferro Inicial no povoado de S. Julião–Vila Verde: Algumas considerações', *Actas do I Congresso Peninsular de Arqueologia, TAE* 34, 3–4: 167–90, Porto: SPAE.

Birot, P. (1950) *Portugal*, Lisbon: Horizonte.

Blanco Freijeiro, A. (1960) 'La cultura castreña', *I Symposium de Prehistoria Peninsular*: 179–95, Pamplona.

Bosch Gimpera, P. (1921) 'Los Celtas y la civilizacion céltica en la Península Ibérica', *Boletín de la Sociedad Española de Excursiones* 29: 248–300.

—— (1932) *Etnologia de la Península Ibérica*, Barcelona: Alpha.

—— (1933) 'Los Celtas en Portugal e sus camiños', *Homenagem a Martins Sarmento*: 54–72, Guimarães: Sociedade Martins Sarmento.

—— (1945) *El poblamiento antiguo y la formación de los pueblos de España*, México D.F.: INAM.

Bouhier, A. (1979) *La Galice. Essai géographique d'analyse et d'interpretation d'un vieux complexe agraire*, Poitiers: Université de Poitiers.

Brun, P. (1987) *Princeps et princesses de la celtique. Le Premier Age du Fer (850–450 av. J.-C)*, Paris: Errance.

Calo Lourido, F. and Sierra Rodríguez, X. C. (1983) 'As orixenes do castrexo no Bronce Final', *Estudios de Cultura Castrexa e de Historia Antigua de Galicia*: 19–85, Santiago de Compostela: Xunta de Galicia.

Carballo Arceo, X. (1986) *Povoamento castrexo a romano da Terra de Trasdeza, Santiago*, Santiago de Compostela: Xunta de Galicia.

—— (1990) 'Los castros de la cuenca media del río Ulla y sus relaciones con el medio físico', *Trabajos de Prehistoria* 47: 161–99, Madrid: CSIC.

Carballo Arceo, X. and Fábregas Valcarce, R. (1991) 'Dataciones de Carbono 14 para castros del Noroeste Peninsular', *Archivo Español de Arqueología* 62: 244–64, Madrid: CSIC.

Cardoso, M. (1958) 'Missão inglesa de escavações num "castro" do norte de Portugal (Sabroso)', *Revista de Guimarães* 68, 3–4: 439–54, Guimaraès: Sociedade Martins Sarmento.

—— (1962) 'Alguns problemas da cultura dos castros no norte de Portugal', *XXVI Congresso Luso – Espanhol Para o Progresso das Ciencias 2, 5*: 391–423, Porto: Associação Portuguesa para o Progresso das Ciências.

Champion, T. C., Gamble, C., Shennan, S. and Whittle, A. (1984) *Prehistoric Europe*, London: Academic Press.

Champion, T. C. and Megaw, J. V. S. (1985) 'Introduction: approaches to the study of Iron Age settlement and society', in T. C. Champion and J. V. S. Megaw (eds) *Settlement and Society. Aspects of West European Prehistory in the First Millennium BC*: 1–8, Leicester: Leicester University Press.

Coffyn, A. (1985) *Le Bronze Final Atlantique dans la Péninsule Ibérique*, Paris: Boccard.

Collis, J. (1989) *La Edad del Hierro en Europa*, Barcelona: Labor.

Corrêa, A. A. M. (1924) 'A cultura dos castros. Sua origem e sua significacão etnológica', in *Os Povos Primitivos da Lusitânia*, Porto: A. Figueirinhas.

Criado Boado, F. (1989a) 'Arqueología del Paisaje y Espacio Megalítico en Galicia', *Arqueología Espacial* 12: 61–117, Teruel: Colegio Universitario.

—— (1989b) 'Asentamiento megalítico y asentamiento castreño. Una propuesta de síntesis', *Gallaecia* 11: 109–37.

Cunliffe, B. (1988) *Greeks, Romans and Barbarians. Spheres of Interaction*, London: Batsford.

Díaz-Fierros, F, Aira Rodríguez, M. J. and Criado Boado, F. (1988) 'Palaeoecological reconstruction of a forested area of Barbanza (Coruña, Spain).

A case study', in F. Salbitano (ed.) *Human influence on forest ecosystems development in Europe*: 31–45, Bologna: Pitagora Editrice.

Esparza Arroyo, A. (1983) 'Sobre el límite oriental de la cultura castreña', in *II Seminario de Arqueología del Noroeste peninsular*: 103–19, Madrid: CSIC.

Fabian, J. (1983) *Time and the Other: How Anthropology Makes its Object*, New York: Columbia University Press.

Fabião, C. (1992) 'O passado proto-histórico e romano', in J. Matoso (ed.) *História de Portugal* 1: 79–91, 190–200, Lisbon: Presença.

Fernández Ochoa, C. (1987) 'Los pueblos prerromanos de la fachada atlántica: la cultura castreña de los pueblos del N y NW en la Segunda Edad del Hierro', in *Historia General de España e América* 1–2: 357–81, Madrid: Ed. Rialp.

Girão, A. A. (1933) *Esboço duma carta regional de Portugal*, Coimbra: Imprenta da Universidade.

Gledhill, J. and Rowlands, M. (1982) 'Materialism and socio-economic process in multilinear evolution', in C. Renfrew and S. Shennan (eds) *Ranking, Resource and Exchange: Aspects of the Archaeology of Early European Society*: 144–9, Cambridge: Cambridge University Press.

Haselgrove, C. (1982) 'Wealth, prestige and power: the dynamics of Late Iron age political centralisation in south-east England', in C. Renfrew and S. Shennan (eds) *Ranking, Resource and Exchange: aspects of the Archaeology of Early European Society*: 79–88, Cambridge: Cambridge University Press.

Hawkes C. (1971) 'North-western castros: excavation, archaeology and history', *II Congresso Nacional de Arqueologia*: 283–6, Coimbra.

—— (1984) 'The castro culture of the peninsular north-west: fact and inference', in T. F. Blagg, R. F. Jones and S. J. Keay (eds) *Papers in Iberian Archaeology*: 187–93, British Archaeological Reports International Series S. 193, Oxford: British Archaeological Reports.

Jorge, S. O. (1980) 'A estação arqueológica do Tapado da Caldeira, Baião', *Portugália*, NS, 1: 29–50, Porto: FLUP.

—— (1987) *O povoado da Bouça do Frade (Baião) no quadro do Bronze Final do Norte de Portugal*, Monografias Arqueológicas 2, Porto: GEAP.

—— (1988) 'Reflexões sobre a Pré-História Recente do Norte de Portugal, Actas do Colóquio de Arqueologia do Noroeste Peninsular', *Trabalhos de Antropologia e Etnologia* 28 (1–2): 85–112, Porto: FLUP.

—— (1990a) 'Pré-história, IV. Desenvolvimento da hierarquização social e da metalurgia', in J. Alarcão (ed.) *Nova História de Portugal* I: 163–251, Lisbon: Presença.

—— (1990b) 'Reflections on northern Portugal's late prehistory', *Arqueologia Hoje, I Etno-Arqueologia*: 38–67, Faro: Universidade do Algarve.

Jorge, V. O. and Jorge, S. O. (1990) 'Statues-menhirs et stèles du Nord du Portugal', *Revista da Faculdade de Letras–História* II: 299–313.

López Cuevillas, F. (1953) *La civilización céltica en Galicia*, Santiago de Compostela: Porto y Cia Editores.

Maluquer de Motes, J. (1973) 'La originalidad de la cultura castreña', *Trabalhos de Antropologia e Etnologia* 22, 3: 335–42, Porto: SPAE.

—— (1975) 'La cultura castreña de la Edad del Hierro', *I Jornadas de Metodología Aplicada a las Ciencias Históricas* 1: 269–84: Madrid: Dirección General de Bellas Artes y Archivos.

Marques, J. A. M. (1987) 'Assentamentos castrejos do Concelho de Monção', *Revista de Ciências Históricas* 2: 77–120, Porto: Universidade Portucalense.

Martins, M. (1988a) *A citânia de S. Julião, Vila Verde*, Braga: Cadernos de Arqueologia – Monografias 2, Braga: VAUM.

—— (1988b) *O povoado fortificado do Lago, Amares*, Braga: Cadernos de Arqueologia – Monografias 1, Braga: VAUM.

—— (1989) *O castro do Barbudo, Vila Verde. Resultados das campanhas realizadas entre 1983 e 1985*, Braga: Cadernos de Arqueologia – Monografias 3, Braga: VAUM.

—— (1990) *O povoamento proto-histórico e a romanização da bacia do curso médio do Cávado*, Braga: Cadernos de Arqueologia – Monografias 5, Braga: VAUM.

Maya, J. L. (1988) *La cultura material de los castros asturianos*, Estudios de la Antigüedad 4/5, Barcelona: Universidad Autònoma.

Peña Santos, A. de la (1992) 'El primer milenio a.c. en el área gallega: génesis y desarrollo del mundo castreño a la luz de la arqueologia', *Complutum* 2–3: 372–94, Madrid: Universidad Complutense.

Pereira Menault, G. (1992) 'Aproximación crítica al estudio de etnogénesis: la experiencia de Gallaecia', *Complutum* 2–3: 35–44.

Ribeiro, O. (1963) *Portugal, o Mediterrâneo e o Atlântico*, Lisbon: Sá da Costa.

Ruiz-Gálvez Priego, M. L. (1984) *La Península Ibérica y sus relaciones con el círculo cultural atlántico*, Madrid: Universidad Complutense.

—— (1987) 'Bronce Atlántico y cultura del Bronce Atlántico en la Península Ibérica', *Trabajos de Prehistoria* 44: 251–64, Madrid: CSIC.

Santa-Olalla, M. (1946) *Esquema Paletnológico de la Península Hispánica*, Madrid: Publicaciones del Seminario de Historia Primitiva del Hombre.

Shanks, M. and Tilley, C. (1987) *Social Theory and Archaeology*, Oxford: Polity Press.

—— (1992) *Reconstructing Archaeology*, London: Routledge.

Silva, A. C. F. (1986) *A cultura castreja no Noroeste Português*, Paços de Ferreira: Câmara Municipal de Paços de Ferreira.

—— (1992) 'Proto-História do Norte e Centro de Portugal', in A. C. F. da Silva and M. V. Gomes (eds) *Proto-história*: 33–100, Lisbon: Universidade Aberta.

Silva, A. R. P. (1988) 'A paleobotânica na Arqueologia portuguesa: resultados desde 1931 a 1987', in *Paleoecologia e Arqueologia*: 5–36, Vila Nova de Famalicão: Câmara Municipal de Famalicão.

Tilley, C. (1990) 'Constituint una arqueologia social: un projecte modernista', in J. Anfruns and E. Lobet (eds), *El canvi cultural a la prehistòria*: 17–44, Barcelona: Columna.

Tranoy, A. (1981) *La Galice romaine, recherches sur le nord-ouest de la péninsule ibérique dans l'antiquité*, Paris: Boccard.

Wells, P. S. (1985) 'Mediterranean trade and culture change in Early Iron Age central Europe', in T. C. Champion and J. V. S. Megaw (eds) *Settlement and Society. Aspects of West European Prehistory in the First Millennium BC*: 69–90, Leicester: Leicester University Press.

—— (1988) *Granjas, aldeas y ciudades. Comercio y orígenes del urbanismo en la protohistoria europea*, Barcelona: Labor.

—— (1990) 'Models del canvi cultural en la Protohistòria europea', in J. Anfruns and E. Llobet (eds) *El Canvi cultural a la prehistòria*: 103–21, Barcelona: Columna.

CHAPTER NINE

MIGRATION REVISITED

Urnfields in Iberia

GONZALO RUIZ ZAPATERO

INTRODUCTION

The Spanish prehistorian Bosch Gimpera (1921, 1925, 1935) reconstructed the ethnic history of European influence in the Iberian Bronze
and Iron Ages. In order to provide a synthesis he tried to integrate the
archaeological, linguistic and historical data. The theoretical basis of his
studies could be summarized in the following way. On the basis of similarities between elements of material culture from Spain and central
Europe he recognized that ethnic movements did take place. These movements could be related to the names of tribes recorded in the written
sources and their routes were understood to be marked by archaeological sites and Indo-European place names. The three pillars of Bosch
Gimpera's interpretation, archaeology, linguistics and ancient history, were
mutually supportive. The starting point which was assumed, but not
demonstrated, was *large-scale* population movements with implicit reference to the barbarian invasions which destroyed the Roman Empire. In
this way, archaeological cultures, identified as 'tribes', were moving
throughout Europe akin to plates in the 'plate-tectonic' theory. Some
tribes were 'pushing' others and initiating an 'invasionist dynamic', which
was 'explained' by the populations' own mobility.

Bosch Gimpera (1942) established the existence of two waves of invasion in Spain. The first, *Urnenfelder* groups, arrived at around 900 BC
through the eastern Pyrenees and affected Catalunya. The second,
comprising Celtic tribes, arrived at around 650–600 BC through the
western Pyrenees and settled in the central Meseta. Later he established
a more complex picture with four migrations (Bosch Gimpera 1944). In
those days Bosch Gimpera's hypothesis was brilliant but imposed a rigid
diffusionist approach. As a consequence, the subsequent debate has largely
revolved around the number of waves which may have taken place.
Almagro (1952) put forward his theory of one great 'Celtic Invasion'

between 800 and 600 BC, which was frequently considered to have been a violent military conquest. It would seem that the 'Celts' were waiting for the right time to invade the Iberian Peninsula! So far, however, nobody has offered solid evidence for the existence of one or several 'waves'. The competing hypotheses of Bosch Gimpera and Almagro have been maintained in Spanish archaeology until quite recently. Before evaluating the Iberian data related to the Urnfields, however, it may be worthwhile to consider the present status of 'migration' in contemporary archaeology.

After the abuses of using migration as a way of explaining major ruptures in the archaeological record during the 1960s and 1970s, the 'New Archaeology' denied invasions and migrations and at the same time stressed local developments and continuities. This attitude, the absence of a real interest in studying population movements, can be explained by two factors. First, a reaction against traditional archaeology and, consequently, migration. Second, a realization of the difficulties inherent in studying population movements through archaeological evidence. The study of migration has been avoided because archaeologists lack the theory and methods which might allow migration to help explain cultural change (Anthony 1990). Instead of developing the necessary tools, therefore, archaeologists have avoided the subject. A new interest in migration developed in the course of the 1980s. The contributions of Neustupny (1982), Rouse (1986) and Ammerman and Cavalli-Sforza (1984) have focused upon population movements as a subject of potential archaeological study. Anthony (1990) and Kristiansen (1989) have addressed two important tasks: first, the need for a proper understanding of the structure of migrations and their behaviour as a process; second, to recognize the variability of population movements, which must be linked to demography and social and economic organization. A consideration of these variables makes it possible to establish the archaeological implications of the different types of population movements. I agree with Kristiansen (1989) when he says that the ability of archaeologists to identify and understand population movements in the archaeological record depends, first, on our ability to explain the social and economic framework within which they operated and, second, on our capacity to carry out comparative studies under historical and contextual control in order to specify the conditions under which they may occur. Only in this way will we be able to discover which types of population movement correspond to specific archaeological correlates.

URNFIELDS IN IBERIA

Returning to the Iberian Peninsula, it is important briefly to consider the situation towards the end of the Middle Bronze Age (c. 1300–1200 BC). The archaeological groups of this period in the northeast of the

Peninsula are still badly defined, although one can distinguish a series of new elements that have their origins on the northern side of the Pyrenees. These elements comprise: (a) ceramics with 'button' handles; (b) multi-legged drinking vessels; (c) edged axes; (d) certain triangular-shaped daggers with central ribbing and rivets (Figure 9.1A).

The ceramics with 'button' handles comprise a well-defined category which has its origin at the heart of the La Polada culture and extends from northern Italy, passing through southeastern France, down to the northeast of the Iberian Peninsula (Maluquer 1942; Barril and Ruiz Zapatero 1980; Maya 1986: Figure 1). Their presence in Pyrenean caves and dolmens proves that they pre-date the first Urnfields of the Late Bronze Age. The multi-legged drinking vessels originate in the French Pyrenees during the Early Bronze Age, although they become wide-spread during the Middle Bronze Age and the very beginning of the Late Bronze Age (Martin 1989). Their rarity in Catalunya suggests a route of penetration via the Segre valley (Maya 1983; Rovira 1988). The edged axes, with an area of distribution similar to that of the ceramics with 'button' handles, have evident parallels in southern France (Chardenoux and Courtois 1979) and a chronology also centred in the Middle Bronze Age (Barril 1982).

The fact that the prototypes of all these artefacts are to be found in southern France and that they are all found in close association with the caves and megaliths of the eastern Pyrenees suggests that they arrived by way of small population movements from southern France. This inter-pretation has some support in the palaeoanthropological evidence, since the European braquicephalic types are clearly distinguishable from Mediterranean types and linked to the archaeological types under discus-sion (Turbón 1981). The evidence seems to indicate that between the fourteenth and twelfth centuries BC, small population groups from the northern side of the Pyrenees infiltrated the passes of the High Segre, and possibly on a lesser scale, the passes of the eastern Pyrenees, and mixed with the established Chalcolithic population.

Clearly, not all the evidence for cultural influence from the northern side of the Pyrenees needs to be related to the arrival of new settlers. In fact some of it is to be explained by adoption and evolution within local populations and traditions. It also appears evident, however, that their appearance in the Peninsula is not to be explained simply through the contact between both sides of the Pyrenees. The new influ-ences are also reflected to a lesser degree in funerary ritual. Together with collective burials in megaliths, caves and niches typical of the Bronze Age (Rovira 1977), there is evidence for a disintegration of the old ritual of collective burial, and with it perhaps a change in reli-gious ideas, such as the individual inhumation 'cist' of the Mig-Arán in the Lleida Pyrenees or the burial in an individual grave also at Can Oliver 3 (Barcelona).

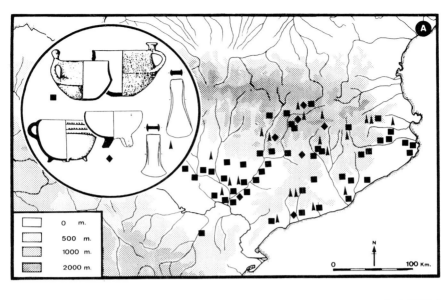

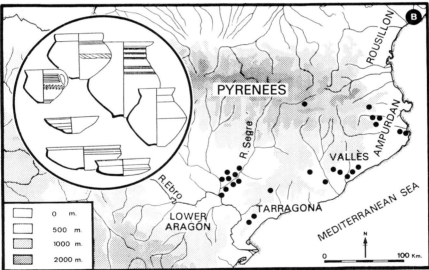

Figure 9.1   A: Archaeological types of the Middle Bronze Age from the region to the north of the Pyrenees: ■ Pottery with 'button' handles, ◆ multi-legged vessels and ▲ edged axes. B: Ancient Urnfield pottery profiles.

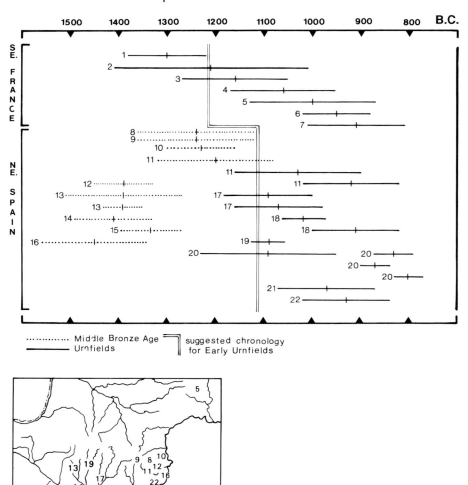

Figure 9.2 Radiocarbon dates from Middle Bronze Age and Urnfield sites in southeast France and northeast Iberia.

Sites: 1. Buffens Cave, 2. Gaougnas Cave, 3. Petite Caougno, 4. Noyer Cave, 5. Hasard Cave, 6. Igne Blanche, 7. Martrou Cave, 8. Cave 120, 9. Les Monges, 10. Fontanilles, 11. Les Pixarelles, 12. Pau IV, 13. Ciquilines IV, 14. Punta Farisa, 15. Riols I, 16. La Fonollera, 17. Carretelá, 18. Genó, 19. del Moro Cave, 20. Los Castellets de Mequinenza, 21. San Sadurní Cave, 22. Mas Castellar de Pontós (after Maya 1992, modified).

Towards the end of the Middle Bronze age two important facts are clear. First, there were ethnic movements from across the Pyrenees, although these could be small, and second, these occurred in the passes of the High Segre and eastern Pyrenees. This suggests that the relations between communities on either side of the Pyrenees were very close, with a fluidity of movement and therefore a good knowledge of the appropriate routes and passes. This situation helps us understand the arrival of the first groups of Urnfields, as they appear to follow identical patterns of penetration (Figure 9.1B).

At the start of the Late Bronze Age, there is a process of major cultural change in northeast Spain associated with the introduction of the Urnfields from southern France (Lenerz-de Wilde 1987; Ruiz Zapatero 1985; Pons and Maya 1988; Maya 1990; Rovira 1991). The archaeo-logical record reveals the introduction of a new funeral rite comprising the cremation of bodies and the burial of ashes in urns placed in holes in the ground, as well as new ceramic forms with groove decoration and new bronze objects. Some novelty is also seen in the methods of subsis-tence (Maya 1992: 285–7), types of dwelling and the organization of settlement (Belarde 1993). The radiocarbon dates associated with the first Urnfields (Carretelá, Lleida: 1090 ± 90 and 1070 ± 90; Genó, Lleida: 1020 ± 45 and 910 ± 90; Los Castellets, Zaragoza: 1090 ± 140; and Cueva del Moro de Olivena, Huesca: 1090 ± 35 BC), seem to suggest an initial chronology at around the end of the twelfth and beginning of the eleventh centuries BC (Maya 1992). This chronology was proposed by Almagro Gorbea (1977) on the basis of parallels with the ceramic typologies of southeast France. The radiocarbon dates of the first Iberian Urnfields are slightly later than the earliest dates of Urnfields in the Languedoc and Rousillon (e.g. Cuevas de Gaougnas: 1210 ± 200 and Petite Caougno: 1160 ± 100 BC), which suggests that there was a rapid expansion from

Table 9.1 Radiocarbon dates

Site	Type	Laboratory	Material	Date BC	Ref.
Carretelá	S	I-12,449	?	1090 ± 90	González et al. 1983
Carretelá	S	I-12,448	?	1070 ± 70	González et al. 1983
Genó	S	GRN–18061	charcoal	1020 ± 45	Maya 1992
Genó	S	GRN–18062	charcoal	910 ± 90	Maya 1992
Castellets	C	GRN–12116	charcoal	1090 ± 140	Royo 1991a, 1991b, 1992
Moro Cave	Ca	GRN–13997	charcoal	1090 ± 35	Baldellou Utrilla 1985

Key: S = settlement C = cemetery Ca = cave

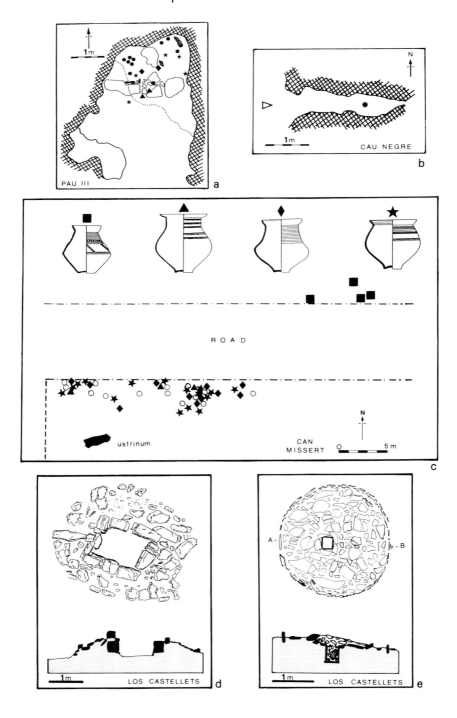

French territories to the northeast of the Iberian peninsula (Figs. 9.2, 9.3 and Table 9.1).

The Urnfields in Iberia are first detected principally through the funerary ritual of cremation and ceramics with rilled decoration. Both constitute the clearest indication of change at that time.

The funerary ritual of cremation

From the end of the second and the beginning of the first millennia BC, the appearance of the cremation ritual introduces a new factor, which combines with indigenous funerary traditions and the process of mutual influence to produce a blend of rituals before urn-cremation cemeteries become widespread throughout the Iberian northeast. Thus, in opposition to traditional opinions, which saw a homogenization in the cremation ritual as characterized by the Urnfields of northeast Spain, the panorama today appears to be more complex and to have developed more gradually (Maya 1993: 14). To begin with, one must say that the first Urnfields in the region do not suppose the implantation of extensive cemeteries comprising cremations in urns. The funerary complexity at the start of the Late Bronze Age comprises the survival of inhumation and hybrid rituals as well as new cremation burials.

The cremation ritual is found in the typical cemeteries with urns in holes, such as Can Missert in Tarrassa (Figure 9.3) and Bovila Roca in El Vallès and in the tumular cemeteries with cists like Torre Filella and Los Castellets de Mequinenza (Figure 9.3) on the plains of the Lower Segre. The old funerary traditions continue with some collective burials in megaliths and with collective and individual burials in caves. Lastly, the mixing of new and old ritual aspects is recognizable in cremations in urns placed within small caves, like Pau III and Cau Negre in Girona (Figure 9.3) and individual inhumations in tumulus-like structures with grave goods typical of Urnfields, such as those at Los Castellets de Mequinenza (Figure 9.3). It is true that these mixed rituals are scarce and somewhat exceptional, yet they can be understood in a period, or periods, of crisis and change. The evidence thus suggests that the new cremation ritual was adopted neither absolutely nor in a uniform manner. Its implantation must have been conditioned by various factors and have undergone modifications due to local pre-existing funerary practices (Rovira and Cura 1989). In the long run, however, cemeteries comprising cremations in urns placed in holes or within tumuli appeared widely. Typological parallels for urns from the earliest cemeteries with ceramics

Figure 9.3 Early Urnfield burial types: (a–b) Pau III and Cau Negre, cremation in cave; (c) Can Missert Urnfield cemetery, phases :1 ■, 2 ▲, 3 ◆ and 4 ★: (d) Los Castellets tumulus 14 with inhumation and (e) tumulus 4 with cremation.

from southeast France and a few radiocarbon dates (Los Castellets de Mequinenza) allow us to date the earliest cremations in the northeast of the Iberian Peninsula to around the ninth century BC.

Little is known about the first Urnfield cemeteries because the documented burials were uncovered in rare early excavations, which lacked scientific rigour and which lack analyses of the cremated bones. At the cemeteries of flat tombs in El Vallès there is no apparent ordering of the funeral space or regular spacing between burials. In contrast, the excavations of the mound cemeteries of the Segre–Cinca region reveal that there were significant groupings of mounds, perhaps denoting the lineage of those interred. The drinking-vessels deposited at the foot of many structures (Fernández et al. 1991) suggest that the funeral area was designed to be seen and visited. Discoveries at Can Missert (Figure 9.3) and other later cemeteries indicate that '*ustrina*' were commonly used for the cremation of the body although this does not preclude cremation in the grave itself in some cases. Perhaps one should suppose that open-air pyres were also used, without any type of preparation apart from the location of the pyre near the place of burial.

The rare burials dating to the oldest phase (Early Urnfields, c. 1100–900 BC) consists of only the urn, filled with ashes and bone remains, and covered with a coarsely carved stone lid. In one exceptional case a tomb at Can Missert also included three small drinking-vessels for offerings and a bronze pin. It is difficult to discern the status of the deceased from this kind of evidence (Maya 1993: 16). The general impression, adduced from the uniformity of grave goods, is that they reflect an egalitarian society with insufficient personal resources to express differences in rank in burial. Lastly, the small number of tombs in the Early Urnfield cemeteries, never more than fifteen or twenty, is a reliable archaeological indicator of the small size of the farming communities at the beginning of the Late Bronze Age. Thus, if the massive and sudden implantation of a new funerary ritual can be considered as evidence of the arrival of new peoples replacing indigenous rituals, then one cannot talk of great population displacements in the Late Bronze Age of northeast Iberia.

Grooved ceramics

The presence of Urnfields in northeast Iberia has been detected in large measure by the appearance of rilled ceramics. In principle, the equation that *Urnfields* = *grooved ceramics* appears valid. However, the proposition that *grooved ceramics* = *cremation ritual* does not now seem sustainable, given that the spread of cremation ritual and the expansion of ceramic types are two distinct phenomena. In other words, cremation is associated with rilled ceramics, but the typical grooved ceramics do not always appear to be tied to contexts of funerary cremation.

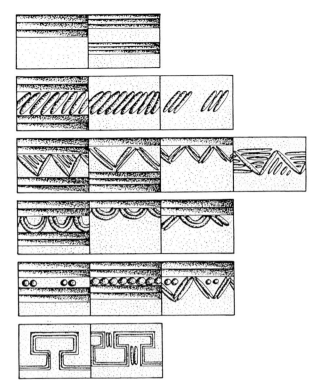

Figure 9.4   Decorative motives on Early Urnfield grooved ware (after Ruiz Zapatero 1985).

How and why did these ceramics spread? To answer this question, let us consider briefly the forms and decoration of grooved ceramics in northeast Iberia. One of the more distinctive aspects of ceramic vessels of the Early Urnfields of the Segre, Vallès and Empordá is the strong similarity of profiles. The most characteristic and common form is the biconic urn, and to a lesser extent, the urn with a cylindrical neck ('Sassenay type'). If one considers grooved decoration, the most important characteristic is the limited range of motifs. The most frequent are horizontal grooving and line-filled triangles. Other designs include zig-zags, geometric borders, short oblique lines, perforations, garlands (floral motifs) and geometric shapes. Regional distribution allows us to establish small nuances of difference in the most common designs and in their compositional syntax. But as in the case of ceramic forms, the clear conclusion that emerges from a comparative analysis is that of an impressive homogeneity, as much in the relative proportions of the simple designs as with the compound ones (see Figure 9.4).

The typological and ornamental similarities must be indications of common origins and swift development with close links between different groups. The existence of such similar decorative codes can only be explained by the adherence to a common ceramic tradition that has hardly undergone local development, despite spreading into different areas. This implies a relatively short time span, perhaps only a few generations of potters, as is otherwise verified by the radiocarbon date of the Early Urnfields. In conclusion, therefore, it appears that the homogeneity of the earliest grooved ceramics in the Iberian northeast must be explained as the result of small groups bearing a common pottery tradition which spread over various regions quite rapidly.

SETTLEMENT AND SUBSISTENCE

The Middle Bronze Age settlements in northeast Iberia are poorly known and we have only limited information about the Early Urnfield settlements. In spite of this, the general impression of the Early Urnfield settlement pattern is its diversity (Belarde 1993; Junyent 1989; Pons and Maya 1988). Some basic trends can be outlined. First, there are different types of settlement in each region, which are always small in size and usually have local precedents (Rovira and Santacana 1989). Thus in the Empordá one finds small clusters of huts with stone walls and partially cut into the bedrock (La Fonollera); in the Segre valley settlements comprise rectangular stone houses flanking a central street within some kind of urban layout (Genó); in El Vallès there are sunken huts; finally, in the mountainous areas of the Pyrenees, central and southern Catalunya, most of the known settlements are cave dwellings. Second, settlements are, in general, occupied on a more permanent basis than in the former period. In some ways they reflect the establishment of close links between Late Bronze Age communities and the territory, probably as a consequence of new subsistence strategies, particularly the growing importance of cereal agriculture. Finally, the number of Early Urnfield settlements is greater than in the Middle Bronze Age period. In some areas where we have wider evidence, such as El Vallès and the Lower Segre valley, the emergence of new settlements reflects a substantial growth in population.

There is little subsistence data to allow a comparison to be made between Middle Bronze Age and Early Urnfield strategies. In any event, the most significant fact is the growing importance of extensive cereal agriculture, and this can be deduced from the location of major settlement densities in areas with fertile soils, the presence of domestic lithic equipment for processing vegetables, and the existence of large vessels for grain storage or silos in such areas as central Catalunya.

Macrobotanical analysis in La Fonollera confirms the importance of wheat and barley with some pulses and provides an impression of what was probably the agricultural model in northeast Iberia. Traditionally, the beginning of the Late Bronze Age has been associated with the introduction of the plough, such new agricultural techniques as crop-rotation and manuring, and new animal species (Maluquer 1971). There is only direct archaeological evidence for the introduction of millet (Maya 1992: 291). However, the use of the plough seems a reasonable inference, given the iconographic evidence on Mailhacian pottery from southeast France (Mendoza 1989).

Livestock is dominated by sheep and goats, together with lesser numbers of cows and pigs. The analysis of faunal remains at La Fonollera provided the following percentages (NISP): 43 per cent ovicaprine, 29 per cent bovine, 10 per cent pig and the rest dog, horse and donkey. At Les Monges cave: 53 per cent ovicaprine, 21.5 per cent bovine and 23 per cent pig. At both sites deer hunting is also of some importance. It has been claimed that new animal species were introduced (Celtic pig and bovine *marinera*) but there is no definitive zooarchaeological evidence. At some sites hunting dogs and cattle protection have been identified. The horse is present at several sites for riding and animal traction. Although there is no conclusive evidence, it seems probable that the horse was probably introduced by Urnfield peoples in northeast Iberia, as it is not known from Middle Bronze Age contexts.

ANTHROPOLOGY AND LANGUAGE

The adoption of cremation as funerary ritual in the Late Bronze Age has meant that there are no opportunities for the anthropological study of the Urnfield population, and cremated bones have only recently begun to be studied. The population of the Bronze Age in northeast Iberia is basically composed of 'gracile Mediterranean' types (Turbón 1981). Only from the Middle Bronze Age is there evidence of central European brachicephalic types in the late megalithic period of north-central Catalunya, associated, as we have seen above, with elements from the north side of the Pyrenees. Recent anthropological analysis of the cemetery of Los Castellets in the Lower Segre indicates that all of the more than forty individuals studied are of gracile Mediterranean type and that they were of autochthonous origin (Lorenzo 1991). In my opinion this can be misleading, because if there were individuals from the north side of the Pyrenees at Los Castellets they must have come from southeast France and therefore they will also be of gracile Mediterranean type. In other words, populations from Languedoc and Catalunya belong to the same basic 'stock', with little evident difference between them. Even if one were to accept the arrival of new populations, they would have been of little importance in demographic terms, and certainly would not have changed the indigenous substratum.

In any event, there is insufficient information to allow the anthropological map of the Late Bronze Age to be drawn. The new analyses of human populations are a useful tool for reconstructing the past and some interesting suggestions have been made for the history of Iberian population (Bertranpetit and Cavalli-Sforza 1991; Calafell and Bertranpetit 1993). It may prove useful for identifying general trends over long periods of time, such as the emergence and establishment of the Basque population, but it will be of little value in documenting specific historical events (Bertranpetit and Cavalli-Sforza 1991: 64). The future developments of population genetics, archaeology and historical linguistics must collaborate in order to produce a better understanding of past historical populations.

We can only guess at the identity of the language (or languages) spoken by Urnfield people, although such linguists as Villar (1991) think that it may have been of Indo-European origin. The hydronimia related to '*Alteuropäisch*' could be an argument to support that point of view (Ruiz Zapatero 1985: 1001). But there a curious fact is apparent: northeast Iberia, a region with the strongest Urnfield influences and which is therefore linguistically Indo-European in the Late Bronze Age (de Hoz 1992), is an area of Iberian language from at least *c.* 500 BC. There are several possible explanations for this. In my opinion the 'failed Indo-Europeanization' hypothesis (Villar 1991: 465) is the most consistent (Ruiz Zapatero 1992). In this it is assumed that the Indo-European linguistic elements of the Urnfield people were in a minority, perhaps forming 'linguistic islands' and without power to transform the pre-Indo-European local languages of the region. This makes it easier to understand why northeast Iberia is inscribed within the Iberian linguistic domain from the Early Iron Age onwards.

CONCLUDING REMARKS: SCENARIOS FOR THE EMERGENCE OF URNFIELDS

In conclusion, the presence of Urnfields in Iberia is, to a great extent, a result of migration (Ruiz Zapatero 1983):

a New pottery styles and metallic objects are introduced on a large scale.
b A new funerary rite, cremation in an urn, is gradually adopted, although with complex mixed rituals and the maintenance of old inhumation rituals.
c These new cultural elements have a core origin in Languedoc, southeast France (Gasco 1988), where the same elements developed contemporaneously (Late Bronze Age II or Early Urnfield).
d Some stratigraphic sequences clearly reveal the intrusive but non-violent introduction of new elements, as well as a break with former cultural tradition, as is proved by the geographical distribution of Urnfield sites which imply the occupation of new areas.

On the whole it must be acknowledged that discontinuities are clear in pottery tradition, metallic objects and funerary ritual, but the indigenous component is strong in settlement and dwellings. Evidence concerning subsistence patterns is inconclusive and much more information is needed.

If the Urnfields in Iberia are a consequence of a migration process, we need to be precise in our definition of the nature of that migration. The traditional explanation of mass migrations through the Pyrenees does not accord with the archaeological data. The small Urnfield settlements and cemeteries in northeast Iberia suggest the movement of small groups. Although it is not possible to extrapolate demographic data from the archaeological record, one would perhaps be safe in estimating that there were a few thousand newcomers in an extensive region of more than 30,000 km². Probably the gradual adoption of cremation and the spread of rilled ware in northeast Iberia during the Late Bronze Age is the archaeological evidence of an elusive new social and economic organization. Even if we accept the coming of new populations in small proportions, the key factor for the spread of new ideas must be a new social organization, probably a gentilicial one.

In sum, plausible models for the explanation of Iberian Urnfields are the following:

a Leap-frog migration. Whole populations move from distant areas and settle in 'no man's land', ignoring indigenous societies, as in Bosch Gimpera's hypothesis.
b Gradual and slow acculturation. This represents the incorporation of cultural elements by contact between neighbours and without population movements. Some French prehistorians have defended this explanation for southeast France and, by extension, for northeast Iberia.
c Small-scale penetration from neighbouring areas. Limited movements of small groups moving short distances between neighbouring regions and with a different impact in their interaction with the population of the new areas. Thus, my proposal (Ruiz Zapatero 1985) explains the cultural affinities and the chronological '*décalage*' between Languedoc and Catalunya and the initially limited migrant component.

In my opinion it is the last model which best suits the archaeological evidence for Iberian Urnfields.

REFERENCES

Almagro, M. (1952) 'La invasión céltica en España'. In R. Menéndez Pidal (ed.) *Historia de España* I, II: 141–240, Madrid: Espasa-Calpe.
Almagro Gorbea, M. (1977) *El Bronce Final y el Periodo orientalizante en Extremadura*, Madrid: Biblioteca Praehistorica Hispana.

Ammerman, A. J. and Cavalli-Sforza, L. L. (1984). *The Neolithic transition and the genetics of populations in Europe*, Princeton: Princeton University Press.

Anthony, D. W. (1990) 'Migration in archaeology: The baby and the bathwater', *American Anthropologist* 92: 895–914.

Baldellou, V. and Utrilla, P. (1985) 'Nuevas dataciones de radiocarbono de la Prehistoria oscense', *Trabajos de Prehistoria* 42: 83–95.

Barril, M. (1982) 'Las hachas de rebordes del noreste peninsular', *4° Col.loqui Internacional d'Arqueologia de Puigcerdà*: 157–70.

Barril, M. and Ruiz Zapatero, G. (1980) 'Las cerámicas con asas de apéndice de botón del noreste de la Península Ibérica', *Trabajos de Prehistoria* 37: 181–221, Puigcerdà: Institut d'Estudis Ceretans.

Belarde, M. C. (1993) 'Arquitectura domèstica al Bronze Final i Primera Edat del Ferro a Catalunya: habitacions construïdes amb materials duradors: estat de la qüestió', *Pyrenae* 23: 115–40.

Bertranpetit, J. and Cavalli-Sforza, L. L. (1991) 'A genetic reconstruction of the history of the population of the Iberian Peninsula', *Annals of Human Genetics* 55: 51–67.

Bosch Gimpera, P. (1921) 'Los celtas y la civilización céltica en la Península Ibérica', *Boletín de la Sociedad Española de Excursiones* 29: 248–300.

—— (1925) 'Els Celtes i les cultures de la primera edat del Ferro a Catalunya', *Butlletí de l'Associació Catalana d'Antropologia, Etnología i Prehistoria* III: 207–14.

—— (1935) 'Los celtas y la cultura de las urnas en España', *Anuario del Cuerpo de Archiveros, Bibliotecarios y Arqueólogos* III: 1–41.

—— (1942) 'Two Celtic waves in Spain', *Proceedings of the British Academy* 26: 1–126.

—— (1944) *El poblamiento antiguo y la formación de los pueblos de España*, Mexico D.F.: INAM.

Calafell, F. and Bertranpetit, J. (1993) 'The genetic history of the Iberian Peninsula: a simulation', *Current Anthropology* 34, 5: 735–45.

Champion, T. (1992) 'Migration revived', *Journal of Danish Archaeology* 9: 214–18.

Chardenoux, M.-B. and Courtois, J.-C. (1979) *Les Haches dans la France Méridional*, Prähistorische Bronzefunde, IX, 11, Munich: C. H. Beck.

Fernández, M., Lafuente, A., López. J. B. and Plens, M. (1991) 'La necròpolis d'incineració de La Colomina 1 (Gerb, La Noguera). Metodologia i classificació de les estructures tumulars', *Limes* 1: 86–115.

Gasco, J. (1988) L'Âge du Bronze Final en Languedoc Occidental. Etat de la question. In P. Brun and C. Mordant (eds) *Le Groupe Rhin–Suisse–France Orientale et la notion de civilisation des Champs d'Urnes*, Nemours: Memoires du Musée de Préhistoire de l'Île de France, 465–79, Associacion pour la promotion de la Recherche Archéologique en l'Île de France.

González, J. R., Junyent, E., Maya, J. L. and Rodríguez, J. I. (1983) 'Carretelà (Aitona, Segrià)', *Arqueología 82*: 173, Madrid: Ministerio de Cultura.

Hoz, J. de (1992) 'The Celts of the Iberian Peninsula', *Zeitschrift für Keltische Philologie* 45: 1–37.

Junyent, E. (1989) 'La evolución del hábitat en la Catalunya occidental durante la Edad del Bronce, primera Edad del hierro y época ibérica'. In *Habitat et structures domestiques en Méditerranée occidentale durant la protohistoire, Colloque International (pré-actes), Arles-sur-Rhône*, 95–105, Arles-sur-Rhône.

Kristiansen, K. (1989) 'Prehistoric migrations – the case of the single grave and corded ware cultures', *Journal of Danish Archaeology* 8: 211–25.

Lenerz-de Wilde, L. (1987) 'Die Urnenfelderkultur auf der Iberischen Halbinsel', in *Die Urnenfelderkulturen Mitteleuropas* (Symposium Liblice), 387–96 Praha.

Lorenzo, J. I. (1991) 'Paleoantropología de la necrópolis del Bronce Final-Campos de Urnas de Los Castellets II (Mequinenza, Zaragoza)', *Arqueología Aragonesa* 1988–9: 547–50.

Maluquer, J. (1942) 'La cerámica con asas de apéndice de botón y el final de la cultura megalítica del noreste de la Península', *Ampurias* IV: 171–88.

—— (1971) 'Late Bronze and Early Iron in the Valley of the Ebro'. In *The European Community in Late Prehistory. Studies in honour of C.F.C. Hawkes*: 107–20, London.

Martin, J. M. (1989) *Les Vases polypodes de l'Age du Bronze dans le sud-ouest de la France*, Archives d'Ecologie Préhistorique, Toulouse: Ecole des Hautes Etudes en Sciences Sociales.

Maya, J. L. (1983) 'Nuevos vasos polípodos pirenaicos en Cataluña', *Trabajos de Prehistoria* 40: 59–84.

—— (1986) 'Cerámicas excisas y de boquique en el nordeste peninsular'. In *6° Colloqui Internacional d'Arqueologia de Puigcerdà*: 103–15 Puigcerdá: Institut d'Estudis Cerretans.

—— (1990) 'Primera Edad del Hierro'. In A.D. Domínguez Ortiz (ed.) *Historia de España*: 295–337, Barcelona: Planeta.

—— (1992) 'Aprovechamiento del medio y paleoeconomía durante las etapas metalúrgicas del Nordeste Peninsular'. In A. Moure (ed.) *Elefantes, ciervos y ovicápridos. Economía y aprovechamiento del Medio en la Prehistoria de España y Portugal*: 275–314, Santander: Universidad de Cantabria.

—— (1993) 'En torno al origen del mundo ibérico catalán: problemas de substrato', *Laietania* 8: 9–19.

Mendoza, A. (1989) 'A propos de quelques décors mailhaciens de Camp Redon 1, Lansargues (Hérault)', *Archéologie en Languedoc* 4: 93–5.

Neustupny, E. (1982) 'Prehistoric migrations by infiltration', *Archeologické Rozhledy* 34, 3: 278–93.

Pons, E. and Maya, J. L. (1988) 'L'Age du Bronze final en Catalogne'. In P. Brun and C. Mordant (eds) *Le Groupe Rhin–Suisse–France Orientale et la notion de civilisation des Champes d'Urnes*: 545–57, Nemours: Mémoires du Musée de Préhistoire de l'Île-de-France, 1, APRAIF.

Rouse, I. (1986) *Migrations in Prehistory. Inferring Population Movement from Cultural Remains*, New Haven: Yale University Press.

Rovira, J. (1977) 'Notas sobre las cavidades sepulcrales de la Edad del Bronce en Cataluña', *Cypsela* 2: 49–53.

—— (1988) 'Sobre la cronología y el papel de los vasos polípodos en Catalunya: la Balma de Pegueroles (Navés, Solsonès) y otros puntos de aparición de este elemento', *Espacio, Tiempo y Forma. Prehistoria* I: 269–77.

—— (1991) 'Reflexiones sobre los primeros Campos de Urnas en la Península Ibérica: una arribada maritima', *Cuadernos de Prehistoria y Arqueología Castellonenses* 15: 157–71.

Rovira, J. and Cura, M. (1989) 'El món tumular català des del bronze antic fins època ibèrica. Continuitat versus substitució', *Espacio, Tiempo y Forma. Prehistoria y Arqueología* I (2): 153–71.

Rovira, J. and Santacana, J. (1989) 'From the end of the Bronze Age to the first Age of Iron. Convulsion of the social and economic structures at the Mediterranean coast of the Iberian Peninsula'. In M. L. S. Sørensen and R. Thomas (eds) *The Bronze Age–Iron Age Transition in Europe*, British Archaeological Reports International Series 483: 100–11, Oxford: BAR.

Royo, J. I. (1991a) 'La necrópolis tumular de Los Castellets II (Mequinenza, Zaragoza). Quinta Campaña', *Arqueología Aragonesa 1988–89*: 121–5.

—— (1991b) 'Los Castellets de Mequinenza (Zaragoza). Sexta Campaña de excavaciones arqueológicas', *Arqueología Aragonesa 1988–89*: 127–31.

—— (1992) 'Estudio de materiales de Los Castellets de Mequinenza. Campaña de 1990', *Arqueología Aragonesa 1990*: 81–7.

Ruiz Zapatero, G. (1983) 'Modelos teóricos de invasiones/migraciones en arqueología prehistórica', *Informació Arqueòlogica* 41: 147–57.

—— (1985) *Los Campos de Urnas del nordest de la Península Ibérica*, Madrid: Universidad Complutense.

—— (1992) 'Campos de Urnas, migraciones y lenguas', *Arqrítica* 4: 19.

Snow, D. R. (1995) Migration in prehistory: the northern Iroquoian case, *American Antiquity* 60 (1): 59–79.

Turbón, D. (1981) *Antropología de Cataluña en el II Milenio a. C.* Barcelona: Ediciones de la Universidad de Barcelona.

Villar, F. (1991) *Los Indoeuropeos y los orígenes de Europa. Lenguaje e Historia*, Madrid: Gredos.

CHAPTER TEN

THE IRON AGE IBERIAN PEOPLES OF THE UPPER GUADALQUIVIR VALLEY

A R T U R O   R U I Z   R O D R Í G U E Z

INTRODUCTION

It is the intention of this chapter to analyse the socio-cultural bases which gave rise to an aristocracy in the upper Guadalquivir valley (Figure 10.1), while at the same time undertaking some general considerations on the causes behind the transition between two opposing social and cultural models. I shall distinguish between two aristocratic systems. The first, which appeared in the early stages, is defined as orientalizing and in it kinship relations carried great weight, while the second may be described as heroic and was client-based. Both were chiefdoms, but, I would argue, they cannot be equated, precisely because of the qualitative difference in their social relations outlined above. In the analysis which follows, the high quality of the available spatial archaeological evidence gives us an insight into the different territorial scales at which both operated in order to understand their respective systems of social relations.

The historical-archaeological sequence which is presented here has used the period divisions developed for the Late Bronze Age by Fernando Molina González (1979) and for the Iberian period by Arturo Ruiz and Manuel Molinos (1993). Molina (1979) has divided the final part of the Bronze Age into Late Bronze Age II (850–750 BC) and III (750–600 BC). This last phase could correspond to the first phase of the Early Iron Age, also defined as the Early Orientalizing or Proto-Iberian period. The Iberian sequence is broken down into Iberian I (600/580–500/480 BC), II (500/480–450/425 BC), III (450/425–350/325 BC) and IV (350/325–200 BC).

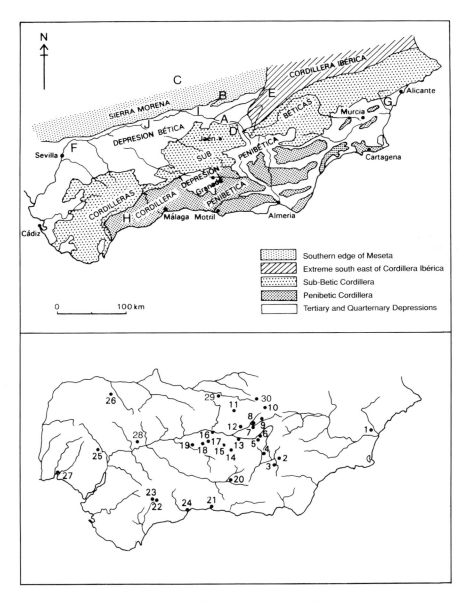

Figure 10.1 Maps showing the geography of the Guadalquivir valley (upper) and the location of sites mentioned in the text (lower).

Upper: A. Campiña of Jaén, B. Despeñaperros, C. La Mancha, D. River Guadalbullón, E. River Guadalimar, F. River Guadalquivir, G. River Vinalopó, H. Ronda, I. Upper Guadalquivir Basin, J. Middle Guadalquivir Basin. **Lower**: 1. Peña Negra (Crevillente), 2. Tútugi/Galera, 3. Baza, 4. Castellones de Ceal, 5. Toya/Tugia, 6. Turruñuelos, 7. El Salto, 8. Giribaile, 9. Olvera, 10. Los Altos del Sotillo (Castellar), 11. Collado de los

THE ORIENTALIZING ARISTOCRACY

Whilst written sources date the arrival of the Phoenicians in the Iberian Peninsula to some time around 1100 BC, from both absolute and sequential chronological references archaeologists date the first material evidence for their presence to the period between the end of the ninth and the beginning of the eighth centuries BC. At this time the first 'factories' were built along the Peninsula's Mediterranean coast, the Phoenicians' political and economic activity began (Aubet 1987), and the indigenous population reverted to the traditional form of concentrated settlement which had predominated during the Early Bronze Age (Nocete 1990). This can clearly be seen in the coastal areas of Andalucía and in the Levant as well as inland along the Guadalquivir valley. In coastal areas this is seen in sites such as Acinipo (Aguayo *et al.* 1986) and in the Levant at sites such as Peña Negra, where the end of the first phase of occupation has been radiocarbon dated to 740 BC (uncalibrated date: González Prats 1985). In the Guadalquivir valley a radiocarbon date obtained from the base of one of the huts at the site of La Plaza de Armas suggests that this settlement must have been formed around 820 BC (Ruiz and Molinos 1993). All this indicates that there emerged a settlement pattern characterized by concentrations of circular or rectangular houses. We know little about the large, Late Bronze Age II (850–750 BC) (Molina González 1979) settlements in the upper Guadalquivir valley because, in all but a few cases, these were located on the sites of large protohistoric centres of population and, as a result, it is difficult to identify many aspects of their internal organisation.

The middle and end of the ninth to the middle of the eighth centuries BC in the southwestern Peninsula saw the appearance of stone *stelae*, which were characterized by engravings of warriors with chariots, weapons, fibulae and combs. In other words, these are representations of some of the most characteristic elements of the process of wealth accumulation generated from the initial contact between natives and colonizers. The *stelae* are completely absent in upper Andalucía, given that the easternmost example in Andalucía was discovered at Juan Abad (province of Ciudad Real). However, some of the products represented in the *stelae*, such as the ivory combs, are well documented in upper Andalucía during this and the following period (Late Bronze Age III, 750–600 BC). This is confirmed at the cemetery of the Cerrillo Blanco

---

Figure 10.1 (cont.)

Jardines, 12. Cástulo, 13. Puente del Obispo, 14. La Plaza de Armas (Puente Tablas), 15. Atalayuelas (Fuerte del Rey), 16. Marmolejo, 17. Los Alcores/Cerrillo Blanco (Porcuna), 18. Torreparedones, 19. Ategua (Córdoba), 20. Cerro de los Infantes (Pinos Puente), 21. Toscanos, 22. La Silla del Moro, 23. Acinipo (Ronda), 24. Guadalhorce, 25. Tejada la Vieja, 26. Cancho Roano, 27. La Joya (Huelva), 28. Setefilla, 29. Oretum, 30. Juan Abad.

in the seventh century (Torrecillas 1985), the Final Bronze Age settlement at the site of El Salto (Hornos *et al.* 1985) and the Cerro de La Plaza de Armas (Ruiz and Molinos 1985).

In the seventh century BC the archaeological record indicates a consolidation of the aristocratic system, with enhanced intra-social differentiation. This is illustrated by the seventeen graves discovered at the cemetery of La Joya, which have an exceptional oriental-style burial offering (Garrido and Orta 1978) and burial mounds, such as mound A in Setefilla (Aubet 1975), a main inhumation around which cremated ashes are distributed and covered by the mound itself. At the same time the old settlements began to erect substantial stone and mud-brick fortifications, a development which took place at the turn of the seventh century BC in southwestern sites, such as Tejada la Vieja (Fernández Jurado 1987), an earlier date than other areas. Other changes were the introduction of the use of iron for agricultural implements and the potter's wheel for the production of ceramics. In addition, houses were henceforth square or rectangular, and were internally divided, and therefore better suited to a more complex division of labour. A particular pattern of mining activity appeared in the Tartessian area in Huelva and somewhat less so along the upper reaches of the Guadalquivir.

Sweeping change took place earlier in the Tartessian area around the lower Guadalquivir basin than in the upper reaches of the river. Examples of sites in the upper Guadalquivir valley are the hillforts of Los Alcores de Porcuna (Arteaga and Blech 1988), Atalayuelas (Castro *et al.* 1987) Puente del Obispo (Crespo *et al.* 1986) and La Plaza de Armas. Our knowledge of settlements in this period comes, however, above all from the last-mentioned hillfort, La Plaza de Armas. It was situated on a large flattened mountain covering an area of more than 5 hectares, the product of uninterrupted occupation by domestic settlement from the ninth century BC. An impressive wall with a number of towers was constructed some time during the seventh century BC. The structure included internal passages and its lower part was made of stone, while the upper reaches were of mud brick. Perhaps its most distinctive feature, however, was a lime-plaster coating which should have given it a powerful and intimidating appearance (Ruiz and Molinos 1986).

La Plaza de Armas is representative of the type of environment and economy of these settlements. It was situated in an area covered by oak (*Quercus ilex*) and pine trees, although other environments have been documented in the surroundings, such as a riverside forest that must have existed near the Guadalbullón, and a decaying sub-desert environment towards the east. An agrarian economic system developed in this area based primarily on cattle and supported by pig, sheep and goat breeding, and mixed cereal and leguminous cultivation (Ruiz and Molinos 1993).

In the Iberian I period (600/580–500/480 BC) the orientalizing aristocracies of the periphery of the Guadalquivir valley were able to minimize the role of the tribal system and imposed their power from the *oppida*. This was a period of great conflict, but also of extensive economic development. In the coastal area changes also occurred. At the end of the seventh century some of the Phoenician 'factories' reinforced their defences. Nevertheless, at the beginning of the sixth century BC 'factories' such as those at Guadalhorce or Toscanos were abandoned (Aubet 1987). The same happened a little to the north in the depressions which separate the Guadalquivir valley from the coast and which had previously been key north–south routes linking the two areas. Here, settlements such as the Cerro de los Infantes in the Granada Depression (Mendoza *et al.* 1981), and Acinipo, situated further west in the Ronda Depression, were also abandoned. In the case of Acinipo, we know that the settlement's inhabitants moved to another site, La Silla del Moro, where they constructed strong defensive fortifications. The pre-existing dispersed rural habitat disappeared, probably because they moved to hill-forts such as La Silla del Moro, mentioned above (Aguayo *et al.* 1990). To the east, in the Levant, in the Vinalopó valley, the indigenous model survived a little longer. Nevertheless, in the middle of the sixth century BC the settlement of Peña Grande was abandoned by its inhabitants, who moved to a hilltop fortification built nearby (González Prats 1985).

The process that took place in the mid-Guadalquivir valley was also to affect the upper valley. By the end of the seventh century BC a particular settlement pattern had become well established in the mid-Guadalquivir valley (Figure 10.2 (a)). This consisted of large, sometimes fortified, settlements linked to a dispersed rural habitat, as at Torreparedones and Porcuna. Towards the end of the seventh century BC and at the beginning of the sixth century BC, this pattern of mixed settlement spread eastwards to the upper Guadalquivir valley, where the Mastieni lived. This has been corroborated by the excavation of settlements such as, on the one hand, Las Calañas de Marmolejo, a small, unfortified and obviously agrarian site, and, on the other, the hillfort of La Plaza de Armas (Molinos *et al.* 1988). At the beginning of the sixth century BC the inhabitants of the upper Guadalquivir valley, which had been an area of indigenous cultural traditions, rather than a direct colonial periphery of Tartessos, established a frontier of towers between the Tartessian mixed settlements of the mid-Guadalquivir valley and the Mastienian settlement pattern of the upper Guadalquivir valley. Shortly afterwards, and certainly before the middle of the sixth century BC, as the Tartessian crisis began to take effect in the lower and mid-Guadalquivir valley, the mixed settlement pattern was abandoned in the upper Guadalquivir (Ruiz and Molinos 1989).

In the lower Guadalquivir valley the changes which occurred at the end of the seventh and the beginning of the sixth centuries are to be considered in the context of the relations between the two political centres, i.e. the colonial (Phoenician) and the indigenous (Tartessian)

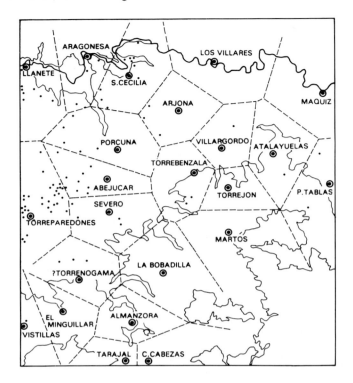

Figure 10.2 (a) Map of the Campiña de Jaén in the sixth century BC. Note the dispersed settlement to the west.

powers. Whilst the best-defined settlements have yet to be studied, the stratigraphic sequence suggested by the remains found at Huelva encourages us to accept the version given by the written sources. These remains include a vast amount of Greek material dating to between 640 and 530 BC (Cabrera 1986), and support the written testimonies of the excellent relations that existed between the Tartessian aristocracy (the mythical king Argantonios) and the Phocaean Greeks and by implication, therefore, the negative effects that these might have had on the existing colonial links between the Phoenicians and the Tartessians, as well as on those between the Tartessians and their indigenous periphery. In this context we must also bear in mind the changes which took place in the Mediterranean a few years later following the fall of Tyre and Carthage's restructuring of the Mediterranean economic system (Aubet 1987). Nor should we forget the growing tension during the early decades of the sixth century BC between the two colonizing powers which would later meet at the battle of Alalia in the mid-sixth century.

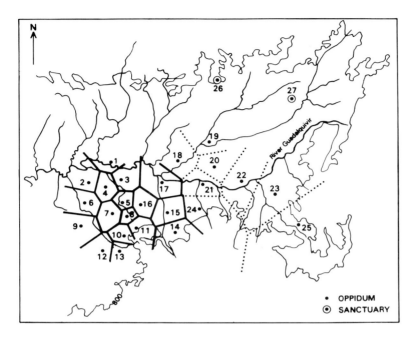

Figure 10.2   (b) Map of the Campiña of Jaén in the fourth century BC showing the distribution of *oppida*.

1. Los Villares de Andújar, 2. San Cristóbal de Lopera, 3. Atalaya de Higuera de Arjona, 4. Arjona, 5. Villargordo, 6. Porcuna, 7. Torrebenzala, 8. Torrejón, 9. Boyero, 10. Martos, 11. Miguelico, 12. Bobadilla, 13. Las Casillas de Martos, 14. La Guardia, 15. Plaza de Armas de Puente Tablas, 16. Atalayuelas, 17. Máquiz, 18. Cástulo, 19. Giribaile, 20. Baeza, 21. Gil de Olid de Puente del Obispo, 22. Ubeda la Vieja, 23. Toya, 24. Cerro Alcalá, 25. Castellones de Ceal, 26. Despeñaperros, 27. Castellar.

This is not to suggest, as the culture-historical archaeological inter-pretation of diffusionism did until relatively recently, that the model was exclusively dictated by the colonizer to the detriment of the indigenous population. The model presented here is based on an articulated dialec-tical system of relations between external centres and peripheries and between different social groups, which precludes the causal and linear vision inherent in the old culture-historical model. The crisis of the system took the form of a chain of conflicts between Phoenicians and Tartessians and in the latters' orientalizing aristocracy, leading to the crisis in the system of client groups. At the beginning of the sixth century BC, therefore, the impact of the crisis was first felt in the Phoenician area; in the second half of the century it reached the indigenous centre, Tartessos, and finally affected the indigenous periphery in the upper Guadalquivir valley. The last can be seen from the destruction of the sculpture at Porcuna in the mid-fifth century BC. This happened at a time when the relations between the colonizers and the indigenous population were being transformed into a different network of Mediterranean relations being created during the fifth century by Greeks and Carthaginians.

THE HEROIC ARISTOCRACY

The destruction of the Porcuna sculptures, an archaic Greek-style work completed only a little earlier, seems to have been the result of a clash between groups belonging to the same ethnic unit; for not only did warriors on both sides wear and use the same armour and weapons, but the defeated warriors seem not have had time to unsheath their swords, which suggests that they were taken by surprise (Negueruela 1990). The importance of these sculptures is that they bring to light the internal conflicts which took place between two different social systems during the fifth century BC: the orientalizing aristocratic system which was in the process of disappearing and the new heroic aristocratic system.

From the last quarter of the fifth century (Iberian III, 450/425–350/325 BC) a very similar settlement pattern is found in both the upper and mid-Guadalquivir valley. The basic and unique element of this was the form of settlement referred to in the written sources as the Iberian *oppidum*, which was quite different to the Celtic *oppidum* found in central Europe at the end of the second century BC (Collis 1984). In the Guadalquivir valley, the *oppida* developed from the primitive settlements established in the eighth century BC. These had evolved through the reinforcement of the fortifications built either in the orientalizing period in the seventh century, at sites such as La Plaza de Armas, or shortly afterwards, as in the case of Atalayuelas. In a few, exceptional cases, new settlements were created. One example is Castellones de Ceal. This was a small settlement which, on the basis of the grave goods in its cemetery, was very prosperous (Chapa and Pereira 1992). The settlement was constructed on terraces and not on the top of a flat mountain, and was situated in what was then a very arid terrain, albeit one which included an area of low-lying fertile land (*vega*) that still survives today. Castellones de Ceal epitomized the results of the economic system generated by the Tartessian crisis. By opening up the routes leading from the Levant to Cástulo (Ruiz *et al.* 1987), and hence the westward path towards the rich mining zone later exploited by Tartessos, this system reinforced the role of the *oppidum* of Toya as the economic centre of the upper Guadalquivir valley. Thus the foundation of Castellones de Ceal at the beginning of the fourth century was connected to the intensification of contacts with coastal areas of the Levant and to the development of the route through the southeast of the Guadalquivir valley. This route linked the large centres found there (Toya and Cástulo) with those in the north of the province of Granada (Tútugi, Galera) and from there with the Levant.

In general terms, the settlements can be classified into three different types according to their size: approximately 1, 6 and 18 hectares. The largest units – i.e. the *oppida* – in the westernmost part of the valley were essentially regularly spaced with an average distance of 8 kilometres between each. In the eastern part of the valley the *oppida* were distributed some 10 kilometres apart in a linear pattern. In terms of the relations between the different types of settlement this phase was characterized, on the one hand, by the disappearance of the dispersed rural settlements of the type identified in the Tartessian mixed settlement model of the sixth century, and, on the other, by the predominance of a polynuclear pattern formed by each nuclear centre (*oppidum*) and the settlements around it. This spatial pattern reflects the power of an aristocratic group over its dependent client groups (Ruiz and Molinos 1993).

The structure of the settlements is the best-known aspect of the internal functioning of the new model. At the site of La Plaza de Armas there is a clearly identifiable zone which may have been the space occupied by the aristocracy, characterized by a large building with porch and central patio. The system of streets and blocks which radiated from this were organized on a rectilinear 'Hippodamian' pattern. We are fortunate to have an almost perfect knowledge of one of these blocks. This contained a large two-storey house, a storage area and a number of small one-storey houses with large courtyards at either the front or rear. Activities relating to consumption and production would have been carried on in these courtyards. In conclusion, these blocks could have been an area belonging to the aristocratic group, that is to say, an area of the settlement where groups of aristocrats and their client groups came into contact. This spatial distribution thus reflects the complexity of the social system.

A more detailed picture of the structure of these aristocratic groups and their dependent client groups has been provided by the analysis of the cemetery of Baza (Figure 10.3). Baza is located in the province of Granada, close to the southeast limit of the province of Jaén. This cemetery is well known because of the 'Lady of Baza' sculpture found there. The spatial distribution of the tombs and of the different items at this cemetery allows us to distinguish two types, or levels, of aristocratic tombs. One is characterized by the presence of Greek kraters, chariots, bronze braziers and large cist tombs. The tombs of the second type are much smaller and, whilst they do contain Greek kraters, they lack the chariots. In terms of their spatial distribution, the first type of tomb formed a nucleus around which the second type of aristocratic tombs were distributed. The rest of the tombs were dispersed around these. In this last category of non-aristocratic tombs, weapon-types and distinct forms of Greek ceramics played a different role: membership of the group

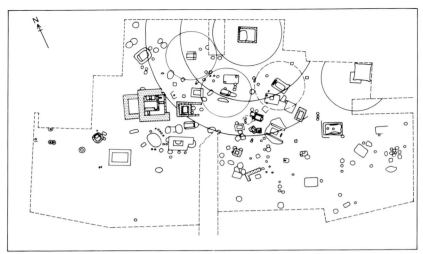

1

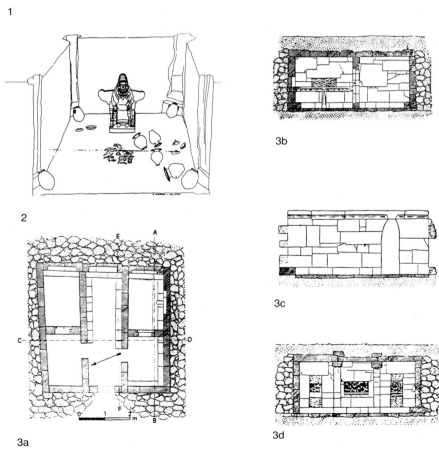

2

3a

3b

3c

3d

gave each person buried within the area of the segment of the circle defined by the aristocratic group the right to be buried with these objects (Ruiz *et al.* 1992).

In contrast to the previous phases (Iberian I and II), both at settlement and burial sites, the products derived from trade or those of great symbolic or economic value now circulated among the whole community. However, depending on their quality, goods were distributed differently between aristocrats and clients. This meant that the aristocratic group ended up controlling the system by allowing its client groups to share in the wealth in circulation, although it still established the rules for access to each type of product. From the point of view of the settlement pattern, the new aristocratic model renounced the structures of the supra-ethnic model or supra-settlement model (i.e. renounced the tribal structure). However, this old ethnic system continued to be relevant, as can be seen from the significant presence of kraters in the entire zone, and of large burial chambers, in contrast to the absence of both in other areas such as the Levant (provinces of Alicante and Murcia).

The burial chamber of Toya is an important example of this type of burial, paradigmatic of Iberian culture in the same way as the *Lady of Elche* sculpture. The tomb, which was discovered at the beginning of the twentieth century, is believed to be the tomb of an aristocrat from the *oppidum* of Tugia (the name which would later evolve into its present form, Toya). The chamber studied and reconstructed by Juan Cabré Aguiló (1925) has a rectangular floor plan and five compartments in three longitudinal aisles. Little is known about the burial offerings as a whole, as most of them were destroyed or dispersed by their discoverers. However, elements found in the chamber (Athenian red-figure kraters, a stone funeral box and a chariot (Fernández-Miranda and Olmos 1986)) appear to identify this chamber with the elite recognized at Baza.

However, in the upper Guadalquivir this new phase did not entail the transformation or adaptation of the previous economic model. No changes can be perceived either in the basic technology (for example, the traditional domestic mill was still used in what was a cereal economy) or in the agrarian structure, which continued to be based on the large-scale cultivation of cereal and the predominance of bovine livestock.

The treaty of 348 BC, which defined the areas of Greek and Carthaginian influence in the western Mediterranean, suggests that tension developed in Graeco-Roman and Carthaginian relations in the mid-fourth century BC. It has been argued that this led to the sudden loss of access to Greek products by aristocratic circles and to a mass exodus from settlements in the Levant (Tarradell 1961). It is in this

Figure 10.3 1) Plan of the cemetery at Baza showing the hierarchical distribution of burial space; 2) Tomb from the first level at Baza; 3a–d) Different views of the Toya burial chamber.

context that we can best understand the crisis that affected the upper Guadalquivir in the latter half of the fourth century. It not only signalled the end of trading relations with the Levant, but also caused the abandonment of some important Iberian settlements, including La Plaza de Armas. However, an analysis of some aspects of the Iberian economy, such as cereals and bovine livestock for example, suggests that they had gone into decline as early as the beginning of the century, that is, precisely at the time when trading relations had begun to increase. This seems to imply that the roots of the economic crisis had already been planted, and that it was, therefore, structurally determined by the nature of the nuclear aristocratic model itself. Indeed, it is possible to identify contradictions resulting from technological underdevelopment ('primitive' domestic mills or querns, ploughs without iron ploughshares, etc.), the continued application of traditional agrarian strategies (based on extensive agriculture and bovine livestock) and extremely rigid systems of social relations (as revealed by the model of nuclear settlements). In such a domestic context, the sudden loss of Greek products, which had served as a means of maintaining the unity of the aristocratic group, may have been the definitive factor in the breakdown of the system.

In the upper Guadalquivir valley, the second half of the fourth and the entire third centuries BC (Iberian period IV (350/325–200 BC)) were very different in character from what had gone before (Figure 10.2 (b). Tribal or supra-settlement structures, ignored by the polynuclear aristocratic group, reappeared in rural sanctuaries in Collado de los Jardines in Despeñaperros and in the Altos del Sotillo. However, these may not necessarily indicate the persistence of the old ethnic/tribal groups. Rather, they may reflect their development and the dependencies which arose between the *oppida*, or in other words conflicts which arose between different aristocratic groups. Written sources have identified the Oretani, the Bastetani and the Turduli with the Late Iberian ethnic groups of the upper Guadalquivir, with significant differences existing between them.

In this way, the upper Guadalquivir came to be structured around these three different ethnic groups. Writing at a much later date, Ptolemy (*Geog.* 2.6.58) stated that one of these ethnic groups, the Oretani, occupied much of the eastern part of what is now the province of Jaén as well as Ciudad Real, a province located in La Mancha. It seems that the original group may have come from Oretum in the area of La Mancha. Significantly, Pliny (*NH* 3.4.25) talks about them as two separate groups and Strabo (*Geog.* 3.3.2) refers to the existence of two Oretanian capitals, Oretum in La Mancha and Castulo in the eastern area of La Campiña in the upper Guadalquivir valley. At some point in the fourth or third century BC either friction between aristocracies on either side of the Sierra Morena (a mountain range that divides La Mancha and the upper Guadalquivir valley), or a kinship plan, may have given rise to a political system characterized by dependencies between *oppida*. This is perhaps reflected in the construction of the sanctuary of Castellar at the end of the fourth or beginning of the third century BC (Nicolini *et al.* 1987), and a homogeneity of material culture on both sides of the Sierra Morena mountains, evident in such items as stamped pottery (*producciones estampilladas*) or the irregular and angular profiles of the clear-painted pottery (Ruiz and Nocete 1981). In any event, whether it was achieved by Cástulo or by Oretum, the creation of the sanctuaries in the Sierra Morena implied the reconversion of the old polynuclear model found in La Campiña of Jaén and in the eastern part of the upper Guadalquivir valley. The new model not only signified the foundation of new *oppida* such as Giribaile and Olvera on the river Guadalimar and Turruñuelos on the river Guadalquivir itself, but also the creation of a planned dispersed habitat in the area of the river Guadalimar (as documented by Luis Gutiérrez Soler 1996) and even in the hinterland of Toya itself.

The new political and ethnic model also favoured the modification of traditional itineraries and roads, as the position of the sanctuaries opened up two previously unexploited routes. One of these connected the Guadalquivir valley to La Mancha via the pass through the Sierra Morena at Despeñaperros. The other linked it to the Levant via the river Guadalimar. This innovation may have been the reason why the strategic importance of Toya and its hinterland of Castellones de Ceal declined, despite the fact that, as Ptolemy noted, these formed part of Oretania.

In terms of Iberian society, the new model which emerged after the crisis of the fourth century BC and which would determine the settlement pattern which developed in Oretania in the third century BC, established a concept of territorial occupation and control that was very different from the old polynuclear model. It was based on a return to the concept of the supra-settlement. This must have begun with the enhancement of the role of the rural sanctuaries, an ethnic-tribal religious reference which recalls the *ver sacrum* found in other Mediterranean areas. This enabled the aristocracy to maintain its position through the development of a system of communal serfdom among the different *oppida*, as has been documented in texts such as the Roman consul L. Aemilius Paullus' decree on the liberation of the *Turris Lascutana* from its dependency upon Hasta Regia (CIL II 5041). It should be noted, however, that the relations of dependency created were not solely the result of the military domination of some aristocracies by others, but were also based on the construction of new ethnic groups. In any event, the new model of territorial occupation and control must have been much more flexible and efficient than that established in La Campiña. Hence the economic centre shifted towards the eastern part of the upper Guadalquivir valley, as demonstrated by the strategies developed by Carthaginians and Romans both before and during the Second Punic

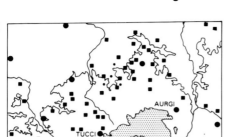

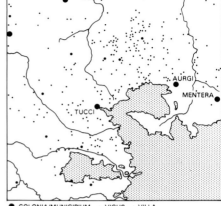

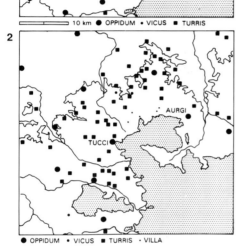

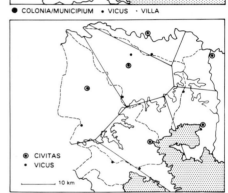

Figure 10.4 Model for the transition from Iberian to Roman settlement in the Campiña de Jaén: 1) second to first centuries BC; 2) first century BC; 3) Flavian period; 4) General panorama of the Campiña of Jaén during the Roman period.

War at the end of the third century BC. An example of these was the marriage of the Carthaginian general Hannibal to Himilce, an Oretanian princess from Cástulo.

In the mid- and upper Guadalquivir valley, that is, in La Campiña of Jaén and Córdoba, settlements such as La Plaza de Armas recovered after the crisis of the middle of the fourth century BC. In this area, however, the new ethnic groups, the Turduli and Bastetani, did not follow the new territorial political model but, on the contrary, continued to adhere to the old polynuclear system. This signified that the polynuclear settlement model, with exceptional inter-*oppida* dependencies, continued to exist much as it had done in the preceding period. However, this was accompanied by significant changes in economic strategy. The analysis of layer VIII at the settlement of La Plaza de Armas reveals that while the economy was still based upon extensive cereal production, sheep and goats replaced bovine cattle as the main elements in livestock farming (Ruiz and Molinos 1993).

This was the new model which the Romans were to encounter when they conquered the Peninsula in the wake of the Second Punic War (218–202 BC). In defining the territories of the different ethnic groups, they sought out the old aristocracies and came to an agreement with them over the forms of indigenous social organization and its dependence (Ruiz *et al.* 1992; Figure 10.4). In this context it is particularly interesting to mention the decline of sanctuaries. Although a residual cult survived in the area of the large sanctuaries at the Sierra Morena, the decline of these from the second century BC and the abandonment of the houses at the foot of the shelter-sanctuary coincided with the creation of the first temple-sanctuaries outside the settlement walls, at Torreparedones (Cunliffe *et al.* 1992), and possibly Giribaile. These developments are indicative of the separation of religious and political power, symptomatic of the transformation of the classic aristocratic system (which had been incapable of carrying out such a division) into a new civil and urban system.

ABBREVIATIONS

CIL II: Hübnor, E. (1869) Corpus Inscriptionum Latinarum 2, Berlin: Academioe Litterarum Rogioe Borussicae.

REFERENCES

Aguayo, P., Carrilero, M. and Martínez, G. (1986) 'Excavaciones en el yacimiento pre y protohistórico de Acinipo (Ronda, Málaga)', *Anuario Arqueológico de Andalucía* II: 333–7, Sevilla: Junta de Andalucía.

Aguayo, P., Carrilero, M., Cabello, N., Diéguez, A., Garrido, O., Morales, F., Moreno, F., Padial, P. and Sanz, L. (1990) 'Excavación arqueológica sistemática en la Silla del Moro. Primera Campaña. 1990', *Anuario Arqueológico de Andalucía* II: 245–51, Sevilla: Junta de Andalucía.

Arteaga, O. and Blech, M. (1988) 'La romanización en la zona de Porcuna y Mengibar, Jaén', in *Los asentamientos ibéricos ante la romanización*: 89–100, Madrid: Ministerio de Cultura and Casa de Velázquez.

Aubet, M. E. (1975) *La necrópolis de Setefilla en Lora del Río, Sevilla. Programa de investigaciones protohistóricas de la Universidad de Barcelona*, Barcelona: Universidad de Barcelona.

—— (1987) *Tiro y las colonias fenicias de Occidente*, Barcelona: Bellaterra.

Cabré Aguiló, J. (1925) 'Arquitectura Hispánica. El sepulcro de Toya', *Archivo Español de Arte y Arqueología* I: 73–101.

Cabrera, P. (1986) 'Los griegos en Huelva: los materiales griegos', in *Homenaje a Luis Siret*: 575–83, Madrid, Sevilla: Ministerio de Cultura, Junta de Andalucía.

Castro, M., López, J., Zafra, N., Crespo, J. and Choclán, C. (1987) 'Prospección con sondeo estratigráfico en el yacimiento de Atalayuelas, Fuente del Rey, Jaén', *Anuario Arqueológico de Andalucía* II: 207–15, Sevilla: Junta de Andalucía.

Chapa, T. and Pereira, J. (1992) 'La necrópolis de Castellones de Ceal (Jaén)', in J. Blánquez and V. Antona (eds) *Congreso de arqueología ibérica. Las necrópolis*: 431–54, Madrid: Universidad Autónoma de Madrid.

Crespo, J., Castro, M., López, J. and Choclán, C. (1986) 'Prospección arqueológica con sondeo estratigráfico en la Finca de Gil de Olid, Puente del Obispo, Baeza (Jaén)', *Anuario Arqueológico de Andalucía* II: 190–2, Sevilla: Junta de Andalucía.

Collis, J. (1984) *Oppida. Earliest Towns North of the Alps*, Sheffield: University of Sheffield.

Cunliffe, B., Fernández, M. C., Poole, C., Brown, L., Davenport, P., Brook, I., Pressey, S., Morena, J. A. and Torres, B. (1992) 'Torreparedones, poblado fortificado en altura y su contexto en la Campiña de Córdoba', *Investigaciones Arqueológicas en Andalucía. Proyectos*: 519–28, Huelva: Junta de Andalucía.

Fernández Jurado, J. (1987) *Tejada la Vieja: Una ciudad protohistórica*, Huelva Arqueológica 9, Huelva: Diputación Provincial de Huelva.

Fernández-Miranda, M. and Olmos, R. (1986) *Las ruedas de Toya y el origen del carro en la Península Ibérica*, Madrid: Ministerio de Cultura.

Garrido, J. and Orta, M. E. (1978) *Excavaciones en la Necrópolis de la Joya*, Excavaciones Arqueológicas en España 96, Madrid: Ministerio de Cultura.

González Prats, A. (1985) 'Los nuevos asentamientos al final de la Edad del Bronce. Problemática cultural y cronología', in *Arqueología en el País Valenciano. Panorama y Perspectivas*, Alicante: anejos de la revista *Lucentum*.

Gutiérrez, Soler, L. (1996) 'Poplamiento Iberico en el curso medio del río Guadalimar', tesis doctoral, Inedita Jaén: Universidad de Jaén.

Hornos, F., Nocete, F., Crespo, J., Zafra, N. and Martínez, P. (1985) 'Excavación de urgencia en el cerro del Salto de Miralrío (Vilches, Jaén) 1985', *Anuario Arqueológico de Andalucía* III: 192–8, Sevilla: Junta de Andalucía.

Mendoza, A., Molina, F., Arteaga, O. and Aguayo, P. (1981) 'Cerro de los Infantes (Pinos Puente, Provinz Granada). Ein Beitrag zur Bronze- und Eisenzeit in Oberandalusien', *Madrider Mitteilungen* 22: 171–210.

Molina González, F. (1979) 'Definición y sistematización del Bronce Tardío y Final en el SE. de la Península Ibérica', *Cuadernos de Prehistoria de la Universidad de Granada* 3: 159–232.

Molinos, M., Serrano, J. L. and Coba, B. (1988) 'Excavaciones arqueológicas en el asentamiento de La Campiña, Marmorejo, Jaén', *Anuario Arqueológico de Andalucía* III: 197–203, Sevilla: Junta de Andalucía.

Negueruela, I. (1990) *Los monumentos escultóricos ibéricos del Cerrillo Blanco de Porcuna (Jaén)*, Madrid: Ministerio de Cultura.

Nicolini, G., Zafra, N. and Ruiz, A. (1987) 'Informe de la campaña de excavación de 1987 en los Altos del Sotillo (Castellar, Jaén)', *Anuario Arqueológico de Andalucía* II: 216–20, Sevilla: Junta de Andalucía.

Nocete, F. (1990) 'Territorio de coerción: el paradigma de las jefaturas', in J. Adánez, C. M. Heras and C. Varela (eds) *Espacio y organización social*: 57–90, Madrid: Universidad Complutense.

Ruiz, A., Castro, M. and Choclán, C. (1992) 'Aurgi-Tucci. La formación de la ciudad romana en la Campiña Alta de Jaén. Conquista romana y modos de intervención en la organización romana y territorial', *Dialoghi di Archeologia* 10 (1–2): 211–29.

Ruiz, A. and Molinos, M. (1985) 'Informe de la campaña de excavación en el Cerro de la Plaza de Armas de Puente Tablas, Jaén', *Anuario Arqueológico de Andalucía* II: 345–52, Sevilla: Junta de Andalucía.

Ruiz, A. and Molinos, M. (1986) 'Informe de la Campaña de excavación en el Cerro de la Plaza de Armas de Puente Tablas, Jaén', *Anuario Arqueológico de Andalucía* II: 401–7, Sevilla: Junta de Andalucía.

—— (1989) 'Fronteras: un caso del siglo VI a.C.', in F. Burillo Mozota (ed.) *Arqueología espacial 13. Fronteras*: 121–36, Teruel: Colegio Universitario de Teruel.

—— (1993) *Iberos. Análisis arqueológico de un proceso histórico*, Barcelona: Crítica.

Ruiz, A., Molinos, M., Hornos, F. and Choclán, C. (1987). 'El poblamiento ibérico en el Alto Guadalquivir', in A. Ruiz and M. Molinos (eds) *Iberos. Actas de las primeras jornadas sobre el mundo ibérico*: 239–56, Jaén: Ayuntamiento de Jaén.

Ruiz, A. and Nocete, F. (1981) 'Un modelo sincrónico para el estudio de la producción cerámica ibérica estampillada del Alto Guadalquivir', *Cuadernos de Prehistoria de la Universidad de Granada* 6: 355–83.

Ruiz, A., Risquez, C. and Hornos, F. (1992) 'Las necrópolis ibéricas en la Alta Andalucía', in J. Blánquez and V. Antona (eds) *Congreso de arqueología ibérica. Las necrópolis*: 397–430, Madrid: Universidad Autónoma de Madrid.

Tarradell, M. (1961) 'Ensayo de estratigrafía comparada en los poblados ibéricos valencianos', *Saitabi* 11: 3–20.

Torrecillas, J. F. (1985) *La necrópolis de época tartéssica de Cerrillo Blanco*, Jaén: Instituto de Estudios Giennenses.

CHAPTER ELEVEN

URBAN TRANSFORMATION AND CULTURAL CHANGE

SIMON KEAY

INTRODUCTION

Transition from the societies of the pre-Roman Iron Age to the Roman period is usually perceived by archaeologists and historians as one of the clearest examples of cultural change in the history of Europe. This is no less true of Iberia. Following the arrival of the Romans in 218 BC a process of cultural change is understood to have swept the Peninsula, culminating in the absorption of northwestern Iberia from the end of the first century BC onwards. Wholesale 'Romanization' is thus the inevitable result of conquest, whether forcibly imposed by Rome or willingly embraced by native communities. Established academic texts continue to emphasize the administrative and historical framework within which this is seen to have taken place and use the archaeological evidence to illustrate these known 'truths'. The implicit assumption seems to be that either it is not possible to engage in the sort of dialogue with their evidence that historians enjoy or that it is only legitimate to do so within certain 'constraints'. In either event the depressing end-result is that much archaeological research is leading to little more than buttressing the accepted picture with little or no room for developing alternative perspectives.

Research into the theory of archaeological interpretation in recent years shows that this view is fallacious. Thus analyses of pre- and protohistoric societies in recent years have shown that archaeology does have an important role to play in our understanding of the past. This may seem to be an obvious point, but it does still need to be made, given that archaeology is still seen by some specialists in the field of classical antiquity to be 'the handmaiden of history' with no original contribution to make to our understanding of the Roman world. History in this context is 'event' dominated and practised at its most traditional without any of the innovatory perspectives introduced by, for example, the Annales school (Braudel 1975: 17–22). As a consequence of this it is salutory to reflect that much of the great data explosion in Spanish and Portuguese archaeology during the 1980s and 1990s consists of little more than the accumulation of data for its own sake. The new discoveries regularly reported in periodic journals published by the autonomous communities of Spain have little, if any, impact upon the 'national' histories of Roman Iberia. This is because excavations, surveys, analyses and the study of individual finds are undertaken with only the briefest of interpretations or reflection, and 'national' or regional histories are largely written by scholars who are unfamiliar with the theoretical frameworks which govern the ways in which archaeological evidence can best be interpreted. At the same time some 'post-processual' archaeologists have begun to express doubts about the accessibility of the past through archaeology and the relationship between material culture and the archaeological record (Barrett 1994 for example). Thus the now 'old' advances of the 'New Archaeology' have had little impact upon the ways in which the evidence is interpreted while the more positive recent advances of 'post-processualist' archaeology have had no impact at all (generally see Dyson 1993).

Those works which have consciously attempted to interpret the archaeological evidence for cultural change, or Romanization, have done so from an implicitly 'functionalist–processual' (Renfrew 1994: 3ff.) point of view in which attention is directed towards the search towards general processes, focusing upon the non-cultural. That is to say that it is the military, taxation, trade or administrative changes, or the environment, which are seen as causal. Work of this kind has tended to focus upon the frontier regions of the Roman Empire, such as Germania (Brandt and Slofstra 1983) and Britain (Millett 1991). Approaches of this kind have been attacked as being too rigid by post-processualists, largely because in the discussion of cultural change the 'system' is stressed at the expense of human cultural change (Hodder 1991: 1–18). Cultural symbols are seen to play an important role, and their relationship to social change has been explored by a number of scholars. Cultural symbolism and its relationship to social change, which play an important role in the post-processual debate, are rarely studied. Instead art and architecture are used as media for analysing the artistic currents between provinces in the Roman world. Alternatively they are completely decontextualized and studied as 'works of art' from a purely aesthetic standpoint.

This chapter explores cultural change from pre-Roman to Roman Iberia through the perspective of urbanization and ideology. Roman towns are, after all, perceived as being different from the broad range of pre-Roman centralized settlements in Iberia and are generally accepted as the most characteristic symbol of the Roman period in the western provinces. They are also understood as playing an important causal role

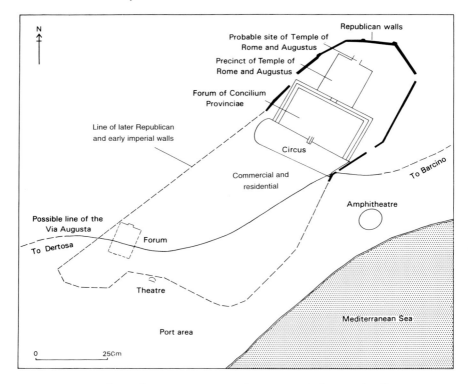

Figure 11.1   Plan of Roman Tarraco (Tarragona) during the first century AD.

in the promotion of cultural change in the Roman Empire. However, little attention has been devoted to their genesis in Iberia apart from analyses of the historical evidence. The crucial period of development during the second and first centuries BC is usually explained in terms of the dates and status of the known *coloniae* and the legal relationship between Roman and native settlements recorded in the classical sources (Knapp 1977; Marín Díaz 1987). This is partly because recognizably *Roman* structures are rare and much of the archaeological evidence for this period reveals little more than the continuity of occupation on native settlements. For many, the archaeological evidence for Roman towns only becomes worth studying when it is obvious and commonplace, that is, from the Augustan period onwards. Even then much of the effort invested is largely directed towards describing town plans and individual buildings rather than attempting to explain their existence in the first place.

This chapter tries to break away from this tradition and to examine the development of Roman towns, and by implication cultural change, through the relationship between cultural symbols and ideology. This is done by looking at ideology as a mechanism of social change and examining its relationship to the development of the provincial capital of Tarraco (Tarragona), in eastern Spain, during the Augustan period (Figure 11.1). It is part of a broader programme of research into the value of imperial ideology as a contributory factor in the Romanization of Iberia in the later Republic and early Empire (for instance, Keay 1995). Specifically the chapter attempts to explain the transformation of urban space and the emergence of a specifically Roman topography at Tarraco in terms of the implementation of a programme of imperial propaganda by the urban elite. Moreover, it is argued that urban transformation at a time of political change ensured social continuity. Tarraco was selected for study as it was the capital of the province of Tarraconensis, and being one of the most influential Roman towns in Iberia, it was the most sensitive to the broader political changes in the Roman Empire. It also possesses a good archaeological and epigraphic record.

IDEOLOGY AS A MECHANISM OF SOCIAL CHANGE

Ideology is a form of power used by a dominant elite to ensure its own stability and continuity by a representation of perceived reality which is favourable to its interests. Representation is by definition misrepresentation since it invariably involves selection according to personal interests and, thus, a range of images, myths or practices are deliberately chosen to present certain values to subject populations as familiar, natural and beyond question (Shanks and Tilley 1987). In this way the 'reality', or 'realities', of the given political or social situations of a subject population is masked. In the current post-processual theoretical climate, where artefacts are not regarded simply as inert works of art or technology but are instead understood as embodying a certain encoded symbolic value which needs to be understood in the context of the society that produced them, overtly ideological symbols have an important role to play in our understanding of past societies.

For the purposes of this chapter ideology is used simply as one explanatory mechanism. It is understood in the non-systemic sense, and emphasis is laid upon the interrelationship between both the Emperor and urban elites in manipulating cultural symbols for their own *personal* ends. There is thus an implicit acceptance that ideological symbols, such as building types, architectural decoration, inscriptions and sculptures, have considerable potential in engendering cultural change in the short to medium term. This naturally contributes to a legitimization of imperial control in the context of a new historical momentum. The degree to which all of this was unquestioningly accepted by subject populations within Tarraco and elsewhere within Tarraconensis lies beyond the scope of this chapter, although it has been touched upon elsewhere (Keay 1995).

It would be difficult to argue that there was no ideology in Iberian society and in Iberia during the Roman Republican period. The communities of northeast Spain had achieved a high degree of social and political complexity by the time of the Roman conquest in the later third century BC, and all the indications are that this formed the framework through which the Romans governed down until the Augustan period. Ideological symbols are, however, harder to find given the more elusive nature of the archaeological record of the last two centuries BC, particularly on native sites where the evidence is largely limited to undecorated ceramics and settlement sites that are still relatively poorly understood. By the first century BC Republican Rome certainly had a growing vision of Empire (Beard and Crawford 1985: 72–84) and a nascent cultural identity expressed in the plastic arts, although this was largely personalized and lacked any standardization or cohesion (Gruen 1992: 131–82).

However, political and religious ideology becomes particularly relevant to the Roman Empire from the reign of Augustus onwards. The political success of this Emperor and, ultimately, the imperial system as a whole prior to the third century AD can be ascribed to a considered misrepresentation of the balance of power in the Roman state. At its very core lay the reality that the legitimacy of the Emperor ultimately resided in his hold over the army of the Empire. The ideology developed to mask, or legitimize, this unpalatable truth was a politico-religious theory which effectively rewrote the past in favour of Augustus and his family. His own military and political achievements were exalted by the side of real and mythological ancestors and woven into a divine framework. The Augustan age was made to be seen as the natural 'culmination' of the Roman historical process through the development of artistic and literary symbols, first at Rome and later in the provinces. A central element was the principle of personal loyalty to the *princeps* which was articulated through public acts of devotion. Initially these were spontaneous personal dedications of altars and buildings, but later they settled down to more systematic public acts which were formalized in the context of the imperial cult. Later Emperors of the Julio-Claudian and subsequent dynasties drew legitimacy by publicly advertising their 'link' to this important formative phase in artistic, architectural and propagandist symbols. Ideology and imperial propaganda were thus a key mechanism in ensuring the continuity of the Empire and, at a provincial level, it played a key role in ensuring the cohesion of subject communities.

DYNASTIC SYMBOLS AND URBAN DEVELOPMENT

Arelate

In a recent paper Gros (1990) suggested that the construction of buildings with strong imperial symbolism in urban landscapes during the Augustan period transformed relationships between traditional structures and determined the long-term axial planning of towns as a whole. This was particularly clear at Athens and Thasos where the insertion of buildings with close imperial connotations into the agora helped to transform old-established town centres. More relevant to the case of Tarraco, however, was the case put forward for the Augustan *colonia* of Arelate (Arles), in southern France. This town was a new foundation of 26 BC, and it is argued that there may have been a dynastic focus to the *forum* at the heart of the town from as early as 26 or 25 BC and that this conditioned subsequent urban development. During its first phase of construction the *forum* focused upon an altar which was housed within a small tetrastyle shrine or *baldacchino*. Gros suggests that this may have housed a marble copy of the bronze shield awarded to Augustus by the Roman Senate in 27 BC (the *clipeus virtutis*), dated to 26 BC and possibly awarded to the town by the Emperor on his way to Hispania. This may, therefore, have been an altar to the *genius Augusti*. It embodied some of the new ideological messages being developed at Rome, such as the return of civil peace with the themes of Victory and Abundance. Slightly later, perhaps in the first years of the first century AD, the altar became the focus for statues, possibly of the heroized nephews of Augustus, Caius and Lucius Caesar.

Between AD 20 and 30 the role of the *forum* as the dynastic focus was continued and reinforced with the construction of a monumental complex at its western end. This comprised a probable temple to the imperial cult on a high podium and two flanking *exedrae*, not dissimilar to the temple of Mars Ultor in the *forum* of Augustus (dedicated in 2 BC) at Rome (Zanker 1984). Overall, Gros underlines the overtly dynastic character of the *forum* of the *colonia*, noting that it progresses from an altar to a temple of the imperial cult.

Tarraco

Gros supports his argument for Arelate by citing Fishwick's hypothesis (1982) concerning the location of the altar and temple of Augustus at Tarraco. Recent discoveries at this town have permitted it to be reassessed in the context of a detailed discussion of the early development of the town (Ruiz de Arbulo 1990). This makes it an ideal candidate for exploring the relationship between dynastic symbols and long-term urban development.

It is now well known that Tarraco had been a substantial pre-Roman settlement and that it was an important town during the Republican period (Keay 1991). During the second and first centuries BC it was a walled settlement comprising a military encampment in what is now the upper town and a civilian settlement on the site of the Iberian centre in what is now the lower town. Little is known about the spatial organization of its interior prior to Augustus, apart from small 'Ibero-Roman' structures close to the site of the Augustan *forum* (Adserias *et al.* 1993). Nevertheless the discovery of an inscription to Pompey the Great (RIT 1) has led some to suggest that there was a forum in the lower town during the Republican period.

The lower town

Despite this paucity of evidence it does seem as if the town was replanned on a large scale under Augustus and his successors and that a dynastic element was the catalyst for this. In the first instance the town, which had acquired colonial status between 45 and 2 BC (Alföldy 1991), was the actual residence of Augustus during his first visit to Hispania in 26–25 BC. His personal presence at Tarraco at this early point in his reign made it effectively the capital of the Empire for a short period. As such it hosted embassies from different parts of the Roman world, one of which came from Mytilene (on Lesbos, off the coast of Asia Minor) in 26 BC with the purpose of honouring Augustus. This was a highly symbolic act at a time when imperial propaganda and imagery were beginning to be developed at Rome with the aim of underwriting the position of Augustus as a 'first among equals'. As Fishwick argues (1982), the value of this very public act of loyalty to the person of the *princeps* was not lost on the inhabitants of Tarraco and may have set the example for the famous altar to Augustus which they dedicated to him in 26 BC (Quintilian *Inst. Orat.* 6.3.77). All of this is of course bound up in the formative stages of the imperial cult in the Empire as a whole.

Nothing survives of the altar. However, images (Burnett *et al.* 1992) on the reverse of coins minted at Tarraco under Tiberius suggest that its front face was decorated with a shield, an oak swag, bucrania and fillets. The first two of these have been identified as the *clipeus virtutis* and the *corona civica*, vocal symbols of Augustan propaganda from 27 BC onwards (Fishwick 1982). On top of the altar was a palm tree, possibly symbolizing the general theme of Augustan victory. The apparent absence of Augustan levels in recent excavations in the upper town at Tarraco (Ruiz de Arbulo 1990) seems to confirm Fishwick's suggestion that this altar to Augustus must have been raised in the *forum* of the lower town. This lies at the heart of the gentle rise marking the site of the old Iberian settlement close to the southwestern corner of the town. However, there is an implicit assumption in his account that it would have been erected

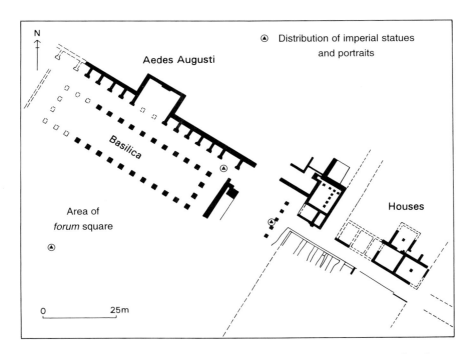

Figure 11.2   Plan of the basilica and *forum* of Tarraco showing the distribution of imperial statues and portraits (after Ruiz de Arbulo 1990).

in a *forum* that was already standing. If so, this would argue against the idea that this dynastic symbol was influential in the subsequent development of the town.

The archaeological evidence for the *forum* is largely restricted to the basilica (Mar and Ruiz de Arbulo 1986) (Figures 11.2, 11.3). This was a large rectangular building with a central space defined by columns with Attic bases and Corinthian capitals and an *ambulacrum*. Statue bases were found inside the central area (Figure 11.2). Its northern side was defined by a series of *tabernae*, which have been identified as merchants' offices. There was also a room let out of the centre of the back wall of the basilica, whose entrance from the main body of the basilica was flanked by two columns. This has recently been identified as a temple to Augustus (*aedes Augusti*), on the basis of Vitruvius' description of a similar room in his basilica at Fano in Italy (*De Architectura* 5.7), which also housed the tribunal (Mar and Ruiz de Arbulo 1986). One assumes that there would have been an image of Augustus at the back of this room, possibly akin to that at the rear of the *sacellum* of the theatre portico at Emerita (Mérida), the capital of Hispania Lusitania (Boschung 1990). In symbolic terms, therefore, the urban magistrates would have been seen to dispense

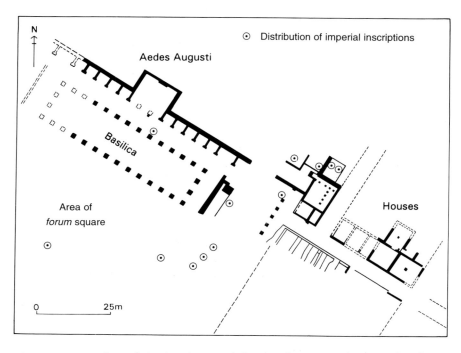

Figure 11.3 Plan of the basilica and *forum* of Tarraco showing the distribution of imperial inscriptions (after Ruiz de Arbulo 1990).

justice on behalf of imperial authority. There was an additional room, or *schola*, located at the eastern side of the basilica. In the course of the Julio-Claudian period this became a gallery with statues, one of which was a veiled portrait of Augustus (Koppel 1985: 44) although the others have yet to be identified with certainty.

As the basilica was excavated in the 1920s (Serra Vilaró 1932), the date of its construction is uncertain, although it is probably Augustan and possibly pre-dating 16–14 BC (Mar and Ruiz de Arbulo 1986; Ruiz de Arbulo 1990; *infra*). Nothing is known about the *forum* area proper which would have lain immediately to the south of this building, as it is obscured by buildings constructed at the turn of the century. It is possible, however, that it was paved and recent research has revealed that somewhere in the *forum* there was a triumphal arch similar to those known at Carpentras and Orange in southern France. This was decorated with barbarian captives, probably commemorating the theme of Augustan victory over barbarian peoples (Koppel 1990). Another building, which was probably located in the *forum*, or its close vicinity, was the *capitolium*, which was already old in the 60s AD (Suetonius *Galba* 8–9) and still extant in the second century AD (RIT 922).

Despite the lacunae in our knowledge of the above, it is possible to suggest that the altar to Augustus preceded, or was contemporary with, the construction of the *forum*. If the identification of the room at the rear of the basilica as the *aedes Augusti* is correct, then it is possible that it may have been built on axis to the altar of Augustus positioned in the *forum* square to the south. It is impossible to know whether this was contemporary with or later than the altar. In either case it is at least possible to argue that the latter was an important determinant in the layout of the *forum* complex. It is also possible that the altar was similarly the precedent for a temple of the municipal imperial cult at Tarraco. The literary sources inform us that Tiberius approved a request for such a temple to Augustus by the people of Tarraco in AD 15 (Tacitus *Annals* 1.78) and the building is illustrated on coins issued by the town (Burnett *et al.* 1992). As this is unlikely to have been built in the upper town, the discussion above suggests that the *forum* in the lower town was the obvious location, possibly along its southern side.

Unlike that in Arelate, the *forum* at Tarraco is not central to the town. It abuts the town wall in the southwestern corner of the town, an off-centre position which was dictated by the geography of the Republican and Iberian settlement. Nevertheless there is evidence that the orientation of the layout of the *forum* conditioned the rest of the street plan of the Augustan town. In the first instance it may have determined the path of the *via Augusta* as it passed diagonally through Tarraco before heading southwards towards Dertosa (Tortosa) and Saguntum (Sagunto). The discovery of a milestone dated to between 16 and 12 BC (RIT 934) in the vicinity of the modern Plaza de Toros a short distance to the southwest of the *forum* suggests that the road left the town at this point, at which it is recorded that a long-destroyed gateway flanked by towers was discovered in the sixteenth century (Ruiz de Arbulo 1990; Pons D'Icart 1572: 91 note 4). If this is correct, then the intra-mural stretch of this important road must also have helped condition other roads within the towns.

Serra Vilaró's excavations of the basilica also uncovered a stretch of street and flanking commercial premises leading away from it in a south-easterly direction. This suggests that the lower town of the *colonia* may have been divided up into *insula* blocks which share the orientation of the *forum*. Sadly, nothing is known about their relationship to the intra-mural path of the *via Augusta* discussed above. Nor is anything known of their chronology, although they must be contemporary with, or post-date, the construction of the *forum*. The same orientation is also shared by the theatre, which lies a few hundred metres to the south on a scarp overlooking the site of the ancient port. This was probably constructed in the Augustan period, in common with many others in Hispania (Jiménez 1993) although doubts have recently been expressed over its chronology (Mar *et al.* 1993) and an alternative late first-century AD date has been proposed. As with the basilica, there is evidence that this building had a strong ideological and dynastic flavour, as was the case with other theatres in Hispania, such as at Emerita, and elsewhere in the western Empire. It has been suggested that the *scaenae frons* was adorned with sculptures of Julio-Claudian princes (Koppel 1985: nos. 1 and 2).

Despite obvious shortfalls in the material evidence there are sufficient grounds to suggest that the *forum* of Tarraco may have been a dynastic centre with imperial symbolism and that, as at Arelate, there was a progression from altar to temple of the imperial cult during the Augustan and Tiberian periods. Furthermore, this development may have conditioned the transformation of the infrastructure of the earlier Republican settlement in the lower town.

The upper town

In contrast to the lower town virtually nothing is known about this sector until the Flavian period. It is clear that this was then replanned on a massive scale and that much of the area within the Republican walls was taken up with an architectural complex intended to serve as a focus for the provincial imperial cult and meetings of the provincial council (*concilium provinciae*). The impetus, if not the actual cost, for such a large undertaking, must surely have come from the Emperor Vespasian, anxious to establish the credibility of his new dynasty in the province of Tarraconensis. This great complex was terraced into the hillside around a central axis and comprised three discrete, but interdependent, architectural entities. There was an uppermost temple and precinct of Rome and Augustus which overlooked a large rectangular enclosure probably reserved for meetings of the provincial council and, at the lowest level, a circus for the celebration of imperial anniversaries and public meetings (TED'A 1989). All of this was built from concrete and local limestone and clad in white Carrara marble. Its association with the provincial imperial cult is attested by the fragments of the architectural decoration of the temple of Rome and Augustus and its precinct (Mar 1993), and corroborated by the many inscriptions of provincial *flamines* which were discovered within the area of the middle enclosure (Alföldy 1973).

The town overall

By the Augustan period Tarraco enclosed an area of at least 70 hectares. The evidence from the lower town suggests that the location of the altar of Augustus in 26 BC at the centre of the earlier Iberian and Republican settlement may have been influential in the development of the *forum* and, ultimately, the layout of much of this part of the town. The contrast between this new layout and earlier traditions is significant in that it epitomizes some of the contradictions inherent in the ideology of the

Augustan age. Nevertheless they accounted for only a small proportion of the urban area. By the end of the first century AD, however, dynastic considerations were sufficiently important for between 25 and 30 per cent of the total area of Tarraco to have been taken up by public buildings which were essentially symbolic in character. A similar process can be observed both at other provincial capitals and, of course, at Rome itself.

THE URBAN LANDSCAPE AS A COGNITIVE MAP

The layout and organization of each of these buildings could have been understood as having symbolized imperial control over a key activity in the daily life of the urban population. Architecture is ultimately concerned with the physical delimitation of space and articulating movement within buildings. Moreover the internal organization of public buildings closely associated with the state, such as the municipal *forum* discussed above, is a symbolic expression of the relationship of imperial power to provincial subject.

Within this system the standardized imperial images and statues played a key role as an important symbol of imperial power, serving to focus public attention both within buildings and in public spaces. The strength of the symbol, however, was that it was not imposed on subject populations. In the Augustan and early imperial period at least, before the 'routine' of imperial celebrations had become established, it was an honour granted by the subjects to their ruler (Price 1984: 175) and thus expressed loyalty of a section of the population to the Emperor. In this capacity, therefore, the statues represented by the portrait heads at Tarraco were an index of the fervour and loyalty of the elite citizens to the Emperor and formed an integral part of the new symbolic urban landscape. It is difficult to be certain if any of those discovered so far were cult images as such, or whether they were more likely to have come from statues in public places not destined for formal ritual. In either case, once the tradition of ritual had become established, imperial statues may have had an added significance. In the Greek-speaking world, for example, imperial statues were perceived to have special properties. They could reveal divine portents and could act as *foci* for refuge and asylum. They also served as 'a potent focal point for evocations of the Emperor' (Price 1984: 195).

It has been argued recently that urban space was structured by the daily activities of the urban elites, rather than the lower-status populace which remained largely immobile. In Rome at least, elites needed to be seen at a set range of public locations, such as the baths and the *forum*, on a daily basis to reinforce their status (Laurence 1994: 129–32). If one accepts that a growing range of public buildings in provincial towns like Tarraco had clear ideological connotations, then daily elite activities served continually to reinforce the geography of imperial power in the town. That in turn conditioned the way the majority of the population perceived the 'reality' that lay around them. In the broader sense, therefore, the situation and interrelationships of *forum*, theatre, streets and imperial cult complex at Tarraco were symbols which may have been understood by its inhabitants as manifestations of power in the broader world at a local level: 'imagery' of this kind may have been reinforced by the symbolism on the silver and bronze coins issued by the town down to the earlier first century AD (Burnett *et al.* 1992).

In this sense, therefore, the topography and planning of Augustan and early imperial Tarraco could have been 'read' as a cognitive map within a mindframe conditioned by the local elite perception of the religious and political ideals of Augustus and his successors. This reasoning may not be as objective as one might like but at least the biases in the construction of the case are clear. Similarly, it may be objected that this model is based upon the translation into a provincial context of the known relationship between symbol and subject in the city of Rome. Nevertheless, this is intended as a model and as such may be tested against future evidence and accepted or rejected.

THE DEVELOPMENT OF A NEW HISTORICAL ORDER

The physical transformation of Tarraco described above implies a break with past social traditions. This is evident in the nature and scale of the buildings, sculptures and inscriptions which now dominated the town. At the same time, however, it can be argued that continuity of the existing social order at Tarraco, and particularly the dominance of the old-established elite families, may have been the primary objective. An important contributory element to this was the systematic creation of a new historical order within the town: after all, this was the context in which the 'cognitive map' discussed above was created. In effect the collective memory and ideological framework of the literate elite at Tarraco were being altered in favour of one which was in tune with the new imperial ideas being generated at Rome. The principal means of doing this, of course, was through inscriptions put up by the town and by ideologically conformist elites. As has been argued elsewhere, inscriptions were not so much a record of history as the means of *creating histories* (Barrett 1993). Side by side with coinage they were one of the means through which public memory was made possible and could be transmitted from one generation to the next. By implication the transmission of public memory would have played an important role in ensuring the reproduction of politico-cultural behaviour from one generation to the next.

Excavations at Tarraco have uncovered a number of inscriptions in the *forum* and its vicinity which clearly associate the town with Augustus and his achievements. One sandstone plaque erected by the Colonia Triumphalis Tarraco commemorates the *victoriae Augustae* (RIT 58) between 26 and 19 BC. It may be a reference to Augustus' victory over the Cantabri in northwestern Spain, an event which undoubtedly contributed towards his military reputation and high status in the eyes of provincials, fuelled his imperial propaganda and ultimately reinforced the new order being established at provincial level. Apart from being an important event in itself, it was a significant step in the new Roman historical process, and by publicly commemorating it, Tarraco associates itself with the new regime and continues to bolster its dominance in the province. Other inscriptions record dedications to individuals closely associated with the *domus Augusta* (RIT 66 and 67). These were seen as public acts of allegiance to the new order, which enhanced the status of the dedicant. The discovery of a dedication to the *numen Augusti* (RIT 48) at the theatre suggests that similar acts of public allegiance took place here too.

These and other commemorative and dedicatory inscriptions would have helped to 'legitimize' the perceived reality of the world implicit in the layout of the *forum*, theatre and walls and the overall organization of space within the town. After all, buildings usually provided the physical context for these kinds of inscription. This would have been reinforced by subsequent dedicatory and commemorative inscriptions to Tiberius (RIT 68, 69, 72 and 145) and later Emperors down to the early fourth century AD. Those dating to the first half of the first century AD mark moments of renewal by commemorating subsequent Emperors in a physical context intimately associated with the constructed imperial vision of the immediate past. The imperial present and, by implication, the future were thus reinforced by the imperial past. Every act of public commemoration of this kind thus represented a conscious acceptance of the ideological status quo and contributed towards its perpetuation. There is little doubt that these were reinforced by the periodic ceremonies associated with the municipal imperial cult. From year to year the symbolic meanings of the inscriptions and buildings would have been reinforced with specific rituals.

The *forum* of the *concilium provinciae* was distinct, in that this particular complex was the ideological focus for the entire province and probably represents a claim to legitimacy by the new Flavian dynasty in an important province after a period of dangerous instability. The majority of the inscriptions discovered here were formally set up by annual high priests (*flamines*) for Tarraconensis in the context of their honorary duties. Like the annual meetings here and the rituals associated with the imperial cult in the adjoining terraces, this was an act which reinforced the legitimacy of the status quo of elites of the province as a whole and, by implication, the state itself.

CONTINUITY AND CHANGE

There seems to be little doubt that the early imperial buildings and monuments at Tarraco were meaningfully constituted cultural symbols, being validated by direct reference to the new ideological and cultural order being developed at Rome itself. They can also be understood as playing an important role in cultural change. In the first instance the contrast with the earlier Iberian and Republican topography could not be clearer. However, there is a tendency to assume that after the completion of the Flavian complex of the upper town the imperial 'mould' of the town's topography was somehow set and that it simply 'continues' as an architectural entity until the town begins a process of topographic decline from the later second or third centuries AD onwards. The archaeological evidence for both monumental complexes in the upper and lower towns is poor, it must be admitted. The former was excavated in the 1920s and much of the interior of the latter is obscured by standing medieval and later buildings. Nevertheless it appears that all the spaces defined by the substantial standing walls of the *forum* and the imperial cult complex appear essentially unchanged until they begin to decline in the fourth and fifth centuries respectively. Nevertheless a combination of literary allusions and inscriptions shows that there was continual development within the new complexes. The Augustan *forum* was probably constantly being remodelled, with new buildings being added, new inscriptions and new imperial reigns being commemorated by new statues. Less is known about the development of the monuments that comprised the imperial cult complex, although the passing of dynasties and the passage of time was marked by inscriptions put up by *flamines* in the *forum* of the *concilium provinciae* (Alföldy 1973) and, presumably, other monuments which have not survived. A conventional interpretation would be to understand these changes in purely formalistic architectural terms, looking for parallels, new influences and so on. An alternative would be to see them in terms of changing ideological landscapes in which the passage of time is marked in both cases by the creation of new points of reference, such as imperial titles, anniversaries, deities, personages within the context of the system of values that were implicit in the original Augustan complex. Structural changes were usually placed in the context of Roman imperial time by allusion to the reigns of the Emperor during which they were completed or consecrated (Duncan-Jones 1990). Perception of the cognitive geography of these monuments therefore changes with time and although the monuments might appear to have remained constant to us, the symbolic meaning for the inhabitants at different periods would have differed. In this sense, therefore, change is taking place within the context of continuity.

THE SOCIAL IMPLICATIONS

It is important to recognize that the impetus behind the cultural transformation of Tarraco was probably the resident elites at Tarraco itself. There is always a temptation to ascribe the construction of major public buildings to the magnanimity of individual Emperors or other major public figures. Although this may sometimes have been the case (Duncan-Jones 1990: 57–76), this should not be assumed unless there is specific epigraphic evidence. Moreover, given that the construction of public buildings linked to the fortunes of the Emperor or state was probably interpreted by contemporaries as an act of political loyalty, and as such would have been central to the success of the Roman Empire, the construction of *fora*, statues, altars and inscriptions were probably spontaneous expressions of personal loyalty to the Emperor, particularly in the period prior to the middle of the first century AD. The underlying motivation for this is, of course, impossible to gauge. It would not be unreasonable, however, to suggest that by being seen to be publicly associated with the Emperor in such a way, elite families were motivated by a wish to ensure the stability of their own social position. After all, ideological conformity with the dominant power in the world may have been understood to guarantee social or political advancement or some other form of recognition from imperial officials in the town. In short, the advent of the new order provided an effective vehicle for ensuring the continued social dominance of the established elite families at Tarraco.

Many of the families involved in this process were Roman citizens, and by definition thus enjoyed close political, legal and linguistic ties with the capital. It is more difficult to ascertain whether they were more recent arrivals or whether they could trace their origin to immigration from Italy in the course of the Republic: the epigraphic record for this period is largely non-existent. It seems probable that a significant proportion emigrated to Tarraco in the Republican period, but that only those families with sufficient landed wealth, who had either survived the turmoil of the later Republic, or who owed their position to the new order, would have had the necessary financial resources publicly to express their loyalty in this manner. However, it would be a mistake to assume that the whole population of the town, urban and rural, were all Roman citizens and shared the same values. In general terms, it has been argued that it is only the dominant classes that are strongly committed to dominant ideologies (Giddens 1979: 72). At the same time the survival of native traditions in material culture until the end of the first century BC in this part of Iberia, as indeed in other parts of the western Mediterranean, is well attested (Keay 1991, for example). The same is implied by the persistence of native-style (non-Roman) urban planning at sites in areas to the west (ancient Iesso) and south (the site at Tossal de Manises) of Tarraco, which suggests that non-Roman elements of the population may have reacted differently to symbols of Roman imperial ideology, implicitly rejecting the social contradictions that it masked and instead adopting elements of the Roman cultural suite (sculptures, theatres, etc.) in a piecemeal fashion.

CONCLUSION

Roman towns are thus important symbols of cultural change which encapsulate some of the problems in trying to understand the transition from native to Roman in Iberia. The essential point of this chapter is that in archaeological terms it is not sufficient merely to chart this or describe it in descriptive or structural terms, but to analyse the archaeological evidence for possible symbolic content. It is commonplace to see the advent of Roman urban form as merely the advent of 'civilization', 'better facilities', or as a development driven by economic or financial agency alone and a means of displaying status. However, this is only part of the answer. One needs to understand towns as the more visible symbols of a radical ideological change in which, in the first instance, major Roman communities in the western Mediterranean participate in the new political and religious values being created at Rome, as well as the *new* historical continuum and concept of time. The driving force for this was a desire for personal advancement within the new political system, both at municipal and imperial level, through overt self-identification with the new embodiment of the Roman state. Its effect must have been to ensure the continued dominance of those elite families that had been sufficiently astute to realize the importance and significance of the new imperial ideology from an early stage. Thus, just as the new imperial ideology ensured a perpetuation of the unequal balance of power between Emperor and the 'executive' body of the state (the Senate) at Rome, so it masked an unequal balance of power between elite families and others in the provinces. At the same time, one must distinguish between Roman families at Tarraco and other major communities, who would have shared the same concepts of ideology, symbolism and time, and those in lesser centres whose perception of them may have been very different. The important point, however, is that the cultural change apparent in the development of architectural forms and sculptural types in politically sensitive centres like Tarraco from the Augustan period onwards actually masks a strong degree of social reproduction. After all, material culture does not reflect cultural behaviour, so much as transform it.

ABBREVIATIONS

RIT: Alföldy, G. (1975) *Römische Inschriften von Tarraco*, Berlin: De Gruyter.

REFERENCES

Adserias, M., Burés, L., Miró, M. T. and Ramón, E. (1993) 'L'assentament pre-romà de Tarragona', *Revista d'Arqueologia de Ponent* 3: 177–227.

Alföldy, G. (1973) *Flamines provinciae Hispaniae citerioris*, Anejos del Archivo Español de Arqueología 6, Madrid: Consejo Superior de Investigaciones Científicas.

—— (1975) *Römische Inschriften von Tarraco*, Berlin: De Gruyter.

—— (1991) *Tarraco*, Fòrum 8, Tarragona: Museu Arqueològic.

Barrett, J. (1993) 'Chronologies of Remembrance: The Interpretation of some Roman Inscriptions', *World Archaeology* 25.2: 236–47.

—— (1994) *Fragments From Antiquity: An Archaeology of Social Life in Britain, 2900–1200 BC*, Oxford: Blackwell.

Beard, M. and Crawford, M. (1985) *Rome in the Late Republic*, London: Duckworth.

Boschung, D. (1990) 'Die Präsenz des Kaiserhauses im öffentlichen Bereich', in W. Trillmich and P. Zanker (eds) (1990): 391–400.

Brandt, R. and Slofstra, J. (1983) *Roman and Native in the Low Countries. Spheres of Interaction*. British Archaeological Reports, International Series 184, Oxford: British Archaeological Reports.

Braudel, F. (1975) *The Mediterranean and the Mediterranean World in the Age of Philip II*, London: Fontana.

Burnett, A., Amandry, M. and Ripollés, P. P. (1992) *Roman Provincial Coinage. Volume 1. From the Death of Caesar to the Death of Vitellius (44 BC–AD 69)*, Part 1, London/Paris: British Museum Publications/Bibiothèque Nationale de Paris.

Duncan-Jones, R. (1990) *Structure and Scale in the Roman Economy*, Cambridge: Cambridge University Press.

Dyson, S. (1993) 'From New to New Age Archaeology: Archaeological Theory and Classical Archaeology – A 1990s Perspective', *American Journal of Archaeology* 97: 195–206.

Fishwick, D. (1982) 'The Altar of Augustus and the Municipal Cult of Tarraco', *Madrider Mitteilungen* 23: 223–33.

Giddens, A. (1979) *Central Problems in Social Theory*, London: Macmillan.

Gros, P. (1990) 'Nouveau Paysage urbain et cultes dynastiques: remarques sur l'idéologie de la ville augustéene à partir des centres monumentaux d'Athènes, Thasos, Arles et Nîmes', in *Les Villes Augustéennes de Gaule. Colloque d'Autun 1985*: 127–40.

Gruen, E. (1992) *Culture and National Identity in Republican Rome*, Ithaca, NY: Cornell University Press.

Hodder, I. (1991) *Reading The Past*, 2nd edition, Cambridge: Cambridge University Press.

Jiménez, J. J. (1993) 'Teatro y Desarrollo Monumental Urbana en Hispania', in S. Ramallo and F. Santiuste de Pablos (eds) *Teatros Romanos de Hispania*.

Cuadernos de Arquitectura Romana 2: 207–17, Murcia: Universidad de Murcia and Colegio Oficial de Arquitectos de Murcia.

Keay, S. (1991) 'Processes in the development of the coastal communities of Hispania Citerior in the Republican Period', in T. Blagg and M. Millett (eds) *The Early Roman Empire in the West*: 120–50, Oxford: Oxbow Books.

—— (1995) 'Innovation and Adaption: The Contribution of Rome to Urbanism in Iberia', in B. Cunliffe and S. Keay (eds) *Social Complexity and the Development of Towns in Iberia. From the Copper Age to the Second Century AD*: 291–338, Oxford: Oxford University Press.

Knapp, R. (1977) *Aspects of the Roman Experience in Iberia, 206–100 BC*, Anejos de Hispania Antiqua IX: Alava/Valladolid: Universidad de Valladolid/Colegio Universitario de Alava.

Koppel, E. (1985) *Die römischen Skulpturen von Tarraco*, Berlin: De Gruyter.

—— (1990) 'Relieves arquitectónicos de Tarragona', in W. Trillmich and P. Zanker (eds) (1990): 327–40.

Laurence, R. (1994) *Roman Pompeii: Space and Society*, London: Routledge.

Mar, R. (1993) 'El recinto de culto imperial de Tárraco y la arquitectura flavia', in R. Mar (ed.) *Els monuments provincials de Tarraco. Documents d'arqueologia classica 1*: 107–56, Tarragona: Universitat Rovira I Virgili.

Mar, R., Roca, M. and Ruiz de Arbulo, J. (1993) 'El teatro romano de Tarragona. Un problema pendiente', in S. Ramallo and F. Santiuste de Pablos (eds) *Teatros Romanos de Hispania. Cuadernos de Arquitectura Romana 2*: 11–23, Murcia: Universidad de Murcia and Colegio Oficial de Arquitectos de Murcia.

Mar, R. and Ruiz de Arbulo, J. (1987). *La basílica de la colonia Tarraco. Una nueva interpretacion del llamado foro bajo de Tarragona*, Fòrum 3, Tarragona: Museu Arqueològic de Tarragona.

Marín Díaz, M. A. (1987) *Emigración, colonización y municipalización en la Hispania Republicana*, Granada: Universidad de Granada.

Millett, M. (1991) *The Romanization of Britain*, Cambridge: Cambridge University Press.

Pons d'Icart, L. (1572) *Libro de las grandezas y cosas memorables de la Metropolitana, Insigne y Famosa de Tarragona*, Lérida (reprinted Tarragona 1981).

Price, S. (1984) *Rituals And Power. The Roman Imperial Cult in Asia Minor*, Cambridge: Cambridge University Press.

Renfrew, C. (1994) 'Towards a Cognitive Archaeology', in C. Renfrew and E. B. W. Zubrow (eds) *The Ancient Mind: Elements of Cognitive Archaeology*: 3–12, Cambridge: Cambridge University Press.

Ruiz de Arbulo, J. (1986) 'El foro de Tarraco', *Cypsela* VIII: 119–38.

Serra Vilaró, J. (1932) *Excavaciones en Tarragona*, Memorias de la Junta Superior de Excavaciones Arqueológicas 116 (1930), Madrid.

Shanks, M. and Tilley, C. (1987) *Social Theory and Archaeology*, Oxford: Polity Press.

TED'A (1989) 'El foro provincial de Tarraco, un complejo arquitectónico de época flavia', *Archivo Español De Arqueología* 62: 141–91.

Trillmich, W. and Zanker, P. (eds) (1990) *Stadtbild und Ideologie. Die Monumentalisierung hispanischer Städte zwischen Republik und Kaiserzeit*, Munich: Bayerische Akademie der Wissenschaften.

Zanker, P. (1984) *The Power of Images in the Age of Augustus*, Ann Arbor: University of Michigan Press.

CHAPTER TWELVE

HISPANIA

From the second century AD *to Late Antiquity*

ISABEL RODÀ

INTRODUCTION

The transformation of the Roman Empire in the course of the Early and Late Imperial periods has been the subject of much debate in recent years. In the case of the provinces of the Hispaniae, prosperity (Figure 12.1), in so far as it is evident in the monumentalization of towns, was the product of two key periods, the reign of Augustus (31 BC–AD 14) and the reigns of the Flavian Emperors (AD 69–96). This ushers in a period, namely the reign of the Emperor Trajan (AD 98–117), which is still little understood in the Iberian Peninsula. In the broader sense, however, it should not be considered so much the moment of the Empire's greatest expansion, as the point at which continual obligations and conquests ultimately led to the collapse of a form of government. The reign of Marcus Aurelius (AD 161–80) represents a contrast with respect to previous periods. On the one hand, it can be said that it saw the generalization of the cultural achievements of Hadrian's reign (AD 117–38). On the other, however, it witnessed wars on the frontiers and military problems in Britain and in the Straits of Gibraltar.

A major break followed during the reigns of the Emperors of the Severan dynasty (AD 193–235). While the use of elements of the iconography and nomenclature of Marcus Aurelius represented a claim to the continuity of the established order, closer inspection reveals increasing difficulties in retaining a unified Empire. Later, the Germanic invasions of the mid-third century AD highlight the inability of the Roman Emperors to find a solution to their frontier problems, although their impact throughout the Empire as a whole should not be exaggerated. However, the gradual loss of territory in the course of the century was significant and is perhaps symptomatic of territorial readjustment. The Tetrarchy (AD 284–305) represents a reaction against this. In an attempt to combat the growing fragmentation of the Empire a new kind of

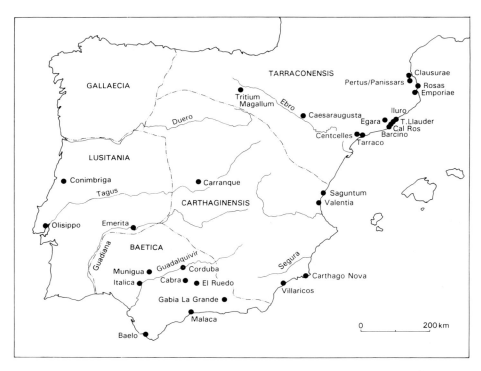

Figure 12.1 Map of the Hispanic provinces of the Late Empire showing the location of places cited in the text.

dynastic principle was implemented for a short time, while the Empire was governed through a rigid system of smaller units. The consequences of this become visible in the later fourth century AD, by which time there had developed an administrative system and cultural mix that was sufficiently resilient to absorb the renewed Germanic invasions at the beginning of the fifth century AD. As a consequence, therefore, the 'collapse' of the Roman Empire has little meaning as a concept, given that the Empire *per se* did not exist by the time that it is supposed to have collapsed.

The study of any individual province in the Empire will invariably bring out characteristics that distinguish it from other parts of the Roman Empire. Epigraphy, on the other hand, tends to illustrate detail and general trends can only be discerned through repetition or by analogy.

This chapter draws upon the picture of the Empire discussed above and attempts to gauge its impact upon the provinces of Hispania. It adopts a long-term perspective on cultural change in the Iberian Peninsula and, rather than attempt a synthesis, explores a number of issues concerning the current state of our archaeological, epigraphic and historical knowledge. There is no attempt to be exhaustive in the themes addressed, although the chapter has sought to follow a chronological sequence, thereby developing into a historical discourse complemented by an analysis of material culture.

THE TRANSITION FROM THE FIRST TO SECOND CENTURIES AD

The later first and the very beginning of the second centuries AD have received most attention from scholars, principally in the context of the concession of privileges to the cities of Hispania by the Flavian Emperors (AD 69–96), the purpose of which is still not clear. The hypothesis put forward by Sasel (1983) is still valid although advances have been made by Guichard (1993) and others. Sasel's hypothesis begins by recognizing Vespasian's (AD 69–79) concession of municipal statutes as exceptional and interprets it as evidence of political gratitude. This Slovenian researcher points out that this gesture is not explained sufficiently by the *Hispani* having supported the Emperor against Vitellius, and suggests that it may possibly represent the fulfilment of a promise, perhaps made earlier by Nero (cf. Seneca *De ben.* 6.19.2). Flavian generosity had been preceded by a short-lived attempt by the Emperor Otho (AD 69) to favour the Iberian Peninsula. Ultimately, therefore, by pragmatically favouring communities in Hispania, Vespasian was establishing a bridge of continuity with the earlier Julio-Claudian dynasty (27 BC–AD 68).

The Flavian period also saw the permanent stationing of the legion created by Galba, and known as *Legio VII Gemina*, in Hispania. This formed a stable army that controlled the rich mining area of the north-west from the moment of its foundation down to its dissolution in the later Empire. This era also saw the maintenance of the roads and the introduction of new priests of the imperial cult. The economic and social effects of all these reforms has been discussed recently by Guichard (1993), while Etienne (1958) has suggested that the apparent continuity of the Flavian period masked a break in the cultic sphere.

These statements provide a basis for explaining Flavian developments. This readjustment also helps explain the decadence of earlier centres, including privileged towns. It seems to have been the consequence of an even greater change than previously suspected, not least due to successive strikes against the central Empire by the Emperors Galba (AD 69) and Otho (AD 69) from bases in the Peninsula and the exploitation of the Peninsula's resources. These must have provoked major economic crises requiring intervention by Rome. Such a situation would have broken Hispania's allegiance to the Julio-Claudian family. In the Neronian period this had been characterized by the presence of portraits of his Empress-mother, Agrippina, throughout the Iberian peninsula (Trillmich 1982). Moreover, the fact that many monuments in Hispania were decorated in marble during the Neronian period emphasizes its special importance: in particular one might cite the example of Olisippo (Lisbon), where the Augustan theatre was renovated at this time (Hauschild 1990). On the other hand, archaeology has now confirmed that much of the programme of urban change which had been thought to have taken place under Vespasian (AD 69–79) in fact occurred under Domitian (AD 81–96). This is true of both the juridical organization of cities and the monumentalization of urban centres, the most exceptional of which was undoubtedly Tarraco.

THE ANTONINE DYNASTY (AD 138–92)

The second period of development seems to have had its origins in the changes of tone introduced into Iberia during the reign of Trajan and the consolidation of the social ascendancy of the *Hispani*. However, it posed serious problems in the economy and in the distribution of property in the towns and regions of origin. It also saw a rise in personal benefaction (euergetism) on a large scale.

The rise of Trajan cannot be understood as a planned goal or the pinnacle of an upward social movement achieved collectively by Hispani and perceived as such within the Empire. Nevertheless there is little doubt that his rise to power was a consequence of the groundwork first laid down in the late Republican period, especially in Baetica, and that his reign had consequences for the elites of Hispania. The social promotion of *Hispani* became increasingly frequent, although it was never the direct cause of one of them becoming Emperor. Trajan's reign was also an important time for the development of aspects of the infrastructure of Hispania, evident in such monuments as the Alcántara bridge (Liz 1986), which was later extensively restored, or the Segovia aqueduct (Alföldy 1992), even though the record of road building is poor (Lostal 1992; Sillières 1990). It may well be that one has to look forward to the reign of Hadrian for the completion of projects which may have been planned, or begun, under Trajan. Urban archaeology has shown this to have been the case at Rome, and, similarly, the *nova urbs* of Italica in Baetica can be reinterpreted within the Hadrianic building programme (León 1988; Keay 1992). The reign of Antoninus Pius (AD 138–61) is characterized by abundant inscriptions and appears to represent institutional consolidation, as the Empire rapidly begins to undergo changes that in Hispania would be manifested regionally.

THE END OF THE SECOND CENTURY AD

It has been pointed out, with reason, that the reign of Marcus Aurelius (AD 161–80) marks an important divide in the development of the Roman Empire. This is manifested politically by growing insecurity within the

Empire, but is also evident in the cultural sphere as the culmination of earlier trends. With regard to Hispania, many scholars believe that this discontinuity is due to the invasion of the Mauri, who crossed into the province of Baetica from Mauretania. Alföldy (1987), for instance, stresses the impact of the *bellum Mauricum* in areas of the Peninsula distant from the scene of the actual incursions. He also points out that the disquiet in Mauretania dated back to the Flavian period and that, later, Hadrian (AD 117–38) had tried to contain potential danger. Once again both sides of the Straits of Gibraltar demonstrate the confluence of their historical development, a reality which the Emperor Claudius (AD 41–54) understood when he simultaneously organized the region of the Gaditanian (the town of Baelo Claudia) and Moroccan coastlines. Nevertheless, the entrance of the Mauri into Baetica in AD 171 has been viewed as a critical moment of change for the Hispanic provinces, all the more so when it is remembered that the expeditions sent to counter them had only a limited success and that a second incursion occurred ca. AD 177. Nevertheless, one must be careful not to exaggerate the importance of this historical event.

THE SEVERAN DYNASTY (AD 193–235)

An evaluation of the archaeological analyses of some Roman cities has recently driven Sillières (1993b) to ask whether people were living amongst ruins at the end of the second century in Hispania. In the first instance the question may seem surprising, but it could not be more pertinent. Attention should be drawn to the ubiquity of abandoned houses dating to the later second and the third centuries, as well as the abandonment of industrial and commercial zones by the third century, as at Munigua (Mulva, Sevilla), Baelo (Bolonia, Cádiz), Emporiae (Empúries, Girona) and Conimbriga (Condeixa-a-Velha). However, it is very difficult to sustain the argument that this kind of evidence represents 'life among the ruins'. Notwithstanding this, it cannot be doubted that a number of public spaces were reconverted during the Severan period, thus bringing about the change which appears to lead to Sillières's conclusion.

Despite the apparently ruinous state of Roman cities at this time, coins and ceramics bear witness to the continuity of life with some measure of prosperity as Sillières (1993a) himself points out. It is very probable that this evidence in fact represents the degeneration of an urban panorama comprising accumulated monuments and relatively sumptuous dwellings, whose restoration had become infrequent, a trend which the state had attempted to counter with legislation for private buildings from the mid first century AD, and for public buildings from the reign of Antoninus Pius (*Digest* 50.10; Janvier 1969). This must have led to the abandonment of public spaces or their conversion into more utilitarian structures.

By contrast, there is also clear evidence for important state involvement in the roads, the monumentalization of public buildings, and the growth of private buildings in suburban and even rural environments. This suggests that there was an adaptation to new needs and realities in the towns of Hispania during the Severan period, rather than an atmosphere of decay. The *continuity* that this implies had already begun to be expressed by Balil (1972) in his time, in the context of the development of the economy of Hispania between the Antonines and the Severans, a view which has had an important subsequent influence.

Reigns as controversial as those of Caracalla (AD 198–217) and Elagabalus (AD 218–22) are reflected in the monumental record and in the development of infrastructure. This is the case of the ample road reform undertaken by the former, who attempted to separate the *conventus* of northwest Hispania in the first attempt at territorial reorganization since Augustus. Elagabalus, for his part, undertook the restoration of the amphitheatre at Tarraco (TED'A 1990). The Severan period is similarly important for urban centres. In some towns, such as Saguntum (Hernández *et al.* 1993; Hernández 1989) and Italica (Corzo 1993; Rodà forthcoming), theatres were refurbished in the first half of the third century. In the case of the latter there is epigraphic proof of a new decorative style and at the former, there was a remodelling that, in the opinion of its excavators, could have been caused by a generic change in the function of the theatres themselves, at a time when they were being adapted to become scenarios for gladiatorial combats. Further north, at Iluro (Mataró), the urban infrastructure was renewed and at the same time, the luxury *villae* at Torre Llauder (Mataró) and Cal Ros de les Cabres (El Masnou) in the vicinity of this town were reformed while retaining their sumptuous character (Prevosti 1981). Indeed, it is becoming increasingly clear that a substantial proportion of the large villas in Hispania experienced continuity more than an abrupt change during the third century, as exemplified by the villas of El Ruedo de Almedinilla (Córdoba) and the 'Mithra' of Cabra (Córdoba), in the province of Baetica (Vaquerizo *et al.* 1994; Jiménez Salvador and Martín Bueno 1992).

It is true to say, however, that in so far as its internal workings were concerned urban life underwent a period of recession. Elites were no longer as concerned about the incentive for social advancement offered by the exercising of magistracies as they had been during the first two centuries AD. Also, the acts of personal benefaction by private citizens that had contributed so much to the monumentalization of urban centres in the first two centuries of Empire became progressively rarer. One must, furthermore, bear in mind that contemporary epigraphic 'saturation' caused the impact of inscriptions to diminish. At the same time the medium of public texts changes, and given climatic conditions in the Iberian Peninsula, it becomes difficult to evaluate the proportion of *painted* texts to those inscribed on stone (Mayer 1993; 1995).

There is an analogous problem with honorific sculpture, whose development was very closely linked to that of inscriptions. Similarly, the funeral portraits that been so commonplace between the first and mid-second centuries AD diminish substantially during the third and fourth. At the same time, however, it should be remembered that there was significant continuity and even an increase of the decorative reliefs on *stelae* or sarcophagi. Studying such changes in fashions is not a frivolous activity, given that they reflect social changes. An analysis of the rich series of portraits from Emerita (Mérida) (Nogales 1993) allows us to gauge these, and to have a better chance of understanding those influences that transform the artistic representation of individuals.

In the context of the early third century, there have been attempts to make known the changes which took place in the commercialization and transport of olive oil from Baetica and to see them as of critical importance to the economy of Hispania (Remesal 1986; Blázquez *et al.* 1994; Sillières 1993b) in the same way that earlier studies had understood Domitian's (AD 81–96) prohibition of provincial viticulture as a way of protecting Italian wine production. However, weaknesses in the data make it hard to gauge their consequences and the degree to which they can be verified. This surely reflects gaps in research, but also suggests that repercussions may have been limited. Competition and changes in the direction of commercial circuits must be evaluated as a whole to avoid generalizations on the basis of local phenomena alone. For example, the production of *garum* fluctuates during the third century, while by contrast, the fourth sees the strong resurgence of the 'salazones' industries in the northeast of the Peninsula, as has been attested at Roses or Barcino (Barcelona) which enjoyed a privileged relationship with the city of Burdigala (Bordeaux) in western Gaul at this time (Nolla and Nieto 1981; Rodà 1991). The tendency for rural establishments to become less dependent upon towns, which begins in the second century and becomes clear in the third, has been considered to be a characteristic fourth-century development. However, this is more an observation than an absolute truth.

THE THIRD CENTURY AFTER THE SEVERANS

The brief reign of the Emperor Maximinus Thrax (AD 235–8) is of particular note for Hispania. This is evident in the road-building programme, given that some ten milestones (*miliaria*) have been discovered across a wide area of Hispania Tarraconensis (Lostal 1992), recording the restoration of bridges and roads with a characteristic epigraphic formula (IRC III, 194). It must also be remembered that this Emperor lent his name to the *Legio VII Gemina* and, as Alföldy (1987) has recently proposed on the basis of an inscription from Dianium (Denia), used the eastern coast as a springboard for dealing with insurrections in Africa, events which ultimately led to his death and the rise to power of the Emperor Gordian (AD 238–44).

The significance of the so-called Gallic Empire (*Imperium Gallicum*) (AD 259–73) for the Iberian Peninsula is largely unknown, and the oft-maintained generalization that Hispania adhered to it during the reign of Postumus is still far from certain (Mayer and Rodà 1990). There are a few known inscriptions mentioning the Gallic usurpers by name and in some areas of Hispania these coincide with those of the Emperor Gallienus (AD 253–68): there is little doubt that a comparison of the distribution of coins issued by both 'parties' would shed light on this problem. The silence of epigraphic sources is clearly illustrated by the contrast between Cantabria and the northwest, on the one hand, and the northeast of the Peninsula on the other. Postumus (AD 259–68) is documented in the former, whilst there is no information from the latter. Thus there are no imperial dedicatory inscriptions at Barcino between the reigns of Marcus Aurelius (AD 161–80) and Claudius Gothicus (AD 270–3), while at Tarraco, the silence of the epigraphic sources is significant with an absence of dedications between Decius (AD 249–51) and Aurelian (AD 270–5). Keay (1981) also notes this curious absence of data and notes the massive presence of Gallienus' coinage in the *conventus Tarraconensis*.

The first 'barbarian invasion' of AD 261/2 has to be understood against this imperfectly known background. Its effect upon urban centres is now thought to have been less devastating than was thought only a few years ago, and has only been specifically noted at such towns as Barcino (Barcelona) and Tarraco (Tarragona). This first invasion also served to highlight the route taken by later waves of barbarian invaders, for whom the sacking of Hispania was only a bridgehead for reaching Africa. There were in later periods other moments of crisis and near civil war in Hispania, such as the repression of Bonosus' uprising in AD 280 by the Emperor Probus (AD 276–82), recorded in the *Historia Augusta* (*Quadr. Tyr.* 14). At the same time, however, there was a degree of stability in the Peninsula during these troubled times which is reflected in the epigraphic record of the reigns of Probus (AD 282–3), Carus (AD 282–3), Carinus (AD 283–5) and Numerian (AD 283–4).

During these decades of the third century, there were important relations with the present-day Maghreb region of North Africa, and Emerita (Mérida) and coastal Tarraconensis were amongst the principal points of contact for African influence. The letter of St Cyprian speaks eloquently for the region of Emerita (*epist.* 67), while African martyrs are known from a number of towns in Tarraconensis (Mayer 1991b; Sotomayor 1979). This close link between early Christianity in Hispania and Africa was echoed by Prudentius at a later date (*Perist.* 4). It has to be understood in the context of the abundant presence of African ceramics and other material culture which have been discovered on contemporary Mediterranean coastal sites and in Baetica, and was to be especially characteristic from the fourth century onwards. By contrast, the markets of the interior were stocked with local products, such as the so-called late *sigillata hispanica*. This was manufactured on the outskirts of Tritium

Magallum (Tricio La Rioja), a centre of great importance which distributed its products principally in the Ebro valley and the Duero basin (Garabito 1978; Mayet 1984; Palol 1986; López 1985; Fuentes 1989).

THE TETRARCHY AND THE FOURTH CENTURY

In Hispania, as in other parts of the Empire, the years of Tetrarchic rule (AD 284–305) brought about a series of changes which marked the end of the organizational system initiated under Augustus. The reforms of Diocletian (AD 284–305) represented a last attempt to match political and administrative realities. The most illustrative of these changes was a new administrative framework which included the *Hispaniae* and *Mauretania Tingitana* within the *diocesis Hispaniarum*, and a reorganization of provincial territories which saw Emerita (Mérida) emerge as the centre of political gravity in the Peninsula. These and other details are recorded in the famous *laterculus Veronensis* document (Seeck 1962): in reality, however, this tells us little more than the bare outlines. The *Nova Provincia Maxima* documented in Siresa (CIL II 4911), or the episode concerning the Balearic isles in the fourth century (Laterculus Polemius, *Silui*, 4.7, ed. O. Seeck) are symptomatic of how little is known.

The construction of defensive walls at a substantial number of cities at the end of the third and the beginning of the fourth centuries AD has been attributed to a reaction against the first barbarian threat to Hispania (AD 261/2). At present, however, the tendency is to date them to a later period. The extreme lateness of the chronology proposed for those at Barcino, however, must be re-examined, since the evidence is weak, and in the event that the proposed mid-fifth-century date proves to be correct, it could be interpreted as the repair or monumentalization of a stretch of wall (Granados 1993).

It is now clear that the cities of Hispania were not abandoned during the fourth century, and that on the contrary this should in some cases be seen as a new period of prosperity, whose broader context needs to be better defined in the future. An urban renaissance took place within a phase of commercial and cultural renewal, and extensive urban cemeteries and Christian religious buildings began to appear. Also it is now possible to show that some towns which had hitherto been believed to have been abandoned at the end of the third century in fact continued to be occupied, although later levels are very poor. Outside towns, prosperity is evident in suburban and rural villas which are accompanied by cemeteries, and sometimes sumptuous elite tombs. A certain duality becomes evident in all these developments. Involvement in public building appears to become the responsibility of imperial officials in accordance with contemporary legislation. Private individuals, however, appear to invest resources in the needs of their daily lives, the religious field-funeral rituals or in preparation for the afterlife.

During the third century Christianity had been symbolized by illustrious people, such as Bishop Fructuosus of Tarraco, who suffered martyrdom in AD 259 together with his deacons Augurius and Eulogius (Prudentius, *Perist.* 6; Vives 1969, nos. 304, 321, 326, 333a). Later persecution under the Emperor Diocletian (AD 284–305) was a defining moment for Christianity in Hispania and under the patina of legend a good number of historical events have been obscured, such as the case of the governor Decianus. In the course of the fourth century Christianity was institutionalized and spread widely. In time the aristocracy began to integrate itself into the ecclesiastical hierarchy, as is evident in the ordination of Paulinus of Nola and the episcopate of Pacianus at Barcino (Barcelona) in the later fourth century (Désmulliez 1985; Mayer 1991b). Nevertheless this did not spell the end of paganism, as we are reminded by the letter from Pope Siricius to Bishop Himerius of Tarragona (AD 385), which mentions Christians in the latter's diocese lapsing into paganism (*PLM* 56, 554–62; *PLM* 13, 1142–7; Sotomayor 1979). One should not thus assume that the spread of Christianity was perceived as irreversible by contemporaries.

Within urban centres and their suburbs ecclesiastical buildings progressively gained prominence and importance. A full understanding of this process at episcopal centres is still a long way off, despite recent archaeological advances. At Egara (Terrassa) and Valentia (Valencia), for example, the known church buildings correspond to later phases in the town's development (AAVV 1991; Soriano 1990; Ribera 1987). Alternatively, the significance of the so-called basilica of Barcino needs to be reinterpreted in light of the importance of its baptistry: its layout and orientation suggest that it corresponds to an *arla* and possibly to a catacumenate. Monasticism seems to have been strongly entrenched by the fourth century, despite the ruling of the first council of Caesaraugusta (Zaragoza) of AD 380 against members of the clergy becoming monks (Vives 1963: 17). It would be unwise to identify possible monasteries without supporting archaeological evidence (Fernández-Galiano 1992). Nevertheless, there is something to be said in favour of re-examining the function of the many extra-urban buildings traditionally labelled as 'villas', with this possibility in mind, although other roles might also be explored.

The fourth century sees an increase in the number of lavish villas. Expensive wall and floor mosaics become increasingly common, from Conimbriga (Condeixa-a-Velha) in Portugal, through to Gabia la Grande (Granada), Yecla, Carranque (Toledo) and the villas of the Meseta in central Spain (Alarcão and Etienne 1977; Pérez Olmedo 1994; Fernández-Galiano *et al.* 1994; Cortes 1996). The recently discovered palace at Cercadilla, 1 kilometre from the urban centre of Corduba (Córdoba), is exceptional in terms of its size, although now sadly destroyed. One suggestion is that this was the residence of the Emperor Maximianus Herculeus during his stay of AD 296–8 (Haley 1994; CIL II^2 7.260a). Another is that it dates to the beginning of the fourth century and represents a shift in the urban centre of Corduba northwards (Hidalgo and Marfil 1992). In general terms the hypothesis of polarity between villa and town in late antiquity cannot be sustained today. Towns continue to be indispensable as vehicles for cultural organization and social promotion. But at the same time, the supposed autonomy of the country villas varies, so that in the northern Meseta they play an important role as economic foci, while in coastal areas near to towns and ports, their rural function is tempered by commercial concerns.

The movements of elements of the rural population, known as *Bagaudae*, have been linked, with good reason, to a general sense of insecurity generated during this period by attacks upon coastal regions by pirates and, of course, the barbarian peril that materialized at the beginning of the fifth century. While one must accept that aristocratic landowners, such as the family of the Emperor Theodosius I (AD 379–95), had the capacity to raise armies on their estates, one cannot at present accept the hypothesis that there was a defensive frontier (*limes*) in the Duero basin of Hispania built at their instigation (Blázquez 1980). In many cases, the supposed 'weapons' found at cemeteries along the frontier are little more than hunting implements (Fuentes 1989).

The *Notitia Dignitatum* and the Edict on Maximum Prices (*Edictum de Pretiis*) are each in their own field symptomatic of attempts at the systematization which dominated the public life of the fourth century. There has been discussion about the limits of the latter's jurisdiction. The numerous copies in the east have suggested that it was only applied there, although it must have been applied in the west too, perhaps with modifications, given that its preamble speaks in terms of the whole of the Empire. In the administrative section of the *Notitia* there are factual details which are often assumed to describe the administrative infrastructure of the imperial government in the provinces of Hispania. The military information, however, merits careful consideration since it cannot be accepted at face value. It describes an idealized situation in which military units were never at full strength, something that was also true of the early Empire.

It is noteworthy that Hispania had no regular mint after the reign of Claudius (AD 41–54), and that during the fourth and earlier fifth centuries it was supplied with coinage minted in other provinces. Small change was issued on a large scale, supplied predominantly from mints in central and northern Europe. While the coastal regions enjoyed a dynamic commercial relationship with Africa, it should not be forgotten that African ports were an obligatory stop for merchants from the eastern Empire. Hispania thus seems to have had a two-way economic role. In this context one must bear in mind the profound impact of North African influence, both in terms of Christianity and in a wide range of artefacts, such as the mosaics to be found at sites along the Mediterranean coast and in the Balearic islands.

The origins and family ties of the fourth century Emperor Theodosius I (AD 379–95) profoundly shaped his rise to power. Those *Hispani* around him played an important role, and even the usurper Maximus (AD 383–8) was tolerated to a degree in his eyes. The imperial family must surely have retained important ties with the Iberian Peninsula through its multiple interests, amongst which imperial property (*res privata*) must have ranked highly. The origins of this are probably to be sought in the Augustan period, whilst it becomes more significant in the Flavian period, and is well documented in the second century.

There have been attempts to associate the fourth-century mausoleum of Centcelles (Tarragona) with the family of Constantine (Schlunk and Arbeiter 1988), and the villa of Carranque (Toledo) with Cynegius Maternus, one of the Spanish senators in Theodosius' cadre. In Hispania, as in other provinces of the Empire, the hierarchization and institution-alization of the Church brought about the convergence of those families that held power in other spheres. In this way fourth-century bishops came from the senatorial order, as is surely the case of Pacianus of Barcelona, who was the father of Nummius Aemilianus Dexter, Praetorian Prefect and member of the inner circle of the Emperor Theodosius (Mayer 1992).

Sotomayor (1979) has recently pointed out that the council of Elvira (Iliberis, Granada) reflects a situation where Christianity in Hispania had largely adapted to traditional Roman forms, particularly in terms of orga-nization. The council thus treats slavery and the exercise of magistracies and the priesthoods (*flaminatus*) in Roman terms, while marriage is treated from a purely Roman legal standpoint.

The Priscillanist conflict appears to have had a tragic end, owing to the religious and social interests of the Christian hierarchy. The death of Priscillian in AD 387 on the orders of the usurper Maximus (AD 383–8) is a good example of the fluidity of the situation in Gaul and Hispania at that time. One need do little more than remember that Hispania had been affected by the uprising of Magnentius (AD 350–3) and his brother Decentius (AD 351–3), following the death of the Emperor Constans (AD 350), one of the sons of Constantine I. This event is reflected in the mile-stones (*miliaria*) put up by these usurpers and their coinage, which circulated in the Iberian Peninsula in abundance until Magnentius was defeated by Constantius II (AD 337–68) at Mursa (Osijek) in AD 351.

The insecurity of the Pyrenean frontier at the time of the barbarian invasions and the progressive weakening of Gaul must have worried Constantius II, a man called 'Lord of the Pyrenees' by Julian (*Or.* 1.33) and induced him to reinforce the pass linking eastern Hispania and Gaul (Pertus/Pannissars) with fortifications (Mayer and Rodà 1990; Castellví 1995). These should be identified, at least in part, with the so-called *clausurae*, defensive structures located at a strategic point above the river Rom in the foothills of the Pyrenees in southern France (La Cluse Haute and Château des Maures), and just before the division of the road into two branches leading to Pertus and to Pannissars. The scheme had been well conceived, since it was precisely the weakness of the western Pyrenees that allowed the barbarians to enter Hispania on a large scale in AD 408, an event that was to lead to the irretrievable loss of the Hispanic provinces by Rome.

In any event the sentiment expressed by the Hispano-Roman Prudentius in Book 2 of his *Peristephanon* (verses 409–88) differs from what one gleans from Hydatius and Orosius. Prudentius presents an optimistic vision of the fourth century, in which the Roman historical process had been leading up to the moment when the City of Rome would be Christian and there would appear a prince – surely Theodosius I (AD 379–95) – who, as a faithful servant of God, would not permit the worship of pagan gods, would close the doors of temples and would prohibit sacrifices. Although it is expressed in Christian terms this message runs along similar lines to the poem about the revival of Rome which was written by the fifth-century Gaul Rutilius Namatianus.

THE FIFTH CENTURY

By way of conclusion, we will briefly examine developments of the early fifth century, but without dwelling extensively upon Visigothic Hispania. It should be noted, however, that there is a contrast between our extensive knowledge of the Visigothic period in Iberia and the paucity of information for the Byzantine province of Spania in the southeast. The archaeological evidence is rich, and the Byzantine levels at Villarícos (Almería) and at the recently discovered theatre of Carthago Nova (Cartagena) are an index of their archaeological potential (Ramallo and Méndez 1989; Ramallo *et al.* 1993).

The fifth century saw intense cultural contacts with North Africa continue, evident in the decorative schemes of mosaics from the Balearic isles, mosaic burial covers, and sarcophagi and table wares imported from Carthage (Rodà 1990; Aquilué 1991, 1992). The presence of all of these can be related to the existence of influential African communities at Tarraco (Tarragona), Carthago Nova (Cartagena) and Malaca (Málaga). Religious persecution by the Vandals may have led these people to flee from Africa to Hispania, especially the south.

The year 409 is marked by the invasion of the Germanic peoples, the Suevi, Vandals and Alans, a watershed recognized in contemporary historiography (Hydatius 42) and which caused the fragmentation of the Hispanic provinces. The Roman administration must have resisted this in part, although only when the barbarians had crossed into Hispania. In these opening years of the century one cannot help being reminded of a scenario similar to the mid-third-century *imperium gallicum*, with usurpers from southern Gaul intervening in Hispania. However, the early fifth-century situation was far more fluid. Despite arguments to the contrary, it was a time of economic upsurge, and the number of invaders was small, underlining the solidity of the recovery achieved in the course of the fourth century. Whether as a participant or a victim, the marginalization of the *diocesis Hispaniarum* from the centre of the Empire only accentuated these regional movements.

The entry of the Visigoths into Hispania with Athaulf at their head in AD 415 was not an attempt at occupation, but represents instead an act of policing undertaken at Rome's behest. Similarly the retreat of the Visigoths led by Wallia to the so-called kingdom of Tolosa (Toulouse) in southwestern Gaul is proof of the lack of direction in the movements of the Visigoths, as well as the fact that it was possible for the Roman administrative structure in Hispania to survive without barbarian support. In any event it is important to note that the Visigoths entered Hispania when at least part of it was under the power of the puppet Maximus (AD 410–11), a protégé of Gerontius, who was in turn in the service of Constantine III (AD 407–11), a usurper based in southern Gaul. At the same time the Visigoths extended their power from the south of Gaul to the Atlantic and had brought with them Priscus Attalus, another usurper and a puppet of Alaric at the time of the sack of Rome in AD 410. It seems that the Visigoths wished to act within a framework of legality, as Orosius' anecdote about Athaulf indicates (Orosius 7.43. 4–8). When he found that he was unable to create a *Gothia* (Gothic state), he decided to champion the concept of the Roman state (a *Romania*). The episode of Galla Placidia, closely linked to this event, is only important for the history of the lady herself and plays a symbolic role (Mayer 1996). Thus, the Emperor Honorius (AD 393–423) managed to dominate southern Gaul and resettled the Visigoths. The move of the Vandals to Africa and the billeting of the Suevi in northwestern Iberia around AD 453 by the Roman Master of the Soldiers (*magister militum*) Aëtius helped to foster the image of a pacified peninsula. However, this was soon shattered by the entry of the Visigoths under Theodoric II in AD 456. Their aim was to exterminate the remaining Suevi, and in carrying this out, they also affected the Roman population. From this moment onwards, the Visigothic kingdom of Tolosa was continually involved in the affairs of Iberia until the Peninsula was finally absorbed later in the century.

Given that much of the supporting evidence is open to question, this historical sketch is deceptive. Nevertheless it is often taken at face value. This is the case of the troops of the usurper Constantine III, the *Honoriaci*, who crossed the eastern Pyrenees (Orosius 7.40.9; Zosimus 6.5; Sozomenus 9.12; Arce 1980), or Honorius' own letter referring to this same zone (Demougeot 1956). Information of this kind is disjointed and finds little archaeological support when it is used to reconstruct the final years of imperial rule in Hispania; the excavation of rubbish dumps within urban centres has occasionally allowed changes taking place towards the middle of the fifth century to be noted, as for example at Valencia and Tarragona (Ribera 1995; TED'A 1989). There are also isolated reports of activity by the Emperor Majorian (AD 457–61), and anecdotes about the territorial disintegration felt in different parts of Iberia and the impact of the initial dislocation from Italy.

The most important institutional development to have taken place at this time was the establishment of the Hispano-Roman councils, of which that celebrated at Toletum in AD 397 played a pioneering role. The Church at Rome seems to have exercised control over, or to have been well informed about, the events in the provinces of Hispania: this explains the reaction of Pope Hilarius to information concerning a bishop of Tarraconensis in AD 465 (Epist. 1–3 *Hilari Papae*). As early as AD 347, the council of Serdica (Sofia) had made it clear that the bishops of Hispania should be integrated within the new organizational and institutional framework of the Church. The character of these Hispanic councils, and particularly their origins in the Roman administrative tradition, ensured that they soon ceased to be strictly religious assemblies and began to exercise an increasingly secular role. By the time of the Visigothic kingdom, therefore, they acted as legislative, and even fiscal, assemblies, as was the case of the decree *de fisco barcinonensi* of AD 592 (Vives 1963: 53–4).

These institutional developments must be carefully evaluated alongside such episodes as that of the mid-fifth-century usurper Sebastian (AD 444: Hydatius 129). Visigothic rule in Iberia rested upon a solid and traditional ecclesiastical organization that in formal terms was heir to the late Roman tradition. The number of Visigoths actually present in Iberia was limited. The overwhelming majority of the population was Hispano-Roman, and despite the wish of the dominant Visigothic minority to remain aloof and apart, its Germanic cultural forms and Arian Christian beliefs were eventually absorbed.

There was continued instability in fifth-century Hispania, exemplified by the depredations of the Bagaudae and religious disquiet. However, the reports of Hydatius and other contemporary writers show that their activities were of only sporadic and localized importance. In the religious sphere there was an increase in heretical movements. The recently discovered letters of Bishop Consentius to St Augustine of Hippo Regius (Bône, Algeria) recount the vices of Priscillanists and attempts to repress the heresy (Amengual 1987–91). Finally, account must be taken of external circumstances, such as the presence of barbarian peoples.

There is now a clear need to re-evaluate the fifth century, particularly if one is to measure the impact of the Visigoths in the second half of the century. This century, which sees the disappearance of the western Roman Empire, has benefited from many meritorious studies seen from the perspective of Hispania. On the other hand, the nature of available documentation means that syntheses are relatively poor. Nevertheless,

better archaeological and numismatic evidence is improving our understanding of this crucial century in the development of the Iberian
Peninsula, although care must be taken not to extract too much meaning
from the literary sources.

ABBREVIATIONS

IRC III = Fabre, G., Mayer, M., Rodà, I. (1991) *Inscriptions romaines de
Catalogne III. Gérone*, Paris: De Boccard.

REFERENCES

AAVV (1987) *El vi a l'Antiguitat. Economia, producció i comerç al Mediterranean
Occidental (Badalona 1985)*, Badalona: Museu de Badalona.
—— (1991) *Simposi Internacional sobre les Esglésies de Sant Pere de Terrassa (Terrassa
1991)*, Terrassa: Centre d'Estudis Històrics de Terassa.
—— (1993) *Anuari d'intervencions arqueològiques a Catalunya. Època romana, Anti-
guitat tardana. Campanyes 1982–1989*, Barcelona: Generalitat de Catalunya,
Departament de Cultura.
Abascal, J. M. and Espinosa, U. (1989) *La ciudad hispano-romana. Privilegio y poder*,
Logroño: Colegio Oficial de Aparejadores y Arquitectos de la Rioja.
Alarcão, J. de (1974) *Portugal romano*, Lisbon: Verbo.
—— (1988) *Roman Portugal*, Warminster: Aris and Phillips.
Alarcão, J. de and Étienne, R. (1977) *Fouilles de Conimbriga I. L'Architecture*,
Paris: De Boccard.
Alföldy, G. (1969) *Fasti Hispanienses*, Wiesbaden: Franz Steiner Verlag.
—— (1986) *Die römische Gesellschaft*, Habes 1, Stuttgart: Franz Steiner Verlag.
—— (1987) *Römische Heeresgeschichte*, Amsterdam: Verlag J. C. Gieben.
—— (1992) 'Die Inschrift des Aquäduktes von Segovia. Ein Vorbericht', *Zeitschrift
für Papyrologie und Epigraphik* 94: 231–48.
Amengual, J. (1987–91) *Consenci, correspondència amb Sant Agustí* (2 vols),
Barcelona: Fundació Bernat Metge.
Amo, M. D. del (1979–81) *Estudio crítico de la necrópolis paleocristiana de Tarragona*
(2 vols), Tarragona: Institut Ramon Berenguer.
Aquilué, X., Dupré, X., Massó, J. and Ruiz de Arbulo, J. (1991) *Tàrraco. Guia
arqueològica*, Tarragona: El Mèdol.
Arce, J. (1980) 'La notitia dignitatum et l'armée romaine dans la diocesis
Hispaniarum', *Chiron* 10: 593–603.
—— (1986) *El último siglo de la España romana (284–409)* (2nd edn), Madrid:
Alianza Editorial.
—— (1988) *España entre el mundo antiguo y el mundo medieval*, Madrid: Taurus.
—— (1989) 'Retratos imperiales de época tardía en Hispania', In AAVV *Retratos
antiguos de Yugoslavia*: 177–80, Barcelona/Madrid: Caja de Ahorros de
Barcelona.
—— (1993a) 'La ciudad en la España tardorromana: continuidad o discontinuidad?', in J. Arce and P. le Roux (eds): 177–84.
—— (1993b) 'La penisola iberica', in A. Schiavone (ed.), *Storia di Roma 3. L'età
tardoantica. II I luoghi e le culture*: 379–404, Roma: Einaudi Editore.

Arce, J. and le Roux, P. (1993) *Ciudad y comunidad cívica en Hispania. Siglos II y III d.C. Actes du Colloque organisé par la Casa de Velázquez et par le CSIC, Madrid 1990*, Madrid: Casa de Velázquez.

Arnheim, M. T. W. (1972) *The Senatorial Aristocracy in the Later Roman Empire*, Oxford: Oxford University Press.

Bajo, F. (1981) 'El patronato de los obispos sobre ciudades durante los siglos IV–V en Hispania', *Memorias de Historia Antigua* 5: 203–12.

Balil, A. (1970) 'La defensa de Hispania en el Bajo Imperio', *Legio VII Gemina*: 603–20 León: Cátedra de San Isidro.

—— (1972) 'Economía de la Hispania romana (ss. I–III d.C.)', *Studia Achaeologica* 15, Valladolid: Seminario de Arqueología de la Facultad de Filosofía y Letras, Universidad de Santiago de Compostela.

Barral, X. (1978) *Les Mosaïques romaines et médiévales de la Regio Laietana*, Barcelona: Institut d'Arqueología y Prehistória, Universitat de Barcelona.

Begastri. Imagen y problemas de su historia, Antigüedad y cristianismo, (1984) Murcia: Universidad de Murcia.

Blázquez, J.M. (1975) 'Hispanien unter den Antoninen und Severern', *Aufstieg und Niedergang der römischen Welt* II, 3: 452–522, Berlin/New York: Walter de Gruyter.

—— (1978a) 'Conflicto y cambio en Hispania durante el siglo IV', *Transformations et conflits au IVe siècle ap. J.-C.*: 53–93, Bonn: Rudolf Habelt.

—— (1978b) *Economía de la Hispania romana*, Bilbao: Najero.

—— (1980) 'Der Limes Hispaniens im 4. und 5. Jh. Forschungstand. Niederlassungen der laeti oder gentiles am Flusslauf des Duero', *Roman Frontier Studies (1979)*: 345.

—— (1990) *Aportaciones al estudio de la España romana en el Bajo Imperio*, Madrid: Istmo.

—— (1991) *Urbanismo y sociedad en Hispania*, Madrid: Istmo.

Blázquez, J. M., Remesal, J. and Rodríguez, E. (1994) *Excavaciones arqueológicas en el Monte Testaccio (Roma). Memoria campaña 1989*, Madrid: Ministerio de Cultura.

Bravo, G. (1980) *Coyuntura sociopolítica y estructura social de la producción en la época de Diocleciano*, Salamanca: Universidad de Salamanca.

Castellví, G. (1995) 'Clausurae (Les Cluses, Pyrénées-Orientales): forteresses-frontière du Bas Empire romain', *Frontières terrestres, frontières célestes dans l'Antiquité. Etudes réunies et presentées par Aline Rouselle*: 85–104, Paris: De Boccard.

Chastagnol, A. (1965) 'Les Espagnols dans l'aristocratie gouvernamentale à l'époque de Théodose', *Les Empereurs romains d'Espagne*: 269–292, Paris: CNRS.

—— (1992) *Le Sénat romain à l'époque impériale*, Paris: Les Belles Lettres.

Clariana, J. F. (1994) *Iluro, ciutat romana*, Mataró: Grup d'Història del Casal.

Claude, D. (1978) 'Prosopographie des spanischen Suebenreiches', *Francia* 6: 647–76.

Corzo, R. (1993) 'El teatro de Itálica', *Teatros romanos de Hispania*, Cuadernos de Arquitectura romana 2: 161–81, Murcia: Universidad de Murcia/Colegio Oficial de Arquitectos de Murcia.

Curchin, L. A. (1990) *The Local Magistrates of Roman Spain*, Toronto: University of Toronto Press.

Cruz Villalón, M. (1985) *Mérida visigoda: escultura arquitectónica y litúrgica*, Badajoz: Departamento de Publicaciones de la Diputación Provincial de Badajoz.

Demougeot, E. (1956) 'Une Lettre de l'empereur Honorius sur l'*hospitium* des soldats', *Revue Historique du Droit Français et Etranger* XXXIV: 5–49.

Desmulliez, J. (1985) 'Paulin de Nole. Etudes chronologiques (393–7)', *Recherches Augustiniennes* 20: 35–64.

Díaz y Díaz, M. C. (1983) 'L'Expansion du christianisme et les tensions épiscopales dans la Péninsule Ibérique', *Miscellanea Historiae Ecclesiasticae* VI, 1: 84–94.

—— (1985) 'La estructura de la propriedad en la España tardoantigua. El ejemplo del monasterio de Asán', *Studia Zamorensia* 6: 347–62.

—— (1994) 'Monacato y ascesis en Hispania en los siglos V y VI', *Cristianesimo e specificità regionali nel Mediterraneo latino (sec. IV–VI) (Roma 1993)*: 377–84, Roma: Instituto Patristicum Augustinianum.

Drinkwater, J. (1987) *The Gallic Empire: Separatism and Continuity in the North-Western Provinces of the Roman Empire, A.D. 260–274*, Stuttgart: Steiner.

Duncan-Jones, R. (1994) *Money and Government in the Roman Empire*, Cambridge: Cambridge University Press.

Escribano Paño, M. V. (1977), 'Acción política, económica y social de la Iglesia hispana durante el siglo V', *Hispania Antiqua* 7–8: 63–78.

—— (1988) *Iglesia y Estado en el certamen priscilianista. Causa Ecclesiae y Iudicium Publicum*, Zaragoza: Universidad de Zaragoza.

Etienne, R. (1958) *Le Culte impérial dans la Péninsule Ibérique d'Auguste à Dioclétien*, Paris: De Boccard.

Etienne, R. and Mayet, F. (eds). (1993) *Histoire et Archéologie de la Péninsule Ibérique antique. Chroniques quinquennales, 1968–1987*, Paris: De Boccard.

Fernández-Galiano, D. (1984) *Complutum II. Mosaicos, Excavaciones Arqueológicas en España 138*, Madrid: Ministerio de Cultura.

—— (1992) 'Cadmo y Harmonía: imagen, mito y arqueología', *Journal of Roman Archaeology* 5: 162–77.

Fernández-Galiano, D., Patón, B. and Batalla, C. M. (1994) 'Mosaicos de la villa de Carranque: un programa iconográfico', *VI Coloquio Internacional sobre mosaico antiguo (Palencia–Mérida 1990)*: 317–26, Guadalajara: Asociación Española del Mosaico.

Février, P. A. (1983) 'Une Approche de la conversion des élites au IVème siècle: le décor de la mort', *Miscellanea Historiae Ecclesiasticae* 6: 22–46.

Fontaine, J. (1974) 'Société et culture chrétiennes sur l'aire circumpyrénéenne au siècle de Théodose', *Bulletin de Littérature Ecclésiastique* 4: 571–95.

—— (1975), 'L'Affaire Priscillien ou l'ère des nouveaux Catilina. Observations sur le sallustianisme de Sulpice Sévère', in F. T. Brannan (ed.) *Classica et Iberica. A Festschrift in Honor of J. M. F. Marique*: 355–92. Worcester, Mass.: Institute for Early Christian Iberian Studies, College of the Holy Cross.

—— (1981) 'Panorama espiritual del Occidente peninsular en los siglos IV y V: por una nueva problemática del priscilianismo', *Primera Reunión Gallega de Estudios Clásicos, 1979*: 185–209, Secretariado de Publicaciones de la Universidad de Santiago.

—— (1994) 'La Bética cristiana, cuna de latinidades medievales', *Actas del II Congreso de Historia de Andalucía (Córdoba 1991)*: 17–25, Córdoba: Consejería de Cultura y Medio Ambiente de la Junta de Andalucía y Obra Social y Cultural Cajasur.

Fuentes Domínguez, A. (1989) *La necrópolis tardorromana de Albalate de las Nogueras (Cuenca) y el problema de las denominadas 'necrópolis de Duero'*, Cuenca: Diputación Provincial de Cuenca.

Garabito Gómez, T. (1978) *Los alfares romanos riojanos. Producción y comercialización*, Bibliotheca Praehistorica Hispanica XVI, Madrid: Consejo Superior de Investigaciones Científicas.

García Iglesias, L. (1978) *Los judíos en la España antigua*, Madrid: Ediciones Cristiandad.

García Moreno, L. A. (1980) 'España y el Imperio en época teodosiana. A la espera del bárbaro', *I Concilio Caesaraugustano*, Zaragoza: 27–63.

—— (1989) *Historia de la España visigoda*, Madrid: Cátedra.

—— (1993) *Los judíos de la España antigua*, Madrid: Rialp.

Garrido González, E. (1987) *Los gobernadores provinciales en el Occidente bajo-imperial*, Madrid: Universidad Autónoma de Madrid.

Gil, J. (1978–9) 'Relaciones de Africa e Hispania en la Antigüedad tardía', Milan: Centro Ricercha e Documentazione Sull'Antichità Clássica.

González, J. (1986) 'The *Lex Irnitana*: a new Flavian municipal law', *Journal of Roman Studies* LXXVI: 147–243.

Granados, J. O. (1993) 'Barcelona a la baixa romanitat', *III Congrès d'Història de Barcelona (Barcelona 1993)*, Vol. 1: 25–46, Barcelona: Ajuntament de Barcelona.

Guardia, M. (1992) *Los mosaicos de la Antigüedad tardía en Hispania. Estudios de iconografía*, Barcelona: Promociones y Publicaciones de la Universidad.

Guichard, P. (1993) 'Les Effets des mesures flaviennes sur la hiérarchie existant entre les cités de la Péninsule Ibérique', in J. Arce and P. Le Roux (eds): 67–84.

Haley, E. W. (1994) 'A palace of Maximianus Herculeus at Corduba?', *Zeitschrift für Papyrologie und Epigraphik* 101: 208–14.

Hauschild, T. (1990) *Das römische Theater von Lisabon. Planaufnahme 1985–1988*, Mainz: Mitteilungen des Deutsches Archäologisches Institut 31, 345–92.

—— (1993) 'Traditionen römischer Stadbefestigungen der Hispania', in A. Nunnerich-Asmus (ed.) *Hispania Antiqua, Denkmäler der Römerzeit*: 217–31, Mainz: Philipp Von Zabern.

Hernández, E. (1989) *El teatro romano de Sagunto*, Valencia: Generalitat Valenciana.

Hernández, E., López, M., Pascual, I. and Aranegui, C. (1993) 'El teatro romano de Sagunto', *Teatros romanos de Hispania*, Cuadernos de Arquitectura romana 2: 25–42, Murcia: Universidad de Murcia/Colegio Oficial de Arquitectos de Murcia.

Hidalgo Prieto, R. and Marfil Ruiz, P. (1992) 'El yacimiento de Cercadilla: avance de resultados', *Anales de Arqueología Cordobesa* 3: 277–308.

Janvier, Y. (1969) *La Législation du Bas-Empire romain sur les édifices publics*, Aix-en-Provence: La Pensée Universitaire.

Jiménez Salvador, J. L. and Martín Bueno, M. (1992) *La casa del Mitra. Cabra, Córdoba*, Cabra: Ayuntamiento de Cabra.

Jones, A. H. M. (1964) *The Later Roman Empire 284–602. A Social, Economic and Administrative Survey* (2 vols), Oxford: Blackwell.

Jones A. H. M., Martindale, J. R. and Morris, J. (1971) *The Prosopography of the Later Roman Empire I. A.D. 260–395*, Cambridge: Cambridge University Press.

Kampers, G. (1979) *Personengeschichtliche Studien zum Westgotenreich in Spanien*, Münster: Archendorff.

Keay, S. J. (1981) 'The Conventus Tarraconensis in the third Century A.D.: crisis or change?' in A. King and M. Henig (eds) vol. II: 451–86.

—— (1984) *Late Roman Amphorae in the Western Mediterranean: A Typology and Economic Study. The Catalan Evidence*, British Archaeological Reports International Series 196, Oxford: British Archaeological Reports.

—— (1992) *Hispania Romana*, Sabadell: Ausa Editorial

King, A. and Henig, M. (eds) (1981) *The Roman West in the Third Century*, British Archaeological Reports International Series 109 (2 vols), Oxford: British Archaeological Reports.

León, P. (1988) *El Traianeum de Itálica*, Sevilla: Monte de Piedad y Caja de Ahorros de Sevilla.

Lepelley, C. (1993) 'Introduction générale. Universalité et permanence du modèle de la cité dans le monde romain', in J. Arce and P. Le Roux (eds): 13–23.

Le Roux, P. (1982) *L'Armée romaine et l'organisation des provinces ibériques d'Auguste à l'invasion de 409*, Paris: De Boccard.

—— (1993) 'Peut-on parler de la cité hispano-romaine aux IIe–IIIe s.?', in J. Arce and P. Le Roux (eds) (1993): 187–95.

—— (1995) *Romains d'Espagne. Cités et politique dans les provinces IIe siècle av. J.-C.–IIIe siècle ap. J.-C.*, Paris: Armand Colin.

Leveay, P. H., Sillières, P., Vallat, J. P. (1993) *Campagnes de la Méditerranée romaine*, Paris: Hachette.

Lisboa Subterrânea (1994), Lisbon: Museu Nacional de Arqueologia.

Liz, J. (1986) 'Alcántara. Puente, templo y arco honorífico', *Revista de Arqueología* 67: 32–43.

López Rodríguez, J. (1985) *Terra sigillata hispanica tardía decorada a molde de la Península Ibérica*, Salamanca: Secretariado de Publicaciones de la Universidad de Valladolid.

Lostal Pros, J. (1992) *Los miliarios de la provincia Tarraconense*, Zaragoza: Institución Fernando el Católico.

Mackie, N. (1983) *Local Administration in Roman Spain A.D. 14–212*, British Archaeological Reports International Series 172, Oxford: British Archaeological Reports.

MacMullen, R. (1988) *Corruption and the Decline of Rome*, New Haven–London: Yale University Press.

Mañanes, T. (1983) *Astorga romana y su entorno. Estudio arqueológico*, Valladolid: Universidad de Valladolid.

Martindale, J. R. (1980) *The Prosopography of the Later Roman Empire II. A.D. 395–527*, Cambridge: Cambridge University Press.

—— (1992) *The Prosopography of the Later Roman Empire III. A.D. 527–641*, Cambridge: Cambridge University Press.

Matthews, J. (1975) *Western Aristocracies and Imperial Court, A.D. 364–425*, Oxford: Oxford University Press.

Mayer, M. (1991a) 'Aproximació a la societat de les Illes Balears en època romana', *Mallorca i el món clàssic*: 167–87, Barcelona: Promociones y Publicaciones Universitarias.

—— (1991b) 'La història de la Barcelona antiga segons els escriptors clàssics', in J. Sobrequés (ed.): 241–70.

—— (1992) 'Numi Emilià Dextre, un col. laborador barceloní de l'emperador Teodosi', *Revista de Catalunya* 64: 41–50.

—— (1993) 'El paganismo cívico de los siglos II y III en la Hispania Citerior. Su reflejo en la epigrafía', in J. Arce and P. Le Roux (eds): 161–75.

—— (1995) 'Las inscripciones pintadas en *Hispania*. Estado de la cuestión', *Commentationes Humanarum Litterarum* 104: 79–92.

Mayer, M. and Rodà, I. (1990) 'El Pirineu català en època romana. Alguns problemes pendents', *La Romanització del Pirineu. 8 Col.loqui Internacional d'Arqueologia de Puigcerdà 1988*: 227–35, Puigcerdà: Institut d'Estudis Ceretans.

—— (forthcoming) 'Claudio e Hispania', *Colloque 'Claude de Lyon, empereur romain'*, Paris–Nancy–Lyon 1992.

Mayet, F. (1984) *Les Céramiques sigillées hispaniques: contribution à l'histoire économique de la Péninsule Ibérique sous l'Empire romain* (2 vols), Paris: De Boccard.

Melchor Gil, E. (1994) *El mecenazgo cívico en la Bética. La contribución de los evergetas a la vida municipal*, Córdoba: Instituto de Historia de Andalucía, Universidad de Córdoba.

La mirada de Roma, catálogo de la exposición, Tarragona–Mérida–Toulouse 1995, Ministerio de Cultura, Mairie de Toulouse and Museu Nacional Arqueológic de Tarragona.

Nogales Basarrate, T. (1993) 'El retrato privado emeritense: estado de la cuestión', *Actas de la I Reunión sobre Escultura romana de Hispania (Mérida 1991)*: 141–58, Madrid: Ministerio de Cultura.

Nolla, J. M. (1987) *Girona romana. De la fundació a la fi del món antic*, Girona: Ajuntament de Girona – Diputació de Girona.

Nolla, J. M. and Nieto, F. J. (1981) 'Una factoria de salaó de peix a Roses', *Fonaments* 3: 187–200.

Orlandis, J. (1987) *Historia de España. Epoca visigoda (409–711)*, Madrid: Cátedra.

—— (1988) *Historia del reino visigodo español*, Madrid: Rialp.

Orlandis, J. and Ramos Lisson, D. (1986–7) *Historia de los concilios en la España romana y visigodà*, Pamplona: Universidad de Navarra.

D'Ors, A. (1986) *La ley flavia municipal (texto y comentario)*, Roma.

Pallarés, F. (1969) 'Las excavaciones de la Plaza de San Miguel y la topografía romana de Barcino', *Cuadernos de Arqueología e Historia de la Ciudad* XIII: 5–42.

Palol, P. de (1967) *Arqueología cristiana de la España romana*, Madrid, Valladolid: Consejo Superior de Investigaciones Científicas.

—— (1986) *La villa romana de La Olmeda de Pedrosa de la Vega (Palencia). Guía de las excavaciones* (3rd edn), Palencia: Diputación Provincial de Palencia.

Palol, P. de and Ripoll, G. (1988) *Los godos en Occidente*, Madrid: Ediciones Encuentro.

Pérez Olmedo, E. (1994) 'El *opus sectile* parietal del yacimiento romano de Gabia la Grande (Granada)', *Actas del II Congreso de Historia de Andalucía (Córdoba 1991)*: 595–615, Córdoba: Consejería de Cultura y Medio Ambiente de la Junta de Andalucía y Obra Social y Cultural Cajasur.

Pons, J. (1994) *Territori i societat romana a Catalunya (dels inicis al Baix Imperi)*, Barcelona: Edicions 62.

Ponsich, M. (1988) *Aceite de oliva y salazones de pescado. Factores geo-económicos de Bética y Tingitania*, Madrid: Universidad Complutense de Madrid.

Prevosti, M. (1981) *Cronologia i poblament a l'àrea rural d'Iluro* (2 vols), Mataró: Rafael Dalmau.

Ramallo, S. F. (1985) *Mosaicos romanos de Carthago Nova (Hispania Citerior)*, Murcia: Consejería de Cultura y Educación de la Comunidad Autónoma.
—— (1989) *La ciudad romana de Carthago Nova: la documentación arqueológica*, Murcia: Universidad de Murcia.
Ramallo, S. F. and Méndez, R. (1989) 'Fortificaciones tardorromanas y de época bizantina en el sureste', *Histoira de Cartagena, vol. IV*, Cartagena: Ediciones Mediterráneo.
Ramallo, S. F., San Martín, P. A. and Ruiz, E. (1993) 'Teatro romano de Cartagena. Una aproximación preliminar', Teatros romanos de Hispania. Cuadernos de Arquitectura romana 2: 51–92, Murcia: Universidad de Murcia/ Colegio Oficial de Arquitectos de Murcia.
Ramón, J. (1986) *El Baix Imperi i l'època bizantina a les Illes Pitiuses*, Ibiza: Publicacions del Museu d'Eivissa.
Remesal, J. (1986) *La annona militaris y la exportación de aceite bético a Germania*, Madrid: Universidad Complutense de Madrid.
Ribera, A. (ed.) (1987) *L'Almoina. Viatge a la memòria històrica de la ciutat*, Valencia: Generalitat Valenciana.
—— (ed.) (1995) 'La intervenció arqueològica', in *Palau de les Corts*: 129–59, Valencia: Corts Valencianes.
Rodà, I. (1990) 'Sarcofagi della bottega di Cartagine a Tarraco', *Atti del VII Convegno di Studio sull'Africa Romana (Sassari 1989)*: 727–36, Sassari: Edizioni Gallizzi.
—— (1991) 'Les activitats econòmiques', in J. Sobrequés (ed.) (1991): 383–418.
—— (forthcoming) 'Los mármoles de Itálica. Su comercio y origen', *Actas del MMCC Aniversario de la fundación de Itálica*, Sevilla: Consejería de Cultura.
Roldán, J. M. (1989) *Ejército y sociedad en la España romana*, Salamanca: Universidad de Salamanca.
Roure, A., Castañer, P., Nolla, J. M., Keay, S. and Tarrús, J. (1988) *La vil.la romana de Vilauba (Camós)*, Gerona: Centre d'Investigacions Arqueològiques de Girona.
Ruiz de Arbulo, J. (1993) 'Edificios públicos, poder imperial y evolución de las élites urbanas en Tarraco (s. II–IV d.C.)', in J. Arce and P. Le Roux (eds): 93–113.
Saitta, B. (1987) *Società a potere nella Spagna visigotica*, Catania: Tringale Editore.
Sasel, J. (1983) 'La fondazione delle città flavie quale espressione di gratitudine politica', *La città antica come fatto di cultura. Atti del Convegno di Como e Bellagio (1979)*: 79–91 Como (*Opera Selecta*: Narodni Muzej Ljubljana 1992: 332–44).
Sayas, J. J. and García Moreno, L. A. (1981) *Romanismo y Germanismo. El despertar de los pueblos hispánicos (siglos IV–X)*, Barcelona: Labor.
Schiavone, A. (ed.) (1993) *Storia di Roma 3. L'età tardoantica. I, Crisi e trasformazioni. II, I luoghi e le merci*, Roma: Einaudi Editore.
Schlunk, H. and Arbeiter, A. (1988) *Die Mosaikkupel von Centcelles* (2 vols), Madrider Beiträge 13, Mainz: Philipp von Zabern.
Schlunk, H. and Hauschild, T. (1978) *Hispania Antiqua. Die Denkmäler der frühchristlichen und westgotischen Zeit*, Mainz: Philipp von Zabern.
Seeckk, O. (ed.) (1962) *Notitia Dignitatum*, Frankfurt: Editorial Minerva.
Sillières, P. (1990) *Les Voies de communication de l'Hispanie méridionale*, Paris: De Boccard.

—— (1993a) 'La Péninsule Ibérique', in P. Leveau, *Campagnes de la Méditerranée romaine*, Paris: Hachette, 201–49.

—— (1993b) 'Vivait-on dans des ruines au IIe siècle ap. J.-C.? Approche du paysage urbain de l'Hispanie d'après quelques grandes fouilles récentes', in J. Arce and Le Roux (eds): 147–52.

Sivan, H. S. (1985) 'De Laude Pampilone Epistula', *Zeitschrift für Papyrologie und Epigraphik* 61: 274–87.

Sobrequés, J. (ed.) (1991) *Història de Barcelona 1. La ciutat antiga*, Barcelona: Enciclopèdia Catalana.

Solin, H. (1983) 'Juden und Syrer im westlichnen Teil der römischen Welt. Eine ethnisch-demographische Studie mit besonderer Berücksichtigung der sprachlichen Zustände', *Aufstieg und Niedergang der römischen Welt* II, 29/2: 587–1249, Berlin–New York: Walter de Gruyter.

Soriano, R. (1990) *La arqueología cristiana en la ciudad de Valencia: de la leyenda a la realidad*, Quaderns de difusió arqueològica 1, Valencia: Ajuntament de València.

Sotomayor, M. (1979), 'La Iglesia en la España romana', in R. García Villoslada (ed.) *Historia de la Iglesia en España* I: 7–400, Madrid: Biblioteca de Autores Cristianos, La Editorial Católica S.A.

—— (1994) 'Andalucía. Romanidad y cristianismo en la época tardoantigua', *Actas del II Congreso de Historia de Andalucía (Córdoba 1991)*: 537–53, Córdoba: Consejería de Cultura y Medio Ambiente, Junta de Andalucía y Obra Social y Cultural Cajasur.

Stroheker, K. F. (1963) 'Spanische Senatoren der spätrömischen und westgotischen Zeit', *Madrider Mitteilungen* 4: 107–32.

Suberbiola, J. (1987) *Nuevos concilios hispano-romanos de los siglos III–IV. La colección de Elbira*, Málaga: Universidad de Málaga.

Syme, R. (1993) *Élites coloniales. Roma, España y las Américas*, Málaga: Algazara.

TED'A (1989) *Un abocador del segle V d.C. en el fòrum provincial de Tarraco*, Tarragona: Ajuntament de Tarragona.

—— (1990) *L'amfiteatre romà de Tarragona. La basílica visigòtica. L'església romànica*, Tarragona: Ajuntament de Tarragona.

Teja, R. (1978) 'Honestiores y humiliores en el Bajo Imperio: hacia la configuración en clases sociales de una división jurídica', *Coloquio de Historia Antigua (Oviedo 1977). Memorias de Historia Antigua* 2: 113–18.

Thompson, E. (1976) 'The end of Roman Spain 1', *Nottingham Medieval Studies* XX: 3–28.

—— (1977) 'The end of Roman Spain 2', *Nottingham Medieval Studies CCI*: 3–31.

Tranoy, A. (1981) *La Galice romaine. Recherches sur le nord-ouest de Péninsule Ibérique dans l'Antiquité*, Paris: De Boccard.

—— (trans.) (1974) *Hydace, Chronique* (2 vols), Sources Chrétiennes 218, Paris.

Trillmich, W. (1982) 'Ein Kopffragment in Merida und die Bildnisse Agrippina Minors aus den hispanischen Provinzen', *Homenaje a Saénz de Buruaga*: 109–26, Badajoz: Diputación Provincial de Badajoz.

Trillmich, W. and Zanker, P. (eds) (1990) *Stadtbild und Ideologie. Monumentalisierung hispanischer Städte zwischen Republik und Kaiserzeit (Madrid 1987)*, Munich: Bayerische Akademie der Wissenschaften.

Tsirkin, J. B. (1987) 'The crisis of antique society in Spain in the third century', *Gerión* 5: 253–70.

Vaquerizo Gil, D., Quesada, F., Murillo, J.F., Carillo, J.R. and Carmona, S. (1994) *Arqueología cordobesa*. *Almedinilla*, Córdoba: Universidad de Córdoba.

Vilella, J. (1987) *Relaciones exteriores de la Península Ibérica dura la Baja Romanidad (300–711): Prosopografía*, tesis microfichada, Barcelona: Universitat de Barcelona.

—— (1989) 'Hispaniques et non-Hispaniques: motifs itinéraires des voyages et des correspondances dans l'Antique tardive (IVe–VIe s.)', *Ktema* 14: 139–58.

Vives, J. (1963) *Concilios visigóticos e hispano-romanos*, Barcelona–Madrid: Consejo Superior de Investigaciones Científicas.

—— (1969) *Inscripciones cristianas de la España romana y visigoda* (2nd edn), Madrid: Consejo Superior de Investigaciones Científicas.

FURTHER REFERENCES

Marcos, M. (1994) 'Los orígenes del Monacato en la Península Ibérica. Manifestaciones ascéticas en el siglo IV', *Cristianesimo e specificità regionali: nel Mediterraneo Latino (sec. IV–VI)*, *Studia Ephemeridis Augustinianum* 46: 353–76, Roma.

—— (1994) 'Ortodossia ed eresia nel Cristianesimo ispano del quarto secolo: il caso delle donne', *Cristianesimo e specificità regionals: nel Mediterraneo Latino (sec. IV–VI)*, *Studia Ephemeridis Augustinianum* 46: 417–35, Roma.

Teja, R. (1990) 'La carta de S. Cipriano a las comunidadas cristianas de León-Astorga y Mérida: algunos problemas y soluciones', *Cristianismo y Aculturación en el Imperio Romano, Antigüedad y Cristianismo* VII: 115–24, Universidad de Murcia.

—— (1993) 'Mérida cristiana en el siglo III: sus primeros obispos', *Mérida y Santa Eulalia. Actas de las Jornadas de Estudios Eulalienses*: 35–44, Badajoz.

CHAPTER THIRTEEN

OBSERVATIONS ON HISTORIOGRAPHY AND CHANGE FROM THE SIXTH TO TENTH CENTURIES IN THE NORTH AND WEST OF THE IBERIAN PENINSULA

LUIS CABALLERO ZOREDA

INTRODUCTION

As is well known, the historian's work lies in resolving the conflict resulting from the personal selection of the causes and facts used in the reconstruction of the historical discourse, and the need for this discourse to be objective and coherent. I consider that the 'reconstruction' of the transition between the sixth and tenth centuries in the north and west of the Iberian Peninsula represents a paradigm of this conflict. There is still no consensus amongst historians about a series of interrelated historical problems which arise in this period. In this chapter attention will be focused upon the problems posed by architecture and decorative sculpture.[1] This is a field of study with a long history of research whose origins are to be found in the history of art and the 'antiquarian' tradition of archaeology. This is open to criticism, but it must be remembered that it is the very basis of our knowledge and consequently affects all subsequent techniques of research that might be considered more advanced and more 'archaeological'.

The Iberian Peninsula of the Middle Ages is characterized by a well-known process of historical development. From the fifth century onwards, the Hispano-Roman population, which had already begun to undergo a slow process of 'Christianization', witnessed the arrival of groups of barbarians from Europe – Suevi, Vandals and Visigoths – both as allies of the Roman authorities and as invading peoples. With the disappearance of the Roman Empire, the Visigothic people were in a minority, but succeeded in consolidating their position in the Peninsula as a social and political elite which governed from the end of the sixth and throughout the whole of the seventh centuries. This period is known as the 'kingdom of Toledo' on account of its capital being Toledo, at the centre of the Iberian Peninsula. In AD 711 the Peninsula was invaded again, this time by eastern and North African Muslims, including Berbers, who were bound together by the strong political and religious ties of Islam. From this moment onwards in the Peninsula distinctions were to be drawn between 'Christian' and 'Muslim'. The Muslims did not totally succeed in dominating the Christians, who were either integrated or converted themselves into centres of resistance. Throughout the northern part of the Peninsula these centres sought political independence in the form of kingdoms, counties or marches which began to expand towards Muslim territory in the south, a process traditionally known as the 'Reconquest'. Amongst these independent groups was the 'kingdom of Asturias', whose name was taken from the region it occupied in the centre of the Cantabrian coast. This kingdom gained its independence by virtue of being effectively isolated by the Cantabrian mountain chain and the Duero valley. The latter area had undergone a process of depopulation and administrative disorganization. With the advance of the Christian Reconquest and the parallel process of 'repopulation' or administrative reorganization, the kingdom of Asturias gave way to the kingdom of León in the tenth century, a name derived from its capital in the Duero valley. It later became the first county and eventually the kingdom of Castille, on account of occupying the eastern frontier of the Asturian kingdom, near to the source of the river Ebro and the upper reaches of the Duero valley. Meanwhile, in Muslim territory, the Mozarabs, Christians who had retained Latin, Church liturgy and other cultural traditions, rebelled and were persecuted. Those who emigrated to the northern lands were responsible for the transmission of new Muslim cultural forms to the independent Christian kingdoms.

I do not intend to discuss all of these questions in these pages, but to focus instead upon those which have been studied most recently. In particular, I shall consider the architecture and sculptures of those churches which are believed to belong to the 'Visigothic age' and to have been built in the seventh century, those dating from the period between AD 711 (taken as a symbolic date) and the beginning of the tenth century and considered characteristic of the so-called 'Asturian' architecture, and, finally, the architecture from outside Asturias dating from the period of 'the Reconquest'. I hope that a clear understanding of my field of analysis will explain interrelationships with other problems (Figure 13.1).

THE MEANING OF 'DYNAMICS OF CHANGE': CONTINUITY AND RUPTURE

The subject I wish to discuss here is conditioned by the concept 'dynamics of change', which is the subtitle of this book. In accordance with my opening remarks, it should be accepted that any understanding of historical change hinges to a large extent on the historiographical perspectives from which it is studied. The 'dynamic of change' which encompasses these different historiographical perspectives engenders a distinct understanding of the 'dynamic of historical change' in which the opinions of historians and archaeologists are embedded. This connection between the dynamic of historians and the understanding of the historical dynamic should not be forgotten, for the two are so interrelated that it becomes difficult to distinguish one from the other.

In the belief that a historical argument should never be considered definitive, I think that it is necessary to rectify the tendency to conclude every 'historiographical development' once it has defined a new theory, as one of the easiest ways to defend that theory. Rather, I believe that when presenting a theory, the unresolved questions should be stressed so that the way is left open for the development of a new, more conclusive argument. Clearly, this way of writing history implies that the discourse presented will become more complex and ambivalent. However, it also facilitates choice and objectivity, the two requisites of the historian outlined above.

On the other hand, analysis of historical change in a given period of time and space entails establishing whether that change was characterized by continuity (evolutionary change) or rupture (sudden change). In the field of 'material culture', and more specifically in the case of architecture or sculpture, an evaluation of the degree of continuity or rupture must be based upon the varying degrees of similarity between the 'objects' located at each end and at any point during the period under consideration. In other words, the analysis of change takes the form of an evaluation of differences. Change is thus revealed through similarities or continuity on the one hand, and differences or ruptures on the other.

THE GENERALLY ACCEPTED HISTORIOGRAPHY OF THE ARCHITECTURE AND SCULPTURE OF THE HIGH MIDDLE AGES IN SPAIN

Until now the prevailing opinion among students of the architecture of the High Middle Ages has defended the idea, among other things, of

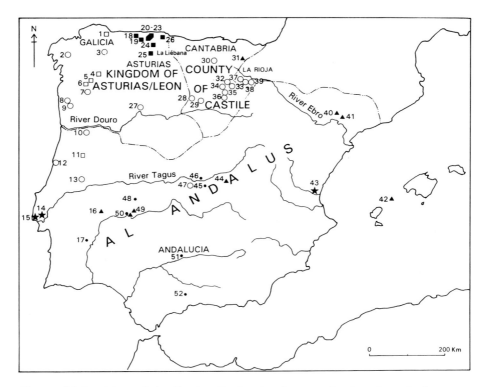

Figure 13.1 Map of the Iberian Peninsula showing the location of places mentioned in the text. Five main categories of buildings and sites with sculptural fragments can be distinguished:

a. *Transitional*: nos. 16 [Torre de Palma (Portugal)], 31 [Treviño (Burgos), 40 [Villa Fortunatus (Fraga, Zaragoza)], 41 [Bovalar (Serós, Lleida)], 42 [Balearic Islands], 44 [Segóbriga/Cabeza del Griego (Saelices, Cuenca), 49 [Casa Herrera (Mérida, Badajoz)]. These are palaeochristian basilicas and churches built c. AD 500 and remaining in liturgical use (with some modifications) until some time between AD 725 and 900.

b. *Buildings whose traditional dates have been altered*: These can be divided into three sub-groups:

1. Buildings and sculpture traditionally considered as Visigothic of the sixth and seventh centuries AD and which are now identified as:
   - Visigothic: the greater part of the sculpture from no. 50 [Mérida, Badajoz]
   - Andalusí or Islamic of the second half of the eighth and ninth centuries AD: the decorative plaques from no. 14 [Cathedral and Rua dos Bacalhaeiros y Sé at Lisbon (Estremadura, Portugal)], and nos. 15 [Chelas (Estremadura, Portugal)] and the secular building at 43 [Plá de Nadal (Valencia)
   - Early Mozarabic of the late ninth and early tenth centuries AD: nos. 17 [Vera Cruz de Marmelar (Alentejo, Portugal), 45 [San Pedro de la Mata, Toledo], 46 [the Credo text sculptural fragment from Toledo], 48 [San Lucía del Trampal (Alcuesar, Cáceres], 50 [a small part of the sculptural suite at Mérida (Badajoz)] and 51 [the Evangelists capital at Córdoba] in Andalusí or Islamic territory; nos. 3 [the decorative plaques at Saamasas, Lugo], 7 [Santa Comba de Bande], 8 [S. Frutuoso

continuity between the architecture of the Visigothic and Asturian eras. This position may be labelled 'Visigothist' or 'continuist'. The so-called *Crónica Albeldense*, which was written at the end of the ninth century, confirms that the Gothic order was restored at the 'church and palace' of Oviedo in the way it had existed at Toledo. This and other kinds of evidence[2] have been taken by researchers as evidence of a continuity or close formal similarity between the architecture and the decorative art of both eras. Visigothic architecture and decoration thus continue in the buildings of the Asturian era, even if some new decorative features can be distinguished (see, for example, the summary by Arias (1993: 94), with regard to the paintings of S. Julián de los Prados, or Arbeiter (1992: 163–4) and especially Bango (1979, 1992)).

Figure 13.1 (cont.)

de Montelios (Braga, Portugal)], 9 [S. Torcato de Guimarães (Minho, Portugal)], 10 [S. Pedro de Balsamão (Beira Alta, Portugal)], 13 [Idanha a Velha (Beira Baixa, Portugal)], 27 [S. Pedro de la Nave (Zamora)], 34 [Quintanilla de las Viñas (Zamora) and 39 [Sta María de Ventas Blancas (La Rioja)] in Christian or Reconquest territory;

- Contradictory or controversial chronology: nos. 12 [S. Gião de Nazaré, Portugal, which is traditionally considered Visigothic but whose architecture betrays Asturian influences and the decoration of which is certainly post-Visigothic], 28 [S. Juan Bautista de Baños de Cerrato (Palencia), traditionally considered Visigothic because an inscription of Recceswinth dated it to AD 652 or 661, but which the writer re-dates as early Mozarabic] and 30 [Stas Céntola and Elena de Siero (Valdelateja, Burgos) at which an inscription with the date of 782 has been re-worked to cut another date, possibly 882].

2. Reused Roman buildings which have been considered Mozarabic and which the writer considers to be early Mozarabic: no. 2 [Mausoleum of Santiago at Santiago de Compostela (La Coruña)].

3. A building which had been considered full Mozarabic, then Visigothic and which has been attributed to early Mozarabic by this writer: no. 47 [Sta María de Melque (S. Martín de Montalban, Toledo)].

c. *Asturian buildings* (dating to between the mid-eighth and the beginning of the tenth centuries AD): nos. 18 [S. Martín de Salas (Asturias)], 19 [Santianes de Pravia (Asturias)], 20 [remains of the Royal Palace in the Cathedral at Oviedo], 21 [S. Julián de los Prados or Santullano (Oviedo, Asturias)], 22 [S. Miguel de Liño (Oviedo, Asturias)], 23 [Sta María de Naranco (Oviedo, Asturias)], 24 [Sta María de Bendones (Asturias)], 25 [Sta Cristina de Lena (Asturias)] and 26 [S. Salvador de Valdediós (Asturias)].

d. *Early Mozarabic buildings*: 1. In Andalusí or Islamic territory (second half of the eighth or ninth centuries AD): no. 52 [Bobastro (Mesas de Villaverde, Málaga). 2. In Christian or reconquered territory (end of the ninth to beginning of the tenth centuries AD): nos 29 [Hérmedes de Cerrato (Palencià)], 32 [S. Felices de Oca (Villafranca y Montes de Oca, Burgos)], 33 [S. Vicente del Valle (Belorado, Burgos)], 35 [S. Pedro el Viejo de Arlanza (Burgos)], 36 [Sta Cecilia de Barriosuso (Silos, Burgos)], 37 [Sta María de los Arcos de Tricio (La Rioja)], 38 [Sta Coloma (La Rioja)].

e. *A selection of Full Mozarabic buildings* (tenth century AD): no. 1 [S. Martiño de Mondoñedo (Foz, Lugo)], 4 [S. Xés de Francelos (Orense)], 5 [S. Martiño de Pazó (Allariz, Orense)], 6 [S. Miguel de Celanova (Orense)] and 11 [S. Pedro de Lourosa (Beira Alta, Portugal)].

This theory has encouraged a search for formal similarities between Asturian buildings and earlier structures outside the region. Spatial and liturgical forms such as those found at the churches of S. Gião de Nazaré (Schlunk 1971), S. Pedro de La Nave (Gómez Moreno 1906, 1966; Camps 1940/1) and Quintanilla de las Viñas (Camps 1939/40; Corzo 1986; Arbeiter 1990; Caballero 1995) and, most recently, Sta Lucía del Trampal (Caballero 1992a, Caballero *et al.* 1991) are evidently related to those of the Asturian churches of S. Julián de los Prados or Santullano, Santianes de Pravia and Sta María de Bendones (Fernández-Conde and Santos del Valle 1987; Bango 1988; Dodds 1989; Arbeiter 1992; Arias 1993). The Visigothic character of the first group of buildings helps to explain the evolutionary continuum described in Asturian chronicles.

In general, the identification of buildings constructed in the territory and epoch of the kingdom of Asturias (AD 718–910) (Figure 13.1.c) is relatively straightforward. They can usually be dated from contemporary documentary sources. They are also clearly uniform in form and technique and geographically very concentrated. In contrast, the characteristics of the buildings now considered to have been Visigothic prototypes (seventh century) are much more varied. From the moment of their discovery, they have thus proved harder to identify. First Gómez Moreno (1906, 1966) and later Camps Cazorla (1939/40, 1940, 1940/1) settled the question by classifying them as Visigothic.

Subsequently, Schlunk (1945, 1970a, 1970b; Schlunk and Hauschild 1978) developed a complex argument that related the sculpture to the architecture of the Visigothic era and presented both as precedents of the sculptural and architectural development which took place in the Asturian period. A key element in his argument is the church of S. Juan de Baños, since this is dated to AD 652 or 661 by an inscription of the reign of King Recceswinth. Schlunk (1970a) argued that the decoration at S. Juan de Baños could be grouped together with the sculpture from the 'centres' of Toledo (the carved Creed) and Córdoba (the Apostles capital), and the churches of S. Pedro de la Nave and Quintanilla de las Viñas. All of these are undated but are ascribed to the Visigothic period on the basis of this argument. Schlunk considered that their figurative decoration in turn reflected or imitated that found in supposedly Visigothic manuscripts which have now disappeared (particularly those of the Apocalypse). All of this evolved and gave rise to high medieval figurative manuscripts and the figurative decoration of Asturian art of the type found at S. Miguel de Liño in Oviedo.

The formation of a 'strategic desert' helps to explain this 'continuity'. According to the chronicles of Alfonso III (AD 866–910), the actions of King Alfonso I of Asturias and above all King Alfonso II, in forcing the emigration of Christians to the northern lands in the second half of the eighth century, led to the Duero valley or northern plain becoming a wilderness: the Berbers' abandonment of the land may have been an additional factor. As a result, the population, techniques and ideological apparatus of Visigothic society moved northwards, so establishing the bases for the formation of a new northern art.

This emigration fits in well with the hypothesis of continuity between Visigothic and Asturian, because it would also explain the lack of Christian art produced in the territory dominated by the Muslims (excluding the church of the supposed Bobastro (Mergelina 1925) and Santa María de Melque (Gómez Moreno 1919; Caballero 1982, 1984; Caballero and Latorre 1980)). In Islamic territory, and doubtless in the uninhabited lands of the Duero valley as well, the activity of workshops responsible for the production of sculptures and stone buildings would have ceased. Outside Asturias this would restart much later, some time in the tenth century, and was largely a result of Islamic influence.

On the basis of all this, and regardless of the well-developed typologies and arguments, my theory proposes a few relatively simple and straightforward norms for the almost automatic 'classification' of any element. Thus, any remains of decorative sculpture found outside Asturian territory should be dated to the Visigothic age. The same applies to those architectural features found outside the region which suggest Asturian planning. They should be considered as dating to the Asturian period and having their origins in the Visigothic era. Only the absence of decoration, the presence of features not found in Asturian architecture, or those generally accepted as Visigothic, should be identified as having been brought by the Muslims and, thus, belonging to a new cultural trend. These features include closed 'horseshoe' arches, interior 'horseshoe' apses or the absence of sculpted decoration. These are only to be found in Bobastro and Santa María de Melque (mentioned above), and are both symptomatic of an art of 'rupture', that is, Mozarabic art. Both buildings would be exceptional, and strictly speaking the only true Mozarabic examples. In other words, they would be the only Christian churches built in lands under Islamic control.

The end of the Asturian monarchy at the beginning of the tenth century coincided with the breakdown of this evolutionary continuum, thus leaving the way clear for Muslim influences. Subsequently, the caliphate art of Al-Andalus would have a decisive influence in the north and would give rise to what is generally known as the Mozarabic art of León in the Duero valley. This artistic movement was reliant upon the arrival of new peoples from the south, the Mozarabs, who were also Christians. However, their cultural 'baggage' was no longer strictly 'Visigothic', but Muslim, or, at least, was a predominantly Muslim-inspired cultural blend which had evolved from Visigothic roots. From AD 910 onwards, therefore, the Mozarabic examples in the area under consideration represented a break with the previous line of evolution. However, this does not mean that there had not been any attempts to introduce some features of this new style into Asturian territory, as for

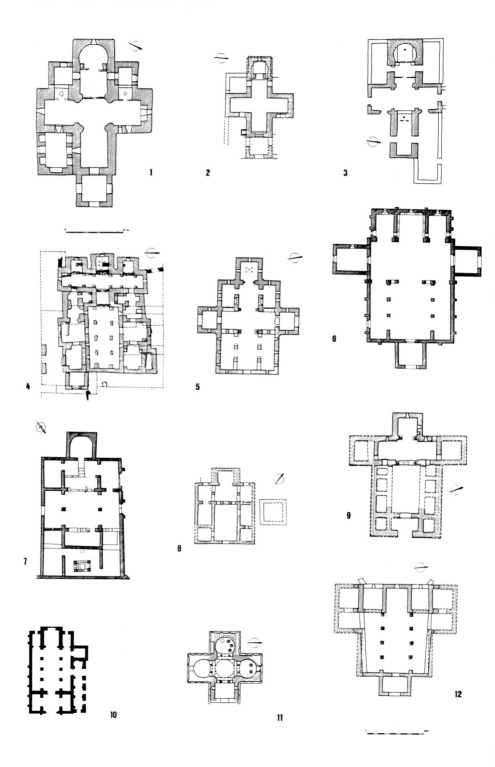

example in the church of S. Salvador in Valdediós (Gómez Moreno 1919: 76–81). It is clear that, traditionally, the term Mozarabic was used to define two distinct realities. On the one hand, it refers to art produced by the Christians in Islamic territory in which the Visigothic tradition was still predominant. On the other, it corresponds to that produced by Arabized Christians who fled from the reconquered territories of the north of the Peninsula from the tenth century onwards (Bango 1974).

Despite its apparent cohesion, this theory does not resolve all the problems. New information has brought to light new relationships which are not adequately explained by this theory. The first piece of information concerns the evident contradictions in the typological relationships between the elements that constitute the cultural/chronological groups. Thus there are both marked differences between elements said to belong to the same group and, conversely, marked similarities between elements supposed to belong to distinct groups. Other types of analysis and documentary evidence have gradually led to the emergence of a number of new arguments which also challenged the theory. The most important are:

a Very similar typological characteristics in what have been hitherto considered Visigothic or Asturian decorative elements and which seem to be contemporary. This is the case with S. Frutuoso de Montelios (Schlunk 1980), S. Torcato de Guimarâes, Chelas, Lisbon, Saamasas, Quintanilla de las Viñas and S. Pedro de la Nave in Spain, which were supposedly Visigothic (Figure 13.2). Those in Oviedo and S. Miguel de Liño are supposedly Asturian.

b A very close relationship between architectural plans hitherto considered Visigothic and Asturian. Thus, Quintanilla de las Viñas, S. Pedro de la Nave, S. Gião de Nazaré, S. Pedro de la Mata and Sta Lucía del Trampal, which are supposedly Visigothic and comparable to S. Julián de los Prados.

c Features of buildings included in the Visigothic group which diverge from this typology and which are closer to those of post-Visigothic date: S. Pedro de Balsemão and S. Gião de Nazaré in Portugal and at least part of Sta Comba de Bande.

d The discovery of a growing number of cases on the northern plain and in the Galician–Portuguese hills which resemble or recall

---

Figure 13.2   Plans of the principal churches cited in the text:

No. 1. Sta María de Melque (Toledo); 2. Sta Comba de Bande (Orense); 3. S. Pedro de la Mata (Toledo); 4. Sta Lucía del Trampal (Cáceres); 5. S. Pedro de la Nave (Zamora); 6. S. Julián de los Prados or Santullano (Oviedo, Asturias); 7. church within the Roman villa of Villa Fortunatus (Fraga, Zaragoza); 8. S. Gião de Nazaré (Estremadura, Portugal); 9. Quintanilla de Viñas (Burgos); 10. S. Salvador de Valdediós (Asturias): the supposedly later lateral porch has not been differentiated; 11. S. Frutuoso de Montelios (Braga, Minho); 12. S. Juan Bautista de Baños de Cerrato (Palencia).

those considered to be Visigothic, but that fit better into 'Asturian', 'Reconquest' or 'Mozarab' typologies. For example, the *ajimezadas* windows, whose arches, single or twin (simple (*medio punto*) or horse-shoe (*herradura*)) are cut from one block of stone, Castilian and Riojan buildings with pendentive domes, or figurative decoration (see below).

e The absence of evidence which would confirm the existence of Visigothic miniatures representing figured scenes in the second half of the seventh century AD. These miniatures are needed to support Schlunk's (1970b) Visigothic dating of the church of S. Pedro de la Nave, the decorative sculpture of which was supposedly carved in imitation. However, the figured scenes on the church's capitals are very similar to late ninth- and tenth-century Mozarabic miniatures.

f The documented dating of supposedly prototypical Visigothic churches, such as Quintanilla de las Viñas and S. Pedro de la Nave, to the Reconquest period could lead us to suggest a later chronology. Further examples include churches now being studied in La Rioja and Castille (see below).

g The absence of detailed analyses of architectural monuments which clearly mark distinct stages in the development of walls and clarify their chronology. This characterizes individual elements and stages of development when monuments are assigned to a single, supposedly 'Visigothic' category. The church at Sta Comba de Bande (Caballero 1992a, 1992b) is a paradigmatic case.

h The absence of archaeological excavations at these buildings and at contemporary sites, and consequently the difficulty in obtaining absolute dates.

A DIFFERENT HISTORIOGRAPHICAL OPINION[3]

This theory was espoused by most authorities and came to be accepted as being the most accurate. Soon, however, it was criticized by a minority of researchers.[4] They highlighted and attempted to resolve the contra-dictions in the 'Visigothist' theory. The position of Puig i Cadafalch is of particular interest. In 1961 he published a study written in the 1940s, *L'Art wisigothique et ses survivences*, a title which could mislead one into thinking that it accepted the official 'Visigothist' thesis. However, both this and a study by Camón Aznar (1963) challenged the dominant theory.

Puig maintained that the supposedly paradigmatic 'Visigothic' build-ings in the Duero valley (S. Pedro de la Nave and Quintanilla de las Viñas), were in fact 'pre-Mozarabic', and that they were constructed soon after the end of the Asturian period and immediately preceding the 'Mozarabic' art of the tenth century. He included the churches of Sta Comba de Bande and S. Pedro de La Mata, in the Tagus valley, in the same 'pre-Mozarabic' group. Moreover, he argued that the same applied to some decorative sculpture. Thus he rejected the Visigothic classification of such significant churches as those at Lisbon, Chelas and Saamasas, as well as that of the decoration of those of Quintanilla de las Viñas and S. Pedro de la Nave. Puig also modified the generally accepted view of the relationship between Asturian churches and those which had hitherto been considered to be Visigothic. He rejected the idea of an evolutionary development from the centre of the Peninsula, where the majority of the 'Visigothic' buildings are found, to the north, where the Asturian buildings are located, a movement which followed the direction of Visigothic/Christian emigration in the mid-eighth century. Instead, he argued that the influence was in the opposite direction, from north to south. Thus the prototypes were to be found at northern Asturian sites, especially S. Julián de los Prados, and the buildings of the Duero valley evolved from them under their influence. They were consequently built later and were considered to be 'pre-Mozarabic'. The documentary evidence available for dating these buildings would appear to support this theory. Puig (1961) only maintained the Visigothic classification for two important examples of known churches, namely S. Juan de Baños and S. Frutuoso de Montelios. This opinion may have been influenced by a desire not to leave the Visigothic space completely 'empty' and by the positive dating of these two sites, one by a dated inscription and the other from historical references. Nor did Puig ignore the need to relate Asturian and Visigothic art, hence the title of his book. He tried to clarify their relationship in a different way, by noting the connection with existing comparable buildings in French territory, such as Vaison and Valcabrère, or with pre-Visigothic buildings, which were in fact Palaeochristian, such as the churches in the Balearic Islands. His arguments were implicitly rejected and were not even cited in order to be refuted.

More recently, some Portuguese researchers (Real 1995) have perceived the same problems and have made clear their support for the theory proposed by Puig i Cadafalch (1961).[5] I myself found contradictions in the official theory, principally concerning the close affinity and contemporaneity of decorations classed as Visigothic and those very confidently dated as Asturian. I recently outlined some of these contradictions (Caballero 1992a, 1995), indicating the way in which the two opposing explanations were rooted in two different approaches or 'referential frameworks'.

Earlier in the 1970s I analysed and excavated the surroundings of a high medieval church, that of Sta María de Melque which lies in the middle of the Tagus valley near Toledo (Figure 13.1.b3). Gómez Moreno (1919: 14–27) maintained that this building was Mozarabic, on the grounds that some of its features differed from those judged to be Visigothic, and that it should be classified as Muslim-influenced, particularly taking into account its southerly location. The excavation uncovered a number of decorative elements (chancel screens or, more probably, barriers formed by carved stone pillars, posts or plaques), which were compatible with art considered to be Visigothic. For that reason I stressed its archaic characteristics and, in contrast to the general consensus, defended its Visigothic date. As with other characteristics considered to be typical of Visigothic art, I found parallels for its distinguishing features (rounded corners and stuccos) at Ravenna, and I emphasized their close relationship to the architectural and liturgical planning of two other buildings considered to be Visigothic, namely those at Sta Comba de Bande and S. Pedro de la Mata (Caballero 1982, 1984; Caballero and Latorre 1980: 734–6).

Although there are no definitive arguments against this theory, it was rejected by all but a few specialists, such as Dodds (1989: 62) and Fontaine (1977: 75–7). They attempted an intermediate solution and it was Fontaine who accepted it later (Fontaine 1987: 142). Schlunk and Hauschild (1978) do not cite it, whereas Palol (1991: 387) points out the contradictions inherent in dating the church to the Visigothic period by means of the traditional theory. Only very recently has Garen (1992) dated Sta María de Melque to the late eighth century. She does this on the grounds that the features which differentiate it from the Visigothic style (rounded pillars and corners, stucco decoration) were directly derived from the Syrian art of the Ummayad dynasty, specifically from the last Ummayad palace of Jirbat al Mafyar (Israel), built in AD 739 (Hamilton 1959). Hence, neither Gómez Moreno (1919), who attributed it to a later period close to the so-called 'Mozarabic' era of the tenth century, nor I, who dated it to the seventh century (Caballero 1982), were correct.

Similarly, the true merit of Garen's argument is to have acted as a catalyst stimulating further advances which have weakened the 'Visigothist' thesis. Let us consider how. By identifying Melque as Visigothic, I incorporated this building into a network of relationships and into a group of decorative elements and architectural features of the Visigothic era. However, this network did not encompass all the features considered to be Visigothic. It could be said that at Sta María de Melque I identified a partial 'subsystem' within the total system of what is officially considered to be Visigothic. Garen's work presented a problem for my own theory. Whilst I believed that much of what she said could be refuted in accordance with the traditional arguments, she did suggest a very attractive perspective or insight into Ummayad influence. This idea helped me to consider the possibility of the existence of a 'third interpretation' which would resolve the contradiction and would answer the question as to whether the subsystem in which I included Sta María de Melque and other buildings could have been chronologically later and have had Ummayad origins.

In my view this third interpretation is the correct one. Space does not permit me to present this theory in detail as I have done elsewhere (Caballero forthcoming, 1994/5). Here I will simply present a brief summary of the main conclusions. I do believe that it is possible to trace a direct connection between the decorative elements of the group that up till now had been considered to be representative of Visigothic sculpture (Sta María de Melque, S. Pedro de la Mata, and Sta Lucía del Trampal; Chelas and Lisbon; Saamasas, S. Fructuoso de Montelios and S. Torcato de Guimarâes), and the most developed decoration of Ummayad Syria. This whole Iberian group, therefore, would not date to the Visigothic period, as hitherto believed, but from some time after AD 760 (Abd–El–Rahman I arrived in the Peninsula in 755), and derive from Islamic influence. The strength of this influence was such that part of the group may in fact be considered Islamic, and not Christian. That is to say that it is neither Christian of the Visigothic period, prior to the arrival of the Muslims, nor Christian of the Reconquest period, which was a later phase in the assimilation of Islamic influences by Christian artisans. Here I am thinking specifically of Chelas and Lisbon and probably the Valencian building in Plá de Nadal (Juan and Pastor 1989).

If this argument is correct, it would also apply to a great many of the buildings still considered Visigothic, including practically all those in the northern Meseta. These buildings thus cease to be considered Visigothic because they have to be redated to the period after AD 760. In this way they belong to an art which 'broke' with what had gone before and which should either be considered fully Islamic or, given that they were Christian churches, as having directly or indirectly accepted Islamic cultural influences. We can perceive, therefore, the formation of a new system initially defined by its Islamic influence and within which, in turn, a number of different groups or subsystems can be distinguished.

The first group is defined by exhibiting very direct Ummayad influence and was the work of either Muslims or Christians. It should be joined by the groups of decorative Asturian sculpture. These elements are generally considered to be Visigothic or Visigothic-derived styles, an identification which I consider to be untenable (*contra* Jiménez (1990): illustration captions). This is the group comprised by Asturian decorative sculpture preserved in the churches of Santianes de Pravia, Sta María de Bendones and Sta Cristina de Lena; the two masters of S. Miguel de Liño, closely related to S. Frutuoso de Montelios (Schlunk 1980: 140–1), Sta María del Naranco and, lastly, the lateral porch of S. Salvador de Valdedios. All of them exhibit the impact of direct Muslim influences which were either a combination of other, perhaps original, prototypes or went on to evolve into their own style. We must also include the decoration of such buildings as S. Fructuoso de Montelios, S. Torcato de Guimarâes (Barroca and Real 1992), S. Pedro de la Nave and Quintanilla de las Viñas within this development on account of their connections to the Asturian group.

The 'Visigothist' theory was akin to a whirlpool which sucked in everything which fell within its grasp, converting everything into Visigothic, and thereby reinforcing its own attractiveness as a theory. The elements assimilated in this way were used to make comparisons with others which then ended up being defined as Visigothic. These, in turn, drew in other elements and thus the process continues. When the theory was first developed, this would have been what happened with the churches of S. Pedro de la Nave and Quintanilla de las Viñas, the griffin plaque in S. Miguel de Liño (Aragoneses 1957), S. Gião de Nazaré, the pieces of the first Asturian decorative group in Santianes de Pravia, and with my own theory about Sta María de Melque. Alternatively one might mention the case of the civil building, or palace, of Plá de Nadal (Juan and Pastor 1989) and the church of Sta Lucía del Trampal (Caballero *et al.* 1991), both of which were recent discoveries.

THE IMPLICATIONS OF THE 'NON-VISIGOTHIST' THEORY FOR OUR UNDERSTANDING OF HISTORICAL CHANGE IN THE HIGH MIDDLE AGES

I wish to compare the implications of the 'Visigothist' and 'non-Visigothist' theories for the changes under discussion. The former theory needed to assimilate as many of the examples from outside Asturian territory as possible into the Visigothic era. At the same time, it had to play down as far as possible the presence of Mozarabic constructions in Islamic territory. Sta María de Melque and Bobastro were the two exceptions which confirmed the rule. Bango (1974) demonstrated the contradictions this entailed, for this is precisely the territory that should be called Mozarabic. Even in these two cases, the culturally Mozarabic would be heavily influenced by the persistence of typically Visigothic features, as Gómez Moreno (1919: 18, 22, 23, 27) accepted as true of Sta María de Melque. It was in this way that the Visigothic decorative 'centres' of Córdoba, Mérida and Toledo, the northern Meseta and Galicia, were identified. All the examples from these centres, and even some of those in Asturias, should be considered truly Visigothic. My proposal of a Visigothic date for Sta María de Melque (Caballero 1982, 1984; Caballero and Latorre 1980) conformed to this need to classify as Visigothic everything that was neither Asturian nor Mozarabic from the tenth century.

Given that the implications of the first, officially accepted theory are well known and widely accepted, I wish to concentrate here on some of the implications of the second, or 'non-Visigothist' theory.

The reduction and disappearance of elements considered Visigothic

In accordance with the 'non-Visigothist' theory, the number of examples of 'Visigothic era' architecture and sculpture is not only considerably reduced in the north of the Peninsula (in Asturias, Galicia, northern

Portugal and the northern Meseta), where they practically disappear, but would also be considerably diminished at centres such as Toledo, Mérida and in Andalucía.[6]

All of this poses a question which requires an adequate and objective answer in order for the theory to be established on a scientific basis. Which sites can be classed as examples of the 'Visigothic era' and how do we define them? If we leave the northern Meseta without churches which can be considered as Visigothic, which are the sixth- and seventh-century Visigothic churches and what form do they take? Perhaps the solution lies in the continued use of the churches that Palol defines as 'transitional' (1967: 69–104, 1986a: 2005–6, 1991: 285–338) (Figure 13.1.a). Examples of these are to be found at the churches of the villa Fortunatus at Fraga, El Bovalar at Serós, whose abandonment is dated by coins of AD 713–15 (Palol 1986b), or the southern churches with a 'counterpoised apse' or 'double apse', as at Casa Herrera near Mérida and the Torre de Palma in Portugal (Ulbert 1978). These bridge the chronological and typological gap between true basilical and wooden-roofed 'Palaeochristian' churches of the fourth and fifth centuries, and the supposedly 'Visigothic', cruciform, domed churches of the seventh century, such as Quintanilla de las Viñas, S. Pedro de la Nave and S. Frutuoso de Montelios. In my view, the transitional churches would have been built around the year AD 500 and as a result of their continual use they would have gradually changed and evolved in response to new liturgical requirements and construction styles until their abandonment at some time after AD 711. Our image of them corresponds to the final stage of their evolution, that is, at the end of the eighth, the ninth, or even at the beginning of the tenth centuries. Examples of this type include the urban basilica of Segóbriga, which is similar to Carolingian models, or the church of the villa Fortunatus at Fraga (Palol 1986a: 2000–4) that recalls the layouts of the 'Asturian' of S. Julián de los Prados and those like S. Gião de Nazaré, Sta Lucía del Trampal y Quintanilla de las Viñas, which I would now consider to be post-Visigothic. We ought perhaps to analyse other material evidence more closely, as Azkárate (1988: 485–92) has done with the cave churches of Treviño, convincingly dating them to the sixth century. If proved to be correct, it may be further corroborated by Domínguez Perela's (1992) suggestion that some of the series of capitals considered to be Mozarabic of the tenth century may, in fact, belong to sixth-century buildings. In both cases these buildings could have continued in use throughout the Visigothic era.

Architecture and sculpture: distinguishing between Visigothic and Islamic with Ummayad influences (Figure 13.1.b)

From this perspective we must re-examine the production which we now believe to have been carried out in the 'Visigothic centres', above all at the most prolific of these, Mérida (Cruz 1985). This will allow two different groups to be distinguished, one dating from the Visigothic era and the other from the Islamic epoch. The latter may be either 'Andalucían Ummayad' Spanish (if this term may be used), or may reveal Ummayad influences. I should point out that I am not interested in defining that Visigothic architecture and sculpture which may have been executed after AD 711. Rather than simply correcting the final date of Visigothic production, I am instead proposing the existence of a culturally distinct production, and one which already incorporates Islamic influences.

As already mentioned above, the pieces from Lisbon and Chelas belong to one of several Islamic rather than Visigothic buildings. An analysis of the decorative sculpture suggests that the same could be true of the Valencian building of Plá de Nadal. In the rest of the 'centres' considered to be Visigothic, we should look for 'pure' Ummayad elements which may be identified as linking Syrian and Andalusí Ummayad styles. Taking Garen's (1992) pro-Ummayad proposal to its ultimate conclusion, the decorative sculpture of Sta María de Melque would not be Visigothic. Thus its counterparts in Sta Lucía del Trampal, Mérida and Córdoba should now be identified as belonging to this new cultural and chronological category. Their decoration is defined by the use of circles drawn with lines of pearls in the form of a chain and enclosing motifs of stars, canes and fleurs-de-lis. Consequently, I consider this decorative group, which stands apart from that considered to be Visigothic, to have been Mozarab in the sense that it was carved with Islamic themes and techniques for churches built in Islamic territory.

However, the implications of this definition may not just be restricted to our understanding of buildings and their decoration. It may also affect the cultural classification of other artefacts conventionally dated to the Visigothic era and which should now be considered post-Visigothic. Given the great number of variables involved, however, this is a much harder question to answer. For example, in the case of burial offerings in cemeteries it is perhaps easiest to accept the idea that Visigothic elements survived and were combined with new Islamic customs: this idea is currently gaining credence. The same may apply to other personal objects, such as belt-buckles with fretwork decoration of the seventh-century Byzantine group, which are continually used to establish parallels with the decoration of S. Pedro de la Nave (refined by Schlunk (1945: 242–3) and Fontaine (1973: 208–9)). As I have already suggested, it may also affect the supposedly Visigothic date of the bronze liturgical objects mainly found in Asturias and Cantabria and which would now be considered as belonging to the era of the Asturian monarchy. Finally it could also modify the chronology and classification of ceramics. Those productions believed to be late Visigothic in date would now be assigned to a later post-Visigothic period, with Berber or Islamic influences. As I pointed out above, at present these definitions are still only very tentative. For that very reason, I believe that simply posing these questions facilitates the search for the correct answer to them.

'Early Mozarabic' (Figures 13.1.b and d)

The definition of an 'early Mozarabic' period (considering this term as analogous to 'pre-Mozarabic' as used by Puig i Cadafalch (1961)) is another of the consequences that help us to describe the change taking place in the late Middle Ages. In adopting this term, I do not seek to open a debate on terminology which, as I have argued elsewhere, ought to be discussed in an appropriate forum by specialists (Caballero 1989: 113–14). For the time being, I use this and other terms for their relative value, without any intention of establishing them as definitive.

I consider that if certain examples of Christian art truly exhibit Islamic influence, they should be loosely labelled 'Mozarabic'. Indeed, they can more properly be labelled Mozarabic than the tenth-century art traditionally given the same name, and in which Islamic influence is less evident. This is particularly true of examples found in what was actually Mozarabic, that is, Islamic, territory still to be reconquered by the Christians. The remaining examples would have been produced in territory that was not actually Mozarabic, the same paradoxical situation mentioned in connection with tenth-century Mozarabic buildings. We should therefore distinguish this Mozarabic production from that traditionally accepted as such, that is, dated to the tenth century: hence the introduction of the concept of 'early' Mozarabic. As I sought to explain above, we should also distinguish this from very similar Ummayad Andalusí groups of the period of the emirate. In terms of its date it must be pointed out that we are analysing an evolutionary process. The oldest of the 'groups' or 'subgroups' discussed below was developed in Islamic territory and is of late eighth-century date. On the other hand, the earliest documented date of the more recent, Castilian, group developed in territory reconquered by the Christians is around the last decades of the ninth century, one very close to that traditionally ascribed to Mozarab.

The accurate classification of these remains presents its greatest difficulties in Galicia, where it is also hard to distinguish some of them from examples of Asturian work. The fact that the Reconquest in this part of northwestern Iberia was closely linked to the Asturian monarchy may explain why these Asturian and early Mozarabic forms are most closely linked. In my view the mosaic floor is similar to Ummayad examples at Qusayr'Amra in the Jordanian desert and dated to around AD 715 (Almagro *et al.* 1975: 53), and the herringbone technique, used on the walls of the mausoleum in Santiago de Compostela (dating from *c.* AD 800; Hauschild 1992), is the most representative prototypes of early Mozarabic style in Galicia. Although this is still not definitively proven, it is tempting to accept the theory that this mausoleum was neither Roman, as is still maintained by some, nor Asturian, as Hauschild believes. Instead it may have been the product of an Ummayad workshop which may also have been the source of the tenth- and eleventh-century Galician and northern Portuguese masonry technique which recalls the engraving technique of Sta María de Melque. Examples of this are to be found at S. Martiño in Mondoñedo, S. Martiño in Pazó, the dismantled church of S. Xés de Francelos in Celanova (Nuñez 1978: 169–78), S. Pedro de Lourosa and the castles of northern Portugal recently studied by Barroca (1990/1) (Figure 13.1.e).

The well-known Saamasas plaques also characteristic of Galicia cannot be Visigothic because of their implicit Islamic influence. Their stylistic similarity to the gryphon chancel of S. Miguel de Liño and, by implication, the sculpture of S. Frutuoso de Montelios and S. Torcato de Guimarães, is an argument against considering this group as Visigothic, and in favour of them being Asturian or from the period of the Asturian Reconquest. Nevertheless, they exhibit unmistakable Mozarab traits, which is why they are included in this section. In my opinion, all the evidence suggests that Sta Comba de Bande should not be considered Visigothic, despite the fact that a work as recent and interesting as that of Dodds still defends this idea (1989: 16, 17, 19, 21, 55–6, although she expresses some doubts: 125–6). I continue to believe that its floor plan must be similar to that of Sta María de Melque and, to a certain extent, S. Pedro de La Mata, as Gómez Moreno (1919: 18, 1966: 122, 126) argued. The differences between its decoration and that of the Visigothic style of Mérida (Cruz 1985), as well as its equally well-known similarity to S. Pedro de la Nave, suggest that it should be considered post-AD 711: this date is confirmed by documentary evidence. Since its floor plan and that of Sta María de Melque belong to the same group, it should be considered Mozarabic. It seems clear that different groups can already be distinguished, and that these may correspond to distinct chronological stages.

Another group would be the Riojan–Castilian group otherwise known as the 'Condal' group on the grounds that it was produced during the development of the county (*condado*) of Castille. Quintanilla de las Viñas and S. Pedro de la Nave are the prototypical buildings of this group. Their masonry was worked with a different technique from that used in Asturian stonework, and the second master decorator in S. Pedro de la Nave was quite clearly influenced by Ummayad models, as Puig (1961) intimated. However, both Quintanilla de las Viñas and S. Pedro de la Nave also display similarities to Asturian art which I will later evaluate. These two churches are not, however, isolated cases. There is a theory which suggests that they form a group with other churches now being studied. We now know that the reconquest of the Duero valley developed around 'churches', which must have included Quintanilla de las Viñas and S. Pedro de la Nave, many of which were monastic or dependent

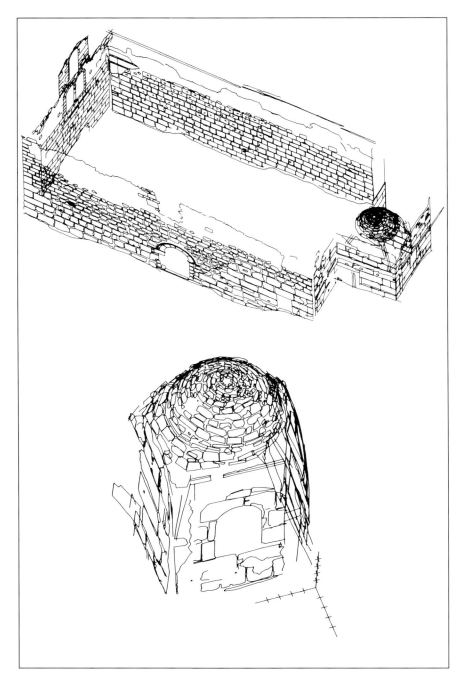

Figure 13.3 A perspective view of the church of S. Pedro el Viejo de Arlanza and details of its dome.

upon monasteries, whilst others were secular churches. The pendentive tufa domes over the apse appear to be the most characteristic feature of this group of churches. It is an element typical of the Syrian Ummayad style and is also found in the stonework at Sta María de Melque. Apart from Quintanilla de las Viñas, it is also found at a number of other churches including Sta María de Ventas Blancas (considered Visigothic by Schlunk and Hauschild 1978: 228), Sta Coloma (Fontaine 1977: 251–2, 416), Sta María de los Arcos de Tricio, S. Vicente del Valle, S. Felices de Oca, S. Pedro el Viejo de Arlanza (Figure 13.3) and Sta Cecilia de Barriosuso, as well as at Hérmedes de Cerrato. Documentary evidence indicates that these buildings must date from some time before the last quarter of the ninth century and the first quarter of the tenth, or perhaps a little later. The unity of the group is evident not only in the domes but also in the technique of reusing blocks of Roman stone, a practice previously considered Visigothic. This unity, the documentary information, and the close correlation between the architecture and decoration of the two principal churches in the group (Quintanilla de las Viñas and S. Pedro de la Nave) and Ummayad or Asturian styles, all support the idea of a date at around this period. Thus, given its Asturian references, this group cannot be considered pure Mozarabic. Finally, the other group would be the true 'early Mozarabic' in Andalusí territory. The coherence of the architectural and decorative typologies evident in the buildings of Sta María de Melque, S. Pedro de la Mata (as Puig 1961: 137 already argued), Sta Lucía del Trampal, Vera Cruz de Marmelar, S. Gião de Nazaré and Idanha a Velha means that these cannot be buildings of Visigothic date, but, on the contrary, must be Mozarabic buildings constructed before the tenth century, possibly in the second half of the eighth century or at the beginning of the ninth. S. Gião de Nazaré, with its Asturian and 'Reconquest' architectural features, stands out from all of these on account of the distinct morphology of its decorative sculptures. This suggests that it was perhaps constructed somewhat later.

The 'Mozarabism' of Asturian art

Gómez Moreno (1919: 71–92) dedicated a chapter of his work on Mozarabic churches to Asturian art. In it he identified the Mozarabic features of this artistic tradition. It was suggested that the prototypes of these were the elements found in the portico of S. Salvador de Valdediós dated from c. AD 910, which was one of the last Asturian churches. However, the Ummayad influence can already be appreciated in the first decorative Asturian sculpture, found in the church of Santianes de Pravia (which an inscription from King Silo dates to c. AD 780 (Fernández-Conde and Santos del Valle 1987)). Here the motifs of tangential circles enclosing stars, spirals of digitate leaves and fleurs-de-lis with speared leaves recall late Ummayad techniques and the Sta María de Melque and Sta Lucía del Trampal group of decoration. In my opinion, the reliefs preserved in Asturian territory and hitherto considered Visigothic either belong to this same group of Santianes de Pravia, such as those of Sta María de Bendones, or derive from it, such as those of Sta Cristina in Lena. In Santianes de Pravia there is a relief which has been correctly identified by Fernández-Conde as Asturian, decorated with the facade of a palace, in which this same influence is visible in the form of triangular Islamic battlements.

If there was strong Islamic influence at Santianes de Pravia and in other Asturian sculptures, it can hardly have taken twenty-five years (from AD 755 to 780) for the art brought by the last of the Ummayads to have had an impact in the north of the Peninsula, unless the dating of the decoration of Santianes de Pravia is to be put back several decades.

Traces of this more developed decorative influence can also be found on such elements as the lattice work and the decoration of S. Miguel de Liño and in the round mouldings of Sta María del Naranco, as Puig (1961) has already argued. We have already seen that one of the 'masters' of Liño can be linked to S. Frutuoso de Montelios and S. Torcato de Guimarães, as well as to Lisbon and Chelas. That is to say that the Asturian architectural decoration derived from Islamic prototypes in Lisbon. The proof for this is that the group of S. Miguel de Liño and S. Frutuoso de Montelios, and that of Santianes de Pravia, exhibit very close stylistic similarities to the decoration of the church of S. Martín de Salas, studied by Gómez Moreno (1919: 88–9). This should not be dated to the late tenth century, but rather to the reign of Alfonso III (AD 866–910) a century earlier, and more precisely, to the year AD 896.

It is also possible that Ummayad influences should be identified in Asturian painting. The painted buildings in S. Julián de los Prados may perhaps best be explained with reference to the mosaics in the mosque of the Dome of the Rock at Jerusalem (Creswell 1969), whilst its geometric panels and the motifs of interior arches and archivolts may be related to Ummayad pictorial decoration and mosaics, such as those of Jirbat al Mafyar (Israel) (Hamilton 1959).[7] It is possible that the non-iconographic character of these paintings is not simply related to Christian tendencies, but is more likely to have been because the principal influence was Islamic. However, I want to make clear that this Mozarabic perspective in Asturian art does not presuppose the absence of well-established Carolingian and Italian influences. As they both formed part of the same fashion of the era, it is possible that they were able to mix without undue difficulty.

The relation between 'early Mozarabic' and Asturian art

It should be recognized that there is a close relationship between Asturian art and that which we have defined as 'early Mozarabic'. Asturian art came first and some of the features of the latter are derived from it. For example, despite the claims of Dodds (1989: 34–7), the floor plan of S. Julián de los Prados in Oviedo is not unique, and I believe that it must be related to those of the churches of Sta Lucía del Trampal, S. Pedro de la Mata, S. Pedro de la Nave and, more remotely, to S. Gião de Nazaré, or to the final post-Visigothic phase of that at Fraga. Other elements of Asturian buildings, such as the rooms on top of the apses or the provision of a three-way division of the western side (narthex) for the emplacement of a high choir, can be found in S. Pedro de la Nave, Quintanilla de las Viñas (which certainly had a high choir – not identified by Arbeiter (1990)) and S. Gião de Nazaré. All of this suggests that in principle the art of the Asturian metropolis influenced that of its Castilian frontier, rather than vice versa.

However, there are some indications which suggest that the influence flowed in the opposite direction. For example, figurative decoration seems more important in S. Pedro de la Nave and Quintanilla de las Viñas than in Asturian territory, and there is the masonry technique developed in the Galician, Portuguese and Castilian areas (the supposed 'Gothic spirit': *more gothico*). Moreover, pendentive domes are not found in Asturias, although tufa domes were used. I now believe that the style of the second master of S. Pedro de la Nave could have derived from the style of S. Miguel de Liño, as both are geometric. However, I also think that this style and the form of the windows of S. Pedro de la Nave are related to Ummayad themes, such as those found in the palace at Amman in Jordan dated to AD 700–25 (Almagro 1983).

The immediate question is whether these elements form a homogeneous group which emerged from the Asturian world or whether they were the product of diverse Carolingian, Ummayad and Asturian influences which spread along different routes. The pendentive domes, the masonry technique and the schools of decorative styles in which we have detected an Islamic influence may all have been the work of Islamic, or perhaps Christian, artisans, whether or not they were Mozarabic in the strict sense. In relation to the figurative decoration in particular, we should discount for the time being the hypothesis of the existence of miniatures from the Visigothic epoch. Rather, we should see this as an indigenous development influenced by both north European and Andalusí styles. The same may also be true of the complex architectural design of Sta Lucía del Trampal or S. Julián de los Prados, which could have been the result of the simultaneous influence of the two principal styles.

Contradictions

Methodologically speaking, I believe that the presentation of a new theory should include an indication of those unresolved questions which may provide the basis for counter-arguments or, indeed, the future refinement of the theory. There are two unexplained facts which contradict my own argument and for which I do not have a logical interpretation. I am referring to the two *in situ* inscriptions that have been used to date the buildings of S. Juan Bautista de Baños and of Stas Céntola and Elena in Siero.

The first of the two inscriptions (dated to AD 652 or 661, Palol 1991: 366–9) could be said to form the nucleus of Schlunk's (1970a) argument. It was this which persuaded Puig (1961) to retain this interesting building in the Visigothic architectural group. It was decorated with chancel-screen plaques discovered by Palol (1988), but not known by Puig. However, the decoration of the church of S. Juan de Baños fits perfectly into the Ummayad-influenced decorative group. It should be remembered that Palol did not find any evidence to suggest that the church stood on the remains of an earlier one, for he proposed that only the main hall and its rectangular upper end belonged to the Visigothic building. The lateral sacristies and a second decoration were understood as later Mozarabic additions, perhaps as a way of explaining post-AD 711 references to the building. Puig (1961: 35, note 1), did indicate that the present position of the inscription in the building was illogical, although without explicitly referring to the problems of chronology. The question remains open, although it is possible that the inscription was taken from an unknown Visigothic building, and reused in the Reconquest church.

The date of AD 782 given in the inscription at the small church of Santas Centola and Elena in Siero (Iñiguez 1934, 1955: 64, 156), which is almost identical to that attributed to Santianes de Pravia, seems too early for the suggestion that its decorative theme was an evolution of that at Quintanilla de las Viñas (Noak 1987), dated to AD 900. Somewhat strangely, only the date of the inscription, which is carved in relief, has been reworked down to the surface of the base. The best explanation is perhaps that the date was modified after an initial mistake (AD 882?), as it makes no sense to talk of a '*damnatio*' as such, given that neither the names in the dedication nor the decoration were altered. Barroca (1990: 127, note 13) expressed a similar opinion and was obliged to suggest a date after the eighth century on the basis of its window typology.

CONCLUSIONS

How secure is the theory that I have expounded here? Inevitably, I have still not forgotten that which I was taught as a student, and with which I began my research. Equally, the alternative which I now propose is too fresh in my own mind for me to be certain. Comparing the two, I am unsure of the conclusions I should draw concerning the dynamics of change in this period.

As the construction of buildings in the northern half of the peninsula during the Visigothic era is well established, I am not attempting to deny the importance of the information available in this respect. The fact that I deny the Visigothic dating of a building like S. Frutuoso de Montelios does not mean that I reject the fact that Bishop Frutuoso commissioned the construction of the building. The same could be said of the information given by Bango (1979) concerning the reconstruction of pre-existing buildings carried out by those who repopulated the area in the ninth century. What we must assess, therefore, is the actual capacity to build in the Visigothic era. It may be that it was not sufficiently great for reliable evidence to have survived. Equally, we must evaluate the character of this production. The origins of Visigothic building are now obscure, and it is possible that it was a continuation of that which immediately preceded it. This would mean that the supposed change from Palaeochristian to Visigothic architecture, the so-called period of transition, never really took place. If this was indeed the case, we would be faced by a dynamic of continuity lasting from the late Roman times to AD 760.

The weakness of the Visigothic kingdom, combined with the new and more complex visions of Visigothic settlement as reflected in their cemeteries and a notable absence of urban life, may lead us to conclude that the area was more similar before and after AD 711 than previously thought. It is possible that the Duero valley was a wilderness before this date and that the differences in the area before and after that date are not as dramatic as once thought. Here too, we can accept the idea of continuity, in which change only implied a rapid acceleration of a pre-existing process. The field of archaeological research in the Duero valley ought to be extended to include the search for the same type of cultural manifestations in the Visigothic era as those sought for the period of the Reconquest.

On the other hand, and contrary to the idea that there was no Roman influence in Asturias, archaeologists are now discovering more and more Roman and late Roman remains in the region (for example Fernández Ochoa *et al.* 1992). For example, ever more striking examples of late Roman ceramics of Gallic and North African origin are being discovered. This, however, may prove misleading. New information on the late Roman civilization in Asturias suggests a panorama that increasingly resembles that of the other peripheral zones in the Peninsula. However, we cannot conclude that there was a direct link between late Roman and Asturian civilization from this alone. I have stated above that this is true in the case of sculpture. I do not believe that any of the sculptural remains discovered in Asturias date to the Visigothic era. Moreover,

I think that this may also be true of other art forms such as painting. The discovery of Roman frescos in Asturias is not related to the existence of pictorial decorations dating to the kingdom of Asturias. Something similar occurs when we look at the northwest quadrant and the northern Meseta. As I have already tried to explain, sculpture and architectural fragments classed as Visigothic in fact date from the Reconquest period, and no Visigothic prototype seems to exist. Thus the birth of Asturian and 'Reconquest' art represented a rupture rather than a more gradual change.

The concept of continuity must also be accepted in Asturian art, although a much more complex explanation of this may be needed. Whilst the continuity of the Gothic order defended in the chronicles of Alfonso III cannot be rejected, this does not imply that we must accept that the material culture dating from before and after AD 711 remained exactly the same. It is possible that this similarity, or continuity, was only a characteristic of the ideological framework and not of material production. The earliest manifestations of material culture in Asturian territory (possibly around AD 775 with King Silo or more probably with Alfonso II around AD 800) in fact seem to reflect a sharp break in the panorama of apparent continuity which appeared to have existed hitherto. There is no reason why these new forms of cultural expression should have forced the Asturian kingdom to renounce the use of Gothic legitimacy as a means of justifying itself, above all if this was done *a posteriori* by Alfonso III (AD 866–910). This question, however, is relevant to the work of historians who use other kinds of sources.

I do not believe that there was the 'technology' necessary to carry out the material manifestations that the new settlers needed and produced either in Asturian territory in the second half of the eighth century, or in the Duero valley in the ninth. Some traditional materials, capable of satisfying basic and primary needs, would have existed. But for the production that we know took place from 775 or 800 onwards they had to assume new techniques and new fashions, breaking with the continuity maintained until then, if in fact this had not already disappeared. The contribution of new techniques and labour (in part Muslim or Mozarabic and in part Carolingian) signified the real change, the point of rupture. In my opinion, this meant the influence of distant Sassanid models which had been adapted from a base of strong Roman 'neo-classical' roots in Syrian territory, as a result of the Islamizing trend. This also explains why, in order to account for these forms, researchers continually resort to 'classical' models; Ravenna for S. Frutuoso de Montelios or Sta María de Melque; Rome for Asturian paintings and lattice work; or Hispano-Roman buildings for the great mosque in Córdoba or the mausoleum in Santiago de Compostela.

The rupture of form signified the replacement of earlier centres of production at Mérida and Toledo with new ones, first at Córdoba and

Asturias, and somewhat later in Galicia, Portugal and Castille. At the same time new relationships were created, which gave rise to the formal similarities briefly outlined above. The population that slowly advanced to fill the Duero valley imposed itself on, or replaced, the few remaining inhabitants, who were incapable of meeting the new needs as they lacked the necessary resources. This change manifested itself in new systems of settlement (the hamlet and the monastery) in which churches were an essential element (Martínez Ochoa 1977–8; Escudero and Martín 1990; Pastor 1990). The documentation for repopulation and the archaeological evidence for this process of settlement and church construction, seems to have been considerable, if compared to the little available for the Visigothic era.

NOTES

1 Descriptions of all the buildings discussed in the text and the basic bibliography can be found in the following syntheses: Gómez Moreno 1919; Camps 1940; Puig 1961; Fontaine 1973, 1977; Schlunk and Hauschild 1978; Ferreira de Almeida 1986; Dodds 1989; Nieto 1989; Palol 1991; Arias 1993.

2 Especially the 'Beatos', illuminated copies of the *Commentary on the Apocalypse* written by Beato, the abbot of Liébana: interest in this manuscript was such that it was frequently reproduced and is today known by the name of its author.

3 It is clear that these historiographical changes must be understood in conjunction with the polemic between Américo Castro and Sánchez Albornoz about the birth of Spanish identity (see Menéndez Pidal 1960; Moxó 1979; Reyes and Menéndez Robles 1991).

4 For example cited in the bibliography, not the text, of Fontaine 1973; Schlunk and Hauschild (1978) hardly cited it in any of their bibliographies or the text; not cited by Palol (1991); alternatively it is noted by Bango (1974).

5 Here I must acknowledge the great influence which my friend, the Portuguese researcher Manuel Luis Real, has had on the development of my ideas.

6 This is compatible with the evidence Barroca (1990) presented for the theory that 'ajimezadas' windows did not have Visigothic precedents but rather belonged to an artistic current dating from after AD 711. The southern examples of Toledo, Mérida and Niebla should also be included in this current dating.

7 Ummayad designs can be seen in the stuccoes of Melque, as Schlunk (1964) and Garen (1992) sought to demonstrate. However, as already noted (Caballero and Latorre 1980: 724), they were inspired by Damascus and Jerusalem and not al-Mafyar.

REFERENCES

Almagro, M., Caballero, L., Zozaya, J. and Almagro, A. (1975) *Qusayr'Amra. Residencia y baños en el desierto de Jordania*, Madrid: Ministerio de Asuntos Exteriores.

Almagro Gorbea, A. (1983) *El palacio omeya de Amman, 1. La Arquitectura*, Madrid: Instituto Hispano-Arabe de Cultura.

Aragoneses, M. J. (1957) 'El grifo de San Miguel de Lillo y su filiación visigoda', *Boletín del Instituto de Estudios Asturianos* 31: 259–68.

Arbeiter, A. (1990) 'Die Westgotenzeitliche Kirche von Quintanilla de Las Viñas. Kommentar zur architektonischen Gestalt', *Madrider Mitteilungen* 31: 193–427.

—— (1992) 'Sobre los precedentes de la arquitectura eclesiástica asturiana en la época de Alfonso II', *III Congreso de Arqueología Medieval Española* II: 161–73, Oviedo: Universidad de Oviedo.

Arias, L. (1993) *Prerrománico Asturiano. El arte de la monarquía asturiana*, Gijón: Ediciones Trea.

Azkárate Garai-Olaun, A. (1988) *Arqueología cristiana de la Antigüedad tardía en Alava, Guipúzcoa y Vizcaya*, Vitoria-Gasteiz: Diputación Foral de Alava.

Bango Torviso, I. G. (1974) 'Arquitectura de la décima centuria: ¿repoblación o mozárabe?', *Goya* 122: 69–75.

—— (1979) 'El neovisigotismo artístico de los siglos IX y X: la restauración de ciudades y templos', *Revista de Ideas Estéticas* 37: 319–38.

—— (1988) 'Alfonso II y Santullano', *II Jornadas sobre Arte prerrománico y románico en Asturias (1985)*: 207–37, Villaviciosa: Ayuntarniento de Villaviciosa.

—— (1992) 'Los reyes y el arte durante la alta Edad Media: Leovigildo y Alfonso II y el arte oficial', *Ephialte* 19–32.

Barroca, M. J. (1990) 'Contribuçâo para o estudo dos testemunhos pré-românicos de entre Douro-e-Minho. 1. Ajimezes, gelosias e modilhões de rolos', *IX centenário da dedicaçâo da Sé de Braga. Congresso Internacional. Actas* 1: 101–45, Braga: Universidade Católica Portuguesa, Cabido Metropolitano e primacial de Braga.

—— (1990/1) 'Do castelo da Reconquista ao castelo românico (Séc IX a XII)', *Portugalia* 11–12: 89–136.

Barroca, M. J. and Real, M. L. (1992) 'As caixas-relicário de Sâo Torcato, Guimarâes (séculos X–XIII)', *Arqueologia Medieval* 1: 135–68.

Caballero Zoreda, L. (1982) 'Santa María de Melque y la arquitectura visigoda', *II Reunió d'Arqueologia Paleocristiana Hispànica (Monserrat, 1978)*: 303–32, Barcelona: Institut d'Arqueologia i Prehistòria.

—— (1984) 'Un tipo cruciforme de iglesia visigoda: Melque, La Mata y Bande', in T. F. C. Blagg, R. F. J. Jones and S. J. Keay (eds) *Papers in Iberian Archaeology*, British Archaeological Reports International Series 193: 578–98, Oxford: BAR.

—— (1989) 'Pervivencia de elementos visigodos en la transición al mundo medieval. Planteamiento del tema', *III Congreso de Arqueología Medieval Española, Oviedo*: 113–34, Oviedo: Universidad de Oviedo.

—— (1992a) '¿Visigodo o asturiano? Nuevos hallazgos en Mérida y otros datos para un nuevo 'marco de referencia' de la arquitectura y la escultura altomedieval en el N. y O. de la Península Ibérica', Seminario Internazionale di Studi su: 'Aspetti e problemi di archeologia e storia dell'arte della Lusitania,

Galizia e Asturie tra Tardoantico e Medioevo', 39 Corso di Cultura sull'Arte Ravennate e Bizantina: 139–90, Ravenna, Edizioni del Girasole.

—— (1992b) *Sobre Santa Comba de Bande (Orense) y las placas de Saamasas (Lugo)* 75–116, Santiago de Compostela: Xunta de Galicia.

—— (1994/5) 'Un canal de transmisión de lo clásico en la alta Edad Media española (I) y (II)', *Al-Qantara* 15.2: 321–50; 16.1: 107–24.

—— (1995) *Zamora en el tránsito de la Edad Antigua a la Edad Media, siglos V–X*: 339–430, Historia de Zamora, I: 107–24 Zamora: Diputación Provincial.

—— (forthcoming) 'Algunos aspectos de cultura material de época visigoda y postvisigoda. A propósito de la datación de Santa María de Melque, en el siglo VIII', *Islam y Occidente, un primer encuentro (Madrid y Alcalá de Henares, 1993)*, Madrid: Casa de Velázquez y Universidad de Alcalá de Henares.

Caballero Zoreda, L. and Latorre Macarrón, J. I. (1980) *La iglesia y el monasterio visigodo de Santa María de Melque (Toledo). Arqueología y arquitectura. S. Pedro de la Mata (Toledo) y Sta Comba de Bande (Orense)*, Excavaciones Arqueológicas en España 109, Madrid: Ministerio de Cultura.

Caballero Zoreda, L., Almagro Gorbea, A., Madroñero de la Cal, A. and Granada Sanz, A. (1991) 'La iglesia de época visigoda de Santa Lucía del Trampal, Alcuéscar (Cáceres)', in J. J. Enríquez Navascués and A. Rodríguez Díaz (eds) *I Jornadas de Prehistoria y Arqueología en Extremadura (1986–1990), Extremadura Arqueológica* 2: 497–523, Mérida–Cáceres: Junta de Extremadura and Universidad de Extremadura.

Caballero Zoreda, L, Cámara Muñoz, P., Latorre González-Moro, P. and Matesanz Vera, P. (1991/2) 'La iglesia prerrománica de S. Pedro el Viejo de Arlanza (Hortigüela, Burgos)', *Numantia* 5: 139–66.

Camón Aznar, J. (1963) 'Arquitectura española del s. X. Mozárabe y de la repoblación', *Goya* 52: 163–219.

Camps Cazorla, E. (1939/40) 'El visigotismo de Quintanilla de las Viñas', *Boletín del Seminario de Estudios de Arte y Arqueología* 22–4: 125–34.

—— (1940 (1963)) 'El arte hispanovisigodo', in R. Menéndez Pidal (ed.) *Historia de España* III: 493–668, Madrid: Espasa Calpe.

—— (1940/1) 'El visigotismo de San Pedro de la Nave', *Boletín del Seminario de Estudios de Arte y Arqueología* 7: 73–80.

Corzo Sánchez, R. (1986) *San Pedro de La Nave. Estudio histórico y arqueológico de la iglesia visigoda*, Zamora: Instituto de Estudios Zamoranos and Diputación de Zamora.

Creswell, K. A. C. (1969) *Early Muslim Architecture, Ummayyads:* AD *622–759, 1*, Oxford: Clarendon Press.

Cruz Villalón, M. (1985) *Mérida visigoda. La escultura arquitectónica y litúrgica*, Badajoz: Diputación Provincial de Badajoz.

Dodds, J. D. (1989) *Architecture and Ideology in Early Medieval Spain*, Pennsylvania: Pennsylvania State University Press.

Domínguez Perela, E. (1992) 'Capiteles hispánicos altomedievales. Las contradicciones de la cultura mozárabe y el núcleo bizantino del Noroeste', *Archivo Español de Arqueología* 65: 223–62.

Escudero Chico, J. S. and Martín Martín, A. (1990) 'Toponimia y repoblación en el territorio burgalés durante la alta Edad Media', *II Jornadas burgalesas de Historia, Burgos en la alta Edad Media (1991)*: 521–37, Burgos: Asociación Provincial de Libreros.

Fernández-Conde, F. J. and Santos del Valle, M. C. (1987) 'La corte asturiana de Pravia. Influencias visigodas en los testimonios arqueológicos', *Boletín del Instituto de Estudios Asturianos* 41: 315–44.

Fernández Ochoa, C., García Díaz, P. and Uscatescu Barrón, A. (1992) 'Gijón en el período tardoantiguo: cerámicas importadas de las excavaciones de Cimadevilla', *Archivo Español de Arqueología* 65: 105–49.

Ferreira de Almeida, C. A. (1986) *Arte da Alta Idade Media, historia da arte em Portugal 2*, Lisboa: Publicações Alfa.

Fontaine, J. (1973) *L'Art prérroman hispanique 1*, La Pierre-Qui-Vire (Yonne): Zodiaque.

—— (1977) *L'Art prérroman hispanique 2*, La Pierre-Qui-Vire (Yonne): Zodiaque.

—— (1987) 'Origines et évolution de l'architecture mozarabe', *Seminario Internazionale di Studi su 'Archeologia e Arte nella Spagna tardoromana, visigota e mozarabica', 34 Corso di Cultura sull'Arte ravennate e bizantina*: 139–54, Ravenna: Edizioni del Girasole.

Garen, S. (1992) 'Santa María de Melque and church construction under Muslim rule', *Journal of the Society of Architectural Historians* 51: 288–306.

Gómez Moreno, M. (1906) 'S. Pedro de la Nave, iglesia visigoda', *Boletín de la Sociedad Castellana de Excursiones* 2: 365–73.

—— (1919) *Iglesias mozárabes. Arte español de los siglos IX a XI*, Madrid: Centro de Estudios Históricos.

—— (1966) 'Primicias del arte cristiano español', *Archivo Español de Arte* 39: 101–39.

Hamilton, R. W. (1959) *Khirbat al Mafjar: An Arabian Mansion in the Jordan Valley*, Oxford: Clarendon Press.

Hauschild, Th. (1992) 'Archaeology and the Tomb of St. James', *The Codex Calistinus and the Shrine of St. James*: 89–103. Tübingen: Gunter Narr Verlag.

Iñiguez Almech, F. (1934) 'La ermita de Santas Céntola y Elena', *Archivo Español de Arqueología* 28: 135–8.

—— (1955) 'Algunos problemas de las viejas iglesias españolas', *Cuadernos de Trabajos de la Escuela Española de Historia y Arqueología en Roma* 7: 8–100.

Jiménez Garnica, A. M. (1990) 'La cultura visigoda en Asturias', in F. J. Fernández Conde (ed.) *Historia de Asturias* 15: 254–72, Oviedo: La Nueva España.

Juan, E. and Pastor, I. (1989) 'Los visigodos en Valencia. Plá de Nadal, ¿una villa aúlica?', *Boletín de Arqueología Medieval* 3: 137–79.

Martínez Ochoa, R. M. (1977–8) 'La ordenación del territorio en la mas vieja Castilla en los siglos IX a XI', *Boletín de la Institución Fernán González* 56 and 57: 273–339 and 81–117.

Menéndez Pidal, R. (1960) 'Repoblación y tradición en la cuenca del Duero', in M. Alvar (ed.) *Enciclopedia Lingüística Hispánica* 1: 39–67, Madrid: Consejo Superior de Investigaciones Científicas.

Mergelina, C. de (1925) 'De arquitectura mozárabe. La iglesia rupestre de Bobastro', *Archivo Español de Arqueología* 1: 159–76.

Moxó, S. de (1979) *Repoblación y sociedad en la España cristiana medieval*, Madrid: Rialp.

Nieto Alcaide, V. (1989) *Arte prerrománico asturiano*, Salinas: Ayalga Ediciones.

Noak, S. (1987) 'En torno al "arte mozárabe"', *II Congreso de Arqueología Medieval Española* 3: 581–8, Madrid: Comunidad de Madrid.

Nuñez, M. (1978) *Arquitectura prerrománica, Historia da Arquitectura galega*, Santiago de Compostela: Colexio de Arquitectos de Galicia.

Palol i Salellas, P. de (1967) *Arqueología cristiana de la España romana*, Madrid and Valladolid: Instituto Enríque Flórez.

—— (1986a) 'La arqueología cristiana en la Hispania romana y visigoda. Descubrimientos recientes y nuevos puntos de vista', *IX Congrès International d'Archéologie Chrétienne* 2: 1975–2027, Roma: Pontificio Istituto di Archeologia Cristiana and École Française de Rome.

—— (1986b) 'Las excavaciones del conjunto de 'El Bovalar', Serós, (Segría, Lérida) y el reino de Akhila', *Actas de la semana internacional de estudios visigóticos 'Los visigodos, Historia y civilización', Antigüedad y Cristianismo* 3: 513–25, Murcia: Universidad de Murcia.

—— (1988) *La basílica de San Juan de Baños*, Palencia: Diputación Provincial de Palencia.

—— (1991) III, 'Arte y Arqueología', in R. Menéndez Pidal (ed.) *Historia de España* 3, 2: 271–430, Madrid: Espasa Calpe.

Pastor Díaz de Garayo, E. (1990) 'Estructura del poblamiento en la Castilla condal. Consideraciones teóricas', *II Jornadas Burgalesas de Historia, Burgos en la alta Edad Media (1991)*: 633–51, Burgos: Asociación Provincial de Libreros.

Puig i Cadafalch, J. (1961) *L'Art wisigothique et ses survivances*, Paris: F. de Nobele.

Real, M. L. (1995) 'Innovação e resistência: dados recentes sobre a Antiguedades Cristã no Ocidente Peninsular', *IV Reunió d'Arqueologia Cristiana Hispànica* (Lisbon 1992): 107–24, Barcelona: Institut d'Estudis Catalans.

Reyes Téllez, F. and Menéndez Robles, M. L. (1991) 'Aspectos ideológicos en el problema de la despoblación del valle del Duero', in J. Arce and R. Olmos (eds) *Historiografía de la Arqueología y de la Historia Antigua en España (siglos XVIII–XX)*: 203–7, Madrid: Ministerio de Cultura.

Schlunk, H. (1945) 'Observaciones en torno al problema de la miniatura visigoda', *Archivo Español de Arte* 71: 241–65.

—— (1964) 'Die Auseinandersetzung der christlichen und der islamischen Kunst auf dem Gebiete der Iberischen Halbinsel bis zum Jahre 1000', *L'Occidente e L'Islam nell'alto Medioevo, Settimane di studio del Centro italiano di studi nell'alto Medioevo, 1965*, 12, 2: 903–31, Spoleto: Centro Italiano sull' Alto Medioevo.

—— (1970a) 'Beiträge zur kunstgeschichtlichen Stellung Toledos im 7. Jahrhundert', *Madrider Mitteilungen* 11: 161–86.

—— (1970b) 'Estudios iconográficos en la iglesia de San Pedro de la Nave', *Archivo Español de Arte* 43: 245–70.

—— (1971) 'La iglesia de S. Gião, cerca de Nazaré', *II Congresso Nacional de Arqueología*: 509–28, Coimbra: Ministério da Educação Nacional.

—— (1980) 'El arte asturiano en torno al 800', *Actas del Simposio para el estudio de los códices del 'Comentario al Apocalipsis' de Beato de Liébana* 1, 1 and 2: 135–64 and 87–120, Madrid: Colección Joyas Bibliográficas.

Schlunk, H. and Hauschild, Th. (1978) *Die Denkmäler der frühchristlichen und westgotischen Zeit, Hispania Antiqua*, Mainz am Rhein: Philipp von Zabern.

Ulbert, T. (1978) *Frühchristliche Basiliken mit doppelapsiden auf der Iberischen Halbinsel*, Archäologischen Forschungen 5, Berlin: Deutsches Archäologisches Institut.

CHAPTER FOURTEEN

THE ORIGINS OF AL-ANDALUS (EIGHTH AND NINTH CENTURIES)

Continuity and change

VICENTE SALVATIERRA CUENCA

INTRODUCTION

Al-Andalus is the name the Arabs gave to their domains in the Iberian Peninsula (Figure 14.1), a territory that gradually decreased as the Christian feudal societies progressed in their steady advance southward. Beginning in AD 711, the Arabs shattered Visigothic control of the Peninsula and in the ninth century, during the Ummayad emirate, the 'Islamic' border moved back to the Duero, largely because of the acute political crisis of the Ummayad emirate in the last thirty years of the century. Under Abd al-Rahman III (AD 912–61), the first caliph of Al-Andalus, the central authority emerged again, settled the border on the Duero and harassed the Christian kingdoms. In the eleventh century, by which time the caliphate had been replaced by the *Taifa* kingdoms, the border was formed by the river Tagus, only undergoing minor variations during the twelfth century on account of the Berber (Almoravid and Almohad) counter-offensives. From the thirteenth century onwards, Al-Andalus became reduced to the Nasrid kingdom, and in the fourteenth century was finally limited to the provinces of Almería, Granada and southern Jaén, before it disappeared in the late fifteenth century (Figure 14.2).

The analysis of the written sources of that time, which were mostly of a political and military nature, has overlooked the study of the territory and the settlements. As a result, some scholars have thought that

Figure 14.1 Map showing the withdrawal of the frontier of Al-Andalus between the mid-eighth and thirteenth centuries.

the invaders occupied the already existing nuclei of population. In terms of residence and economy, the population is understood to have been largely urban-based from the beginning, with few subsequent changes. In recent years, however, archaeological research in south and eastern Iberia has focused upon this issue and suggests a substantially different picture.

THE POTTERY

An important avenue of investigation for this matter in recent times has been pottery. However, its chronological imprecision makes the analysis of the evolution of the settlements quite difficult. Until recently, most

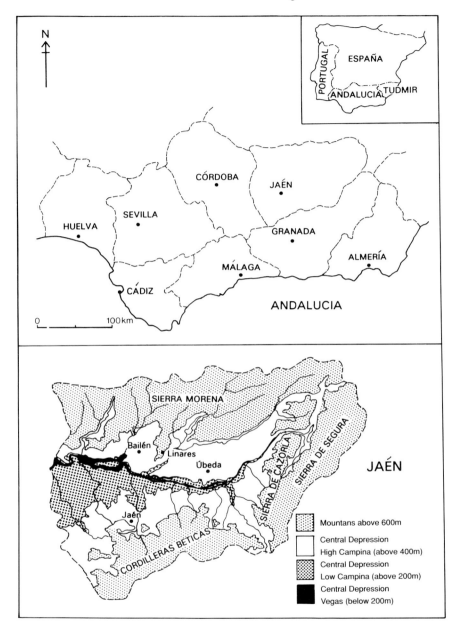

Figure 14.2 Map showing the location of Jaén province in Andalucía (above) and its principal geographical features (below).

studies analysed decorated pottery, whose many types cover the period between the tenth and the fifteenth centuries, although the duration of each type is still only understood in approximate terms.

Nevertheless, different pottery types have been the basis of a chronology for associated coarse wares. The general pattern of development for some of these types has been traced, the jars of the east Spanish coastal area, for instance, even though the individual phases are still too broad (Bazzana 1986). On the whole, most of the already existing studies are catalogues of sites with imprecise chronologies and seldom show stratigraphical sequences. However, the concentration of thirteenth-century sites in a relatively small area of the province of Murcia has led to a deeper understanding of the material of that period and region (Navarro Palazón 1986). In any case, the limited advance in this field is evident from the fact that the first synthesis of Islamic pottery, which was published by Guillem Rosselló Bordoy in 1978 for Mallorca, is still the main frame of reference.

The analysis of the period between the fifth and the tenth centuries, that is, between the last of the *terra sigillatas* and the appearance of green-and-white decorated pottery, presents greater difficulties as there is neither comparative nor stratigraphic evidence. However, recent research in the south and southeast of the Peninsula has led to fairly complete type-series for the period between the seventh and the ninth centuries (Gutiérrez 1988; Acién and Martínez Madrid 1989). They were systematized at the Conference held in Salobreña in 1990, after which our understanding of the Arab conquest and the development of Islamic society, a key period in the history of the Peninsula, was advanced.

THE STATE OF THE QUESTION:
A PRELIMINARY APPROACH

The ultra-nationalistic historiography which prevailed in Spain until the middle of this century has often studied the origin of a 'disaster', such as the destruction of the Visigothic kingdom in the course of the Muslim invasion of the Peninsula. Explanations are full of references to the 'decadence' or 'vices' of the Visigothic ruling class and even to fanciful tales of treachery.

Apart from taking for granted the social structure and military potential which lay behind the irresistible conquests of the Arabs, the interpretation of these events is currently understood in terms of the disintegration of the state. This thwarted the Visigothic king's efforts to make rapid use of all his power (Thompson 1969). Many authors consider that this process implies the existence of a true process of feudalization.

This avenue of investigation makes us pay only secondary attention to the immediate cause of the Visigoths' defeat, namely the military factor.

Clearly this issue is less interesting for historical analysis than one which analyses Visigothic society and the ways in which confrontation and integration were resolved after the conquest. This matter has been the subject of different interpretations (Sánchez Albornoz 1974; Barbero and Vigil 1978; García Moreno 1989), although there is a consensus that the invaders were 'westernized'. That is to say that society in Al-Andalus was more akin to Christian feudal society than to its Islamic counterpart. As archaeology is an exclusively positivist science and centred upon the object of its study alone, it has not been able to make a contribution to the debate (Salvatierra 1990).

When Pierre Guichard published his historical and anthropological study in 1976 and demonstrated the sharp contrast between Christian feudal society and its contemporary in Al-Andalus, he opened up a new area of research. This renewed existing concepts and defined some new areas of research in which archaeology could play a key role. In the subsequent years, two French researchers, André Bazzana and Pierre Guichard himself, began an important project in eastern Spain with the aim of confirming some of the latter's hypotheses. Whatever the value of this project, it has clearly influenced most current Spanish researchers (Guichard 1990, 1991; Bazzana 1992).

In this sense, archaeological analyses of the territory over the last ten years have provided results which are essential to understanding an extremely complex process and which have occasionally led to new interpretations of the written sources. Differences among the three main groups in Al-Andalus after the invasion are thus clearly revealed: Arabs, Berbers and the Romano-Goths. In the main these were differences generated by preceding social structures, although some confrontations take on the appearance of religious wars.

THE TERRITORY

If we wish to understand the historical reasons behind the ocupation of the territory during the first centuries of the Islamic period, it is important to take into account the preceding situation. During the Roman period, in particular from the first century BC, the settlement pattern comprised a large number of cities and an intensive occupation of the low-lying land. During the following five centuries various important transformations took place, brought about by a change in Hispano-Roman society and its economic structure, even though the town–country relationship was largely restricted to the lowlands (below 600/700 m). The crisis of the Roman Empire and the Visigothic occupation of the Iberian Peninsula from the fifth century AD brought about a new series of changes. In the rural environment there is a movement of population away from the lowlands into the more mountainous areas. In the urban context there is a debate as to whether the ancient cities decayed and disappeared or whether they continued to be occupied. Both these themes will be examined below with the aid of available archaeological evidence.

The countryside

In his studies of the Spanish Levant Pierre Guichard showed that hill-top settlements first appeared as early as the fifth century (Guichard 1983), and developed in the following centuries (Torró and Ferrer 1986). These sites have been interpreted as representing the abandonment of late Roman economic structures, perhaps as the result of the weakening of the state, which was unable to maintain trade or to restrict the more independent activity of the agrarian communities which in their turn evaded the payment of taxes to the state. In a way, this means the return to pre-Roman economic structures or, perhaps, a process similar to the Italian *incastellamento* (Toubert 1973; Francovich and Milanese (eds) 1990).

The same process took place along the coast of Granada. The network of harbours and anchorages was abandoned and the coastal towns lost their power, while a number of settlements appear on hills inland. The economy of these new settlements was probably based on cattle raising, hunting, the exploitation of the natural resources, and marginal agriculture (Malpica 1984; Malpica and Gómez Becerra 1991). The tendency to abandon the plains and settle in upland areas increased considerably during the seventh century, eventually becoming widespread all over the territory. This might be related to the frequent migration of slaves and peasants recorded in the written sources. It was not entirely due to the weakening of the state and a quest for greater autonomy, but also represents the defensive reaction of rural nuclei against increased pressure and economic coercion by the Visigothic aristocracy (Bertrand 1987; Gómez Becerra 1989), in a process of feudalization. The Arab conquest saw the consolidation of these upland settlements, with the maintenance of those already in existence and the emergence of new ones. Arab records allude to this, mentioning the flight of the population of Málaga to the mountains after the fall of the city (Acién 1991, 1993). These rural communities frequently developed a complex system of irrigated lands which underwrote their prosperity and attracted the ambition of the new ruling classes (Barceló 1989; Cressier 1991).

After the consolidation of the conquest and the establishment of agreements between the Arabs and the old Visigothic aristocracy, control over these communities began to be established. This became stricter during the eighth and ninth centuries with the building of Arab hill settlements which were considerably more complex and better fortified: Arab sources called these *ummahat al-husun* and described them as being ruled by *ashab* (lords). This distinguishes them clearly from the simple *husun*, which were merely unfortified refuges. Besides this, Acién points out that local society exercised a degree of 'contamination' over the Arab environment, so that some Arab and Berber dynasties became aristocratic, created their own *ummahat al-husun* and also extorted rural communities (Acién 1989). This process, which with due reservations could be considered feudalizing in the same sense as in contemporary Carolingian Europe, ran parallel to attempts by the Ummayads (especially after Abd al-Rahman II (AD 822–52)) gradually to implant an Islamic society, drawing upon urban communities.

Recent research in several countries has revealed the great potential of archaeology in providing useful documentation for the study of towns and their development. However, in contrast to the long-standing tradition of recent decades in countries such as Britain and Italy, urban archaeology in Spain was not undertaken systematically until the 1980s and even then was mainly focused on levels corresponding to the Roman era, with considerable disregard for those of the medieval period. To a certain extent this explains why current documentation is sparse, fragmentary and in many cases largely irrelevant.

The urban environment

Urban studies are based on the spatial distribution of, and relationship between, towns. There is only a limited understanding of rural sites, the demographic importance of towns with respect to their territories, and their development through time. This is due to a lack of detailed studies of individual territories. Only once we have this kind of information will it be possible to discover whether towns really existed in the initial periods of Andalucían Islam, and if so, what role they played.

Nevertheless, preliminary studies are beginning to reveal the existence of strong interregional differences. Corral points to the disappearance of many towns around the Middle March (corresponding to the central watercourse of the river Ebro) (Corral 1987, 1991), coinciding with traditional theories in this respect. In the Tudmir region (southeast of the Peninsula), by contrast, towns exhibit continuity into the early Islamic periods (Llobregat 1991; Gutiérrez 1993, forthcoming). In the Guadalquivir valley to the west, it has been postulated that the flattest lands were exhausted by the end of the second century AD (Choclán and Castro 1988), and that this led to the early disappearance of towns bordering the river, such as Salaria, while others such as Isturgi and Cástulo become simple villages (Salvatierra 1995, and forthcoming). We have already referred to the weakening of some southern coastal towns, which seems to become generalized at a later date, and to have spread to the larger centres. It has been recorded that a beach which developed at the jetty of the port of Roman Málaga in the third century later became the site of an early Islamic cemetery (Acién 1993). The town of Baria on the Almerían coast also underwent a process of transformation which continued up to the fifth century. This is still imperfectly understood, but saw the occupation of high lands in the surrounding hills (Olmo and Menasanch 1993). With a few exceptions, such as at Cástulo, those towns which were bishoprics persisted into the Visigothic period, being converted into centres of religious, civil and military administration, or residences for the *duces*.

Acién (1989) has analysed the role played by towns after the conquest. Initially they were occupied by the Muslims, usually by means of pacts, and the bishops were used to control the population. This is illustrated by the census of Málaga undertaken by Bishop Hostegenesis on a population which had fled to the hills. Shortly afterwards large enclosures were built, such as the enormous 'Hoya de Archidona' (with a perimeter of 4000 m) near Málaga or the Punt del Cid and Els Tossals de Bullentó on the east coast, about which one should note 'the intention to imitate the medina, i.e. to be in harmony with Islamic society' (Acién 1989).

At a second stage (Acién forthcoming), the old towns were abandoned and their special relationship to the bishops was sundered when the Muslims became aware that the peasants and their rents were really under the control of the landowners who had left the towns long before. Almost simultaneously the original function of the large enclosures diminished during the disputes of the first half of the eighth century, when Islamic solidarity broke down and people separated into Arab or Berber tribes and clans (Acién 1984, 1989; Aguirre and Salvatierra 1989). This was the time when the people settled in the *qarya*, an event which written sources confirm occurred after the conquest, and which archaeological research shows to have been established by the middle of the eighth century. However, it is possible that *qarya* may have referred to the aforementioned enclosures.

Subsequent policy of the Ummayad emirs sometimes led to the construction of new towns near the sites of earlier ones. This occurred in the upper Guadalquivir, where Ubbadat (present-day Ubeda) was founded near Salaria, and Andújar a few kilometres from Isturgi (Aguirre and Salvatierra 1989; Salvatierra *et al.* 1988–90). In both cases their occupation seems to begin with a small nucleus dating to the end of the seventh or the early eighth centuries, although sources first refer to them only in the ninth century, in one case explicitly stating its 'foundation' by the caliph Abd al-Rahman I and in another referring to the restoration of its walls. A similar situation can be seen in the Tudmir region, where the ancient towns were abandoned (Gutiérrez 1993) and the new capital of the region, Murcia, was built. Also, Corral (1987, 1991) reports the existence of a deliberate policy of urbanization in the Middle March in response to pressure from the Christian centres in the north, although he also recognizes the incomplete nature of the archaeological documentation.

If little is known about the demographic structure of the territory, our understanding of the appearance of what are generally recognized as the main centres in the eighth and ninth centuries is little better. At present, the outlook for medium-term research into Al-Andalus as a whole is reasonably good, since several sites of mainly Visigothic date but with early Islamic levels are being excavated. Amongst the most prominent of these are Recopolis, the royal town of King Leovigild (Olmo 1983, 1985) and El Tolmo de Minateda (Abad *et al.* forthcoming) in Albacete.

Most Islamic towns, however, lie beneath the present-day centres. This is illustrated by research undertaken in Jaén province which revealed that nearly all towns with more than 5,000 inhabitants are either of Islamic origin or existed during that period (Salvatierra *et al.* 1992). Thus our knowledge of this area must come from urban archaeology. If this situation is true for the medieval era as a whole, it is considerably worse for the eighth century, since in addition to the difficulties mentioned above, distinguishing superimposed occupation levels also presents a challenge.

If there is some truth in the image of half-deserted towns with large open spaces and random occupation which is defended by many authors and apparently confirmed in some places by current studies, it is difficult to obtain a clear image of them. The main problem is that later development, particularly that which took place from the eleventh century onwards, tended to cover these same areas, making it impossible to ascertain whether the absence of earlier levels is due to the deliberate demolition of previous structures or simply the result of a lack of previous occupation. Despite these problems, the general character of some towns is now becoming clear. The clarity of our understanding varies from town to town, as can be seen from the cases of Barcelona and Jaén. The analysis of urban evolution in Barcelona from the Roman to the medieval eras is based on relatively complete archaeological data, although the lack of information at present for some areas prevents an overall study from being undertaken (Granados 1987).

The location of the city of Jaén (Ibero-Roman Aurgi) was without doubt selected because of a large spring which was always situated within the city. The Romans almost certainly channelled it and arranged the spatial layout of the city around it. One of the main problems they must have encountered, however, would have been arranging the transport of surplus water to areas outside the city. The Islamic town initially remained within the limits of the Roman town and either used or reorganized the original system of water distribution. From the eleventh century onwards, the water supply developed as the northeast/southeast watercourse was divided into smaller lateral channels along which the water was conducted to five of the city's *hammam* (baths), after which it was used to irrigate the numerous orchards both inside and outside the city walls (Figure 14.3). Given the proximity of the water level to the surface, there were

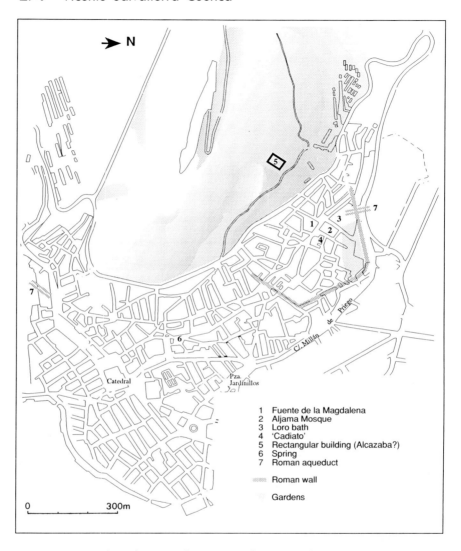

Figure 14.3 Plan showing the extent of Jaén in the ninth century.

probably wells in most dwelling-places (Salvatierra and Alcázar 1993; Salvatierra *et al.* forthcoming). Likewise, in the tenth century, Palma de Mallorca, the capital of the Balearic Islands, was organized around an extensive canal system (Riera 1993).

It seems that both Jaén and Palma de Mallorca initially covered an area of approximately 6 hectares, although it is more difficult to calculate the number of inhabitants. Nevertheless, the population of the ninth century can be calculated from the size of the *aljama* mosque, which was built at this time. These calculations are based on a system developed by Lézine (1971) which has been recently applied to Madinat al-Zahra by Acién (1987), and whose example is followed here. Although the exact appearance of the mosque is unknown, Pavón's reconstruction seems acceptable (Pavón 1984). According to his calculation the oratory would have covered an area of *c*. 530 m^2 which, on the basis of Lézine's system, would imply 576 prayer-places. If we suppose, as is customary, that the size of the mosque was calculated to accommodate all the males in the town, as it was they who were obliged to attend, and that the average family had four or five members, we obtain a population of approximately 2,300 to 2,900 people. Although the courtyard and porches were also used for prayer during later periods, we can assume that the estimate is reasonably accurate for the period when the mosque was built. Since the population would have been even smaller in the previous century, this could be estimated at about 2,000 inhabitants. This figure is quite high for that period, but can be considered as acceptable in the current state of knowledge (Salvatierra forthcoming).

The onset of the caliphate of Abd al-Rahman III in the tenth century was to a great extent the result of the rise of a strong central power which imposed the state's control over most of the territory and started the process of Islamization in the Peninsula. This new period was clearly different from the previous one, and is little known as far as the matters discussed here are concerned (Acién 1992).

REFERENCES

Abad, L., Gutiérrez, S., Sanz, R. (forthcoming) 'Fortificación y espacio doméstico en un yacimiento tardorromano: El Tolmo de Minateda (Hellín, Albacete)', *Jornadas Internacionales de la Sede de Elo. El espacio religioso y profano en los territorios urbanos de Occidente (Siglos V–VII)*.

Acién, M. (1984) 'La formación y destrucción de al-Andalus', in M. Barceló (ed.) *Historia de los pueblos de España. Tierras fronterizas (I): Andalucia, Canarias*: 21–46, Barcelona: Argos Vergara.

—— (1987) 'Madinat al-Zahra en el urbanismo musulmán', *Cuadernos de Madinat al-Zahra* 1: 11–26.

—— (1989) 'Poblamiento y fortificación en el Sur de al-Andalus. La fortificación de un país de Husun', *III Congreso de arqueología medieval Española* 1: 135–50, Oviedo: Universidad de Oviedo.

—— (1991) 'Recientes estudios sobre arqueología andalusí en el Sur de al-Andalus', *Aragón en la Edad Media* 9: 355–69.

—— (1992) 'Sobre la función de los husun en el Sur de al-Andalus. La fortificación en el califato', *I Coloquio Hispano-Italiano de arqueología medieval*: 263–74, Granada: Patronato de la Alhambra y el Generalife.

—— (1993) 'La cultura material de época emiral en el sur de al-Andalus. Nuevas Perspectivas', in A. Malpica (ed.) *La cerámica altomedieval en el Sur de Al-Andalus*: 153–72, Granada: Universidad de Granada.

—— (forthcoming) 'El poblamiento indígena en al-Andalus e indicios de primer poblamiento andalusí', *Coloquio: El siglo VIII. Islám y Occidente, un primer encuentro*, Madrid: Casa de Velázquez.

Acién, M. and Martínez Madrid, R. (1989) 'Cerámica islámica arcaica del sureste de al-Andalus', *Boletín de Arqueología Medieval* 3: 123–35.

Aguirre, F.J. and Salvatierra, V. (1989) 'Cuando Jaén era Yayyan', in *Jaén. II, Historia* 2: 453–90, Jaén: Junta de Andalucía.

Barbero, A. and Vigil, M. (1978) *La formación del feudalismo en la Península Ibérica*, Barcelona: Crítica.

Barceló, M. (1989) 'El diseño de espacios irrigados en al-Andalus: Un enunciado de principios generales', in *El agua en zonas áridas: Arqueología e Historia*: XIII–L, Almeria: Instituto de Estudios Almerienses, Diputación de Almería.

Bazzana, A. (1986) 'Essai de typologie des ollas valenciennes', *II Coloquio Internacional: La cerámica medieval en el Mediterraneo Occidental*: 93–8, Madrid: Ministerio de Cultura.

—— (1992) 'Maisons d'al-Andalus', *Habitat médiéval et structures du peuplement dans l'Espagne orientale*, Madrid: Casa de Velázquez.

Bertrand, M. (1987) 'Los covarrones-refugio de Guadix. Primeros datos cronológicos', *II Congreso de Arqueología Medieval Española* II: 451–76, Madrid: Comunidad de Madrid.

Choclán, C. and Castro, M. (1988) 'La Campiña del Alto Guadalquivir en los siglos I–II d.C. Asentamientos, estructura agraria y mercado', *Arqueologia Espacial* 12: 205–21, Tervel: Colegio Universitario de Tervel.

Corral, J.L. (1987) 'El sistema urbano en la Marca Superior de al-Andalus', *Turiaso* VII: 23–64.

—— (1991) 'Las ciudades de la Marca Superior de al-Andalus', *Symposium Internacional sobre la ciudad islámica*: 253–87, Zaragoza: Institución Fernando el Católico.

Cressier, P. (1991) 'Agua, fortificaciones y poblamiento: El aporte de la arqueología a los estudios sobre el Sureste peninsular', *Aragón en la Edad Media* IX: 403–27.

Francovich, R. and Milanese, M. (eds) (1990) *Lo scavo archeologico di Montarrenti e i problemi dell'incastellamento medievale*, Florence: All'Insegna del Giglio.

García Moreno, L.A. (1989) *Historia de España visigoda*, Madrid: Cátedra.

Gómez Becerra, A. (1989) 'Poblamiento Altomedieval en la costa de Granada: El yacimiento de Pico Aguila (Gualchos–Castell de Ferro)', *Revista del Centro de Estudios Históricos de Granada y su Reino* 3: 69–78.

Granados, J.O. (1987) 'La transformación de la colonia Bárcino. Reformas entre el siglo V y el IX', *II Congreso de Arqueología Medieval Española* II: 353–61, Madrid: Comunidad de Madrid.

Guichard, P. (1976) *Al-Andalus. Estructura antropológica de una sociedad islámica en Occidente*, Barcelona: Barral.

—— (1983) 'Orient et Occident: peuplement et société', in A. Bazzana, P. Guichard, and J.M. Poisson (eds) *Habitats fortifiés et organisation de l'espace en Méditerranée médiévale*: 177–96, Lyon: Gis–Maison de l'Orient.

—— (1990) *Les Musulmans de Valence et la Reconquête (XI–XIII siècles)* I, Damascus: Adrien Maisonneuve.

—— (1991) *Les Musulmans de Valence et la Reconquête (XI–XIII siècles)* II, Damascus: Adrien Maisonneuve.

Gutiérrez, S. (1988) *Cerámica común paleoandalusí del sur de Alicante (Siglos VII–X)*, Alicante: Diputación de Alicante.

—— (1993) 'De la Civitas a la Madina: destrucción y formación de la ciudad en el Sureste de al-Andalus. El debate arqueológico', *IV Congreso de Arqueología Medieval Española* I: 11–35, Alicante: Diputación de Alicante.

—— (forthcoming) 'La formación de Tudmir desde la periferia del Estado islámico', *II Jornadas de Madinat al-Zahra. Al-Andalus antes de Madinat al-Zahra*.

Lézine, A. (1971) *Deux villes D'Ifriqiya*, Paris: Librairie Orientaliste Paul Geuthner.

Llobregat, E. (1991) 'De la ciudad visigótica a la ciudad islámica en el Este peninsular', in *Symposium Internacional la ciudad islámica*: 159–88, Zaragoza: Institución Fernando el Católico.

Malpica, A. (1984) 'Modificaciones en la estructura de poblamiento de la costa granadina a raíz de la conquista castellana', *Arqueología Espacial* 5: 201–24, Teruel: Colegio Universitario de Teruel.

Malpica, A. and Gómez Becerra, A. (1991) *Una cala que llaman La Rijana. Arqueología y Paisaje*, Granada: Ayuntamiento de Gualchos–Castell de Ferro and Diputación de Granada.

Navarro Palazón, J. (1986) *La cerámica islámica en Murcia*, Murcia: Ayuntamiento de Murcia.

Olmo, L. (1983) 'Restos defensivos de la ciudad visigoda de Recópolis', *Homenaje al Prof. Martín Almagro* IV: 71–2, Madrid: Ministerio de Cultura.

—— (1985) 'La ciudad de Recópolis y el hábitat en la zona central de la Península ibérica durante la época visigoda', in *Wisigoths, Aquitains, et Francs en Aquitaine, Septimanie et Espagne. VII Journées nationales d'archéologie mérovingienne*, Toulouse.

Olmo, L. and Menasanch, M. (1993) 'El poblamiento tardorromano y el altomedieval en la cuenca baja del rio Almanzora (Almería)', in *Investigaciones Arqueológicas en Andalucía 1985–1992*: 675–80, Huelva: Consejería de Cultura de la Junta de Andalucía.

Pavón, B. (1984) 'Jaén medieval, Arte y Arqueología árabe y mudejar', *Al-Qantara* 5: 329–66.

Riera, M. (1993) *Evolució urbana i topografía de Madina Mayurqa*, Palma: Ajuntament de Palma.

Rosselló, G. (1978) *Ensayo de sistematización de la cerámica árabe de Mallorca*, Palma de Mallorca: Diputación Provincial de Baleares.

Salvatierra, V. (1990) *Cien años de Arqueología Medieval. Perspectivas desde la periferia: Jaén*, Monográfica Arte y Arqueología 7, Granada: Universidad de Granada.

—— (1995) 'Continuidad y discontinuidad urbana romano-islámica. La Campiña de Jaén', in E. Boldroni and R. Francovich (eds), *Acculturazione e Mutamenti Prospettive nell' Archeologia Medievale*: 107–19, Florence: Edizioni All'Insegna del Giglio.

—— (forthcoming) 'Arqueología y urbanismo andalusí en el siglo VIII. Teoría y realidad', in *Coloquio: El siglo VIII. Islám y Occidente, un primer encuentro*, Madrid: Casa de Velázquez.

Salvatierra, V. and Alcázar, E. (1993) 'La distribución del agua en Jaén durante el periodo islámico', in *Formas de habitar e alimentação no sul da Península Iberica (Idade Media) Arqueologia Medieval* 4, 95–106.

Salvatierra, V., Castillo, J.C. and Pérez, M.C. (1988–90) 'El desarrollo urbano en al-Andalus: El caso de Andújar', *Cuadernos de Madinat al-Zahra* 2: 85–107.

Salvatierra, V., Castillo, J.C. and Castillo, J.L. (1992) 'Arqueología urbana e historia. El caso del Jaén islámico', *I Coloquio Hispano-Italiano de Arqueología Medieval*: 109–22, Granada: Patronato de La Alhambra y el Generalife.

Salvatierra, V., Pérez, M.C., Castillo, J.L., Alcázar, E. and Cano, J. (forthcoming) 'Formación y evolución de una ciudad islámica: Jaén', *IV Congreso de Arqueología Medieval Española* II, 87–92, Alicante: Disputación de Alicante.

Sánchez Albornoz, C. (1974) *En torno a los Orígenes del Feudalismo I. Fideles y gardingos en la monarquía visigoda*, Buenos Aires: Editorial Universitaria de Buenos Aires.

Thompson, E.A. (1969) *The Goths in Spain*, Oxford: Oxford University Press.

Torró, J. and Ferrer, P. (1986) 'Asentamientos altomedievales en el Pic del Negre (Cocentaina, Alicante). Aportación al estudio del tránsito a la época islámica en el ámbito montañoso de las comarcas meridionales del país valenciano', *I Congreso de Arqueología Medieval Española* III: 129–46, Colección Actas 9, Zaragoza: Diputación General de Aragón.

Toubert, P. (1973) *Les structures du Latium médiéval: le Latium méridional et la Sabine du IX siècle à la fin du XIIe siècle*, Rome: École Française de Rome.

CHAPTER FIFTEEN

ALL CHANGE?

A commentary on Iberian archaeology

ROBERT CHAPMAN

The presentation of this group of papers at the *Euro*TAG conference in Southampton in 1992 marked only the second occasion on which Iberian archaeology had received such attention at the annual meetings of the Theoretical Archaeology Group. At that time, it was twenty years since I had first visited Spain as a zealous young Ph.D. student. This began my involvement in research and fieldwork on the prehistoric archaeological record of that country. The Spain (and indeed Portugal) which exists now is a very different place archaeologically, politically, economically and culturally from what it was in the early 1970s. The chapters in this volume gave me the opportunity to reflect on those changes, and to examine the external context within which Iberian archaeology exists. I use the word 'external' in two senses, first, in relation to the local context of archaeology within Spanish and Portuguese society, and second, to refer to the nature and effects of interaction between local archaeology and that practised within the international community. The main emphasis in this chapter is on the second of these meanings. How has Iberian archaeology changed in response to this interaction? Has it really been 'interaction', rather than a one-way process of intellectual colonization? Why is a knowledge of contemporary Iberian archaeology important, both empirically and theoretically? During the course of this commentary on the chapters, I shall try to answer these questions. If the balance of my comments leans too much towards Spain rather than Portugal, then this reflects my own cultural and archaeological experiences.

Anyone who has visited Spain and Portugal since the early 1970s will have clear, visual impressions of the political, cultural and economic changes which have taken place since the deaths of the the two right-wing dictators, Franco and Salazar. With the ending of cultural, intellectual and economic isolation, and membership of the EC, both countries are looking to push their economies into the late twentieth century, while at the same time maintaining their individual identities. In the same year as *Euro*TAG, Spain played host to the Olympic Games in Barcelona and Expo-92 in Seville, and celebrated the 500th centenary of Cristobal Colon's voyage of discovery to the New World. The modernization of the transport and communications infrastructure has been given a major boost by these events. My friend Vicente Lull and I had the strange experience of arriving in the Vera basin that year to be confronted by a new motorway and major road system which initially made us feel like strangers in a region we had both known for twenty years. Other changes have been as diverse as the decline in the influence of the Catholic Church, the major demographic shift from the country to the towns (e.g. fifty years ago, some 50 per cent of the Spanish population earned its livelihood from the land, but this figure has now shrunk to 10 per cent, see Fox 1991: 25), the cultural influence of Uncle Sam (Macdonalds, Levis, politically incorrect Sony Walkmen, etc.), the adoption of 'yuppie' into Castilian, the spread of hard-core pornography and the recreational use of pharmaceutical products.

Collectively, such changes have produced a Spain which is no longer the country of Hemingway, Gerald Brennan and Robert Graves (a point to which I shall return later). 'Modernization' also produces a challenge to both Spanish and Portuguese society: how can some kind of independent, distinctive identity be maintained within the context of participation within an intrusive and pervasive world system? A similar question is posed for the archaeology of the Iberian Peninsula (and here I make no distinction from prehistory, although this is normally the tradition within both countries). When it comes to archaeological theory and methodology, is it simply a matter of intellectual colonization from the Anglo-Saxon World, receiving the Holy Wisdom, adopting the latest trends and 'isms', following the agenda set in northwest Europe and the United States? Although the chapters in this volume were presented at a *Euro*TAG, with active participation of European archaeologists, the Big Debate at the beginning of the conference still sent clear signals (whether intended or not) that the agenda was firmly in the hands of Anglo-Saxons (in this case, Lew Binford and Colin Renfrew versus Chris Tilley and John Barrett). A similar message was conveyed by Ian Hodder's edited volume, *Archaeological Theory in Europe* (1991), in which regional European traditions were used to make critical points in a tired old debate between 'processual' and 'post-processual' archaeology. If open discussion and 'democratization' are the aims, then why could this not have been reflected in the editorial process? Are the other European authors there simply to provide ammunition for a battle which is not of their own making, or could they not be involved more actively in debate (e.g. making shorter contributions, based on a reading of all of the papers, at the end of the book)?

Within Spain, and to a lesser extent Portugal, issues of theory and methodology have surfaced in the literature and in meetings, beginning slowly in the 1970s, but increasing in tempo since the first major Congress at Soria in 1981 (for the best reviews of this recent history, see Lull 1991; Vázquez Varela and Risch 1991). This exposure to external debate came about for a variety of reasons, including the reopening of cultural contact, access to books and periodicals from the Anglo-Saxon world, increase in familiarity with the English language, the publication of Castilian translations of major texts, periods of study in England or the United States and the participation in Spanish archaeology of a small number of theoretically minded Anglo-Saxon scholars. While there are still those to whom issues of theory and methodology are anathema (note that Risch's comment that ' "traditional" anti-theoretical archaeology still controls large parts of the power structures in archaeology' (Vázquez Varela and Risch 1991: 33) has a familiar ring to those of us in Britain), a younger (and increasingly middle-aged!) generation has established these issues in the university curriculum.

This process of adoption has been marked by a diversity of responses to the 'external' world, including fierce critique of the latest trends from the English-speaking world. The evolution of Spanish archaeology into a 'mirror-image' of that practised in Britain and the United States is rejected (except perhaps at the level of introductory textbooks, which stress conformity, methods and techniques rather than theoretical debate (e.g. Fernández Martínez 1989). As Risch has written,

> Spanish, and more widely Mediterranean (also including North African) and Latin American social thought has produced a marginal and critical tradition sufficient to develop its own approaches, rather than just reproduce out of context the models of the English-speaking world which are now so much in fashion. The aim should be to widen and diversify international communication, which is still very poor and controlled by particular 'bosses'.
>
> (Vázquez Varela and Risch 1991: 46–7)

Given the tradition of social thought to which Risch refers, it is not surprising that historical materialism is the dominant perspective within Spanish theoretical archaeology.

As the main theoretical approaches which have been debated in the Anglo-Saxon world in the last three decades, it is processualism and post-processualism which have attracted the major critiques (for detailed references, see Vázquez Varela and Risch 1991). Gurus from both camps have come under the cosh, as Spanish archaeologists react to wider debates and try to make original contributions to them. Evidence of this 'auto-development' can be seen in a variety of publications on formation processes and taphonomy (Castro *et al.* 1993), spatial archaeology (an ongoing series of edited volumes, beginning with Burillo 1984), units of analysis in the archaeological record (Estévez *et al.* 1984; Ruiz

Rodríguez *et al.* 1986), archaeology as social science (Estévez *et al.* 1984), archaeological theory (e.g. Lull 1988; Lull *et al.* 1990; Vicent 1982), the archaeology of death (Lull and Picazo 1989) and gender archaeology (for a list of references, see Díaz-Andreu 1994). Indeed I have to say that I see a greater subtlety of thought in many of these publications, and a greater understanding of European philosophers and social scientists, than I do in their English-speaking counterparts. Matched with this subtlety of thought, there is a more realistic approach to the relationship between theory and practice, and a willingness to enter into critical self-consciousness and the evaluation of ideas against an empirical record.

On the other hand, there is also evidence of a prominent weakness inherited from the Anglo-Saxon world, namely to treat the 'isms', or paradigms, of archaeology as hermetically sealed units. Like normative views of culture, insufficient attention is devoted to variability within paradigms, as if debate only occurs between them. In an otherwise thoughtful review of the theory and practice of contemporary archaeology in Jaén, Ruiz *et al.* (1986) treat New/Processual Archaeology as a monolithic entity, with no recognition of the differences of opinion between leading members of this 'school'. Similarly, in a contribution to a volume of *Revista de Occidente* concerned with contemporary archaeology, Antonio Gilman (1988: 52) identifies population pressure as a central concept within New Archaeology, without acknowledging the role played by scholars inspired by this approach in collecting the data which contradicts the importance of such pressure in cultural change (e.g. state origins in Mesoamerica). And if our approaches are such closed systems, then how do we cope with two papers by David Clarke which anticipated by more than a decade the inference of gender differences from settlement data (1972), and the analysis of the external context within which archaeology exists (1973)? Dividing the academic world into 'good' guys and 'bad' guys may make sense in the context of disciplinary politics, but it is neither subtle nor realistic when trying to understand theoretical and methodological issues. It may also impose artificial barriers to communication.

Note that Risch argued that we should 'widen and diversify international communication' (Vázquez Varela and Risch 1991: 46–7), and it is here that I would like to consider the issue of language. Anthropologists have long recognized how misunderstandings caused by linguistic problems can cause difficulties during fieldwork. Those of us who have undertaken research in foreign countries can all empathize with the anthropologist Nigel Barley, who wanted to say to the Dowayo chief in Cameroon 'Excuse me, I am cooking some meat', and actually said 'Excuse me, I am copulating with the blacksmith' (Barley 1986: 57)! I can remember getting the pronunciation of a popular Spanish ice-cream wrong, and amusing all listeners by asking for a part of the female anatomy! Such communication problems are inevitable with any language.

The British are lucky, because theirs is the major international language for scholarly debate, but they are also more language-bound than most of their European counterparts. How many European languages can we read and understand? Can we understand the ideas and concepts which Spanish, Portuguese, Italian, French, German, etc. archaeologists are trying to express, or the theoretical and methodological structures they are creating? Theory can be difficult enough in your own language, let alone in another one. Clearly, without understanding there can be no debate, and Anglo-Saxon archaeologists often forget that the use of their own language for debate imposes an inequality on their relationships with non-English-speaking scholars.

One solution is an increase in the publication of translations of major works. This has characterized Spanish archaeology since the 1980s (e.g. Binford 1988; Clarke 1984; Hodder and Orton 1990), but even then it was nearly two decades since some of the major processual archaeology texts had been published in English. The failure to review such books (whether in English or Spanish) in the major Spanish periodicals is argued to have contributed to the slow local take-off of theoretical debate (Ruiz Zapatero 1987). But how many Spanish books have been translated into English? Aubet's book on the Phoenicians in the western Mediterranean (1987) was published by Cambridge University Press in 1993, and will be followed by Ruiz Rodríguez and Molina's synthesis of the southern Iberian Iron Age (published in Spanish in 1993), but these are about the only two examples which spring to mind. Access to and control of publication still helps to control the research agenda.

In spite of all these problems, there is no doubt that awareness of the Spanish and Portuguese archaeological records is now reaching a much wider audience in Europe and beyond. Conference publications in English are gaining momentum (e.g. Lillios 1995b; Cunliffe and Keay 1995; Balmuth et al. forthcoming), and translated papers are addressing important theoretical issues (e.g. Nocete 1994). As is pointed out by Díaz-Andreu (this volume), there is a noticeably greater participation of both Spanish and Portuguese archaeologists in international congresses, both in Europe and the United States. Whether this really means, as she claims, that there is a 'European integration of the southwest periphery' is debatable, given the communication problems mentioned above. But the chapters in this volume illustrate something of the relevance of the Iberian archaeological record, and its study, to foreign scholars. Issues of wider interest include an understanding of local historiographies, knowledge of prehistoric and historic cultural change within Iberia, and an appreciation of how 'big' theoretical issues are being tackled in relation to a specific empirical record.

One of the pleasing trends of 1980s scholarship in archaeology was the recognition that there was not one history of archaeology, but many histories of the subject. I was educated myself on histories of Britain and northwest Europe, of the kind produced by Glyn Daniel. Indeed I can remember David Clarke jokingly referring to the genre as 'the history of eccentric Welshmen'! But now there are more histories of regional traditions (e.g. Trigger and Glover 1981). Díaz-Andreu's chapter is one of a series of articles she is writing about the history of archaeology in Spain (for works on Portuguese archaeology written in English, cf. Lillios 1995a). She raises the issues of intellectual colonialism and communication problems which are mentioned above, only this time in relation to that dramatic period of discovery of the Iberian archaeological record in the last two decades of the nineteenth, and the first decade of the twentieth centuries. Publication of these great discoveries was often in languages other than Spanish, local scholars were rarely cited and ethnocentrism dominated the foreigners' thinking. The interaction of these archaeological 'colonists' with those of other regional traditions in western Europe helps to fill many gaps left by previous histories of this period.

The conception of Spanish peasants as 'living fossils', expressed by Pierre Paris in 1910 (see Díaz-Andreu, this volume), has, I suspect, been held more broadly by foreign archaeologists working in Spain and Portugal (let alone other areas of the Mediterranean). Indeed I have the feeling that the 'traditional' view of the Iberian Peninsula, which attracted Hemingway, Brennan and Graves, has been part of a pan-Mediterranean 'ethnographic present' which has been projected back into the historic and prehistoric past. To take one example, there was a period of time from the mid-1960s until the late 1970s when the briefest glimpse of a herd of sheep going up a mountainside would lead prehistorians to infer the existence of seasonal movements along the same routes over millennia (e.g. Jarman *et al.* 1982). It did not matter that historical records showed the specific contexts of such large-scale movements within the medieval and modern economies. What mattered was long-term continuity, whether it was in Greece, Italy or Spain. Now there is no denying that continuity does occur in human behaviour, but so does change, and it is up to us as archaeologists to try to measure the nature and degree of such change. Clinging too closely to the ethnographic present keeps us from the challenge of an 'other' past (see p. 285, in relation to early agricultural societies in the Mediterranean basin).

Moving on to other issues of the Iberian archaeological record, there is no doubt that any scholar of the European Palaeolithic cannot fail to put new Spanish publications towards the top of his/her current reading list. As Enamorado's chapter (this volume) makes clear, the latest radiocarbon evidence supports the case for Neanderthals existing in southern Spain until *c.* 30,000/28,000 BP while anatomically modern humans appeared in the north some ten thousand years earlier. Given the non-Dordogne nature of the Upper Palaeolithic assemblages in southern Spain, such a late survival of Neanderthals was always a possibility, but the new dating evidence makes biological and cultural regional variation within the Peninsula *c.* 40,000–30,000 BP a key problem in the European research agenda. Iberia has also become 'central' rather than 'peripheral' in relation to three other Palaeolithic problems. Enamorado cites the new radiocarbon dating for Spanish Solutrean assemblages, compelling us to rethink questions of origins and regional interaction. Two other fundamental discoveries, those relating to the earliest humans in Europe (the site of Orce, in Granada, see Roe 1995), and the Upper Palaeolithic open-air art from the Coa valley in northern Portugal (Bahn 1995), came too late for Enamorado's chapter, but in both cases they have had a continental-wide impact.

Another widely debated issue, the nature of early agricultural societies in Europe, is raised by Ribé *at al.* (this volume). Here we are concerned with the kinds of issues which have been raised in influential papers by Zvelebil and Rowley-Conwy (1984, 1986), and which have been discussed most recently for the Iberian Peninsula by Zilhão (1993). As with later prehistoric periods, the challenge before us is to reconstruct (or perhaps, more correctly, to construct, or in Lull's terms, to represent) a past which is not simply the 'ethnographic present' projected backwards a few millennia. How different were early agricultural societies from those 'traditional' farmers of the present century, who existed within von Thünen-like territories and practised some form of transhumance? Did a major break in settlement–subsistence systems occur at the beginning of the Neolithic, over seven thousand years ago, or, as I have argued elsewhere (Chapman 1990: 221–7), some two thousand years later? Ribé *et al.* attempt to construct regional systems (cf. Bosch 1994) for the Neolithic in Catalunya, while acknowledging ambiguities in the details of such systems. More open-air sites are now being discovered for this period, but the dynamics of change remain unclear. Where along the spectrum from 'mobile' to 'sedentary' did these Neolithic societies lie? If the changes in the archaeological record of the Neolithic some five thousand years ago are not simply an artefact of the archaeological record, then can we start to model the change in terms of social rather than just economic systems? In many areas of Europe, thinking about Neolithic subsistence is still normative and ignores the social context of production. Who actually adopted the new resources first, and were these resources equally available to all members of local communities and regional populations? To what extent were there differences in access to and control over production? It is about time such questions were being asked of the archaeological record both in Iberia and in other parts of Europe.

The nature of Neolithic production systems is also basic to an understanding of the changes inherent in the emergence of hereditary social inequalities. The development of complexity in prehistoric Europe is widely debated as a 'big' problem: when, where and why did it occur? Such questions assume that there is agreement on what 'it' is, and yet there is a lot of loose or undefined use of terms, so that comparative analysis proves difficult. In recent papers on Copper and Bronze Age societies in Iberia, neither Kunst (1995) not Díaz-Andreu (1995) give clear definitions of what they mean by 'complexity', nor do they address the variable material expression of this concept in the archaeological record. These problems are also highlighted in a recent, edited synthesis of the Mediterranean Bronze Age (Mathers and Stoddart 1994; for a review of these problems, see Chapman 1995).

The chapters which discuss more 'complex' societies in the later prehistory of Iberia (Hernando, Hurtado, Jorge and Jorge) together illustrate how regional analysis in the Peninsula has been extended beyond the traditional 'centres' of southeast Spain and southern Portugal. The majority of this research has been undertaken within the last three decades, and in some cases has yielded an archaeological record which was previously unsuspected (e.g. the Bronze Age sequences and sites of La Mancha and Albacete). This does not mean that regional and local 'lacunae' have ceased to exist, as Hurtado stresses with regard to knowledge of settlement patterns through field survey, reconstruction of environmental change and analysis of the material traces of past subsistence activities. To this list can be added the systematic application of radiocarbon dating, which even in the 'heartland' of southeast Spain has only been a characteristic of research within the last decade. In turn, the issue of dating directs our attention to what exactly it is that we want to date. What are our units of analysis, in time and space? In many respects we are still constrained by the three-age system, using major 'breaks' in cultural sequences (e.g. Copper to Bronze Ages) to structure our analyses of environmental and subsistence materials, or thinking in terms of 'an economy' for a particular cultural phase.

Two of the most interesting observations to emerge from southeast Spain in recent years have been the intra-regional variation in cultural, economic and demographic change (e.g. Chapman 1990; Ruiz et al. 1992), and the movement from site-oriented cultural sequences to the dynamics of regional political systems. Variation in one variable, 'risk for a peasant way of life', is at the heart of Hernando's chapter, as she compares and contrasts the archaeological sequences of Sardinia, southeast Spain and La Mancha from the fourth to the second millennia BC. In particular she argues that there is, or was, a correlation between agricultural risk and 'the investment of energy in the symbolic use of the world of the dead', thus helping to 'explain' interregional variation in the 'transformation of society'. While I am the first to applaud comparative analysis, it seems to me that Hernando's hypothesis has to face severe challenges. Even if her correlation were to hold true cross-culturally, the 'symbolic use of the world of the dead' in mortuary rituals may not necessarily be given material form in burial and other practices, which in turn may not be equally represented in the known archaeological record of each region under study. And what is 'risk for a peasant way of life'? It seems to be neither defined nor measured, and begs a lot of questions about the social organization of production systems, especially as we move to regional political systems based on hereditary inequalities. And if we take the correlation at face value, then how do we explain the occurrence of some of the most monumental tombs in the Iberian Peninsula in areas which are less arid, and therefore less 'risky' than southeast Spain (e.g. the Antequera megaliths in western Granada)?

Two further problems faced by students of later prehistory, and greater 'complexity', in Iberia (and indeed elsewhere in Europe) are also raised in these chapters, although they are not necessarily given the explicit attention they deserve.

First, there is the degree to which Iberian archaeologists are moving beyond formal definition of artefact or site types to an understanding of variation in these types and the extent to which they 'mean' or symbolize the same thing in different contexts. Let us take, as an example, Copper Age fortified sites. Ask any third-year undergraduate student to name some famous prehistoric sites in Iberia, and s/he will almost certainly mention Los Millares and Zambujal. Initially known in southeast Spain and southern Portugal, such sites have been characterized as 'typical' of the Copper Age in these regions and sometimes referred to as 'semi-urban'. In recent times such sites have been found over much wider regions of southwestern Spain, southern Portugal, the western part of the northern Meseta and northern Portugal (for a catalogue, map and discussion, see Oliveira Jorge 1994). Does this mean that 'semi-urban' society was everywhere in southern and western Iberia in the Copper Age? Was warfare endemic? Clearly a lot depends on context. There is much variation in energy expenditure devoted to the construction of walling around these sites, with Los Millares and Zambujal being exceptions rather than the rule. Just because there are concentric walls around a site does not imply that such sites all had the same functions, that they were all permanent settlements or centres, or that they were all part of local 'complex' Copper Age societies. The formal similarity is indeed interesting, but then so is the variability and local context, as indicated in the chapters by Hurtado and by Jorge and Jorge.

Second, the pan-regional nature of such fortified sites is only one example of a problem which has yet to find a post-diffusionist solution, namely the nature and effects of large-scale, interregional political, social and economic networks across the Iberian Peninsula. During the Copper Age we see this problem also in the distribution of symbolic artefacts (e.g. figurines/idols), while in the Bronze Age the distribution patterns of different bronze artefacts (as mentioned by dos Reis Martins in this volume) have been discussed in terms of diffusion (e.g. Savory 1949) and more recently through the use of a core–periphery model (Rowlands 1980). Hurtado (this volume) also mentions the most famous example of pan-regional distribution patterns within the Peninsula, that of Beaker pottery. While the quest for 'origins' still occupies the minds of archaeologists (and not just in Iberia), the recognition of local variations within wider styles in areas such as the middle Guadiana (Hurtado, this volume) and Almería (Arribas and Molina 1987) raises more interesting questions. Is such local variation purely 'random', as potters try to produce examples of a widespread style of decoration, with cumulative variation through time? Or are we witnessing intentional production of local Beaker styles, which signal their part in a wider tradition, but which also stress distinctive local identity? In other words, how far is a pan-regional style of pottery decoration being manipulated to the (social) benefit of local groups?

By the time we reach the first millennium BC, the position of Late Bronze Age and Iron Age societies within larger-scale Mediterranean and European networks has the kind of empirical support which is often lacking in the archaeological record of earlier periods. In the case of Late Bronze Age Urnfields discussed by Ruiz Zapatero (this volume), severe methodological problems remain unsolved in the inference of population movements from burial evidence. For the Iron Age societies, there is increasingly well-documented evidence for interaction with the Phoenicians, Greeks, Carthaginians and finally (in more than one sense of the word) the Romans. The known archaeological record really has changed remarkably in the last three decades, and only now is it beginning to be published for and in the English-speaking world. A comparison of Arribas's book on *The Iberians* (1963) with that of Ruiz Rodríguez and Molinos (1993) shows just how much new data on indigenous settlements, settlement patterns, economic interaction and social differentiation have been collected through excavation and field survey. Ruiz Rodríguez's chapter in this volume gives a flavour of this new data, and shows how European Iron Age scholars need to expand their traditional west–central European focus. Indeed the different nature of *oppida* in Spain, as compared with central Europe (Ruiz Rodríguez, this volume), is only one example where an expanded focus will put such variation into context. The degree to which the social organization of local Iron Age societies intensified, both economically and socially, in response to expanding, colonial powers has been a long-standing theme of Iron Age studies in west–central Europe (for a famous model, see Frankenstein and Rowlands 1978). But I would hazard a guess that the data for both colonizers (e.g. Aubet 1987, 1993; López Castro 1992) and colonized in Iberia is now as good as, if not better, than that in the 'classic' area to the north and east. Comparative analysis of regional sequences is clearly a matter of urgency.

With the onset of Roman colonization in Iberia we enter the 'historical' world, in which written texts have assumed an unmerited dominance over the material evidence of the archaeological record. Of the two chapters in this volume which discuss Roman Iberia, it is Keay who is openly critical of this dominance and who seeks to re-evaluate the material evidence for urban transformation within a less event-oriented and aesthetic approach to art and architecture. The material evidence from Roman towns now becomes, in Keay's hands, the ideological battle-ground for local elites 'manipulating cultural symbols for their own personal ends' (p. 195). In some respects this is a similar kind of approach to that which I recommended above in relation to the Beaker 'problem'. Keay honestly acknowledges the empirical weaknesses of his model, and in particular the difficulties in tracing the dynamics of change from immediately pre-Roman local communities to Roman urban formations. But it is a model for evaluation against the empirical record, and takes us in interesting, new directions. One such challenging problem concerns the relationship between, and possible primacy of, such ideological power struggles, and the equally powerful world of economic control and tribute mobilization within the provinces and between them and the imperial centre.

With the collapse of the Roman Empire, both written sources and material evidence have been used to identify cultural and population changes, in the form of the arrival of the Visigoths (Caballero, this volume) and later the Arabs (Salvatierra, this volume). Both are assumed to represent major disruptions for the local populations, and the political history of the early medieval period has tended to dominate the accounts of this period. Indeed, one celebrated synthesis of the conflict between European and African kingdoms at this time almost totally ignored the Iberian Peninsula (Hodges and Whitehouse 1983). While this bias against Iberia must, like the earlier Iron Age world, reflect the availability of sources published in English, it would also be fair to comment on the very recent 'take-off' of medieval archaeology within Spain and Portugal. The majority of the references cited by Salvatierra date to the 1980s and 1990s, when the (mainly) urban and (to a lesser extent) rural archaeology of the post-Roman periods began. As in the Roman period, it is the archaeological research which is challenging and complementing the accepted wisdom of the historical sources.

By way of a conclusion to this commentary, it ought to be clear to the reader that the period from the 1970s to the 1990s in Spain and Portugal has seen critical political, economic and social changes, and that archaeology has undergone changes in its practice, its practitioners, its institutions and its theoretical approaches. Archaeology in the Iberian Peninsula has emerged from isolation to begin a task of modernization. The local adoption of what had been seen as 'standard' methods in other parts of Europe (e.g. field survey, radiocarbon dating, environmental and subsistence reconstruction) has produced a quantitative leap in archaeological data for most periods. In many cases, as mentioned above, the empirical record demands, and is getting, attention on a European scale.

The same cannot yet be claimed for local debates on theoretical issues. While lively, challenging and important (or so I believe), these debates are not yet impinging upon those in the linguistically bound Anglo-Saxon world. At the same time, within Spain and Portugal, it is debatable whether the structure of power within archaeology, or indeed its 'clout' within society as a whole (to judge by the Coa valley fiasco), has changed much since the 1970s. For these reasons, Spanish and Portuguese archaeologists face internal and external struggles over the next decade. Those of us who undertake our research in either country have an obligation to be aware of these struggles, to be supportive in the area of international cooperation, and to remember that politically and intellectually we now live in a post-colonial world.

REFERENCES

Arribas, A. (1963) *The Iberians*, London: Thames and Hudson.

Arribas, A. and Molina, F. (1987) 'New Bell Beaker discoveries in the south-east Iberian Peninsula', in W. Waldren and R. C. Kennard (eds) *Bell Beakers of the Western Mediterranean* 1: 129–46, BAR International Series 331, Oxford: BAR.

Aubet, M. E. (1987) *Tiro y las colonias fenicias de Occidente*, Barcelona: Ediciones Bellaterra.

—— (1993) *The Phoenicians and the West. Politics, Colonies and Trade*, Cambridge: Cambridge University Press.

Bahn, P. (1995) 'Cave art without the caves', *Antiquity* 69: 231–7.

Balmuth, M., Gilman, A. and Prados Torreira, L. (eds) (forthcoming) *Encounters and Transformations: The Archaeology of Iberia in Transition*, Monographs in Mediterranean Archaeology, Sheffield: Sheffield Academic Press.

Barley, N. (1986) *The Innocent Anthropologist. Notes from a Mud Hut*, London: Penguin.

Binford, L. R. (1988) *En Busca del Pasado*, Barcelona: Crítica.

Bosch, A. (1994) 'El Neolítico antiguo en el nordeste de Cataluña. Contribución a la problemática de la evolución de las primeras comunidades neolíticas en al Mediterráneo occidental', *Trabajos de Prehistoria* 51: 55–75.

Burillo, F. (ed.) (1984) *Arqueología Espacial* 1, Teruel: Seminario de Arqueología y Etnología Turolense, Colegio Universitario de Teruel.

Castro, V., Lull, V. and Micó Pérez, R. (1993) 'Arqueología: algo más que Tafonomía', in *Arqueología Espacial* 16–17: 19–28, Teruel: Seminario de Arqueología y Etnología Turolense, Colegio Universitario de Teruel.

Chapman, R. (1990) *Emerging Complexity. The Later Prehistory of south-east Spain, Iberia and the West Mediterranean*, Cambridge: Cambridge University Press.

—— (1995) Review of Mathers, C. and Stoddart, S. (eds), *Development and Decline in the Mediterranean Bronze Age*, *Antiquity* 69: 423–4.

Clarke, D. L. (1972) 'A provisional model of an Iron Age society and its settlement system', in D. L. Clarke (ed.) *Models in Archaeology*: 801–69, London: Methuen.

—— (1973) 'Archaeology: the loss of innocence', *Antiquity* 47: 6–18.

—— (1994) *Analítica Arqueología*, Barcelona: Bellaterra.

Cunliffe, B. and Keay, S. (eds) (1995) *Social Complexity and the Development of Towns in Iberia*, Proceedings of the British Academy 86, Oxford: Oxford University Press.

Díaz-Andreu, M. (1994) 'Mujer y Género. Nuevas tendencias dentro de la arqueología', *Arqritica* 8: 17–19.

—— (1995) 'Complex societies in Copper and Bronze Age Iberia: a reappraisal', *Oxford Journal of Archaeology* 14: 23–39.

Estévez J., Gasull, P., Lull, V., Sanahuja, M. E. and Vila, A. (1984) 'Arqueología como arqueología', in *Primeras Jornadas de Metodología de Investigación Prehistórica*: 21–8, Madrid: Ministerio de Cultura.

Fernández Martínez, V. M. (1989) *Teoría y método de la arqueología*, Madrid: Síntesis.

Fox, R. (1991) *The Inner Sea. The Mediterranean and its People*, London: Sinclair-Stevenson.

Frankenstein, S. and Rowlands, M. J. (1978) 'The internal structure and regional context of Early Iron Age society in south-western Germany', *Bulletin of the Institute of Archaeology* 15: 73–112.

Gilman, A. (1988) 'Enfoques teóricos en la arqueología de los ochenta', *Revista de Occidente* 81: 47–61.

Hodder, I. (ed.) (1991) *Archaeological Theory in Europe*, London: Routledge.

Hodder, I. and Orton, C. (1990) *Análisis espacial en arqueología*, Barcelona: Crítica.

Hodges, R. and Whitehouse, D. (1983) *Mohammed, Charlemagne and the Origins of Europe*, London: Duckworth.

Jarman, M. R., Bailey, G. N. and Jarman, H. N. (eds) (1982) *Early European Agriculture: Its Foundations and Development*, Cambridge: Cambridge University Press.

Kunst, M. (1995) 'Central places and social complexity in the Iberian Copper Age', in K. T. Lillios (ed.) (1995b): 32–43.

Lillios, K. T. (1995a) 'The historiography of late prehistoric Portugal', in K. T. Lillios (ed.) (1995b): 7–19.

—— (ed.) (1995b) *The Origins of Complex Societies in Late Prehistoric Iberia*, International Monographs in Prehistory, Archaeological Series 8, Ann Arbor: University of Michigan Press.

López Castro, J. L. (ed.) (1992) *La colonización fenicia en el sur de la península Ibérica. 100 años de investigación*, Almería: Instituto de Estudios Almerienses.

Lull, V. (1988) 'Hacía una teoría de representación en arqueología', *Revista de Occidente* 81: 62–76.

—— (1991) 'La prehistoria de la teoría arqueológica en el Estado español', in A. Vila (ed.) *Arqueología*: 231–50, Madrid: Consejo Superior de Investigaciones Científicas.

Lull, V., Micó, R., Montón, S. and Picazo, M. (1990) 'La arqueología entre la insoportable levedad y la voluntad de poder', *Archivo de Prehistoria Levantina* XX: 461–74.

Lull, V. and Picazo, M. (1989) 'Arqueología de la muerte y estructura social', *Archivo Español de Arqueología* 62: 5–20.

Mathers, C. and Stoddart, S. (eds) (1994) *Development and Decline in the Mediterranean Bronze Age*, Sheffield Archaeological Monographs 8, Sheffield: J. R. Collis Publications.

Nocete, F. (1994) 'Space as Coercion: the transition to the state in the social formations of La Campiña, upper Guadalquivir valley, Spain, c. 1900–1600 BC', *Journal of Anthropological Archaeology* 13: 171–200.

Oliveira Jorge, S. (1994) 'Colónias, fortificacões, lugares monumentalizados. Trajectória das concepcões sobre um tema do Calcolítico peninsular', *Revista do Faculdade de Letras* XI: 447–546.

Roe, D. (1995) 'The Orce basin (Andalucía, Spain) and the initial Palaeolithic of Europe', *Oxford Journal of Archaeology* 14: 1–12.

Rowlands, M. J. (1980) 'Kinship, alliance and exchange in the European Bronze Age', in J. C. Barrett and R. J. Bradley (eds) *Settlement and Society in the British Later Bronze Age*: 15–55, British Archaeological Reports International Series S83, Oxford: British Archaeological Reports.

Ruiz, M., Risch, R., González Marcén, P., Castro, M., Lull, V. and Chapman, R. (1992) 'Environmental exploitation and social structure in prehistoric south-east Spain', *Journal of Mediterranean Archaeology* 5: 3–38.

Ruiz Rodríguez, A. and Molinos, M. (1993) *Los Iberos. Análisis arqueológico de un proceso histórico*, Barcelona: Crítica.

Ruiz Rodríguez, A., Molinos, M. and Hornos, F. (1986) *Arqueología en Jaén (Reflexiones desde un proyecto arqueológico no inocente)*, Jaén: Diputación de Jaén.

Ruiz Zapatero, G. (1987) 'La recension de publicaciones arqueológicas: S.O.S.', *Trabajos de Prehistoria* 44: 313–21.

Savory, H. N. (1949) 'The Atlantic Bronze Age in south-west Europe', *Proceedings of the Prehistoric Society* 15: 128–55.

Trigger, B. and Glover, I. (eds) (1981) 'Regional traditions of archaeological research', *World Archaeology* 13 (2, 3).

Vázquez Varela, J. M. and Risch, R. (1991) 'Theory in Spanish archaeology since 1960', in I. Hodder (ed.) *Archaeological Theory in Europe*: 25–51, London: Routledge.

Vicent, J. M. (1982) 'Las tendencias metodológicas en prehistoria', *Trabajos de Prehistoria* 39: 9–54.

Zilhão, J. (1993) 'The spread of agro-pastoral economies across Mediterranean Europe: a view from the far west', *Journal of Mediterranean Archaeology* 6: 5–63.

Zvelebil, M. and Rowley-Conwy, P. (1984) 'The transition to farming in northern Europe: a hunter-gatherer perspective', *Norwegian Archaeological Review* 17: 104–28.

—— (1986) 'Foragers and farmers in Atlantic Europe', in M. Zvelebil (ed.) *Hunters in Transition. Mesolithic Societies in Temperate Eurasia and their Transition to Farming*: 67–93, Cambridge: Cambridge University Press.

INDEX

academia: role of the structure of the academic profession in theoretical change 2

agriculture: ancestors, role of in regulating access to land 88–90, 93–4; link between people and land 88–9; Middle Neolithic economy 76–7; nature of early agricultural societies in Europe, discussion of 285–6; origins of in Iberia 66–7, 69–71; origins of, discussion of the conceptualisation of 88; 'peasant way of life', discussion of the dynamics of in Spain from the Neolithic to the Bronze Age 85–94; risks of early agriculture 87–8; Urnfield culture and the introduction of the plough into Iberia 169; *see also* domestication, economy, Neolithic

Al-Andalus: and the development of Mozarabic art 241; early Islamic elite social structure 270, 271; historiography of, discussion of 265, 267, 268–9; history of the Islamic province of 265, 267; Islamic conquest of 268, 270; Islamic destruction of the Visigothic kingdom, traditional account of 268–9; Islamic hill-top settlements, construction of 270–1; Jaén, town of 273–5; pottery chronology of 267–8; towns, abandonment of in the early Islamic period 271–2, 273; towns, construction of new towns in the Islamic period 272; towns, role of after the Islamic conquest 272; Ummayad emirate, effects of on 265, 271, 272

Alentejo: Bell-Beakers, appearance of in 134; chiefdoms, emergence of during the Chalcolithic in 134; early metallurgy in 129; fortified settlements, evidence of during the Neolithic/Chalcolithic transition 132; hill-top settlements during the Neolithic/Chalcolithic transition 129; megalithic tomb types during the Neolithic/Chalcolithic transition 129, 131; megaliths, symbolism of the grave goods in 131; Mother-Goddess cult, evidence of in 131; Neolithic/Chalcolithic transition, discussion of the archaeological record for 128–9, 131–4; role of ritual in the legitimation of social hierarchy during the Chalcolithic 133–4; settlement pattern of during the Neolithic/Chalcolithic transition 132, 133; social instability, evidence of during the Neolithic/Chalcolithic transition 129; subsistence technology during the Neolithic/Chalcolithic transition 132–3

Algarve: Bell-Beakers, appearance of in 134; chiefdoms, emergence of during the Chalcolithic 134; early metallurgy in 129; fortified settlements, evidence of during the Neolithic/Chalcolithic transition 132; hill-top settlements during the Neolithic/Chalcolithic transition 129; megalithic tomb types during the Neolithic/Chalcolithic transition 129, 131; megaliths, symbolism of grave goods in 131; Mother-